Validity Generalization
A Critical Review

Validity Generalization
A Critical Review

Edited by

Kevin R. Murphy
Pennsylvania State University

LEA LAWRENCE ERLBAUM ASSOCIATES, PUBLISHERS
2003 Mahwah, New Jersey   London

Lawrence Erlbaum Associates, Inc., Publishers
10 Industrial Avenue
Mahwah, New Jersey 07430

Cover design by Kathryn Houghtaling-Lacey

Library of Congress Cataloging-in-Publication Data

Validity generalization : a critical review / edited by Kevin R. Murphy.
     p. cm. — (Applied psychology series)
    Includes bibliographical references and index.
    ISBN 0-8058-4114-8 (alk. paper)
    1. Psychology—Research—Methodology. I. Murphy, Kevin R., 1952–
 II. Series in applied psychology

BF76.5 .V35 2003
150'.7'2—dc21

2002024474
CIP

Books published by Lawrence Erlbaum Associates are printed on acid-free paper,
and their bindings are chosen for strength and durability.

Printed in the United States of America
10 9 8 7 6 5 4 3 2 1

Dedicated to the memory
of Jack Hunter (1939–2002)
who gave so much to the field of
Industrial and Organizational Psychology
—Frank Schmidt, University of Iowa

SERIES IN APPLIED PSYCHOLOGY
Edwin A. Fleishman, George Mason University,
Jeanette N. Cleveland, Pennsylvania State University
Series Editors

Gregory Bedny and David Meister
The Russian Theory of Activity: Current Applications to Design and Learning

Michael T. Brannick, Eduardo Salas, and Carolyn Prince
Team Performance Assessment and Measurement: Theory, Research, and Applications

Jeanette N. Cleveland, Margaret Stockdale, and Kevin R. Murphy
Women and Men in Organizations: Sex and Gender Issues at Work

Aaron Cohen
Multiple Commitments in the Workplace: An Integrative Approach

Russell Cropanzano
Justice in the Workplace: Approaching Fairness in Human Resource Management, Volume 1

Russell Cropanzano
Justice in the Workplace: From Theory to Practice, Volume 2

James E. Driskell and Eduardo Salas
Stress and Human Performance

Sidney A. Fine and Steven F. Cronshaw
Functional Job Analysis: A Foundation for Human Resources Management

Sidney A. Fine and Maury Getkate
Benchmark Tasks for Job Analysis: A Guide for Functional Job Analysis (FJA) Scales

J. Kevin Ford, Steve W. J. Kozlowski, Kurt Kraiger, Eduardo Salas, and Mark S. Teachout
Improving Training Effectiveness in Work Organizations

Jerald Greenberg
Organizational Behavior: The State of the Science (new edition coming 2003)

Uwe E. Kleinbeck, Hans-Henning Quast, Henk Thierry,
and Hartmut Häcker
Work Motivation

Martin I. Kurke and Ellen M. Scrivner
Police Psychology into the 21st Century

Manuel London
*Job Feedback: Giving, Seeking, and Using Feedback for Performance
Improvement (new edition coming 2003)*

Manuel London
How People Evaluate Others in Organizations

Manuel London
Leadership Development: Paths to Self-Insight and Professional Growth

Robert F. Morrison and Jerome Adams
Contemporary Career Development Issues

Michael D. Mumford, Garnett Stokes, and William A. Owens
Patterns of Life History: The Ecology of Human Individuality

Kevin R. Murphy and Frank E. Saal
Psychology in Organizations: Integrating Science and Practice

Kevin R. Murphy
Validity Generalization: A Critical Review

Ned Rosen
Teamwork and the Bottom Line: Groups Make a Difference

Heinz Schuler, James L. Farr, and Mike Smith
*Personnel Selection and Assessment: Individual and Organizational
Perspectives*

John W. Senders and Neville P. Moray
Human Error: Cause, Prediction, and Reduction

ontents

Series Foreword

Series Editors

Jeanette N. Cleveland
Pennsylvania State University

Edwin A. Fleishman
George Mason University

There is a compelling need for innovative approaches to the solution of many pressing problems involving human relationships in today's society. Such approaches are more likely to be successful when they are based on sound research and applications. This Series in Applied Psychology offers publications that emphasize state-of-the-art research and its application to important issues of human behavior in a variety of societal settings. The objective is to bridge both academic and applied interests.

Twenty-five years have passed since the publication of Schmidt and Hunter's (1977) ground-breaking article laying out a model for meta-analysis and its special case of validity generalization (VG). This article and the work that followed changed the face of personnel psychology and has had a profound impact on many other disciplines. There have been many papers, chapters, and books describing, extending, and applying the methods pioneered by Schmidt and Hunter in the last 25 years, but there has never been a comprehensive review describing how this method works, what it has accomplished, and where it is likely to be heading. The present volume fills this void.

Kevin Murphy has assembled a distinguished set of authors, many of whom have made important contributions to the meta-analysis and validity generalization literature, and asked each of them for constructive, critical evaluations of the VG method, its applications, and its future development. The resulting chapters present a wide-ranging review of VG research and applications, as well as a number of new developments, unique perspectives, and insightful suggestions for the future of VG.

This book provides historical overviews of how this method was developed and how it has been applied. Of particular interest are the discussions of the impact of VG on the science and practice of personnel psychology, as well as the evolving relationship between VG research and professional standards for testing, assessment and personnel selection. Several chapters show, for example, how VG research has revolutionized research and applications linking personality measures and personnel selection. These are just a few examples of the unique contributions of this volume.

The book is critical in the best sense of the word. Each chapter presents fresh insights and balanced evaluations of the strengths and weaknesses of the VG method. It is clear from these chapters that VG is here to stay, and that it is likely to continue making important contributions. It is also clear that there are important problems yet to be solved; this book provides well-articulated frameworks (e.g., Bayesian statistics, generalizability theory) for attacking many of these issues. This timely and well-balanced set of chapters will be particularly valuable for both researchers and doctoral students in Industrial and Organizational Psychology. Further, human resources managers will find a number of chapters as a must-read as they design and finetune their testing and selection systems.

The present volume is welcomed for its coverage of new quantitative methods, developed in the context of the thriving areas of meta-analytic and VG research, which are clearly relevant and applicable to these important scientific issues. Psychologists, students, and others dealing with many areas of human performance will find much of value in this important and timely contribution.

Preface

It has been 25 years since the publication of Schmidt and Hunter's (1977) article "Development of a General Solution to the Problem of Validity Generalization" (*Journal of Applied Psychology, 62*, 643–661). That article, and the subsequent stream of research, debate, and discussion about the meaning of validity generalization (VG), changed the face of personnel psychology. Prior to 1977, it was assumed that a new validity study would be needed virtually every time a test or selection procedure was tried out in some new setting. After 1977, it was often argued that a new local validity study was not only not needed, but that it might even add to the confusion rather than shedding new light on the validity of the test.

Developments in validity generalization led to wholesale changes in psychologists' assumptions about what conclusions could or could not be drawn from examining the cumulative literature. Prior to 1977, researchers often despaired of making sense of substantial bodies of research, largely because of the apparent instability of results from study to study. A test or intervention that seemed to work well in one organization would appear to fail in other similar settings, and given the extensive variability in study outcomes, it seemed that few good conclusions could be gained from looking at the research literature. Psychologists who wanted to know how a test or intervention would work in some particular setting would simply have to try it out there and see. VG research suggested that the fundamental relationships among tests and criteria and among the constructs they represent were simpler and more regular than they appeared, and that the combined effects of sampling error, measurement error, and other statistical artifacts had blinded applied psychologists to the true worth of selection tests. More important, these statistical artifacts had blinded psychologists to the consistency in relationships between tests and between constructs.

The methods and conclusions of VG researchers have often been the subject of intense controversy. This controversy has in turn stimulated a number of developments and refinements of the concepts and calculations that underlie VG research. There are several good books describing VG methods, and numerous review articles that incorporate them, but there is no single source that provides an overview of the method, the controversies, the current status of VG, and the probable future of validity generalization research. The purpose of this volume is to provide that overview. Twenty-one authors have contributed chapters that outline the history and the contributions of the VG model, applications of this model to diverse domains, challenges to validity generalization, and alternative methods for attacking the key problems faced when using existing research to draw conclusions about the relationships among measures and among constructs.

In putting this volume together, I asked authors to take a critical view of VG, with the goal of describing what we do well with VG and identifying areas where more progress is needed. They more than met the challenge. The chapters in this volume document the many accomplishments and contributions of VG research, but they also provide concrete suggestions for further improving the process of validity generalization. More important, they provide a road map of where this method is likely to go in the future. It is clear from reading these chapters that VG is alive and well, but that daunting challenges remain to be faced in developing methods for extracting the most reliable information from the cumulative research literature. The authors of these chapters have helped lay the foundation for attacking these challenges and for building on the 25 years of progress that followed Schmidt and Hunter's original VG article.

During the production of this volume, I received the sad news that Jack Hunter had died. His contributions to psychology will live on, but we mourn his passing.

—*Kevin R. Murphy*

1 The Logic of Validity Generalization

Kevin R. Murphy
Pennsylvania State University

A few minutes in any college library is enough to illustrate one of the important characteristics of research in the behavioral and social sciences (i.e., that the number of books, papers, chapters, and reports published in these areas is simply enormous). For example, the various journals of the American Psychological Association publish tens of thousands of pages of peer-reviewed studies each year. The sheer volume of published work often makes the task of summarizing, integrating, and making sense of this research daunting. For example, a recent keyword search of the *PsychInfo* database using the term *attitude change* returned 1,800 citations. A search using the term *psychotherapy* returned more than 54,000 citations. In industrial and organizational psychology, a similar phenomenon has been noted, especially in the area of selection test validity. There have been thousands of studies examining the validity and utility of tests, interview methods, work samples, systems for scoring biodata, assessment centers, etcetera (e.g., a *PsychInfo* using the term *personnel selection* yielded more than 2,300 citations), and the task of interpreting this body of research is a challenging one.

For much of the history of personnel psychology, the task of interpreting this literature fell on the authors of textbooks and narrative reviews (notably Ghiselli, 1966, 1970). Throughout the 1960s and 1970s, reviews of literature on the validity and utility of tests and other selection methods highlighted two recurrent problems: relatively low levels of validity for tests that seemed highly relevant to the job, and substantial inconsistencies in validity estimates from studies that seemed to involve similar tests, jobs, and settings. This pattern of findings led personnel psychologists to conclude that it would be difficult to predict or determine what sorts of tests might or might not be valid as predictors of performance in a particular job, that the validity of particular tests varied extensively across settings, organizations, etcetera, even when the essential nature of the job was held constant, and that the only way to determine whether a test was likely to be valid in a particular setting was to do a local validity study. The application of meta-analytic methods, and in particular, the validity generalization model to these same validation studies has led some very different conclusions about the meaning of this research. Applications of meta-analysis, and particularly validity generalization analyses, to studies of the validity of tests, interviews, assessment centers, and the like has led to the conclusions that (1) professionally developed ability tests, structured interviews, work samples, assessment centers, and other structured assessment techniques are likely to provide valid predictions of future performance across a wide range of jobs, settings, etcetera, (2) the level of validity for a particular test can vary as a function of characteristics of the job (e.g., complexity) or the organizations, but validities are often reasonably consistent across settings; and (3) it is possible to identify abilities and broad dimensions of personality that are related to performance in virtually all jobs (for reviews of research supporting these points, see Hartigan & Wigdor, 1989; Hunter & Hunter, 1984; McHenry, Hough, Toquam, Hanson, & Ashworth, 1990; Nathan & Alexander, 1988; Ree & Earles, 1994; Reilly & Chao, 1982; Schmidt & Hunter, 1999; Schmidt, Hunter, & Outerbridge, 1986; Schmitt, Gooding, Noe, & Kirsch, 1984; Wigdor & Garner, 1982. For illustrative applications of VG methods, see Callender & Osburn, 1981; Schmidt, Hunter, Pearlman, & Shane, 1979). Schmidt and Hunter (1999) reviewed 85 years of research on the validity and utility of selection methods and concluded that cognitive ability tests, work samples, measures of conscientiousness and integrity, structured interviews, job knowledge tests, biographical data measures and assessment centers all showed consistent evidence of validity as predictors of job performance.

The purpose of this chapter is to discuss the methods used by researchers to study the cumulative literature in areas such as test validity, and in particular, to lay out the logic behind the methods used in research on validity generalization (VG). Research on validity generalization is based on an integration of meta-analysis and psychotric theory, and in order to understand the methods and results of VG research, it is important to examine the method and its logic in some detail.

METHODS OF META-ANALYSIS

The problem of making sense of the outcomes of hundreds or thousands of studies is in many ways similar to the problem of making sense of the data collected in any particular study. For example, if you conduct a study in which 200 subjects each complete some task of measure, the first step in making sense of the data you have collected is often to compute a variety of statistics that both describe that you found (e.g., means, standard deviations) and lend support to inferences you might make about what those data mean (e.g., confidence intervals, significance tests). One of the key insights of methodologists in the 1970s and 1980s was that the same could also be applied to the problem of making sense of a body of research. That is, if you wanted to make sense of the results of 125 different validation studies, each of which reported the correlation between some test and some measure of performance, one thing you would probably do would be to compute the mean and the standard deviation of the validities across studies. Many of the current methods of meta analysis take a more sophisticated approach to the problem than simply computing the average across all studies (e.g., they might weight for sample size), but the starting point for virtually all methods of meta analysis is essentially to compute some descriptive statistics that summarize key facets of the research literature you hope to summarize and understand. Differences in approaches to meta-analysis start to emerge as we move from descriptive statistics (i.e., what happened) to inferential ones (i.e., what does this mean).

The term *meta-analysis* refers to a wide array of statistical methods that are applied to the outcomes of multiple studies to describe in some sensible fashion what these studies have typically found, and draw inferences about what those findings might mean. Validity generalization represents a specialized application of meta-analysis that attempts to integrate both psychometric and statistical principles to draw inferences about the meaning of the cumulative body of research in a particular area (this method is sometimes also referred to as *psychometric meta-analysis*). In particular, validity generalization analyses attempt to draw inferences about the meaning of a set of studies, each of which has attempted to draw conclusions about fundamental relationships among the constructs being studied on the basis of imperfect measures, finite samples, and studies that vary on a number of dimensions (e.g., the level of reliability of the measures used).

There are a number of methods of quantitatively summarizing the outcomes of multiple studies, any or all of which might be referred to as meta-analysis. For example, Rosenthal (1984) developed methods of combining the p values (i.e., probability that experimental results represent chance alone) from several independent studies to obtain an estimate the likelihood that the particular intervention, treatment, etcetera has some effect. Glass, McGaw, and Smith (1981) developed methods of combining effect size estimates (e.g. the difference between the experimental and control group means, expressed in standard deviation units) from multiple studies to give an overall picture of how much impact treatments or interventions have on key dependent variables. Schmidt and Hunter (1977) developed methods of combining validity coefficients (i.e., correlations between test scores and criterion measures) from multiple studies to estimate the overall validity of tests and other selection methods. Several variations on the basic VG model proposed by Schmidt and Hunter have been reviewed by Burke (1984) and Hedges (1988). Hedges and Olkin (1985) elaborated a general statistical model for meta-analysis that includes as a special case a variety of procedures similar to those developed by Schmidt and Hunter. Brannick (2001) discussed applications of Bayesian models in meta-analysis (see also Raudenbush & Bryk, 1985). Finally, Thomas (1990) developed a mixture model that attempts to describe systematic differences in validity among specific subgroups of validity studies.

The methods developed by Schmidt and Hunter have been widely applied, particularly within the field of personnel selection. For example, Schmidt (1992) noted that "meta-analysis has been applied to over 500 research literatures in employment selection, each one representing a predictor-job performance pair" (p. 1177). The most frequent application of these methods has been in research on the relationship between scores on cognitive ability tests and measures of overall job performance; representative examples of this type of validity generalization analysis include Pearlman, Schmidt, and Hunter (1980), Schmidt, Gast-Rosenberg, and Hunter (1980) and Schmidt, Hunter, and Caplan (1981). However, applications of meta-analysis and validity generalization analysis have not been restricted to traditional test validity research. Hunter and Hirsh (1987) reviewed meta-analyses spanning a wide range of areas in applied psychology (e.g., absenteeism, job satisfaction). Other recent applications of meta-analytic methods have included assessments of the relationship between personality traits and job performance (Barrick & Mount, 1990), assessments of race effects in performance ratings (Kraiger & Ford, 1985) and assessments of the validity of assessment center ratings (Gaugler, Rosenthal, Thornton, & Bentson, 1987). Finally, Hom, Carnikas-Walker, Prussia, and Griffeth (1992) combined meta-analysis with structural modeling to assess the appropriateness of several competing theories of turnover in organizations.

VALIDITY GENERALIZATION:
THE BASIC RATIONALE

The basic model developed by Schmidt and Hunter (1977) has gone through several developments and elaborations (Burke, 1984; James, Demaree, Mulaik, & Ladd, 1992; Raju & Burke, 1983; Schmidt et al., 1993), and the accuracy and usefulness of the model has been widely debated (e.g., Hartigan & Wigdor, 1989; James, Demaree, & Mulaik, 1986; Kemery, Mossholder, & Roth, 1987; Thomas, 1990). Although there is still considerable discussion and controversy over specific aspects of or conclusions drawn from validity generalization analyses, the core set of ideas in this method are simple and straightforward.

As noted earlier, the problem the validity generalization model was designed to address is that of making sense of research literature in which many, if not most of the relevant studies are of dubious quality. For example, many studies of the validity and utility of selection tests feature small sample sizes or unreliable criteria. Because sampling error leads to random variations in study outcomes and measurement error artificially lowers (i.e., attenuates) validities, it is reasonable to expect that validity coefficients from different studies will seem to vary randomly from study to study and will generally seem small. However, the effects of sampling error and unreliability are both relatively easy to estimate, and once the effects of these statistical artifacts are taken into account, you are likely to conclude that the actual validity of the test or assessment procedure studied is probably both larger and more consistent than a simple examination of the observed validity coefficients would suggest.

For example, suppose that there are 100 studies of the validity of structured interviews as predictors of job performance, and in each study the reliability of the performance measure is .70 and N (i.e., the sample size) is 40. If the average of the observed validity coefficients is .45, the formula for the correction for attenuation suggests that the best estimate of the validity of the these interviews is probably closer to .54 (i.e., .45 divided by the square root of .70) than .45. Thus, a simple correction for measurement error suggests that the interviews are probably more valid than they seem on the basis of a quick examination of the validity studies themselves.

Because each validity coefficient comes from a fairly small sample, it is natural to expect some variability in study results; this variability can be estimated using a well-known formula for the sampling error of correlation coefficients (Hunter & Schmidt, 1990). For example, suppose that the standard deviation of the validity coefficients coming from these 100 studies was .18. On the basis of sampling error alone, you would expect a standard deviation of .12, given an N of 40 and a mean observed validity of .45 (see Hunter & Schmidt, 1990, for a detailed discussion of the formulas used to make such estimates). One conclusion that is likely to be reached in a validity generalization study is that much of the observed variation is test validities is likely to be due to the effects of sampling error rather than to the effects of real variation in test validity (here, 66% of the observed variability in validities might be due to sampling error).

Although the results of various approaches meta-analytic do not always agree (Johnson, Mullen, & Salas, 1995), these methods lead to similar general conclusions about the validity of selection tests, interviews, assessment centers, etcetera. In particular, it seems highly likely that test validities are generally both larger and more consistent across situations than the results of many individual validity studies would suggest (Hartigan & Wigdor, 1989; Schmidt, 1992; see, however, Murphy, 1993). Indeed, given the nature of much of the available validation research (i.e., small N, unreliable measures, range restriction), this general finding is virtually a foregone conclusion, although it directly contradicts one of the most widely held set of assumptions in personnel psychology (i.e., that validities are generally small and inherently unstable). Similarly, applications of the VG model to quantitative reviews of research on the validity of personality inventories as predictors of performance (e.g., Barrick & Mount, 1991; Hough, Eaton, Dunnette, Kamp, & McCloy, 1990; Tett, Jackson, & Rothstein, 1991) has overturned long-held assumptions about the relevance of such tests for personnel selection. Personnel researchers now generally accept the conclusion that scores on personality inventories are related to performance in a wide range of jobs.

The VG model suggests that there are a variety of statistical artifacts that artificially depress the mean and inflate the variability of validity coefficients, and further that the effects of these artifacts can be easily estimated and corrected for. It is useful to discuss two broad classes of corrections separately, corrections to the mean and corrections to the variability in the distribution of validity coefficients that would be found in a descriptive meta-analysis.

Corrections to the Mean

There are several reasons why validity coefficients might be small. The most obvious possibility is that validities are small because the test in question is not a good predictor of performance. However, there are several statistical artifacts that would lead you to find relatively small correlations between test scores and measures of job performance, even if the test is in fact a very sensitive indicator of someone's job-related abilities. Two specific statistical artifacts that are known to artificially depress validities have received extensive attention in literature dealing with validity generalization, the limited reliability of measures of job performance and the frequent presence of range restriction in test scores, performance measures, or both.

There is a substantial literature dealing with the reliability of performance ratings (Viswesvaran, Ones, & Schmidt, 1996; Schmidt & Hunter, 1996) and other measures of job performance (Murphy & Cleveland, 1995). This literature suggests that these measures are often unreliable, which can seriously attenuate (i.e., depress) validity coefficients. For example, Viswesvaran et al.'s (1996) review showed that the average inter-rater reliability estimate for supervisory ratings of overall job performance was .52. To correct the correlation between a test score (X) and a measure of performance (Y) for the effects of measurement error in Y, you divide the observed correlation by the square root of the reliability of the performance measure. If you use inter-rater correlations as an estimate of reliability, corrected correlations will be, on average, be 38.7% larger than uncorrected correlations (i.e., if you divide the observed correlation by the square root of .52, the correction will lead to a 38.7% increase in the size of r). Murphy and DeShon (2001) questioned the use of inter-rater correlations as estimates of the reliability of ratings, but the general principle that low reliability will lead to what appears to be low levels of validity is beyond debate.

Performance ratings are normally collected in settings where range restriction is ubiquitous, especially when ratings are used to make administrative decisions about ratees (e.g., salary, promotion; Murphy & Cleveland, 1995). For example, Bretz, Milkovich, and Read (1992) concluded that "the norm in U.S. industry is to rate employees at the top end of the scale" (p. 333). Ratees who consistently receive either very high ratings or very low ones are likely to be moved out of the job (e.g., promotions for high-rated employees, transfers or dismissals for low-rated employees), artificially truncating the distribution of ratings. Evidence of leniency and range restriction in performance ratings is so pervasive that several commentators (e.g., Ilgen, Barnes-Farrell, & McKellin, 1993; Jawahar & Williams, 1997) have urged caution in using ratings as criteria in validation studies. Range restriction can also artificially depress validity coefficients.

There has been considerable discussion in the literature about the best ways to correct for attenuation and range restriction (Hartigan & Wigdor, 1989; Hunter & Schmidt, 1990; Schmidt et al., 1993; Viswesvaran et al., 1996), and there are difficult issues with both corrections that have never been satisfactorily resolved (Cronbach, Gleser, Nanda, & Rajaratnam, 1972; Lumsden, 1976). However, the idea that both range restriction and the limited reliability of the measures used in validity studies depress validity coefficients, and that we can at least estimate and partially correct for this effect, is well accepted.

Corrections to the Variance

Meta-analyses of validity coefficients have often shown that the validity for the same type of test or measure varies considerably across jobs, organizations, settings, etcetera. This variability in validity coefficients is one of the chief reasons for the long-held assumption that it was necessary to validate tests in each setting where they were used. The validity generalization model suggests that some, and perhaps all of the variability in validity coefficients, might be explained in terms of a few simple statistical artifacts and that once the effects of these artifacts are removed, you are likely to conclude that the validity of tests is substantially similar across settings. Many potential explanations for variability in test validity have been put forth (e.g., the reliability of performance measures is higher in some organizations than in others, which can lead to apparent differences in validity), but much of the literature dealing with validity generalization has focused on the simplest and probably the most important explanation for differences in validity coefficients across studies (i.e., simple sampling error). Many validity studies, particularly studies from the early 1970s and before, used small samples, and it is well known that statistical results of all sorts, including validity coefficients, are highly unstable when samples are small. Corrections for sampling error and for other artifacts that artificially inflate the variability in test validities often suggest that much of the apparent instability of validities is a reflection of weaknesses of validity studies (small samples, variation in the degree of unreliability and range restriction) rather than a reflection of true differences in the validity of tests across settings. For example, in McDaniel, Whetzel, Schmidt, and Maurer's (1994) analysis of the validity of situational interviews the standard deviation of the validities they reviewed was .14. After applying statistical corrections based on the VG model, this value shrunk to .05.

The cumulative effect of corrections that raise the mean and shrink the variance of the distribution of validities can be substantial. Returning to the example used above, McDaniel et al. (1994) reported that the mean of 16 validity coefficients for situational interviews was .27, and the standard deviation was .14. After correcting for statistical artifacts, the estimated population mean validity rose to .50, and with a standard deviation of .05. These researchers concluded that corrected validity of situational interviews was .43 or larger at least 90% of the time.

VG: THE INFERENTIAL MODEL

Validity generalization research involves developing and applying a particular type of inferential model, with the hope that this model can be used to understand the meaning of the cumulative body of research in a particular area. Traditionally, the model presented by VG researchers has resembled a variation on classic true score models used in psychometric research, in which there is an attempt to decompose the variance of test scores into its component parts. The classic true score theory of reliability states that the variance in observed scores can be broken down into that due to true scores and that due to measurement error, or:

$$\sigma^2_{observed} = \sigma^2_{true} + \sigma^2_{error} \tag{1}$$

which implies that any method that allows you to estimate the variance in scores due to measurement error also allows you to determine how much is due to true scores, or

$$\sigma^2_{true} = \sigma^2_{observed} - \sigma^2_{error} \tag{2}$$

In validity generalization studies, the *scores* to be analyzed are validity coefficients calculated in the different validity studies. In VG, the equivalent to Equation 1 is given by

$$\sigma^2_{observed} = \sigma^2_{true} + \sigma^2_{artifacts} \tag{3}$$

That is, the observed variance in validities from study can be broken down into true differences in validity from setting to setting and variance due to a number of statistical artifacts, such as sampling error, differences across settings in the amount or range restriction, the reliability of tests, etcetera. If this variance can be estimated, it is possible to draw inferences about the true variability in test validity on the basis of an equivalent to Equation 2, or

$$\sigma^2_{true} = \sigma^2_{observed} - \sigma^2_{artifacts} \tag{4}$$

As in traditional reliability theory, Equations 3 and 4 are based in part on the assumption that artifacts such as range restriction, test reliability, etcetera are independent of the true validity of tests. This assumption is probably not justified (James et al., 1992), but there is not much evidence that these artifacts are systematically correlated with test validity, and it is probably a reasonable approximation of the true state of affairs. Many of the modifications and refinements of the basic VG equations over the years (e.g., Schmidt et al., 1993) have been developed to capture more fully and accurately the variance due to statistical artifacts, which in turn should lead to better estimates of the true variability in test validity across jobs, settings, etcetera.

An alternative method of tackling the same problem (i.e., to understand the observed distribution of test validities) is to try and develop a process model. That is, the task of the VG researcher can be described as one of developing a that could explain key features of the observed distribution of test validities, then see if the model fits well enough to accept it as at least a reasonable approximation. Here, the *data* to be modeled are a set of correlations between (for example) scores on some test and measures of job performance, all obtained from relatively small and presumably independent samples. The mean of this distribution is likely to be relatively small and the variance of this distribution is likely to be relatively large (see, e.g., Ghiselli, 1966). The problem is to generate a model of the process that might lead to this observed distribution of test-performance correlations.

Validity generalization analyses implicitly involve a process model of the sort previously described. For example, suppose you started with the assumption that scores on tests really did tell you a good deal about the job performance of applicants, and furthermore that the relationships between the test and performance were in fact reasonably consistent in their actual performance across settings. This implies that if you had a set of validity studies that combined essentially perfect measures, large and well-defined samples, minimal range restriction, etcetera you would find consistently large correlations between tests and performance. Suppose, however, that most researchers use unreliable measures of performance. This would tend to lower the correlations. Suppose, also, that there was substantial levels range restriction in many studies. This would also lower the correlations, yielding a distribution with a small mean (but also a small variance). Suppose further that the amount of range restriction, criterion unreliability, etcetera varied from study to study. This would lead to some variation in the observed distribution of correlations. Suppose further that validity studies often employed small samples. This would lead to further variation in validity coefficients. The net effect of all of these statistical artifacts would be to produce exactly what reviewers in the 1960s and 1970s bemoaned, validity coefficients that were often both small and variable. Yet none of the processes described above reflect real deficiencies in tests. Rather, they reflect deficiencies in validation research (i.e., small samples, unreliable measures). Furthermore, it might be hard to identify plausible alternative models that would explain this state of affair, although several possibilities are considered in the following.

Suppose, for example, you made the same assumption as was traditionally made by personnel psychologists in the 1960s and 1970s (i.e., that tests that "worked" in one setting might turn out to be virtually useless in other similar settings). If the validity of tests did in fact vary from setting to setting, the process model described earlier would lead one to expect an even more pessimistic set of conclusions than those reached by researchers at the time. That is, if there were real and meaningful differences in the validity of tests across most of the settings in which they were applied, the observed distribution of correlations should show even more variability than they typically do. It is certain that some of the variability in results across settings is due to the often lamentable quality of the validity studies themselves, and if this artifactual variance in validity was piled on top of true and meaningful differences in validity across settings, it seems certain that the outcomes of validity studies would be much more varied that they have turned out to be. The VG model provides a coherent explanation of the observed distribution of validities, but a model that starts with the assumption that validity truly varies from job to job probably cannot fit the data, given the known effects of sampling error, limited reliability, etcetera.

Are Alternative Models Plausible?

One strength of the VG model is that it provides a coherent explanation for the observed distribution of validities. That is, if you start with a test that in fact works pretty well and pretty consistently, then carry out a large number of validity studies, each combining small N with unreliable performance measures, you will get pretty much what is actually known to occur (i.e., validity coefficients that are generally small and highly variable). Thus, the model "works," in the sense that it explains how the observed distribution of validities could arise from a population in which the actual validity is relatively large and relatively consistent. Any alternative model will have to take into account the known effects of low reliability, small sample sizes, differences in reliability across settings, and so forth, when explaining why validity coefficients are typically low and variable. This means, for example, that a model that takes the observed distribution of validities at face value (i.e., that concludes that validity truly is low and variable) is unlikely to be correct; if there was substantial real variation in validity across settings, the VG model suggests that the observed variance in validities should be much larger than it actually is.

There are, of course, other processes that might lead to the same outcome as the VG model. The most obvious possibility is a self-censorship model. Suppose, for example, that you are studying the validity of a cognitive ability test, and you know that other studies in your area typically report uncorrected validity coefficients in the ballpark of .30. You obtain a validity coefficient of −.20 (or, for that matter, a coefficient of .70). It is likely that researchers who find validity coefficients that are very different from those normally reported with reanalyze their data, check their assumptions, evaluate their measures closely, etcetera, whereas researchers who obtain values that are closer to the norm will take them at face value. This process would lead to a tendency to doubt, revise, or discard validity estimates that were too far out of the range of researchers' expectations and to keep those that fell within the distribution of results researchers were more comfortable with, distorting the distribution of *reported* validity coefficients (meta-analysts typically have no way of knowing whether the final result reported in a validity study is the result of data checking, transformations, or other sorts of data manipulation) in such a way that the observed distribution was similar to the distribution one would expect if the VG model was true.

A variation on this theme might be to argue that external censorship would produce the same result (i.e., a tendency to report results hat conform to establish patterns and to withhold publication of results that deviate sharply). As a journal editor, I receive frequent reminders of reviewers' tendencies to question findings that deviate sharply from current trends in the literature and to take at face value results that conform to those trends, and it is reasonable to argue that this tendency will favor the publication of studies that report similar results to those of existing studies and work against the publication of studies with discordant results. The result will be a body of published literature in which the observed variation in outcomes is less than the variation in outcomes of all studies.

It is not the argument that a self-censorship or an external censorship model is correct, or that these sort of processes plays any meaningful role in validity research. Rather, the point is made that demonstrating that the VG model could be used to explain the observed distribution of validities is a different matter than demonstrating that the VG model does explain this distribution. The VG model is certainly plausible, if certain assumptions are met, but the data that have been analyzed by VG researchers does not demonstrate that this model is correct. To make such a demonstration, one must either show that no plausible alternative exists or show that the model corresponds so closely to the phenomenon being studied that no alternatives would both explain the observed distribution of validities and correspond to the process by which validity coefficients were obtained in the first place.

There have been few attempts to generate, much less test alternative models for explaining the observed distribution of validity coefficients. Because few serious contenders have even been put forth, it is difficult to know how a proponent of the VG model could truly demonstrate that no alternatives exist. A more fruitful direction to pursue might be to compare some of the key features of the model with the known characteristics of validity studies. The closer the match, the lower the likelihood that meaningful alternative models could be constructed that would explain the observed distributions of validity coefficients and lead to substantially different conclusions about the true value and validity of tests.

Key Assumptions of the VG Model

The assumptions that underlie meta-analyses in general and validity generalization analyses in particular are rarely articulated (for an exception see Hedges & Olkin, 1985), and it is likely that some researchers will dispute any conclusions that other researchers reach about the assumptions that underlie these techniques. The approach taken here is to examine the similarities and differences between statistical analyses in meta-analysis and comparable analyses in primary research. The statistical model for meta-analysis is usually a simple extension of the same model that would be used in analyzing data from a single study, and an explicit comparison of the problems of statistical inference when the data are individual observations versus the results of multiple studies can help to illustrate the challenges faced my meta-analysts in creating a useful model to explain their data.

For the purpose of illustrating the similarities and differences in the assumptions at different levels of analysis, consider two studies, one that involves collecting and analyzing data from a pool of subjects (primary analysis) and the other involving a meta-analysis of published and unpublished studies in a particular area. In the first study, 100 subjects are asked to carry out some experimental task, and their responses are recorded and analyzed. In the second study, the results form 100 existing studies are recorded and analyzed. In both cases, the goal of these statistical analyses is to both describe what happened in this particular study or set of studies and to draw inferences about what these findings mean in some broader sense.

The most obvious set of assumptions have to do with sampling. In a primary study, we treat subjects as a random sample from some particular population. In a meta-analysis, studies are treated as repeated samples from a common population. Regardless of the level of analysis, the population is rarely well-defined, and the process by which subjects are sampled from that population is rarely a random one. On this basis alone, some skepticism about the accuracy and meaningfulness of inferential statistics is often warranted, and there are as many reasons to worry about the results of primary analyses as about those of meta-analyses. A second sampling assumption, the independence of observations, is likely to pose more serious problems in interpreting meta-analyses (Hedges & Olkin, 1985) than in interpreting primary research.

In traditional between-subjects research designs, it is reasonable to assume that the responses of subject i are independent of those of subject k. There are, of course, many designs (e.g., within-subjects or mixed designs, group data collections) in which this assumption is violated, and there is a rich methodological literature dealing with the problems caused by nonindependence and potential solutions to these problems. In meta-analysis, the assumption of independence is obviously inappropriate. For example, if there are 100 studies of the relationship between self-esteem and job performance, it is unreasonable to assume the researchers who design and carry out the 101st study will do so with complete disregard to the methods, results, and conclusions of previous studies (indeed, one of the factors motivating the development of meta-analysis and VG was researchers' inability to properly consider the implications of existing research when evaluating their own studies). It is often not clear how nonindependence will influence the design, analysis, or reporting of study results, but it is virtually certain that the results of studies in a particular area will be influenced by the body of available research. At present, there are no good methods for modeling, much less for correcting the effects of this nonindependence on the observed distribution of validity coefficients.

A second set of assumption involves the data themselves. It is usually assumed that data from multiple sources, either multiple subjects or multiple subjects, can be aggregated without fundamentally changing the nature of the variables being analyzed. This assumption is likely to be a serious problem in a meta-analysis. Except in special cases where a meta-analysis focuses on some specific test or measure (e.g., the validity of Minnesota Multiphasic Personality Inventory, 2nd edition [MMPI-2] scales for predicting social adjustment), it is common for the studies included in an analysis to feature many different operational definitions of the independent and dependent variables. For example, a study of the validity of spatial ability tests as predictors of job performance would certainly include a wide range of measures of both ability and performance. This raises the question of whether these can or should be combined, and if so, what the combined results mean.

Suppose, for example, that the meta-analysis described earlier includes 12 different (and nonequivalent) measures of spatial ability, five different measures of performance, and samples that differ in important ways from study to study. Even if the validities turn out to be reasonably consistent (i.e., not much more different than one would expect on the basis of sampling error and other artifacts), it is still unclear what population parameter is being estimated. It is conventional to describe this sort of study as an examination of the validity of spatial ability tests as a predictor of job performance, and given the results described here, one might conclude that this relationship in invariant across the settings studied. However, it is difficult to describe precisely what this relationship really means. The population that is defined by the sorts of studies included in this validity generalization analysis is probably best described as studies involving a range of things that are referred to as spatial tests as predictors of another range of things referred to as performance measures, and even if the empirical results turn out to be reasonably consistent from study to study, the conventional interpretation (i.e., spatial ability predicts job performance) is not justified in terms of any specific statistical model.

In principle, there would be nothing to stop you from doing a grand meta-analysis of the relationship between all X variables and all Y variables studied in the social and behavioral sciences. Indeed, given the sample sizes typical in this research (e.g. Sedlmeier & Gigerenzer, 1989) it is likely that a large proportion of the variability in the r_{xy} values (for randomly chosen Xs and Ys) reported in all behavioral science research will probably be due to sampling error. The problem with this sort of meta-analysis is that its results would be impossible to interpret. The same general problem is, however, faced in all meta-analyses. Whenever studies that are nominally similar (e.g. *quantitative* and *job performance* in the title) are grouped together, there will be some ambiguity in describing exactly what the *population validity* estimated on the basis of that set of studies truly means. As a rule of thumb, it will probably be easier to interpret the results of meta-analyses that combine validity studies of relatively standardized tests or assessments (e.g. commercially published cognitive ability tests) than those that combine studies of tests or assessment procedures that are highly diverse (e.g. selection interviews, work sample tests, simulations).

Testing Meta-Analytic Models

There is an extensive literature dealing with the accuracy, bias, and efficiency of various meta-analytic procedures, and an examination of the methods used to test these models both confirms the importance of the assumptions laid out earlier and points out critical weaknesses of these tests. The method of choice for evaluating VG models, or meta-analytic procedures in general is to conduct Monte Carlo studies (for a sample of illustrative applications, see Brannick, 2001; Callender & Osburn, 1981; Kemery et al., 1987; Law, Schmidt, & Hunter, 1994; Osburn, Callender, Greener, & Ashworth, 1983; Oswald & Johnson, 1998). A typical Monte Carlo study mirrors quite precisely the assumptions laid out above. That is, it is normal to generate data from a known set of population parameters, to create a large number of independent replications, to calculate validity coefficients in each of the samples generated, then to see whether various meta-analytic models do a better or worse job of accounting for characteristics of the observed distribution of validities. These methods can be extremely useful, and they often lead to important insights into the relationships among the various approaches to meta-analysis and validity generalization. If the assumptions that guided these models were at least reasonable approximations of the actual process by which studies are conducted, there would be little controversy about the accuracy of VG estimates or about the advantages and disadvantages of different models for meta-analysis and VG.

The central weakness of most tests of the accuracy of VG estimates is the gap between the assumptions needed to develop and test these models and the actual process by which validity results are produced and generated. The same, of course, can be said of most statistical models used in primary research. Assumptions of normality, random sampling, independence, and so forth are routinely violated in most studies in the behavioral and social sciences. Concerns about the possible effects of such violations have led to the development of a wide range of nonparametric techniques, and also to a large literature dealing with the robustness of statistical tests under various sorts of violations of statistical assumptions (Hunter & May, 1993; McDonald, 1999; Wilcox, 1992; Zimmerman & Zumbo, 1993; Zwick & Marascuilo, 1984). Some studies of the sensitivity of meta-analytic procedures to violation these assumptions have emerged (e.g., Oswald & Johnson, 1998), but even these are often limited by their dependence of the Monte Carlo framework. That is, most assessments of the accuracy and reasonableness of conclusions from VG analyses have been carried out in environments where assumptions of random sampling, independent observations, etcetera are literally met. The problem of determining the usefulness of these models under more realistic conditions is just starting be addressed (e.g., Steel & Kammeyer-Mueller, 2002), and it is likely that this effort will require a very different set of methods than the standard Monte Carlo simulations that are now used to evaluate VG models.

Some Conclusions About VG Models and Their Alternatives

In examining the literature dealing with alternative interpretations of VG results, three conclusions are discussed here. First, no serious contender has been put forth that accounts for the observed

distribution of validities as well as the likely effects of statistical artifacts such as limited reliability and sampling error. Right now,
the only explanation that has been put forth and has survived serious scrutiny is the explanation offered by VG researchers (i.e., that
statistical artifacts mask the level and the consistency of validity
coefficients).

Second, the fact that the VG model can explain the observed distribution of validities does not imply that it does explain this distribution. Key assumptions of the VG model are obviously wrong, and
the discrepancies between the model and the reality it tries to explain are far from trivial. In particular, the results of validity studies
cannot be thought of as independent observations sampled from
some well-defined population. Rather, the results of any particular
study are likely to be affected by whatever was known (or thought to
be known) about the phenomenon at the time the study was performed, and these dependencies are likely to complicate the interpretation of meta-analytic findings.

Third, one potential route for developing and testing alternate
models might be to focus on violations of key assumptions. The censorship models put forward earlier as a potential explanations for
the observed variance in validities are an example. Mixture models
(e.g., Thomas, 1990) designed to examine potential changes in validity as the operational definitions of X and Y change provide another example of using differences between the assumptions of the
VG model and the reality it is designed to explain to generate alternative explanations.

VALIDITY GENERALIZATION VERSUS
SITUATIONAL SPECIFICITY OF VALIDITIES

Murphy (1994) noted that researchers and practitioners sometimes
confuse the claim that validity generalizes with the claim that validity is essentially constant across situations. This confusion has
arisen largely because of changes, over time, in the way personnel
researchers have conceptualized and discussed validity.

In the early years of validity generalization research (e.g., late
1970s to mid 1980s), researchers often talked about validity as if it
were a dichotomous variable, that is, tests are either valid or not
valid. This way of thinking closely mirrors the treatment of validity
in the legal system, in which tests that led to adverse impact were
held to be illegal unless they were shown to be valid. If such a showing was made, it did not matter much whether the test was just

above the minimum threshold for defining validity or if it was a highly sensitive predictor of performance. Early research on validity generalization focused largely on the question of whether test validities exceeded some minimum level in most validity studies. Later research has focused more strongly on the consistency of validity across situations, in particular on the hypothesis that the level of validity achieved by a test might be situationally specific.

Distinguishing Between Validity Generalization and Situational Specificity

In the VG literature, the existence of substantial variability in the level of validity across situations (after correcting for statistical artifacts) is referred to as situational specificity. If the correlation between test scores and job performance truly depends on the job, organization, or the situation, validity is said to be situationally specific. Validity generalization, on the other hand, refers to the classification of tests or other assessment devices as *valid* or *not valid*. If a test demonstrates at least a minimal level of validity in a sufficiently wide range of situations, validity is said to generalize. If a test cannot be consistently classified as *valid*, validity generalization fails.

The processes involved in testing the validity generalization and situational specificity hypothesis overlap in many ways. In both cases, you start by calculating the mean and variance of the observed distribution of validities. Next, you correct for unreliability, range restriction, and other statistical artifacts that might affect the mean of the validity distribution, and correct for sampling error, variation across studies in range restriction and unreliability, and other statistical artifacts that might affect the variance of the distribution of validities (see Hunter & Schmidt, 1990, for formulas and sample calculations). At this point, the two processes diverge.

Tests of the situational specificity hypothesis involve a comparison between the observed variance in validities and the variability expected solely on the basis of sampling error and other artifacts. If the variability expected on the basis of statistical artifacts is as large, or nearly as large as the observed variability in validities, the situational specificity hypothesis is rejected. Schmidt, Hunter, and their colleagues suggested a "75% rule," in which the situational specificity hypothesis is rejected if the variability expected on the basis of statistical artifacts is at least 75% as large as the observed variance in validities (e.g., Schmidt et al., 1979). Other authors (e.g., Hedges & Olkin, 1985) use statistical tests of the homogeneity of correlations coefficients to evaluate this hypothesis. In many meta-analyses, the observed variance in validity coefficients is equal to or less than the variance that would be predicted on the basis of statistical artifacts alone, and this is often taken as evidence that true validities do not vary. Several aspects of the situational specificity hypothesis, including the decision rules used to evaluate the consistency of validities, are discussed in sections that follow.

The procedure for determining validity generalization is quite different from those used to evaluate situational specificity. After applying corrections for unreliability, sampling error, etcetera, the test of validity generalization involves comparing the bottom of the corrected validity distribution (e.g. the value at the 10th percentile of the corrected distribution) to some standard that represents a minimal level of validity (e.g. a validity coefficient of .00, or .10). For example, if the value at the 10th percentile of a corrected validity distribution was greater than .10, proponents of validity generalization would conclude that you could be 90% confident that the test would be at least minimally valid in essentially all new applications.

Gaugler, Rosenthal, Thornton, and Bentson (1987) conducted a meta-analysis of assessment center validities; results from this study can be used to illustrate the procedures used to evaluate validity generalization vs. situation specificity. Their review included 44 correlations (from 29 separate studies) between assessment center ratings and measures of job performance. The mean and the standard deviation of these validity coefficients were .25 and .15, respectively. After correcting for sampling error, unreliability, and other statistical artifacts, Gaugler et al. (1987) reported that: (a) the best estimate of assessment center validity was given by a corrected mean validity of .36, (b) the corrected validities varied substantially across studies (i.e., a corrected standard deviation of .14), and (c) 90% of the corrected validities were greater than .18. This set of results led them to conclude that the assessment center method was at least minimally valid in virtually all reported applications (i.e., assessment center validity generalized) but that the level of validity was not consistent across studies, suggesting that characteristics of the jobs, organizations, assessment exercises, and so forth could substantially affect the validity of assessment center ratings.

In principle, there is no necessary relationship between tests of situational specificity and tests of validity generalization. The most common finding, at least in the area of ability testing, has been that validities are both: (a) generalizable, in the sense that such tests appear to be at least minimally valid predictors in virtually all settings, and (b) consistent, in the sense that the level of validity is reasonably comparable across settings (Hunter & Hirsch, 1987; Hunter & Hunter, 1984; Schmidt, 1992). However, it is also possible to conclude that validities are generalizable, but not consistent. That is, tests might show some validity in virtually all settings, but might be substantially more useful in some jobs, organizations, etcetera than in others.

On the whole, it is easier to demonstrate validity generalization than to demonstrate consistent levels of validity across situations. Mean validities are reasonably high for most structured selection procedures (see Hunter & Hunter, 1984; Reilly & Chao, 1982; Wiesner & Cronshaw, 1988), which means that the lower bound of the validity distribution is almost always greater than 0, .10, or whatever other standard is used to define minimal validity for this class of tests and assessment procedures. Demonstrations of situational specificity, on the other hand, are typically more difficult and controversial.

What Inferences Can Be Drawn From Tests of Situational Specificity?

Earlier it was noted that whereas many methods of meta-analysis provide what are basically descriptive statistics, VG analyses focus on inferential statistics (i.e., estimates of unknown population parameters). The descriptive-inferential distinction highlights one of the most difficult problems in using the results of VG analyses to draw inferences about situational specificity (i.e., the problem of deciding the conditions under which inferences can be drawn from the sample of studies included in a meta-analysis to the specific application in mind).

The logic of using situational specificity tests to make projections about the validity of a particular test in a particular situation is straightforward. If validities have not varied (except for variation due to sampling error and other statistical artifacts) across a large number of studies included in a VG analysis, it is reasonable to conclude that they will also not change when we apply the test in a new and different situation. This description suggests that there are four key questions that need to be answered in determining whether inferences about the level of validity you can expect from a particular test can be on the basis of VG analyses: (1) did the VG analysis provide convincing evidence to refute the hypothesis of situational specificity?; (2) is the sample of validity coefficients included in the analysis sufficiently large and diverse to provide a reasonable picture of the population?; (3) is the test you are trying to validate a member of the same population of measures as that included in the VG analysis?;

and (4) is the situation in which you wish to apply this test drawn from the population of situations sampled in the VG analysis?

First, it is important to ask whether a VG analysis provides credible evidence about situational specificity. Analyses that are based on relatively weak studies (e.g., studied with small N and unreliable criteria) may not allow you to convincingly sort out variance due to statistical artifacts from variance due to meaningful changes in validity across jobs, organizations, or settings. For example, many early validity generalization analyses featured average sample sizes of approximately 60 to 75 (see Table 1 in McDaniel et al., 1986), whereas more recent studies often have sample sizes ranging from approximately 600 to 750, depending on the criterion (Schmitt et al., 1984). Meaningful inferences about situational specificity depend first and foremost on the quality of the database that supports those inferences, and even studies that include a very large number of studies (as has been the case in some meta-analyses of the ability-performance relationship) may not provide a firm basis for making inferences about situational specificity if most of the underlying studies are poorly designed.

Second, it is important to ask whether the sample of studies included in a meta-analysis spans the population of potential applications of the test. VG analyses that are based on a small number of validities, or that are based on studies taken from a very restricted range of potential applications may not provide a useful basis for making inferences about the consistency of test validity. For example, McDaniel et al. (1994) drew inferences about the validity of situational interviews on the basis of 16 validity coefficients, and about psychological interviews on the basis of 14 coefficients. They were appropriately cautious in interpreting these findings, and potential consumers of meta-analysis must also be cautious about over-interpreting consistency in a small set of validity studies. They must be even more cautious about drawing broad inferences when the sample of validity studies spans only a small part of the range of situations in which a test might be used. For example, validity studies are more likely to be done in lower-level jobs (e.g., clerical jobs, semiskilled labor) than in managerial or professional jobs. When drawing inferences from a VG analysis, it is important to have detailed information about the range of jobs, situations, and so forth represented by the set of validity studies examined. Unfortunately, this sort of information is virtually never presented in the publications describing meta-analyses or VG analyses, and it is often necessary to go back to the original validity studies to determine what sorts of populations have actually been studied.

Third, it is important to determine whether the test you are hoping to use is a member of the same population of instruments that was examined in the body of literature summarized in a VG analysis. For example, there are probably hundreds of tests currently available that measure or claim to measure cognitive abilities (Murphy & Davidshofer, 1998). These tests do not all measure the same abilities (although they probably overlap substantially in their measurement of general cognitive ability, or g: Ree & Earles, 1994), and some tests are certainly better measures than others. Meta-analyses and VG studies rarely provide a detailed, explicit description of the population of tests, measures, etcetera they are designed to sample, and the process of determining whether the test you are hoping to use is really a member of the population of instruments sampled in a meta-analysis is sometimes little more than guesswork. In general, inferences that the test will work in the same way as tests sampled in the literature have worked are most likely to hold up if your tests is highly similar to the tests included in this meta-analysis.

Finally, it is important to consider whether the situation in which you hope to use a test is essentially similar to the situations sampled by the validity studies included in the VG analysis. For example, suppose that in most validity studies, range restriction is a relatively small concern (or is one that has been corrected for), and that validity coefficients reported in a meta-analysis are consistently in the .40's. In your organization, applicants go through extensive screening, and only a handful of candidates are allowed to go on for testing. Should you conclude that the correlation between test scores and performance is likely to be .40 in your organization? Probably not.

In sum, use of meta-analytic results suggesting that validity is essentially constant in a particular sample of studies to infer that it will remain essentially constant in some new setting depends on the same sorts of assumptions and concerns that pertain to all inferential statistics. In particular, concerns over whether the test, situation, etcetera, that you have in mind is a member of the same population sampled in the meta-analysis are vital in determining what inferences can or cannot be made on the basis of meta analyses in particular and VG analysis in particular. Meta-analytic methods are tremendously useful in describing general trends in the research literature, and these trends often give selection practitioners a very good idea of what will or will not work. However, it is easy to overinterpret VG analyses and to make inferences about how well particular tests will work in particular settings that are not empirically justified. One of the great challenges in this sort of analysis is determining what inferences can be made (e.g., the inference that cognitive ability tests are at least minimally valid in most jobs seems a safe one) and what sort cannot be made on the basis of meta-analyses of validity studies.

STRONG INFERENCES FROM WEAK DATA

The methods and conclusions of meta-analysis in general and VG in particular have been the source of some controversy (e.g., Hartigan & Wigdor, 1989; Schmidt et al., 1985). To some extent, this controversy can be a reflection of general concerns about the logic of meta-analyses, particularly those that attempt to pull together very diverse sets of studies (e.g., studies employing a wide range of independent and dependent variables) to estimate a single population parameter (Eyesenck, 1978). This controversy also reflects the distaste of many reviewers for the answers provided by VG analyses (e.g., Hartigan & Wigdor, 1989, comment extensively on the social implications of VG research). However, the most lasting source of controversy is likely to be one that reflects the audacity of the endeavor itself. VG researchers frequently draw what appear to be very strong conclusions on the basis of what appear to be relatively weak data (e.g., see Schmidt's, 1992, widely cited paper telling us "what the data really mean"). That is, VG researchers often draw relatively strong conclusions about the relationships among constructs on the basis of the cumulative weight of what are often poorly conducted studies. For example, VG analyses have led some researchers to conclude that cognitive ability is related to job performance in virtually all jobs (Schmidt & Hunter, 1999). Schmidt, Hunter, and Pearlman (1981) went further concluding that the validity of selection tests for predicting performance was virtually invariant across jobs. This conclusion was based largely on the basis of findings that the observed variance in validities in large-scale databases did not greatly exceed the variance expected on the basis of statistical artifacts. Subsequent research demonstrated that validity levels did in fact vary as a function of job level and complexity (Gutenberg, Arvey, Osburn, & Jenneret, 1983).

Can we really draw strong inferences from weak data? The VG model suggests that we often can. The VG model explains the pattern of results usually found when examining individual validity studies (validity coefficients that seem so weak and variable) in terms of the known effects of statistical artifacts. Once the effects of these artifacts are estimated and removed, there is often little room for other variables (e.g., differences in operationalizations of independent and dependent variables across studies) to have much effect on validities. The fact that the observed data fits this particular model well is an important argument in favor of accepting this explanation. On the other hand, the fact that a model fits the data pretty well is no assurance that it is the correct model (Birnbaum, 1973). There is a clear and immediate need for serious research on alternatives to the VG model. We have gone about as far as we can with demonstrations that it fits; the next step in drawing strong inferences must be an assessment of alternative explanations for these same data. Our ability to draw strong inferences will in the end depend on the explanation provided by the VG model is not only plausible, but that it is also right.

One of the unique strengths of the VG method is its marriage of meta-analysis and psychometrics. Schmidt and Hunter (1977) convincingly argued that we cannot draw appropriate conclusions simply by looking at correlations obtained using unreliable measures in finite, range-restricted samples. There is no doubt that analyses of appropriately corrected correlations would be more informative than analyses of observed correlations, and the theory that underlies these corrections is generally straightforward. However, there are reasons to believe that the operational procedures used to estimate reliability and perhaps range restriction effects do not provide the sorts of estimates that psychometric theory demands (Murphy & DeShon, 2000a, 2000b). For example, numerous VG analyses in recent years have used inter-rater correlations (which typically run in the .50 to .55 range) to estimate the reliability of performance ratings, which implies that observed correlations very substantially underestimate the true correlations between tests and performance measures. Interrater reliabilities are common in many areas of psychology, and there may be good reasons to use them in some settings (e.g., where raters are roughly parallel), but it is clear that they do not estimate the sort of reliability coefficient that underlies the basic psychometric theory and many of the corrections that are at the heart of VG analyses. The greatest single difficulty in consummating a marriage between meta-analysis and psychometric theory may be in developing procedures that can be used to correctly estimate the sources of variance in the sorts of criteria routinely used in VG analysis. Murphy and DeShon (2000b) noted that validity research has not yet caught up with developments and refinements in psychometric thinking that have occurred over the last 30 years, and that we many be farther from obtaining credible estimates of population validities than a casual reading of the VG literature would suggest.

REFERENCES

Barrick, M. R., & Mount, M. K. (1991). The big five personality dimensions and job performance. *Personnel Psychology, 44,* 1–26.

Birnbaum, M. H. (1973). The devil rides again: Correlation as an index of fit. *Psychological Bulletin, 79,* 239–242.

Brannick, M. (2001). Implications of empirical Bayes meta-analysis for test validation. *Journal of Applied Psychology, 86,* 468–480.

Bretz, R. D., Milkovich, G. T., & Read, W. (1992). The current state of performance research and practice: Concerns, directions, and implications. *Journal of Management, 18,* 321–352.

Burke, M. J. (1984). Validity generalization: A review and critique of the correlational model. *Personnel Psychology, 37,* 93–113.

Callender, J. C., & Osburn, H. G. (1981). Testing the constancy of validity with computer-generated sampling distributions of the multiplicative model variance estimate: Results for petroleum industry validation research. *Journal of Applied Psychology, 66,* 274–281.

Cronbach, L. J., Gleser, G. C., Nanda, H., & Rajaratnam, N. (1972). *The dependability of behavioral measurements: Theory of generalizability for scores and profiles.* New York: Wiley.

Eyesenck, H. J. (1978). An exercise in mega-silliness. *American Psychologist, 33,* 517.

Gaugler, B., Rosenthal, D., Thornton, G. C. III, & Bentson, C. (1987). Meta-analysis of assessment center validity. *Journal of Applied Psychology, 72,* 493–511.

Glass, G. V., McGaw, B., & Smith, M. L. (1981). *Meta-analysis in social research.* Beverly Hills, CA: Sage.

Ghiselli, E. E. (1966). *The validity of occupational aptitude tests.* New York: Wiley.

Ghiselli, E. E. (1970). The validity of aptitude tests in personnel selection. *Personnel Psychology, 26,* 461–477.

Gutenberg, R. L., Arvey, R. D., Osburn, H. G., & Jenneret, P. R. (1983). Moderating effects of decision-making/information processing job dimensions on test validities. *Journal of Applied Psychology, 68,* 602–608.

Hartigan, J. A., & Wigdor, A. K. (1989). *Fairness in employment testing: Validity generalization, minority issues, and the General Aptitude Test Battery.* Washington, DC: National Academy Press.

Hedges, L. V. (1988). Meta-analysis of test validities. In H. Wainer & H. Braun (Eds.), *Test validity* (pp. 191–212). Hillsdale, NJ: Lawrence Erlbaum Associates.

Hedges, L. V., & Olkin, I. (1985). *Statistical methods for meta-analysis.* New York: Academic Press.

Hom, P. W., Carnikas-Walker, F., Prussia, G. E., & Griffeth, R. W. (1992). A meta-analytical structural equations analysis of a model of employee turnover. *Journal of Applied Psychology, 77,* 890–909.

Hough, L. M., Eaton, N. K., Dunnette, M. D., Kamp, J. D., & McCloy, R. A. (1990). Criterion-related validities of personality constructs and the effect of response distortion on those validities. *Journal of Applied Psychology, 75,* 581–595.

Hunter, J. E., & Hirsh, H. R. (1987). Applications of meta-analysis. In C. L. Cooper & I. T. Robertson (Eds.), *International review of industrial and organizational psychology* (pp. 321–357). Chichester, UK: Wiley.

Hunter, J. E., & Hunter, R. F. (1984). Validity and utility of alternative predictors of job performance. *Psychological Bulletin, 96,* 72–98.

Hunter, J. E., & Schmidt, F. L. (1990). *Methods of meta-analysis: Correcting error and bias in research findings.* Newbury Park, CA: Sage.

Hunter, M. A., & May, R. B. (1993). Some myths concerning parametric and nonparametric tests. *Canadian Psychology, 34,* 384–389.

Ilgen, D. R., Barnes-Farrell, J. L., & McKellin, D. B. (1993). Performance appraisal process research in the 1980s: What has it contributed to appraisals in use. *Organizational Behavior and Human Decision Processes, 54,* 321–368.

James, L. R., Demaree, R. G., & Mulaik, S. A. (1986). A note on validity generalization procedures. *Journal of Applied Psychology, 71,* 440–450.

James, L. R., Demaree, R. G., Mulaik, S. A., & Ladd, R. T. (1992). Validity generalization in the context of situational models. *Journal of Applied Psychology, 77,* 3–14.

Jawahar, I. M., & Williams, C. R. (1997). Where all the children are above average: The performance appraisal purpose effect. *Personnel Psychology, 50,* 905–926.

Johnson, B. T., Mullen, B., & Salas, E. (1995). Comparison of three major meta-analytic approaches. *Journal of Applied Psychology, 80,* 94–106.

Kemery, E. R., Mossholder, K. W., & Roth, L. (1987). The power of the Schmidt and Hunter additive model of validity generalization. *Journal of Applied Psychology, 72,* 30–37.

Kraiger, K., & Ford, J. K. (1985). A meta-analysis of race effects in performance ratings. *Journal of Applied Psychology, 70,* 56–65.

Law, K. S., Schmidt, F. L., & Hunter, J. E. (1994). A test of two refinements in procedures for meta-analysis. *Journal of Applied Psychology, 79,* 978–986.

Lumsden, J. (1976). Test theory. *Annual Review of Psychology, 27,* 251–280.

MacDonald, P. (1999). Power, Type I, and Type III error rates of parametric and nonparametric statistical tests. *Journal of Experimental Education 67,* 367–379.

McDaniel, M. A., Hirsh, H. R., Schmidt, F. L., Raju, N., & Hunter, J. E. (1986). Interpreting the results of meta-analytic research: A comment on Schmitt, Gooding, Noe, and Kirsch (1984). *Personnel Psychology, 39,* 141–148.

McDaniel, M. A., Whetzel, D. L., Schmidt, F. L., & Maurer, S. D. (1994). The validity of employment interviews: A comprehensive review and meta-analysis. *Journal of Applied Psychology, 79,* 599–616.

McHenry, J. J., Hough, L. M., Toquam, J. L., Hanson, M. A., & Ashworth, S. (1990). Project A validity results: The relationship between predictor and criterion domains. *Personnel Psychology, 43,* 335–355.

Murphy, K. R. (1993). The situational specificity of validities: Correcting for statistical artifacts does not always reduce the trans-situational variability of correlation coefficients. *International Journal of Selection and Assessment, 1,* 158–162.

Murphy, K. (1994). Advances in meta-analysis and validity generalization. In N. Anderson & P. Herriot (Eds.), *International handbook of selection and appraisal: Second Edition* (pp. 323–342). Chichester, UK: Wiley.

Murphy, K. R., & Cleveland, J. N. (1995). *Understanding performance appraisal: Social, organizational and goal-based perspectives.* Thousand Oaks, CA: Sage.

Murphy, K. R., & Davidshofer, C. O. (1998). *Psychological testing: Principles and applications* (4th ed). Englewood Cliffs, NJ: Prentice Hall.

Murphy, K., & DeShon, R. (2000a). Inter-rater correlations do not estimate the reliability of job performance ratings. *Personnel Psychology, 53,* 873–900.

Murphy, K., & DeShon, R. (2000b). Progress in psychometrics: Can industrial and organizational psychology catch up? *Personnel Psychology, 53,* 913–924.

Nathan, B. R., & Alexander, R. A. (1988). A comparison of criteria for test validation: a meta-analytic investigation. *Personnel Psychology, 41,* 517–535.

Osburn, H. G., Callender, J. C., Greener, J. M., & Ashworth, S. (1983). Statistical power of tests of the situational specificity hypothesis in validity generalization studies: A cautionary note. *Journal of Applied Psychology, 68,* 115–122.

Oswald, F. L., & Johnson, J. W. (1998). On the robustness, bias, and stability of statistics from meta-analysis of correlation coefficients: Some initial Monte Carlo findings. *Journal of Applied Psychology, 83,* 164–178.

Pearlman, K., Schmidt, F. L., & Hunter, J. E. (1980). Validity generalization results for tests used to predict job proficiency and training success in clerical occupations. *Journal of Applied Psychology, 65,* 373–406.

Raju, N. S., & Burke, M. J. (1983). Two new approaches for studying validity generalization. *Journal of Applied Psychology, 68,* 382–395.

Raudenbush, S. W., & Bryk, A. S. (1985). Empirical Bayes metaanalysis. *Journal of Educational Statistics, 10,* 75–98.

Ree, M. J., & Earles, J. A. (1994). The ubiquitous predictiveness of g. In M. G. Rumsey, C. B. Walker, & J. H. Harris (Eds.), *Personnel selection and classification* (pp. 127–136). Hillsdale, NJ: Lawrence Erlbaum Associates.

Reilly, R. R., & Chao, G. T. (1982). Validity and fairness of some alternate employee selection procedures. *Personnel Psychology, 35,* 1–67.

Rosenthal, R. (1984). *Meta-analysis procedures for social research.* Beverly Hills, CA: Sage.

Schmidt, F. L. (1992). What do data really mean? Research findings, meta-analysis, and cumulative knowledge in psychology. *American Psychologist, 47,* 1173–1181.

Schmidt, F. L., Gast-Rosenberg, I., & Hunter, J. E. (1980). Validity generalization results for computer programmers. *Journal of Applied Psychology, 65,* 643–661.

Schmidt, F. L., & Hunter, J. E. (1977). Development of a general solution to the problem of validity generalization. *Journal of Applied Psychology, 62,* 643–661.

Schmidt, F. L., & Hunter, J. E. (1996). Measurement error in psychological research: Lessons from 26 research scenarios. *Psychological Methods, 1,* 199–223.

Schmidt, F. L., & Hunter, J. E. (1999). The validity and utility of selection methods in personnel psychology: Practical and theoretical implications of 85 years of research findings. *Psychological Bulletin, 124,* 262–274.

Schmidt, F. L., Hunter, J. E., & Caplan, J. R. (1981). Validity generalization results for two groups in the petroleum industry. *Journal of Applied Psychology, 66,* 261–273.

Schmidt, F. L., Hunter, J. E., & Outerbridge, A. N. (1986). Impact of job experience and ability on job knowledge, work sample, performance, and supervisory ratings of job performance. *Journal of Applied Psychology, 71,* 432–439.

Schmidt, F. L., Hunter, J. E., & Pearlman, K. (1981). Task differences as moderators of aptitude test validity in selection: A red herring. *Journal of Applied Psychology, 66,* 166–185.

Schmidt, F. L., Hunter, J. E., Pearlman, K., & Shane, G. S. (1979). Further tests of the Schmidt-Hunter Bayesian validity generalization procedure. *Personnel Psychology, 32,* 257–281.

Schmidt, F. L., Hunter, J. E., Pearlman, K., Hirsch, H. R., Sackett, P. R., Schmitt, N., Tenopyr, M. L., Kehoe, J., & Zedeck, S. (1985). Forty questions about validity generalizations and meta-analysis with commentaries. *Personnel Psychology, 37,* 407–422.

Schmidt, F. L., Hunter, J. E., Pearlman, K., & Shane, G. S. (1979). Further tests of the Schmidt–Hunter Bayesian validity generalization procedure. *Personnel Psychology, 32,* 257–281.

Schmidt, F. L., Law, K., Hunter, J. E., Rothstein, H. R., Pearlman, K., & McDaniel, M. D. (1993). Refinements in validity generalization procedures: Implications for the situational specificity hypothesis. *Journal of Applied Psychology, 78,* 3–14.

Schmitt, N., Gooding, R. Z., Noe, R. D., & Kirsch, M. (1984). Metaanalyses of validity studies published between 1964 and 1982 and the investigation of study characteristics. *Personnel Psychology, 37,* 407–422.

Sedlmeier, P., & Gigerenzer, G. (1989). Do studies of statistical power have an effect on the power of studies? *Psychological Bulletin, 105,* 309–316.

Steel, P., & Kammeyer-Mueller, J. (2002). Comparing meta-analytic moderator search techniques under realistic conditions. *Journal of Applied Psychology, 87,* 96–111.

Tett, R. P., Jackson, D. N., & Rothstein, M. (1991). Personality measures as predictors of job performance: A meta-analytic review. *Personnel Psychology, 44,* 703–742.

Thomas, H. (1990). A likelihood-based model for validity generalization. *Journal of Applied Psychology, 75,* 13–20.

Viswesvaran, C., Ones, D. S., & Schmidt, F. L. (1996). Comparative analysis of the reliability of job performance ratings. *Journal of Applied Psychology, 81,* 557–574.

Wiesner, W. H., & Cronshaw, S. F. (1988). A meta-analytic investigation of the impact of interview format and degree of structure on the validity of the interview. *Journal of Occupational Psychology, 61,* 275–290.

Wigdor, A. K., & Garner, W. R. (1982). *Ability testing: Uses, consequences, and controversies.* Washington, DC: National Academy Press.

Wilcox, R. R. (1992). Why can methods for comparing means have relatively low power, and what you can you do to correct the problem? *Current Directions in Psychological Science, 1,* 101–105.

Zimmerman, D. W., & Zumbo, B. D. (1993). The relative power of parametric and nonparametric statistical methods. In G. Keren & C. Lewis (Eds.), *A Handbook for Data Analysis in the Behavioral Sciences: methodological Issues* (pp. 481–518). Hillsdale, NJ: Lawrence Erlbaum Associates.

Zwick, R., & Marascuilo, L. A. (1984). Selection of pairwise comparison procedures for parametric and nonparametric analysis of variance models. *Psychological Bulletin, 95,* 148–155.

2

History, Development, Evolution, and Impact of Validity Generalization and Meta-Analysis Methods, 1975–2001[1]

Frank Schmidt
University of Iowa

John Hunter
Michigan State University

EARLY HISTORY AND DEVELOPMENT

Background and Origins

In the Industrial/Organizational (I/O) PhD program at Purdue and other universities in the 1960s, the textbooks and most courses taught that selection procedure validities were situationally specific. The dominant theory held that the validity of the same test for what seemed to be the same job varied from employer to employer, region to region, across time periods, and so forth. It was believed and taught that the same test could have high validity in one location or organization and at the same time have zero validity in another for the same or very similar jobs. This belief was supported by the finding that observed validity coefficients for similar tests and jobs varied substantially across different validity studies and the finding that some of these validity coefficients were statistically significant and others were not. The explanation for this puzzling variability was that jobs that appeared to be the same differed in important but subtle ways in what was required to perform them. The conclusion, we were taught, was that the validity of selection

---

[1]For ease of expression this chapter is written in the first person singular of the first author. However, the test reflects the views of both authors.

procedures had to be estimated anew for each different situation or setting by a validity study conducted in that setting. It was impossible to generalize validity from one setting to others.

For most of my undergraduate career I was a biology major. Perhaps partly for this reason, I found it hard to believe that general and generalizable relationships did not exist in this area because it seemed to me that the goal of research in science was the discovery of generalizable relationships and the explanation of these relationships through theory. In a course on personnel selection taught by Hubert Brogden, I asked for his explanation for the variability of validity estimates. He replied that he thought most of the variability was due to sampling error stemming from use of small samples in civilian validity studies. Brogden's background was different from that of the other faculty: He formerly had been the research director of what is now the Army Research Institute (ARI). His own research had employed the large samples characteristic of military research, and he reported that validities behaved in a lawful and predictable manner. There were no puzzles: If a test was valid for a job in one study, it was valid in all such studies. Other faculty did not accept this view.

After moving to U.S. Office of Personnel Management (OPM) from the Michigan State I/O program in 1974, I began research on the currently important question of the technical feasibility of criterion-related validity studies. As the employment agency for the federal government, we were under pressure from EEOC (Equal Employment Opportunity Commission) to conduct criterion-related validity studies whenever they were *technically feasible*, a term that had not been adequately defined. It occurred to me that low statistical power to detect validity was a way to define technical infeasibility. Hunter, Urry, and I (Schmidt, Hunter, & Urry, 1976) showed that the typical validity study in the literature had statistical power of only about .50 to detect validity given its presence (meaning that these studies were not technically feasible to begin with). These findings led me back to the question of validity generalizability that I had dropped years ago at Purdue. I realized that these findings explained one aspect of the data supporting the situational specificity theory: the fact that about half of all reported validities were statistically significant and half were not. I began to think about the possibility that most or all of the variability in validity estimates for a given test–job combination might be artifactual.

One day in 1975, sitting in my office looking at a distribution of observed validities reported by Ed Ghiselli (1969) in one of his books, the thought occurred to me that I could estimate the amount of variance due to sampling error variance in that distribution by averaging the amount of sampling error variance in the individual studies. I was shocked to find that this came out to be about 70% of the observed variance. I was also surprised to see that once I had subtracted out sampling variance, the remaining variance was small enough to produce a corrected (residual) standard deviation (SD) of validities small enough that almost all observed validities were positive. Then, when I corrected the mean validity for criterion unreliability and mean range restriction (using reasonable estimates of these based on figures in the literature), I saw that almost all the validities were not only positive but also substantial in magnitude.

Excited about this result, I called Jack Hunter at Michigan State. In his opinion, there were no errors in my calculations. He thought this general approach was likely to be fruitful and was also excited about the implications, later sending me an enthusiastic letter to that effect. We discussed ways to refine this procedure so it could be applied systematically to data in the literature. For example, we needed ways to estimate how much variability in validities was due to differences between studies in criterion reliability and range restriction—which I had not at that time taken into account. When we had done this and applied the procedure to several validity distributions from Ghiselli, the resulting paper won the 1976 Society for the Industrial/Organizational Psychology (SIOP) James McKeen Cattell Research Design Award. The following year an expanded version of this paper became our first published validity generalization paper (Schmidt & Hunter, 1977).

About this time we started corresponding with a number of psychologists interested in this topic. (Most of this correspondence is preserved and was available for review in preparing this chapter.) Edwin Ghiselli thought the idea was excellent; he very much regretted that, as a result of a dispute with the Berkeley psychology department, he had just recently destroyed all of his validity files, making it impossible for us to use his data. Bob Guion praised the concept and method, as did Anne Anastasi, who cited the research favorably in subsequent editions of her book *Psychological Testing*, greatly facilitating its acceptance. Marvin Dunnette responded positively and later became an important public defender of this research; he also later confirmed our findings in his own data sets. Lee J. Cronbach wrote saying the method should not be limited to personnel selection and suggesting that we present the method as a general one that could be applied to any research literature; he also brought the related work of Gene Glass to our attention.

However, there was an error in the Schmidt and Hunter (1977) publication, as John Callender discovered via computer simulation in his 1978 dissertation: Our method underestimated the SD of the operational (true) validities. Callender could not pinpoint the cause of the error but we did after he brought it to our attention: We had failed to correct the SD for mean levels of criterion reliability and range restriction, a correction that increases the SD value. We had corrected the mean validity but not the SD of validities. We immediately fixed this problem and presented the corrected results (along with analyses of new data) in Schmidt, Hunter, Pearlman, and Shane (1979).

Callender and Osburn (1980) next published their own quantitative model for validity generalization, a model later shown with real data (Callender & Osburn, 1981; Schmidt, Hunter, & Caplan, 1981) and in computer simulation studies to produce findings very similar to ours, enhancing the credibility of the conclusion that validity was generalizable. This same thing occurred again 2 years later when Raju and Burke (1983) published two additional procedures for assessing the generalizability of validity that again produced very similar numerical results and identical conclusions about generalizability. These developments made it clear that there was not something peculiar about our quantitative model that produced the conclusion that validity was generalizable. Around this same time, Jack Hunter and I (Schmidt, Gast-Rosenberg, & Hunter, 1980) developed a new quantitative VG model—the interactive model—that proved to be slightly more accurate than our original noninteractive model. (The term *interactive* refers to the fact that the new model took into account the fact that the effects of artifacts interact slightly: Specifically, the effects of unreliability are greater when there is less range restriction, and vice versa.)

During these early years, several OPM personnel psychologists were involved in validity generalization research, the first of which was Ken Pearlman. Pearlman (Pearlman, Schmidt, & Hunter, 1980) was lead researcher on a massive VG study of selection for clerical occupations, a study that became perhaps the most frequently cited VG application. He followed this with his dissertation (Pearlman, 1993), which applied VG methods to the Navy's Basic Test Battery, demonstrating the same generalizability in military data that we had found in civilian validity data. Others conducting VG research included Hannah Rothstein (Hirsh), Mike McDaniel, Jim Caplan, Ilene Gast-Rosenberg, Lois Northrop, and (later) Marvin Trattner.

Developments Following Origins

In 1982, heeding Cronbach's advice, we published a book on meta-analysis that extended the method beyond the study of selection procedure validity to all research literatures (Hunter, Schmidt, & Jackson, 1982). This book resulted in the widespread application of these meta-analysis methods to many literatures in I/O psychology and others areas (Schmidt, 1992, 1996). For example, between 1978 and 1997, *Journal of Applied Psychology* published 60 meta-analysis-based studies in areas other than VG, with these studies containing an average of about 15 separate meta-analysis. This development made it difficult for the critics who objected only to the VG studies and their conclusions of generalizability: It was difficult to maintain that these methods were acceptable for application to all types of research literatures except one—validity research literatures. They could point to nothing unique about validity studies that could support such a position.

Nevertheless, the conclusion that validity is generalizable was viewed as radical by many. The theory of situational specificity of validities had been accepted in I/O psychology for over 60 years. In fact, it was typically viewed not as a theory but as an established fact (Schmidt, 1988; Schmidt & Hunter, 1981). So it is not surprising that many found validity generalizability hard to accept. In the early 1980s, Ken Pearlman, Hannah Rothstein, and I began systematically to collect objections and criticism and to set down our responses to them. We recorded all objections although some seemed silly to us—for example, the statement that VG results should always be checked for accuracy by a traditional local validity study. This was like checking the accuracy of the Hubble space telescope from the ground using a pair of hand-held 7x binoculars; we had already shown that traditional local validity studies contained little information (as shown in the wide confidence intervals) and typically had statistical power of only about .50. Milton Hakel, then editor of *Personnel Psychology*, suggested that we publish these objections and our responses in a special issue of that journal. He also suggested that five I/O psychologists respond to our responses—and we to theirs. The result was the article "Forty Question About Validity Generalization and Meta-Analysis" (Schmidt, Hunter, Pearlman, & Hirsh, 1985), at 102 pages perhaps the longest article ever published in that journal.

None of us could have predicted the impact of this article. We were surprised to find that this article caused almost all objections to validity generalization and meta-analysis to melt away—something that our more technical and scientific articles had never been able to achieve. There is a lesson here: Although most editors are loathe to publish such exchanges, they are many times more effective at producing movement and progress in a field than traditional articles. Within 2 years of publication of the Q&As we stopped seeing the negative, skeptical feedback within the field. In less than 10 years, we received both the SIOP and the American Psychological Association (APA) Distinguished Scientific Contributions Awards for this work. This turn-around from having to fight tooth and nail to defend our work to the highest level of recognition was like night and day.

Early applications of validity generalization methods were mostly limited to ability and aptitude tests (e.g., Pearlman et al., 1980; Schmidt et al., 1979; etc.), but applications to a wide variety of different selection procedures soon followed: Work sample tests (Hunter & Hunter, 1984); behavioral consistency and traditional evaluations of education and experience (McDaniel, Schmidt, & Hunter, 1988); assessment centers (Gaugler, Rosenthal, Thornton, & Benson, 1987); integrity tests (Ones, Viswesvaran, & Schmidt, 1993); employment interviews (McDaniel, Whetzel, Schmidt, & Mauer, 1994); job knowledge tests (Dye, Reck, & McDaniel, 1993); biographical data measures (Carlson et al., 1999; Rothstein, Schmidt, Erwin, Owens, & Sparks, 1990); personality scales (Mount & Barrick, 1995); college grade point average (Roth, BeVier, Switzer, & Shippmann, 1996); and others (Hunter & Hunter, 1984). In general, validities for these procedures also proved to be generalizable, although interpretation of generalizability was sometimes more complex (e.g., see Schmidt & Rothstein, 1994). The findings from most of this research is summarized in Schmidt and Hunter (1998).

Selection programs based on validity generalization were introduced by many organizations during the 1980s and 1990s. Examples include the petroleum industry (through the American Petroleum Institute); the electric utility industry (through the Edison Electric Institute); the life insurance industry (through the Association of Insurance Companies); AT&T; Sears; the Gallup Organization; the State of Iowa; ePredix; the Pentagon; and the U.S. OPM. During this period, VG methods were also used in developing and supporting commercial employment tests [e.g., Psychological Services Incorporated (PSI) and the Wonderlic Company included VG results in their test manuals].

VG methods and findings also impacted professional standards. The 1985 edition of the AERA-APA-NCME *Standards for Educational* and Psychological Testing recognized validity generalization and the importance of meta-analysis (p. 12). In the most recent edition of this document (the 5th edition; AERA (American Educational Research Association)-NCME-APA, 1999), validity generalization plays an even larger role (see pp. 15–16 and *Standards* 1.20 and 1.21). The 1987 edition of the *Principles for the Validation and Use of Personnel Selection Procedures*, published by the SIOP, devoted nearly three pages to validity generalization (pp. 26–28). The SIOP *Principles* are currently being updated to incorporate newer research and further developments of this sort can be expected.

Although to our knowledge no up-to-date definitive review is available, validity generalization seems to have fared well in the courts. Sharf (1987) reviewed cases up through the mid-1980s. The most recent case we are aware of is U.S. Department of Justice v. City of Torrance, CA. In that 1996 decision, all basic VG findings were accepted by the court, and the court's rejection of the U.S. Department of Justice (USDOJ) challenge to the Torrance police and fire tests appears to be based mostly on the court's acceptance of VG and related findings. In addition to U.S. court cases, the use of validity generalization as the basis for selection systems was upheld in Canada in 1987 (Maloley v. Canadian Civil Service Commission). A comprehensive review of court decisions related to validity generalization would probably be useful at this point.

In 1990, Jack Hunter and I (Hunter & Schmidt, 1990) published an expanded and updated version of the 1982 book. As meta-analysis applications increased in frequency, this book became widely used and cited, and meta-analysis classes based on this book were introduced at a number of universities. We are now in the process of revising and updating this book again.

The Largest VG Project in History:
The GATB VG Program

In the early 1980s, the U.S. Department of Labor (USDOL) launched the largest and most influential VG program ever and one of the largest employment testing programs in history. This program was based on the U.S. Employment Service's General Aptitude Test Battery (GATB), which was introduced in 1947 for use by state employment agencies. Until the advent of this new VG program, use of the GATB had been based on job-specific validity studies. In the 25 years since its introduction, such studies had been conducted for only about 400 of the more than 12,000 jobs in USDOL's *Dictionary of Occupational Titles* (1977), and hence could be used only with these jobs (about 3% of all jobs). In the late 1970s, officials in USDOL became aware of VG methods and research and wanted to apply these methods to the GATB database so as to extend validity generalization of all 12,000 plus jobs.

USDOL officials approached me in 1979 and wanted me to conduct a large-scale VG project for the GATB. At that time I was directing a research program at the U.S. OPM. As a government employee, I could not accept any compensation from USDOL for such a project; nor could I do it on OPM time. I therefore recommended they contact John Hunter at Michigan State to do the project. They did, and under contract he conducted the massive project for them, producing four USDOL technical reports (Hunter, 1983a; 1983b; 1983c; 1983d). Basic GATB VG results were reported in Hunter and Hunter (1984).

Based on factor analysis, Hunter (1983a) reduced the 12 GATB subtests to three broad abilities [general mental ability (GMA), general perceptual/spatial ability (GSA), and general psychomotor ability(GPA)]. He classified all jobs into five complexity levels (in terms of mental demands). With the exception of GPA in high complexity jobs, generalizable validity was found for all abilities at all five complexity levels. Based on the VG results, Hunter produced separate regression equations for predicting job performance for each of the five complexity levels (job families). The higher the complexity level of jobs, the greater was the regression weight on GMA; the lower the complexity level, the greater was the regression weight on GPA. (GSA received a nonzero weight for only one job family.) Due to the complementary nature of GMA and GPA, the multiple R was high (.50 or higher) for all five job families (Hunter, 1983b).

The VG program was pilot tested in North Carolina (McKinney, 1984) and then was offered nationwide. Ultimately it was adopted and used by state employment services in 42 states, with hundreds of thousands of applicants being screened and referred to employers each year. It was very popular with business and industry, with most Fortune 500 companies and thousands of smaller firms using it (Madigan, Scott, Deadrick, & Stoddard, 1986; *Work America*, 1986a; 1986b; 1986c). Some firms (e.g., Phillip Morris; see McKinney, 1984) conducted studies that showed that employees entering through the VG program averaged higher job performance, better training performance, less absenteeism, and fewer accidents. Using firms signed referral agreements with state employment agencies and were free to use any additional selection procedures in hiring those referred to them by the VG program. The service was free to employers and applicants alike.

Because the GATB VG program was a referral program, not a selection program per se, USDOL did not want to disproportionately screen out minorities before they got to the selection or hiring point. Therefore USDOL adopted a within-group norming system for Blacks, Hispanics, and Whites in which the percentile score for each individual was reported based on norms for his or her group ("race norming"). Despite allegations to the contrary in the press, these adjustments were not secret and were announced openly in materials distributed to employers and states on the program.

In 1987, the U.S. Department of Justice (USDOJ) challenged the score adjustment part of the VG program on grounds it was a form of racial discrimination. USDOL and USDOJ agreed to submit their dispute—and indeed the entire GATB VG program—to a National Research Council (NRC) "blue ribbon" committee of the National Academy of Sciences for study. In its May 1989 report (Hartigan & Wigdor, 1989) the NRC committee endorsed the appropriateness of VG methods, supported the validity and utility of the GATB VG program, and supported the use of score adjustments.[2] The George H. W. Bush administration viewed the score adjustments negatively, and in 1990 Secretary of Labor Elizabeth Dole published a proposal in the Federal Register to suspend the GATB VG program. However, in the public comment period the response was 99% negative—the highest negative response ever—with most of the objections coming from employers, a Republican constituency. Dole was forced to withdraw her proposal.

The following year the 1991 Civil Right Acts (CRA) became law. This new CRA specifically forbade any score adjustments based on race, ethnicity, or sex. In February 1992, 3 months after the effective date of the 1991 CRA, USDOL announced that, in accordance with the law, it was discontinuing score adjustments—but would continue the GATB VG program without the adjustments for any state wishing to continue using it. The following summer, USDOL Secretary Dole unilaterally suspended the GATB VG program and announced a new research program to develop a revised GATB that would not show group score differences. As we know from decades of research, this is an impossible goal for reliable cognitive ability

---

[2]The committee did take issue with some of the technical details of the USDOL VG studies. They questioned aspects of the range restriction corrections and the corrections for unreliability of the job performance measures. However, the committee concluded that when its preferred corrections were applied, validity was still present and still generalized and that selection utility was still substantial. It is now apparent that the committee erred in the technical assessments (e.g., see Schmidt, Ones, & Hunter, 1992).

tests (Sackett, Schmidt, Ellingson, & Kabin, 2001), and no such revised GATB was ever produced.

Thus ended what was the largest, most impactful VG program in history—and also one of the largest employment testing programs in history. It is instructive to examine the reasons behind this development. The termination had nothing to do with the VG methods—all sides agreed that the VG methods and findings were sound. Instead, the termination resulted from what has come to be a national social dilemma, captured in the following statements: (a) Unless we use valid employment tests of cognitive ability, we experience large losses in performance and productivity (as shown by utility studies, including those conducted as part of this project; Hunter, 1983d); (b) We cannot use GMA tests without adverse impact because the 1991 CRA forbids score adjustments by race; and (c) We cannot use GMA tests with unadjusted scores because group differences result in levels of adverse impact that are politically prohibitive—even if they are legally defensible. In the end, the GATB VG program had the effect of greatly clarifying this national dilemma. This dilemma faces the entire U.S. economy, and in 2002 there is still no solution for it.

In the private sector defacto score adjustments are currently made informally and subjectively. Because no literal or formal changes are made in numerical scores, these practices are considered technically not to violate the 1991 CRA. Despite statistical, logical, and even ethical problems (Schmidt & Hunter, 1995, in press-b), significance test-based sliding bands with within-band racial preferences is a popular method for making de facto score adjustments (Sackett & Wilk, 1994). This problem does not exist in many other countries, and large-scale government GMA-based VG programs have been introduced in Canada and some European countries.

RECENT HISTORY: FURTHER DEVELOPMENTS

Meta-analysis (and VG) methods are complex both conceptually and technically. They are complex conceptually because their understanding and proper use requires major changes in the way researchers think about the research enterprise and the meaning of individual studies and research literatures (Schmidt, 1992; 1996). They are complex technically because they combine measurement methods and statistical methods in the same procedure (Hunter & Schmidt, 1990), something rarely done in the past. That is, meta-analysis methods require the simultaneous consideration of both measurement error and sampling error. Most textbook discussions of measurement error (e.g., Nunnally & Bernstein, 1994) assume a very large N, so that the discussion can ignore sampling error and focus solely on measurement error. Similarly, most statistics texts implicitly assume perfect reliability (the absence of measurement error) so that the discussion can focus solely on sampling error and ignore measurement error. Both of these approaches are unrealistic because both types of error exist in all real research data. Partly because of this complexity, meta-analysis methods (and VG methods) remained the focus of technical and research attention after the major questions about the acceptability of the methods were settled in their favor. This section discusses some of these developments in the history of VG methods.

Refinements to Increase Accuracy of the SD$_\rho$ Estimate

All quantitative estimates are approximations. Even if these estimates are quite accurate, it is always desirable to make them more accurate if possible. Perhaps the most complex task performed by meta-analysis methods is the estimation of the SD of the population correlations (SD$_\rho$). In VG studies, this is the estimated SD of the operational (true) validities, and it determines the location of the 90% credibility value in the true validity distribution, the value that is usually used to decide if validity generalizes. One way to make this estimate more accurate is to find a more accurate estimate of the sampling error variance of the correlation coefficient in meta-analysis. Hunter and Schmidt (1994) showed analytically that using mean r ($\bar{r}$) in place of r in the sampling error variance formula for the correlation coefficient increases the accuracy of this estimate in the homogenous case (i.e., the case in which SD$_\rho$ = 0). Because of the complexity of the math, no such analytic demonstration was possible for the heterogeneous case (i.e., the case in which SD$_\rho$ > 0). We therefore tested the heterogeneous case using computer simulation and found that there, too, use of mean r improved accuracy over the traditional sampling error variance formula (Law, Schmidt, & Hunter, 1994b). Aguinis (2001), again using computer simulation, provided an even more complete and thorough demonstration of this fact. This finding that the traditional formula underestimates the amount of sampling error variance and that its accuracy can be improved by using $\bar{r}$ in the formula instead of the observed r from the individual study at hand is important, because the traditional formula has been accepted throughout statistics since around 1900. However, in most VG studies even the more accurate formula still underestimates (and undercorrects for) sampling error variance. Millsap (1989) showed that the presence of direct range restriction increases sampling error variance and therefore causes the formula to underestimate the amount of sampling variance. Aguinis and Whitehead (1997) showed the same thing for indirect range restriction. Hence final corrected true validity SDs are still overestimated in VG studies, and validity generalizability is correspondingly underestimated.[3] (However, in non-VG meta-analyses there may be no range restriction, and if so this problem does not occur.)

The aforementioned improvement increases the accuracy of the estimate of the residual SD (SD_{res})—the SD of observed rs after variation due to artifacts has been subtracted out. Another opportunity to improve accuracy occurs at the step in which the residual SD is corrected to estimate SD_ρ or the SD of operational (true) validities. This opportunity occurs with respect to the correction for range restriction. One can think of the range restriction correction as multiplying the observed correlation by a constant. For example, if the correction increases the r by 30%, then the constant of correction is 1.30. In our earlier methods, if the constant of correction for range restriction for *the mean r* was, say, 1.30, we applied that same constant to all the values in the residual distribution. That is, we assumed (as an approximation) that the range restriction correction would increase all values of r by 30%. Actually, the range restriction correction (unlike the measurement error correction) is nonlinear: it increases small r values by *more* than 30% (in this example) and large values by less than 30% (in this example). Hence applying the constant of range restriction correction of the mean r to all rs resulted in overestimation of SD_ρ. We therefore added a refinement that computed the range restriction correction independently for each separate r value in the residual distribution and tested it using computer simulation methods. This study (Law, Schmidt, & Hunter, 1994a) showed that doing this increased the accuracy of estimates of SD_ρ. Both these accuracy-increasing refinements were then added to our interactive meta-analysis program and that program was then used to reanalyze the extensive database from Pearlman et al. (1980). This research (Schmidt et al., 1993) showed that validity was more generalizable than Pearlman et al. (1980) concluded. Specifically, the true validity SDs were substantially

---

[3]Because there are at least five other uncorrectable factors contributing to underestimation of validity generalizability (see Schmidt et al., 1993, pp. 8–11), it is difficult to calibrate the exact size of this effect in real data. However, see Aguinis and Whitehead (1997) for some attempts to do this.

smaller, 90% credibility values were considerably larger, and the percent of variance accounted for by artifacts was substantially larger. These developments show that the accuracy of even well established methods—methods that are very accurate by the standards of psychological research—can nevertheless be improved. The findings also further undercut the theory of situational specificity of validity. In fact, the average amount of variance accounted for was so large (87%) and the average SD_ρ value was so small (.097) that Schmidt et al. (1993) interpreted their findings as fully disconfirming the situational specificity hypothesis (the hypothesis that $SD_\rho > 0$) for aptitude and ability tests. They reasoned that the tiny amount of remaining variance (.0094 on average) could be explained by the six sources of artifactual variance that could not be corrected for (see pp. 8–11 of that article). [Note: Because the focus in this study was on SD_ρ, and because of space limitations, mean true validity estimates were not reported in this study; however, they can be found in Hunter and Schmidt (1996). The accuracy of estimates of mean true validity is discussed in a later section of this chapter.]

I should note here that disconfirmation of the situational specificity hypothesis is not required for validity generalizability. Even if $SD_\rho > 0$, validity still generalizes so long as the 90% credibility value is greater than zero. However, the fact that in a large validity database (more than 600 studies) created over a span of 6 decades by a wide variety of researchers, essentially all validity variance can be accounted for by statistical and measurement artifacts is a striking scientific finding. It illustrates the extent to which nature can indeed be parsimonious at its fundamental level despite surface appearances to the contrary.

The Argument for Large *N* Studies

Some have argued that the need for meta-analysis and validity generalization studies is merely a consequence of small sample studies with their typically low levels of statistical power. The argument is made that researchers should conduct only large sample studies and that such studies, with their higher statistical power would make meta-analysis unnecessary (e.g., see Bobko & Stone-Romero, 1998; Murphy, 1997). We question this position for three reasons: (a) it leads to reductions in the total amount of information available in the literature for the calibration of validities; (b) it reduces the ability to detect the presence of potential moderators; and (c) it does not eliminate the need for meta-analysis.

Loss of Information. For practical reasons, many researchers cannot obtain large sample sizes, despite their best efforts. If a requirement for large Ns is imposed, many studies that would otherwise be conducted and published will not be conducted—studies that could contribute useful information to subsequent meta-analyses (Schmidt, 1996). This is what has happened in the area of validity studies in personnel psychology. After publication of the Schmidt et al. (1976) study showing that statistical power in traditional validity studies averaged only about .50, average sample sizes of published studies increased from around 70 to more than 300. However, as we expected, the number of studies declined dramatically, with the result that the total amount of information created per year or per decade (expressed as total Ns in a VG study) for entry into validity generalization studies decreased. That is, the total amount of information generated in the earlier period from large numbers of small sample studies was greater than that generated in the later period for a much smaller number of large sample studies. Hence there was a net loss in ability to calibrate validities.

Reduced Ability to Detect Potential Moderators. The situation described earlier creates a net loss of information even if there are no moderator variables to be detected; that is, even if $SD_\rho = 0$ in all validity domains studied. Although $SD_\rho = 0$ is a viable hypothesis in the predictor domains of ability and aptitude tests (Schmidt et al., 1993), this hypothesis is probably not viable in some other predictor domains (e.g., assessment centers, college grades). And it is certainly not viable in many research areas outside personnel selection. If $SD_\rho = 0$, the total number of studies does not matter; all that matters in determining the accuracy of the VG study is the total N across all studies in the VG analysis. As described above, this total N has been reduced in recent years. But if $SD_\rho > 0$, then it is critical to have an accurate estimate of SD_ρ. In estimating SD_ρ, N is the number of studies. Hence, holding the total N in the meta-analysis constant, a small number of large studies provides a less accurate estimate of SD_ρ than a large number of small studies (Hunter & Schmidt, 1990, chap. 9). A large number of small studies samples a much more numerous array of potential moderators—in fact, each small study samples different potential moderators that might contribute to $SD_\rho > 0$. For example, suppose total N for the VG study is 5,000. If this total N consists of 4 studies each with $N = 1250$, the estimate of SD_ρ is based on only four data points: four samples from the distribution of ρ. On the other hand, if this total N consists of 50 studies of $N = 100$ each, then the estimate of SD_ρ is based on 50 data points sampled from the ρ distribution—and is therefore likely to be much more accurate (Hunter & Schmidt, 1990, chap. 9). This greatly increases what Cook and Campbell (1976, 1979) called "external validity."

Bobko and Stone-Romero (1998) argued that this same level of precision of estimation for SD_ρ can be obtained with a single large N study by in effect dividing the one large study into many smaller ones. This is unlikely to be true: The single large study reflects the way a single researcher or set of researchers conducted that one study (same measures, same population, same analysis procedures, etc.). It is unlikely to contain within itself the kinds of variations in the methods and other variables that are found in 50 independently conducted studies. Another way to see this is to consider the continuum of different types of replications of studies (Aronson, Ellsworth, Carlsmith, & Gonzales, 1990). In a literal replication, the same researcher conducts the new study in exactly the same way as the original study. In a operational replication, a different researcher attempts to duplicate the original study. In systematic replication, a second researcher conducts a study in which many features of the original study are maintained but some aspects (e.g., types of subjects) are changed. Literal and operational replications contribute in only a limited way to external validity (generalizability) of findings, but systematic replications are useful in assessing the generalizability of findings across different types of subjects, measures, etcetera. Finally, in the case of constructive replications, the researcher attempts to vary most of the aspects of the initial study's methods, including subject type, measures, and manipulations. Successful constructive replication adds greatly to the external validity of a finding. Breaking up a large study into pieces is similar to the creation of several literal replications and does not contribute much to external validity or generalizability of findings. However, in a meta-analysis of a large number of small studies, the studies in the meta-analysis constitute systematic or constructive replications of each other (i.e., many study aspects vary across studies). Under these circumstances, a finding of a small SD_ρ (or a small SD_δ) provides strong support for generalizability—that is, this result is strong evidence of external validity of the finding. If the number of studies in the meta-analysis is small, even if each study is a large sample study, the meta-analysis is weaker because the number of systematic or constructive replications underlying the final results is smaller and hence external validity is more questionable. This is another approach to understanding why a large number of small studies is better than a small number of large studies.

Meta-Analysis Still Necessary.   Finally, even if all studies conducted are large sample studies, it is still necessary to integrate findings across studies to ascertain the meaning of the set of studies as a whole. Because meta-analysis is the statistically optimal method for doing this, meta-analysis is still necessary. In concluding that meta-analysis would no longer be necessary, advocates of the position I am critiquing appear to be thinking of the fact that large N studies, with their high statistical power, will show agreement on statistical significance tests: If there is an effect, all studies should detect it as statistically significant. But this does not mean meta-analysis is unnecessary. What is important is the estimates of effect size magnitudes. Effect size estimates will still vary across studies,[4] and meta-analysis is still necessary to integrate these findings across studies. Hence we cannot escape the need for meta-analysis.

We conclude therefore that a movement to a smaller number of larger N studies would not contribute to the advancement of cumulative knowledge in the VG area or any other area of research. In fact, it would be detrimental to knowledge generation and discovery.

Bayesian Models in VG

After a VG analysis is completed for a particular predictor-job combination, it is likely that within a short period of time a new primary validity study will appear on that same predictor-job combina-

---

[4] The argument here is general and is not limited to validity generalization studies, much less to VG studies of ability and aptitude tests. That is, the argument is directed to meta-analysis applications in general because the arguments of Bobko and Stone-Romero (1998) were directed to meta-analysis as a general method that can be applied to all behavioral and social science research literatures. As noted later in the text, in VG studies of ability and aptitude measures, (corrected) validity estimates should not vary much across large N studies—because sampling error variance should be small in large N studies, the effects of range restriction and measurement error should be corrected for, and SD_p is small. Low variability of estimated true validities cannot necessarily be expected for VG studies of other selection procedures, even with large N studies. Also, Ns required to reduce sampling error variance to low levels are much larger than typically realized, usually 3000 or more (Hunter & Schmidt, 1990, chap. 1). Studies with Ns of 300, 400, or 500 still contain considerable sampling error and hence show variability across studies. Persistent underestimation of the size of sampling error variance has been a constant theme throughout the 100 year history of I/O psychology (Schmidt, Ocasio, Hillery, & Hunter, 1985).

tion. How should that that new study be combined with the pre-existing VG meta-analysis? After the first few years of work in this area, the answer we adopted is that the VG analysis should be updated (rerun) to include this new study and any others that have appeared since completion of the original VG analysis. This ensures that each new study will be treated and weighted in the same way as other studies. This procedure also has the advantage of being general: It is the procedure of choice for handling new studies in all other research areas (non-VG areas) inside and outside of I/O psychology.

However, there is another possibility, one that we considered in our early publications (e.g., Schmidt & Hunter, 1977): The new study can be combined in a Bayesian way, using Bayes Theorem, with the distribution of operational validities from the original meta-analysis. That is, $\bar{\rho}$ and SD_ρ from the VG study is taken as defining the Bayesian prior distribution and this distribution is multiplied by the results of the new study (the likelihood function) to produce a Bayesian posterior validity estimate. This estimate can be taken as applying to the setting in which the new study was conducted. Brannick (2001) has recently revisited this possibility and has recommended this approach. We discontinued our advocacy of this approach when it became apparent that it leads to overweighting of the new primary study. That is, this approach typically gives much heavier weight to the single new study than it would get if the VG study were rerun including this study. In view of findings casting doubt on situational specificity of validities, it is highly doubtful that such heavy weights are justified. In addition, we believe that any procedure used in VG should have the quality of generality: it should be equally appropriate if applied to non-VG research literatures. It is hard to think of a research literature in which it would be appropriate to give much larger weight to one study simply because that study happened to be conducted after the relevant meta-analysis was completed. Hence we believe that all VG studies (and all meta-analyses in all research areas) should be updated and rerun periodically by incorporating new studies that have become available in the interim. This is the best way to incorporate new data into the cumulative research literature.

It should be noted that even if Bayes Theorem is used as earlier described, it can only be used in the heterogeneous case (i.e., where $SD_\rho > 0$). In the heterogeneous case, only a random effects meta-analysis model can be used; random effects models allow $SD_\rho > 0$, whereas fixed effects models assume a priori that $SD_\rho = 0$. (See discussion below). Brannick (2001) argued that the Bayesian procedure can be used with fixed effects models as well as with random effects models. In fact, it is a logical contradiction to apply Bayes Theorem using the fixed effects meta-analysis model. If the fixed effects model is used, then SD_ρ of the prior Bayesian distribution is by definition zero, and the final (posterior) validity estimate is always the same as the $\bar{\rho}$ from the prior meta-analysis. That is, the new study will always get an effective weight of zero and will not have any effect on the final estimate. Hence the Bayesian model cannot be used with fixed effects meta-analysis models.

Standard Errors of Model Estimates

The two most important parameters estimated for random effects models of VG or meta-analysis are $\bar{\rho}$ and SD_ρ. It is perhaps easy to forget that these quantities are estimates of the parameters, not the parameters themselves, because in VG and meta-analysis reports they are rarely topped off with a circumflex ($\hat{}$). Technically, these values should be written as $\hat{\bar{\rho}}$ and $\hat{SD}_\rho$ but typically are not in the interests of simplifying the symbolism. Every estimate has a standard error (SE), known or unknown, and our models have been criticized for not reporting SEs for these estimates (e.g., F. Drasgow, November 2, 2000). Schmidt, Hunter, and Raju (1988) provided formulas for the SE of mean observed r, but this is not the same statistic. We derived the equations for these SEs (Hunter & Schmidt, 1987a; 1987b) but have not emphasized these statistics. In statistics, the use made of the SE of the mean is in placing confidence intervals around the mean. In VG and meta-analysis, confidence intervals around the mean are not as important as *credibility* intervals—because it is the whole distribution, and not the just the mean, that is important. Our focus has been on credibility intervals (Hunter & Schmidt, 1990; Whitener, 1990). Second, SEs are rarely given for SD estimates in statistical models. This can be seen in the fact that almost all researchers know by heart the formula for the SE of the mean $(SD/\sqrt{n})$ but few can even remember seeing the formula for the SE of a SD. [How many times have you seen a confidence interval placed around a SD? Or seen an SD tested for statistical significance (which also requires the SE estimate)?] In fact, other random effects models—the Hedges-Vevea (1998) model, the Raju and Burke (1983) models, the Callender and Osburn (1980) also did not provide this SE formula.

The formulas for the $SE_{\bar{\rho}}$ are complex but the simple approximations below are fairly accurate. If correlations are corrected individually (see chap. 3 of Hunter & Schmidt, 1990), then:

$$SE_{\bar{\rho}} = SD_{r_c} / \sqrt{k}, \tag{1}$$

where $SE_{\bar{\rho}}$ is the SE of $\bar{\rho}$, SD_{r_c} is the SD of the correlations after each has been individually corrected for measurement error and other artifacts, and k is the number of studies. If artifact distribution meta-analysis (see chap. 4 of Hunter & Schmidt, 1990) is used, then:

$$SE_{\bar{\rho}} = [(\bar{\rho} / \bar{r})SD_r] / \sqrt{k}, \tag{2}$$

where $SE_{\bar{\rho}}$ is the SE of $\bar{\rho}$, $\bar{\rho}$ = the estimate of mean true validity, $\bar{r}$ = the mean observed (uncorrected) validity, SD_r = the SD of the observed (uncorrected) correlations, and k = the number of studies. These formulas have been used in published studies (e.g., Judge & Bono, 2000 used Equation 1). In the case of artifact distribution meta-analysis, an (equivalent) alternative to Equation (2) can be used to compute confidence intervals for $\bar{\rho}$. First, use the formulas presented by Schmidt, Hunter, and Raju (1988) to compute $SE_{\bar{r}}$, the SE of the mean observed correlation. Second, use $SE_{\bar{r}}$ to compute the confidence interval (CI) around $\bar{r}$. Third, correct the endpoints of this CI for mean levels of measurement error and range restriction to yield the CI for $\bar{\rho}$. This method is used in Viswesvaran, Schmidt, and Ones (2002). The formulas for the SE of SD_{ρ} are both more complicated and less useful and I do not present them here because of space limitations.

Fixed and Random Effects Models in VG and Meta-Analysis

Recently two questions have received considerable attention in meta-analysis and VG: (a) the relative appropriateness of fixed versus random effects meta-analysis models (Hedges & Vevea, 1998; Hunter & Schmidt, 2000); and (b) the relative accuracy of different random effects models (Field, 2001; Hall & Brannick, 2002).

Fixed Versus Random Effects Models. As noted previously, the basic distinction here is that fixed effects models assume a priori that exactly the same ρ (or δ) value underlies all studies in the meta-analysis (i.e., $SD_{\rho} = 0$). In the area of VG, this is the same as assuming a priori that there is no situational specificity and that true validities therefore generalize perfectly. Random effects models, on the other hand, allow for the possibility that population parameters (ρ or δ values) vary from study to study; a major purpose of random effects models is to estimate this variance. The random effects model is the more general one: fixed effects models are a special case of random effects models in which $SD_\rho = 0$. In fact, when a random effects model is applied to data in which $SD_\rho = 0$, it becomes mathematically a fixed effects model. Application of a random effects model can result in an estimated SD_ρ of zero, a finding indicating that a fixed effects model would be appropriate for those data. Application of a random effects model can detect the fact that $SD_\rho = 0$; however, application of a fixed effects model cannot estimate SD_ρ if $SD_\rho > 0$. That is, random effects models allow for any possible value of SD_ρ, whereas fixed effects models allow for only one: $SD_\rho = 0$.

All of the models in Hunter and Schmidt (1990) and related publications are random effects models (Hedges & Olkin, 1985, p. 242; Hunter & Schmidt, 2000; Schmidt & Hunter, 1999). These models all assume that population parameters may vary across studies and attempt to estimate that variance. The basic model is subtractive: the estimate of population variance is the variance that is left after variance due to sampling error and other artifacts is subtracted out. Some authors (e.g., Field, 2001; Hedges & Vevea, 1998; Hall & Brannick, 2002) have pointed out that the weights these procedures apply to studies in computing means and variances across studies are somewhat different from those usually applied in random effects models. This is true. The rationale for our study weighting approach (weighting by sample size) is presented in Hunter and Schmidt (1990, chaps. 2 and 3). Although traditional random effects weights produce slightly more accurate estimates of the mean, weighting by sample size produces more accurate estimates of population SDs (SD_ρ values), the accuracy of which is critical to VG and meta-analysis in general. This question is addressed empirically in studies discussed below that examine the accuracy of different models. Like the models in Hunter and Schmidt (1990) and related publications, the Callender-Osburn and Raju-Burke VG models are also random effects models and also weight studies by sample size. All of these models have been shown in computer simulation studies to produce very accurate estimates of mean correlations.

Hedges and Olkin (1985) and Hedges and Vevea (1998) presented both fixed and random effects models. However, as a practical matter their random effects models have almost never been used in the literature. For example, all of the applications of the Hedges-Olkin methods of meta-analysis that have appeared in *Psychological Bulletin* have used their fixed effects models (Hunter & Schmidt, 2000). None have used their random effects models. (All applications of the

Rosenthal-Rubin models in that journal have also used fixed effects models.) Hedges and Olkin (1985) recommended that when the fixed effects model is used, the chi-square homogeneity test should be applied. They state that only if this test is nonsignificant should one conclude that $SD_\rho = 0$ and proceed to apply the fixed effects model. The National Research Council (1992) pointed out that this chi-square test has low power to detect variation in population values and has therefore recommended against the use of fixed effects models and in favor of random effects models. Not only does the chi-square test often fail to detect real heterogeneity, many users of the Hedges-Olkin fixed effects model apply that model even when the chi-square test is significant, indicating the fixed effects model is not appropriate (Hunter & Schmidt, 2000). If the fixed effects model is applied when it is not appropriate (i.e., when $SD_\rho > 0$), confidence intervals are erroneously narrow and all significance tests have Type I biases (National Research Council, 1992). These Type I biases are typically quite large (Hunter & Schmidt, 2000). The upshot of this is that most of the meta-analyses appearing in *Psychological Bulletin* and other journals, based as they are on fixed effects models, are potentially inaccurate and probably should be redone using random effects models (Hunter & Schmidt, 2000).

Accuracy of Different Random Effects Models

However, fixed effects models have never been used in VG research and have rarely been used in any I/O research. So the key question in personnel selection and I/O psychology is which of the random effects models is the most accurate. This question has been addressed over the years by the many computer simulation studies in *Journal of Applied Psychology* and *Personnel Psychology* comparing the accuracy of our noninteractive and interactive models, the Callender-Osburn model, the two Raju-Burke models, and other models. The studies by Law et al. (1994a & 1994b) discussed previously are examples of such studies. The general finding is that all of these random effects models are quite accurate by the standards of social science. (We interpret Law et al., 1994a, as showing that the addition of the two accuracy-increasing features discussed earlier makes our non-interactive model slightly more accurate than the others in most realistic situations.)

It is probably the case that one reason so few researchers conducting meta-analyses in social psychology and other non-I/O areas have used the Hedges-Olkin random effects models is that the

Hedges and Olkin (1985) book developed its fixed effects models more completely than its random effects models. Recently, however, Hedges and Vevea (1998) presented a more complete development and discussion of their random effects model. This has stimulated interest in comparing the accuracy of the Hedges-Vevea (1998) and the Hunter-Schmidt (1990) random effects models.

Field (2001) compared the accuracy of the Hedges-Vevea (H-V) and the Hunter-Schmidt (H-S) random effects models in estimating $\bar{\rho}$. (Strangely, he did not compute or compare estimates of SD_ρ, nor did he include or compare the Raju-Burke models or the Callender-Osburn model.) He found that when the studies were homogenous (i.e., $SD_\rho = 0$), the two models had similar accuracy in estimating $\bar{\rho}$ (see his Table 1). However, he found that when the studies were heterogeneous (e.g., $SD_\rho > 0$), the H-V model overestimated $\bar{\rho}$, often by substantial amounts, while the H-S method slightly underestimated these values. For example, when the actual mean was .30, the H-V estimates ranged from .40 to .43, whereas the H-S estimates were all .29 (all estimates rounded to two places). When the actual mean was .50, the H-V estimates ranged from .64 to .71, whereas the H-S estimates ranged from .47 to .49. The overestimation produced by the H-V model was much larger than the underestimation produced by the H-S model. We believe that the overestimation produced by the H-V model stems from biases induced by use of the Fisher's z transformation (Hunter & Schmidt, 1990, pp. 213–218; Hunter, Schmidt, & Coggin, 1996; Schmidt et al., 1986). Field also concluded this. Our procedures (like those of the Raju-Burke and Callender-Osburn models) do not use the Fisher's z transformation. All calculations are performed directly on the correlation coefficients.

Hall and Brannick (2002) also used computer simulation to compare the H-V (1998) and H-S (1990) random effects models. Like Field, they also did not examine the Raju-Burke or Callender-Osburn random effects models. However, Hall and Brannick did examine the accuracy of SD_ρ estimates, in addition to $\bar{\rho}$ estimates. But because the H-V method estimates SD_ρ in Fisher's z units, and because there is no way to transform a Fisher's z SD estimate into correlation units, they compared the two methods on the basis of credibility intervals, rather than directly on SD_ρ values. They produced credibility intervals in correlation units for the H-V method by back transforming the end points of the Fisher's z credibility intervals. They also examined separately situations in which artifacts attenuated correlations and those in which it was assumed there were no artifacts other than sampling error (i.e., assumed perfect measurement and no range restriction). (The Field study, by contrast, did not examine any artifacts beyond sampling error.) Whether the studies were homogenous or heterogeneous, when there were no artifacts other than sampling error, they found that the H-V method tended to overestimate $\bar{\rho}$ values, whereas the H-S model produced small underestimates—findings similar to Field's, although the H-V model overestimation was less severe in the Hall and Brannick (2002) study.

However, when measurement error and range restriction were present, the H-V model produced very large *underestimates* of $\bar{\rho}$— as would be expected because that model contains no means of correcting for the effects of these artifacts. So Hall and Brannick added the H-S artifact correction methods to the H-V model and then reevaluated that model. With the H-S artifact correction methods grafted on, the accuracy of the H-V model was much improved. However, it still tended to overestimate $\bar{\rho}$—although not by as large a percentage as in the no-artifact condition. The H-S model was generally more accurate than the H-V model.

A major finding in Hall and Brannick (2002) pertained to the credibility intervals produced by the two methods. Hall and Brannick placed considerable stress on credibility values, because they are used to determine the decision as to whether validity generalizes or not. They found that even when the H-V models included the artifact correction modules, the H-S method generally produced more accurate credibility values. The H-V credibility intervals tended to be too wide (compared to the known real values) and to be shifted to the left (see their Figure 1). Again, we believe that this is due to distortions introduced by use of the Fisher's z transformation. The H-S credibility intervals were quite close to the real values. For these reasons, Hall and Brannick (2002) recommended use of the H-S random effects model over the H-V random effects model.

Finally, Hall and Brannick (2002) re-analyzed four published meta-analyses to address the question of whether any of these differences matter with real data. They found that they do; in some cases, the overall conclusions reached differed depending on which random effects model had been applied.

Although they were not included in these studies, there is good reason to believe that the Raju-Burke (1983) TSA models and the Callender-Osburn (1980) model would perform similarly to the H-S model and would likewise prove more accurate than the H-V model. Again, we believe the use of Fisher's z is the key to this difference in accuracy. However, these studies also support the conclusion (Hunter & Schmidt, 1990, chaps. 2 and 3) that use of sample size to weight studies in a random effects model—rather than more traditional random effects study weights (Mosteller & Colditz, 1996), as used in the H-V model—does not negatively affect accuracy and may improve accuracy.

Finally, we note that the Hunter-Schmidt random effects model that both Field (2001) and Hall and Brannick (2002) compared to the Hedges-Vevea random effects model is not our most accurate random effects model. The model these authors evaluated, our multiplicative model, is presented and described in detail on pp. 159–182 of Hunter and Schmidt (1990). This model is derived based on the algebra of the products of independent variables (just as the Callender and Osburn, 1980, model is). Unlike our interactive model, this model does not include the accuracy-enhancing refinements discussed earlier. In preparing Law et al. (1994a), we found through computer simulation that our multiplicative model was not as accurate as our interactive model, even when the accuracy-enhancing refinements were added to it. Because of length concerns by the editor, we did not include the simulation tests of our multiplicative model in Law et al. (1994a), although we did include the somewhat similar Callender-Osburn multiplicative model. Hence we believe that our interactive random effects model will compare even more favorably with the Hedges-Vevea random effects model. (Apparently, the reason why Field, 2001, and Hall and Brannick, 2002, used the H-S model multiplicative rather than our interactive model is that the Hunter-Schmidt (1990) book does not contain a detailed mathematical description of the interactive model; this description being omitted because it was available in earlier journal publications.)

Accuracy of Corrections for Artifacts

The results produced by VG methods could exaggerate the magnitude and generalizability of validity if the artifact distributions used and the corrections made overcorrect for the effects of artifacts. Computer simulation studies do not (and cannot) determine whether the artifact distributions are realistic or not; instead, such studies use these artifact distributions along with initial true validity values to generate simulated observed validities and then determine whether the procedures can accurately recapture the initial true validity distributions. So the question can be raised: Are the artifact distributions that have typically been used likely to overcorrect for the effects of artifacts?

This question usually has been focused on criterion reliabilities and range restriction values (u values, where $u = s/S$, where s = the restricted SD of the predictor and S = the unrestricted SD of the predictor). To our knowledge, no one has questioned the artifact distribution values used for the reliability of predictors—because no correction is made to mean validity for unreliability in the predictors. (The reason for this, or course, is that observed predictor scores must be used in selection because true scores are unknown.)

Overcorrection could occur in two different ways. First, the mean validity could be overcorrected. That is, if one's estimate of criterion reliability were too low, or one's estimate of the mean level of range restriction were too severe, then the corrected mean validity estimate (mean true validity estimate) would be too large. Second, even if mean artifact values and corrections were correct, if one's artifact distributions were too variable, then the amount of variance in observed validities attributed to differences between studies in criterion reliability and range restriction would be too great. It appears clear that this second form of overcorrection cannot be a source of serious distortion in results. Hunter and Schmidt (1990, pp. 224–226) summarize the research showing that even if the artifact distributions are too variable, the effect on the VG final results is negligible. This finding stems from the fact that between-study differences in artifact levels account for very little variance; most between-study variance in validities results for sampling error variance. In addition, empirical studies of range restriction values and criterion reliabilities have found levels of variability similar to those used in VG studies (Alexander, Carson, Alliger, & Cronshaw, 1989; Viswesvaran, Ones, & Schmidt, 1996).

This leaves us with the question of whether there is overcorrection of mean validity for criterion reliability and range restriction. Criteria include both measures of job performance and measures of training performance. Training performance measures are usually quite reliable, and there has been to our knowledge no criticism of the high reliabilities (and corresponding small corrections) we have estimated for training performance measures. The criterion measure of job performance used in most validity studies is supervisory ratings of job performance. Almost invariably one supervisor produces these ratings; it is very rare, for example, that the ratings used are the average ratings from two or more supervisors. Also, it is almost always the case that some of the employees in the sample are rated by one rater, others by another rater, and still others by a third rater, and so forth, introducing rater leniency effects into the variance of ratings. That is, almost never are all subjects in the study rated by the same rater. Starting with our first VG study, whenever ratings reliabilities were not available from the studies in the VG analysis, we have estimated the mean interrater reliability of ratings of this sort at .60. This value was based on our reading of the literature. However, later large sample research studies of ratings found smaller mean reliabilities—values at or near .50 (Rothstein et al., 1990; Viswesvaran et al., 1996). Hence it is very unlikely that there has been overcorrection for criterion unreliability. In fact, it is likely that there has been undercorrection. (Use of the .60 figure when the correct figure is .50 results in a 9% undercorrection.)

In passing, I note that Murphy and DeShon (2000) argued that interrater reliability is inappropriate for ratings of job performance and have stated that intrarater reliability should be used instead. This position entails the rejection of the classical measurement model in I/O research. My colleagues and I (Schmidt, Viswesvaran, & Ones, 2000) have presented the reasons why we believe this position is mistaken. These two articles provide a thorough exploration of the issues involved in this question.

The final question is whether there is overcorrection for range restriction. There are two ways in which the mean correction for range restriction could be erroneous. First, the mean u value ($u = s/S$) used could be too small, leading to an overcorrection for range restriction. When empirical estimates of u values were not available, we have typically estimated the mean u value at .60 to .70, with these values being based on our impressions from reading the literature. However, as the data became available we compared these values to quantitative averages from real studies. In the large VG study that John Hunter conducted for the USDOL on more than 400 General Aptitude Test Battery (GATB) test validity studies, the average u value was .67 (Hunter, 1983b; Hunter & Hunter, 1984). A later empirical study by Alexander et al. (1989) that included available published and unpublished literature found an average u value of .70. Hence the empirical evidence indicates that the mean u values we have used are close to the appropriate values.

The second way in which range restriction corrections can be erroneous is that the range correction formula used can over- or undercorrect. To date the correction equation we have used has been Thorndike's (1949) Case II formula. This is also the formula used in the Callender and Osburn (1980) model and the Raju and Burke (1983) models. This formula assumes direct range restriction (truncation) on the predictor. That is, it assumes that all applicants below a certain score on the predictor are rejected for hire and all others are hired. It has long been known that if range restriction is indirect rather than direct this formula will undercorrect (e.g., see Linn, Harnisch, & Dunbar, 1981), and we have repeatedly pointed out this undercorrection (Schmidt, Hunter, & Pearlman,

1981; Schmidt et al., 1985, p. 751; 1993, p. 7). It is clear that if some or all of the primary validity studies in a VG study are characterized by indirect range restriction, the use of this range correction formula will lead to undercorrection, even if one's u values are accurate. This is important because range restriction is indirect in almost all studies (Thorndike, 1949, p. 175). For example in the USDOL GATB database, all of the 515 validity studies were concurrent, and hence range restriction was indirect. Range restriction is often indirect even in predictive studies: The tests to be validated are often given to incumbents, with the criterion measures being taken months or years later, making the study technically predictive. In our research over the years, we rarely have seen a study in which there had been direct selection on the predictors being validated—the only kind of study for which the Case II range correction formula would not undercorrect.

If the Case II range correction formula used in all VG models (ours, Callender and Osburn's, and Raju and Burke's) undercorrects, then why has this undercorrection not shown up in computer simulation studies? As noted most recently by Hall and Bannick (2002), computer simulation studies have shown that these VG methods are quite accurate. In fact, estimates of $\bar{\rho}$ seem to be particularly accurate. The answer is that all computer simulation studies have assumed (and programmed in) only direct range restriction. There have been no computer simulation studies of VG methods based on indirect range restriction. Hence these simulation studies by definition cannot detect the undercorrection that occurs when range restriction is indirect.

How large is this underestimation of mean true validity? All VG models have in effect implicitly assumed that it is relatively small. Linn et al. (1981) attempted to calibrate empirically the size of the undercorrection in the case of the Law School Admissions Test (LSAT) and concluded that it is probably substantial. However, because they were unable to develop an analytical solution, their estimates were only suggestive. However, an analytical solution has been developed for the most common case of indirect range restriction: the one in which incumbents have been selected on unknown and unmeasured variables (or on a composite of such variables; Hunter & Schmidt, 2001; Mendoza & Mumford, 1987). An example would be a validity study in which there is no formal record of how incumbents were selected but in which $u < 1.00$, indicating the presence of range restriction; this example is in fact the usual case. Unlike the formula we derived (also derived by Mendoza & Mumford, 1987), other equations for correction for indirect range restriction require knowledge of scores on the measure that produced the indirect range restriction; because of this requirement, it is rarely possible to use these equations [e.g., Thorndike's (1949) Case III] with real data.

Our findings indicate that the undercorrection of $\bar{\rho}$ for range restriction is substantial (Hunter & Schmidt, 2001). For example, application of the new equation to the GATB database (Hunter & Hunter, 1984) indicates that the mean true validity of measures of general mental ability has been underestimated by 25% to 30% (Hunter & Schmidt, 2001). Hence the implications of the traditional undercorrection are important. It will probably take a number of years to explore the full implications of this development.

In summary, the evidence indicates that artifact values used for both criterion reliability and range restriction (the u values) do not lead to overcorrection of mean true validities. In fact, there has probably been an undercorrection for criterion unreliability when the criterion was job performance. In addition, even when u values are accurate, the Case II range restriction correction equation used in all VG programs to date undercorrects validities for range restriction, resulting in substantial underestimates of mean true validities. Hence, we have a problem of undercorrection, not a problem of overcorrection.

THE BROADER VIEW: WHERE ARE WE NOW

In keeping with the subject of this book, I have emphasized the history, development, evolution, and impact of validity generalization methods. However, the broader significance of these methods lies not in VG but in meta-analysis. The vast majority of applications of these methods today are not in validity generalization or even in personnel psychology but in a wide variety of research areas inside and outside of I/O psychology (Hunter & Schmidt, 1996; Schmidt, 1996; Schmidt & Hunter, in press-a). The total contribution these methods are making to cumulative knowledge in all these other areas is necessarily much greater than the contributions to calibrating the validity estimates of selection procedures.

There is now widespread realization that random effects meta-analysis models are almost always the only appropriate ones and that fixed effects models are rarely appropriate and typically lead to questionable results and conclusions (Field, 2001; Hall & Brannick, 2002). Virtually all meta-analyses published to date in the behavioral and social sciences outside of I/O psychology have employed fixed effects models and therefore are likely to be inaccurate and in need of re-analysis using random effects models (Hunter & Schmidt,

2000). At the same time, computer simulation tests (Field, 2001; Hall & Brannick, 2002) indicate that our random effects models are more accurate than those of Hedges and Olkin (1985) and Hedges and Vevea (1998). Hence we have a situation in meta-analysis in which we may be on the cusp of major changes.

A second important development has occurred recently. There is now widespread appreciation of the fact that any meta-analysis method that does not provide for corrections for measurement error (and other artifacts) is incomplete and cannot provide accurate results (Field, 2001; Hall & Brannick, 2002). There are probably many reasons for this realization, but widespread use of structural equation modeling (SEM) to test causal and other models is probably an important part of the explanation. Corrections for measurement error are an integral part of SEM methods, are very apparent to users of SEM, and the need for these corrections is clear (Le & Schmidt, 2002). Our methods of meta-analysis, and those of Raju and Burke (1983) and Callender and Osburn (1980), are the only ones that provided for these corrections. There is no such provision in the Hedges-Olkin methods or in the Rosenthal-Rubin methods (Hunter & Schmidt, 1990). These facts will also have increasingly important implications.

The 21st century is now well underway, and the meta-analysis methods we first explored in our 1977 article (Schmidt & Hunter, 1977) are still going strong after 25 years. In the faddish world of social science, 25 years is an eternity. These methods have been applied, and continue to be applied, to research literatures of many kinds inside and outside I/O psychology (Schmidt & Hunter, in press-a), and these applications continue to make contributions to cumulative knowledge.

REFERENCES

Aguinis, H. (2001). Estimation of sampling variance of correlations in meta-analysis. *Personnel Psychology, 54*, 569–590.

Aguinis, H., & Whitehead, R. (1997). Sampling variance in the correlation coefficient under indirect range restriction: Implications for validity generalization. *Journal of Applied Psychology, 82*, 528–538.

Alexander, R. A., Carson, K. P., Alliger, G. M., & Cronshaw, S. F. (1989). Empirical distributions of range restricted SDx in validity studies. *Journal of Applied Psychology, 74*, 253–258.

American Educational Research Association, American Psychological Association, and the National Council on Measurement in Education (1985). *Standards for educational and psychological testing* (4th ed.). Washington, DC: American Educational Research Association.

American Educational Research Association, American Psychological Association, and the National Council on Measurement in Education (1999). *Standards for educational and psychological testing* (5th ed.). Washington, DC: American Educational Research Association.

Aronson, E., Ellsworth, P., Carlsmith, J., & Gonzales, M. (1990). *Methods of research in social psychology* (2nd ed.). New York: McGraw-Hill.

Brannick, M. T. (2001). Implications of empirical Bayes meta-analysis for test validation. *Journal of Applied Psychology, 86,* 468–480.

Bobko, P., & Stone-Romero, E. F. (1998). Meta-analysis may be another useful research tool but it is not a panacea. In G. R. Ferris (Ed.), *Research in personnel and human resources management* (Vol. 16, pp. 359–397). New York: JAI Press.

Callender, J. C. (1978). *A Monte Carlo investigation of the accuracy of two models for validity generalization.* Unpublished doctoral dissertation, University of Houston.

Callender, J. C., & Osburn, H. G. (1980). Development and test of a new model for validity generalization. *Journal of Applied Psychology, 65,* 543–558.

Callender, J. C., & Osburn, H. G. (1981). Testing the constancy of validity with computer generated sampling distributions of the multiplicative model variance estimate: Results for petroleum industry validation research. *Journal of Applied Psychology, 66,* 274–281.

Carlson, K. D., Scullen, S. E., Schmidt, F. L., Rothstein, H. R., & Erwin, F. W. (1996). *Generalizable biographical data: Is multi-organizational development and keying necessary?* Unpublished manuscript, University of Iowa, Iowa City, Iowa.

Carlson, K. D., Scullen, S. E., Schmidt, F. L., Rothstein, H. R., & Erwin, F. (1999). Generalizable biographical data validity: Is multi-organizational development and keying necessary? *Personnel Psychology, 52,* 731–756.

Cook, T., & Campbell, D. T. (1976). The design and conduct of quasi-experiments and true experiments in field settings. In M. Dunnette (Ed.), *Handbook of industrial and organizational psychology* (pp. 223–236). Chicago: Rand McNally.

Cook, T., & Campbell, D. T. (1979). *Quasi-experiments and true experimentation: Design and analysis for field settings.* Chicago: Rand McNally.

Dye, D. A., Reck, M., & McDaniel, M. A. (1993). The validity of job knowledge measures. *International Journal of Selection and Assessment, 1,* 153–157.

Field, A. P. (2001). Meta-analysis of correlation coefficients: A Monte Carlo comparison of fixed- and random-effects methods. *Psychological Methods, 6,* 161–180.

Gaugler, B. B., Rosenthal, D. B., Thornton, G. C., & Benson, C. (1987). Meta-analysis of assessment center validity. *Journal of Applied Psychology, 72,* 493–511.

Ghiselli, E. E. (1969). *The validity of occupational aptitude tests.* New York: Wiley.

Hall, S. M., & Brannick, M. (2002). Comparison of two random effects methods of meta-analysis. *Journal of Applied Psychology, 87,* 377–389.

Hartigan, J. A., & Wigdor, A. K. (Eds.). (1989). *Fairness in employment testing: Validity generalizations, minority issues, and the General Aptitude Test Battery.* Washington, DC: National Academy of Sciences Press.

Hedges, L. V., & Olkin, I. (1985). *Statistical methods for meta-analysis.* NY: Academic Press.

Hedges, L. V., & Vevea, J. L. (1998). Fixed- and random effects models in meta-analysis. *Psychological Methods, 3*, 486–504.

Hirsh, H. R., Northroup, L., & Schmidt, F. L. (1986). Validity generalization results for law enforcement occupations. *Personnel Psychology, 39*, 399–420.

Hirsh, H. R., Schmidt, F. L., & Hunter, J. E. (1986). Estimation of employment test validities by less experienced judges. *Personnel Psychology, 39*, 337–344.

Hunter, J. E. (1983a). *The dimensionality of the General Aptitude Test Battery (GATB) and the dominance of the general factors over specific factors in the prediction of job performance.* Washington, DC: U.S. Employment Service, USDOL. USES Test Research Report No. 44.

Hunter, J. E. (1983b). *Test validation for 12,000 jobs: An application of job classification and validity generalization analysis to the General Aptitude Test Battery.* Washington, DC: U.S. Employment Service, USDOL. USES Test Research Report No. 45.

Hunter, J. E. (1983c). *Fairness of the General Aptitude Test Battery: Ability differences and their impact on minority hiring rates.* Washington, DC: U.S. Employment Service, USDOL. USES Test Research Report No. 46.

Hunter, J. E. (1983d). *The economic benefits of personnel selection using ability tests: A state of the art review including a detailed analysis of the dollar benefit of U.S. Employment Service placements and a critique of the low-cutoff method of test use.* Washington, DC: U.S. Employment Service, USDOL. USES Test Research Report No. 47.

Hunter, J. E., & Hunter, R. F. (1984). Validity and utility of alternative predictors of job performance. *Psychological Bulletin, 96*(1), 72–98.

Hunter, J. E., & Schmidt, F. L. (1982). Fitting people to jobs: Implications of personnel selection for national productivity. In E. A. Fleishman & M. D. Dunnette (Eds.), *Human performance and productivity.* Volume I: Human capability assessment (pp. 233–284). Hillsdale, NJ: Lawrence Erlbaum Associates.

Hunter, J. E., & Schmidt, F. L. (1987a). *The standard error of estimated mean true score correlations in meta-analysis.* Unpublished paper.

Hunter, J. E., & Schmidt, F. L. (1987b). *The standard error of* $\hat{SD}_\rho$ *in meta-analysis.* Unpublished paper.

Hunter, J. E., & Schmidt, F. L. (1990). *Methods of meta-analysis: Correcting error and bias in research findings.* Beverly Hills, CA: Sage.

Hunter, J. E., & Schmidt, F. L. (1994). The estimation of sampling error variance in meta-analysis of correlations: The homogeneous case. *Journal of Applied Psychology, 79*, 171–177.

Hunter, J. E., & Schmidt, F. L. (1996). Cumulative research knowledge and social policy formulation: The critical role of meta-analysis. *Psychology, Public Policy, and Law, 2*, 324–347.

Hunter, J. E., & Schmidt, F. L. (2000). Fixed effects vs. random effects meta-analysis models: Implications for cumulative research knowledge. *International Journal of Selection and Assessment, 8*, 275–292.

Hunter, J. E., & Schmidt, F. L. (2001). *Range restriction and validity generalization.* University of Iowa, Unpublished paper.

Hunter, J. E., Schmidt, F. L., & Coggin, T. D. (1996). Meta-analysis of correlations: Bias in the correlation coefficient and the Fisher z transformation. Unpublished manuscript, University of Iowa.

Hunter, J. E., Schmidt, F. L., & Jackson, G. B. (1982). *Meta-analysis: Cumulating research findings across studies.* Beverly Hills, CA: Sage Publications.

Judge, T. A., & Bono, J. E. (2000). Relationship of core self-evaluations traits—self-esteem, generalized self-efficacy, locus of control, and emotional stability—with job satisfaction and job performance: A meta-analysis. *Journal of Applied Psychology, 86,* 80–92.

Law, K. S., Schmidt, F. L., & Hunter, J. E. (1994a). Nonlinearity of range corrections in meta-analysis: A test of an improved procedure. *Journal of Applied Psychology, 79,* 425–438.

Law, K. S., Schmidt, F. L., & Hunter, J. E. (1994b). A test of two refinements in meta-analysis procedures. *Journal of Applied Psychology, 79,* 978–986.

Le, H., & Schmidt, F. L. (2002). The multi-faceted nature of measurement error and its implications for measurement error corrections: The case of job satisfaction. Manuscript under review.

Linn, R. L., Harnish, D. L., & Dunbar, S. B. (1981). Corrections for range restriction: An empirical investigation of conditions resulting in conservative corrections. *Journal of Applied Psychology, 66,* 655–663.

Madigan, R. M., Scott, K. D., Deadrick, D. L., & Stoddard, J. A. (1986, September). Employment testing: The U.S. Job Service is spearheading a revolution. *Personnel Administrator,* 103–112.

McDaniel, M. A., Schmidt, F. L., & Hunter, J. E. (1988a). A meta-analysis of the validity of methods for rating training and experience in personnel selection. *Personnel Psychology, 41,* 283–314.

McDaniel, M. A., Whetzel, D. L., Schmidt, F. L., & Mauer, S. (1994). The validity of employment interviews: A comprehensive review and meta-analysis. *Journal of Applied Psychology, 79*(4), 599–616.

McKinney, M. W. (1984). *Final Report: Validity generalization pilot study.* U.S. Employment Service, USDOL, Southern Test Development Field Center, Raleigh, NC.

Mendoza, J. L., & Mumford, M. (1987). Corrections for attenuation and range restriction on the predictor. *Journal of Educational Statistics, 12,* 282–293.

Millsap, R. E. (1989). Sampling variance in the correlation under range restriction: A Monte Carlo study. *Journal of Applied Psychology, 74,* 456–461.

Mosteller, F., & Colditz, G. A. (1996). Understanding research synthesis (meta-analysis). *Annual Review of Public Health, 17,* 1–17.

Mount, M. K., & Barrick, M. R. (1995). The big five personality dimensions: Implications for research and practice in human resources management. In G. R. Ferris (Ed.), *Research in personnel and human resources management* (Vol. 13, pp. 153–200). JAI Press.

Murphy, K. R. (1997). Meta-analysis and validity generalization. In N. Anderson & P. Herriot (Eds.), *International Handbook of Selection and Assessment* (pp. 324–342). London: Wiley.

Murphy, K. R., & DeShon, R. (2000). Interrater correlations do not estimate the reliability of job performance ratings. *Personnel Psychology, 53,* 873–900.

National Research Council (1992). *Combining information: Statistical issues and opportunities for research.* Washington, DC: National Academy of Sciences Press.

Ones, D. S., Viswesvaran, C., & Schmidt, F. L. (1993). Meta-analysis of integrity test validities: Findings and implications for personnel selection and theories of job performance. *Journal of Applied Psychology Monograph, 78,* 679–703.

Pearlman, K. (1982). *The Bayesian approach to validity generalization: A systematic examination of the robustness of procedures and conclusions.* Unpublished doctoral dissertation, Department of Psychology, George Washington University.

Pearlman, K., Schmidt, F. L., & Hunter, J. E. (1980). Validity generalization results for tests used to predict job proficiency and training criteria in clerical occupations. *Journal of Applied Psychology, 65,* 373–407.

Raju, N. S., & Burke, M. J. (1983). Two new procedures for studying validity generalization. *Journal of Applied Psychology, 68,* 382–395.

Roth, P. L., BeVier, C. A., Switzer, F. S., & Shippmann, J. S. (1996). Meta-analyzing the relationship between grades and job performance. *Journal of Applied Psychology, 81,* 548–556.

Rothstein, H. R., Schmidt, F. L., Erwin, F. W., Owens, W. A., & Sparks, C. P. (1990). Biographical data in employment selection: Can validities be made generalizable? *Journal of Applied Psychology, 75,* 175–184.

Sackett, P. R., Schmitt, N., Ellingson, J. E., & Kabin, M. B. (2001). High-stakes testing in employment, credentialing, and higher education: Prospects in a post-affirmative action world. *American Psychologist, 56,* 302–318.

Sackett, P. R., & Wilk, S. L. (1994). Within-group norming and other forms of score adjustment in pre-employment testing. *American Psychologist, 49,* 929–954.

Schmidt, F. L. (1988). Validity generalization and the future of criterion-related validity. In H. Wainer & H. I. Braun (Eds.), *Test validity* (pp. 173–190). Hillsdale, NJ: Lawrence Erlbaum Associates.

Schmidt, F. L. (1992). What do data really mean? Research findings, meta-analysis, and cumulative knowledge in psychology. *American Psychologist, 47,* 1173–1181.

Schmidt, F. L. (1996). Statistical significance testing and cumulative knowledge in psychology: Implications for the training of researchers. *Psychological Methods, 1,* 115–129.

Schmidt, F. L., Gast-Rosenberg, I. F., & Hunter, J. E. (1980). Validity generalization results for computer programmers. *Journal of Applied Psychology, 65,* 643–661.

Schmidt, F. L., & Hunter, J. E. (1977). Development of a general solution to the problem of validity generalization. *Journal of Applied Psychology, 62,* 529–540.

Schmidt, F. L., & Hunter, J. E. (1981). Employment testing: Old theories and new research findings. *American Psychologist, 36,* 1128–1137.

Schmidt, F. L., & Hunter, J. E. (1995). The fatal internal contradiction in banding: Its statistical rationale is logically inconsistent with its operational procedures. *Human Performance, 8,* 203–214.

Schmidt, F. L., & Hunter, J. E. (1998). The validity and utility of selection methods in personnel psychology: Practical and theoretical implications of 85 years of research findings. *Psychological Bulletin, 124,* 262–274.

Schmidt, F. L., & Hunter, J. E. (1999). Comparison of three meta-analysis methods revisited: An analysis of Johnson, Mullen, and Salas (1995). *Journal of Applied Psychology, 84,* 114–148.

Schmidt, F. L., & Hunter, J. E. (in press-a). Meta-Analysis. In J. Schinka & W. Velicer (Eds.), *Comprehensive Handbook of Psychology, Vol. 2: Research Methods in Psychology*. New York: Quorum Books.

Schmidt, F. L., & Hunter, J. E. (in press-b). SED banding as a test of intellectual honesty in I/O psychology. In H. Aguinis (Ed.), *Test score banding in human resource selection: Legal technical, and societal issues*. New York: Quorum Books.

Schmidt, F. L., Hunter, J. E., & Caplan, J. R. (1981). Validity generalization results for two job groups in the petroleum industry. *Journal of Applied Psychology, 66*, 261–273.

Schmidt, F. L., Hunter, J. E., & Pearlman, K. (1981). Task difference and validity of aptitude tests in selection: A red herring. *Journal of Applied Psychology, 66*, 166–185.

Schmidt, F. L., Hunter, J. E., Pearlman, K., & Hirsh, H. R. (1985). Forty questions about validity generalization and meta-analysis (with commentary by P. R. Sackett, M. L. Tenopyr, N. Schmitt, J. Kehoe, & S. Zedeck). *Personnel Psychology, 38*, 697–798.

Schmidt, F. L., Hunter, J. E., Pearlman, K., & Shane, G. S. (1979). Further tests of the Schmidt-Hunter Bayesian Validity Generalization Model. *Personnel Psychology, 32*, 257–281.

Schmidt, F. L., Hunter, J. E., & Raju, N. S. (1988). Validity generalization and situational specificity: A second look at the 75% rule and the Fisher Z transformation. *Journal of Applied Psychology, 73*, 665–672.

Schmidt, F. L., Hunter, J. E., & Urry, V. W. (1976). Statistical power in criterion-related validation studies. *Journal of Applied Psychology, 61*, 473–485.

Schmidt, F. L., Law, K., Hunter, J. E., Rothstein, H. R., Pearlman, K., & McDaniel, M. (1993). Refinements in validity generalization methods: Implications for the situational specificity hypothesis. *Journal of Applied Psychology, 78*, 3–13.

Schmidt, F. L., Ocasio, B. P., Hillery, J. M., & Hunter, J. E. (1985). Further within-setting empirical tests of the situational specificity hypothesis in personnel selection. *Personnel Psychology, 38*, 509–524.

Schmidt, F. L., Ones, D., & Hunter, J. E. (1992). Personnel selection. *Annual Review of Psychology, 43*, 627–670.

Schmidt, F. L., & Rothstein, H. R. (1994). Application of validity generalization methods of meta-analysis to biographical data scores in employment selection. In G. S. Stokes, M. D. Mumford, & W. A. Owens (Eds.), *The biodata handbook: Theory, research, and applications* (pp. 237–260). New York: Consulting Psychologists Press.

Schmidt, F. L., Viswesvaran, C., & Ones, D. S. (2000). Reliability is not validity and validity is not reliability. *Personnel Psychology, 53*, 901–924.

Sharf, J. (1987). Validity generalization: Round two. *The Industrial-Organizational Psychologist, 25*, 49–52.

Thorndike, R. L. (1949). *Personnel Selection*. New York: Wiley.

U.S. Department of Labor (1977). *Dictionary of Occupational Titles* (3rd Edition). Washington, DC: Employment and Training Administration.

Viswesvaran, C., Ones, D. S., & Schmidt, F. L. (1996). Comparative analysis of the reliability of job performance ratings. *Journal of Applied Psychology, 81*, 557–560.

Viswesvaran, C., Schmidt, F. L., & Ones, D. S. (2002). The moderating influence of job performance dimensions on convergence of supervisory and peer ratings of job performance: Unconfounding construct-level convergence and rating difficulty. *Journal of Applied Psychology, 87,* 345–354.

Whitener, E. M. (1990). Confusion of confidence intervals and credibility intervals in meta-analysis. *Journal of Applied Psychology, 75,* 315–321.

Work America (1986a, May). Validity generalization: Employment Service is doing new tricks with an old aptitude test. *National Alliance of Business,* 1–4.

Work America (1986b, May). New Jersey zealots just scratch the surface with validity generalization. *National Alliance of Business,* 3.

Work America (1986c, May). Taking the load off GM: Hiring 2,000 is easy with validity generalization. *National Alliance of Business,* 4.

3

Meta-Analysis and Validity Generalization as Research Tools: Issues of Sample Bias and Degrees of Mis-Specification

Philip Bobko
Gettysburg College

Philip L. Roth
Clemson University

The notion of validity generalization is one of the more useful methodologies available to both practitioners and researchers in human resource selection. Such a methodology is very practical because it provides organizations with the possibility of implementing selection systems without the prerequisite time and effort involved in designing and conducting a local, empirical validation study. On the other hand, validity generalization is also a research-based procedure because its invocation requires the user to compile known literature, classify studies accordingly, and analyze the situation at hand. The technique also helps separate variation in study outcomes due to artifacts from variation due to "true" states of affairs. In sum, validity generalization can be considered as a remarkable blend of good science with organizational needs and practicality.

In this chapter, the focus is on meta-analysis as a more general case of validity generalization. The latter is usually quite focused on the transportability or generalization of the validity of selection systems, and the effect size of interest is most often the Pearson product moment correlation coefficient between a selection test and a measure of job performance (the validity coefficient). In contrast, meta-analysis focuses on cumulating knowledge about any organizational interventions, which might include not only selection systems, but training systems, motivational interventions, types of reward structures, and so forth. Meta-analysis can also focus on naturally occurring effects (e.g., the analysis of individual differences across ethnic or gender subgroups). So, meta-analysis differs a bit from validity generalization in that it focuses on a variety of effect sizes (e.g., the standardized mean difference between two groups or two types of interventions) and not just on Pearson correlations (the typical index of empirical validity). (Note: the effects of such a distinction may be more apparent than real because many effect sizes are often transformations of Pearson r's.)

To repeat, the current chapter is written with the more general notion of meta-analysis in mind, although many of the comments apply to the more specific notion of validity generalization. In that regard, Bobko and Stone-Romero (1998) suggested that proponents of meta-analysis (or validity generalization) might be a bit overzealous in claims about what meta-analysis could or could not accomplish. The current authors believe that meta-analysis and validity generalization can be very useful (practically and theoretically) techniques. Indeed, the potential utility of validity generalization can be found in other chapters in this book. However, it is also the case that Bobko and Stone-Romero noted that caveats for meta-analysis and validity generalization are in order. Attention to these caveats will enhance the usefulness, both practical and theoretical, of meta-analyses and validity generalization studies. As such, we build on their earlier work and explicate several of the concerns about meta-analysis already mentioned in the literature. We also go beyond some of these earlier caveats and update the issues, given new developments in the field. Finally, we note that the more specific notion of validity generalization tends to appear in human resources (HR) and selection applications, whereas meta-analysis appears in more general topic domains. We consider some of the more general applications in organizational behavior (OB) and find that OB applications often have more desirable characteristics (e.g., a more complete set of variables in their nomological nets) than HR applications. We show that some valuable lessons for HR can be learned from such a comparison.

CONCERNS ABOUT META-ANALYSIS

In their prior chapter, Bobko and Stone-Romero (1998) listed a variety of concerns about meta-analysis. In this chapter we build on several of those concerns in light of new developments in the field and discuss other issues, as well. Bias is considered due to incongruous sample types, some general methodological issues regarding method and construct confounds, and the importance of specifying a wider range of variables in meta-analytic research.

Bobko and Stone-Romero (1998) pointed out six issues along which meta-analysis was considered to be a useful technique but not a panacea. Specifically:

a. Meta-analysts presume to avoid trappings of traditional significance testing by using confidence intervals, yet many researchers continue to interpret confidence bands in traditional, significance testing ways. Thus, concerns about significance testing will be repeated, not removed.

b. There are many judgment calls involved in meta-analysis that could substantially influence the results and outcomes of the analysis (see Wanous, Sullivan, & Malinak, 1989).

c. Meta-analysis operates by cumulating effect sizes across studies. Some of the traditional effect sizes, such as Pearson product moment correlations, are not fully informative (context is ignored).

d. There are major construct validity issues when cumulating results. For example, averaging study results when those studies use different measures of the same construct is problematic. That is, the notion of averaging makes sense when the phenomenon of interest contains random error (e.g., sampling error). However, if there is some common bias or deficiency in one of the measures, then averaging studies with that bias will keep the bias in the result, not average it out.

e. The statistical power to detect moderators is quite low (e.g., Spector & Levine, 1987). This is ironic given that one of the motivations for conducting meta-analytic (and validity generalization) studies is to avoid the low statistical power associated with primary studies.

f. It was suggested that fewer, but more comprehensive, studies could be of greater benefit to the field than the meta-analytic cumulation of limited scope studies, even if those limited studies were more numerous. The more comprehensive studies can systematically and planfully build in variation across factors (e.g., factors such as potential moderators) and incorporate more variables (assuming increased sample size). Thus, these more comprehensive studies will have just as much efficiency to estimate the primary relationship of interest yet be better able to accommodate concerns about model misspecification and the investigation of nonlinear relationships.

As already mentioned, this chapter is focused on the further explication of three of these issues (effect sizes, construct validity, and study scope—points c, d, and f, respectively) and we link our thoughts, when possible, to new developments in the field. When finished, we believe that researchers will have a greater appreciation for the positives and negatives associated with meta-analysis (and validity generalization), and they will be better armed to conduct studies that will be useful to both academics and practitioners.

BIAS IN CUMULATED EFFECT SIZES: THE ISSUE OF INCONGRUOUS SAMPLES

The core concern in this section is that samples used in research studies can differ dramatically from one another and that studies conducted in one type of sample (e.g., concurrent) may not accurately represent what happens in other contexts (e.g., applicant populations). So, by bias (what we call *sample bias* in the title of this chapter), we mean that an effect size may be well-estimated in one type of sample but generalization of results to another type of sample may not accurately apply to that other context. For example, statistics based on applicant samples may accurately represent applicant parameters. However, statistics computed from incumbent samples may not accurately represent applicant parameters.

Bobko and Stone-Romero (1998) already noted that effect sizes (e.g., average value of *r* in validity generalization) by themselves do not tell the entire story relevant to practitioners because the effect sizes are generally context (and metric) free and subject to misinterpretation in regards to the actual magnitude of the effect. More recently, researchers in industrial/organizational psychology and human resources selection have come to realize that many effect sizes that are cumulated in meta-analyses and validity generalization studies are also potentially biased. This is an extremely important problem. That is, in arithmetically combining effect sizes, the hope (assumption) is that cumulating across findings from multiple primary studies will have the effect of "averaging out" some of the random variation in study-to-study results. However, by definition, bias is not random—it is some systematic perturbation that makes each effect size too small or too large. If there is a common bias across several studies in a meta-analysis, then the average of this bias will be the bias itself (*not* zero)—and the cumulated effect size will remain biased by the same amount.

To see how this issue manifests in practice, consider ethnic group (or gender) difference research in personnel selection and the types of samples often used in this research. The most typically used effect size is *d*. For our purposes, *d* is defined as the standardized mean difference in scores between two subgroups (e.g., Blacks and Whites; males and females). For example, the mean Black score is often subtracted from the mean White score. The difference in means is then divided by the sample-weighted average of the standard deviations for the two subgroups.

Many individuals in the field assume that $d = 1.0$ for Black–White differences on cognitive ability tests in selection contexts (see Herrnstein & Murray 1994; Sackett & Wilk, 1994). This would mean that minority and majority groups differ, on average, by about one standard deviation. In fact, the d of 1.0 has been used in analyses of meta-analytically generated matrices (e.g., Bobko, Roth, & Potosky, 1999; Schmitt, Rogers, Chan, Sheppard, & Jennings, 1997). However, many of the samples used to support this estimate of the standardized ethnic group difference were drawn from the U.S. population. For example, the sample in the National Longitudinal Study of Youth is designed to be representative of the U.S. population as a whole. The SAT test is also given to a wide range of individuals in the U.S. as well.

Samples from the U.S. population as a whole may not be representative of individuals in employment settings. That is, figures compiled on national samples may systematically differ from samples of job applicants and job incumbents. Although data on Black–White differences in the U.S. population as a whole often yields estimates near $d = 1.0$ (Roth, BeVier, Bobko, Switzer, & Tyler, 2001), analysis of within-job studies of applicants shows smaller values. For example, low-complexity jobs are associated with a d of .86 whereas the value of d for medium complexity jobs is about .73 (Roth et al., 2001). And, accurate estimation of the d statistic within any particular context is important in the selection literature, as it is one way to index the adverse impact potential of a selection measure (Sackett & Ellingson, 1997).

As another example of a biasing factor (and incongruous samples), and perhaps one with a larger biasing influence, is the difference between job applicant and job incumbent values. The issue at hand concerns the fact that many studies are concurrent in nature (i.e., they are based on samples of job incumbents), but researchers use such data to make inferences about applicants. That is, some values of d for cognitive ability tests might be estimated using a sample of job incumbents. To the extent that these incumbents have already been selected based on a measure of cognitive ability (or some other measure positively associated with cognitive ability), then the range of scores will be restricted (directly or indirectly). In turn, the value of d will be biased downward (because of the aforementioned relationship between d and r (see Bobko, Roth, & Bobko, 2001). In fact, a recent study by Carretta (1997) illustrates the potential magnitude of the problem. That author managed to obtain and report values of ethnic group d's on cognitive ability for both incumbents and applicants; the respective values of d were .46 and 1.19. A recent meta-analysis of Black–White cognitive ability differences found similar results, such that the estimated incumbent d was .38 and the applicant d was .82 across levels of job complexity (Roth, BeVier, et al., 2001).

So, a meta-analysis that cumulates values across studies—some of which are concurrent in nature and some of which are based on applicant populations—could be averaging inappropriate values. The overall estimate of effect sizes for applicants may be too low in some contexts, particularly as the number of concurrent studies increases. As noted in the prior paragraph, aggregating across studies that have such characteristics will not remove any bias due to incongruous samples—at most, researchers will obtain a more precise estimate of the biased effect size. This is a major problem that many meta-analyses fail to address when reporting effect sizes.

The issue of sample types and the range restriction associated with sample types is not confined to cognitive ability tests. Roth, Van Iddekinge, Huffcutt, Eidson, and Bobko (2002) considered the minority–majority effect size of d for job interviews. The overall value of d for structured interviews reported in prior work by Huffcutt and Roth (1998) was .23 and the specific value for behavioral interviews was .10—values that might seem encouraging when compared to the above values of d for cognitive ability. However, Roth et al. also noted that there is evidence of prior selection for 21 of the 31 studies in the original meta-analysis. Thus, the value of d reported in prior work is not particularly helpful if one is considering an interview at the initial hurdle of a selection system (e.g., as is sometimes done in college recruiting) or when the interview is being considered as an alternative to cognitive ability tests (e.g., as in Schmitt, Rogers, Chan, Sheppard, & Jennings, 1997). Indeed, in contrast to the above values, Roth et al. reported an average d of .46 as an estimate of the effect size for interviews in their applicant population.

The literature on biodata is yet another example of potential bias in effect sizes. Note that the method of biodata is also sometimes considered as an alternative to cognitive ability tests for selection (the mixing of methods and constructs is ignored in this analysis but discussed later in the chapter). Test consultants claim that biodata tests have lower adverse impact potential than measures of cognitive ability. However, Roth, Bobko, Switzer, and Dean (2001) again considered this issue and noted that most major analyses of the d for biodata inventories have been obtained from concurrent studies only. They found only one study that reported an estimated value of d for applicant populations (Dean, 1999). In fact, in that study, although the range-restricted (second stage of selection) value of the biodata d was .34, the estimated applicant population value of d was .73. This value is more than double the restricted value and is reminiscent of the above d for cognitive ability tests for medium complexity jobs.

The bottom line to the examples regarding the estimation of d is that many of the meta-analyses and validity generalization studies may yield biased estimates of effect sizes for applicant populations if they are based largely on concurrent studies. This is particularly salient if the d's are calculated for tests that are being considered as alternatives to, or in composites with, cognitive ability measures. In fact, in computer simulations across a variety of values of selection ratio, predictor intercorrelations, and population values of d, Roth, Bobko, Switzer, et al. (2001) found that bias in effect size estimates of d ranged from 30% to 70%. It is important to understand that the same issues apply for other effect size indices—such as the r typically used in validity generalization. Applicant and incumbent studies may represent two different populations, and applicant validity estimates may be biased by inclusion of concurrent validities in the cumulation. For example, in the personality literature, Hough (1998) reported a concurrent validity of .39 for dependability, but a .23 estimate for predictive validity studies—more than a 40% reduction. As another example, in the literature on situational judgment tests, McDaniel, Morgeson, Finnegan, Campion, and Braverman (2001) reported an estimated concurrent validity of .35 and an estimated predictive validity of .18—a 48% reduction.

METHODS AND CONSTRUCT CONFOUNDS

Clearly understanding the "constructs versus methods" issue is just as important in meta-analysis as it is in primary studies (Bobko & Stone-Romero, 1998). For example, the constructs represented in an interview or biodata inventory are often not well-specified and may vary considerably across studies (e.g., constructs such as cognitive ability, personality factors, interests, etc.). When estimating r and d in primary studies in selection, the importance of formally noting the constructs being analyzed and the methods of measurement has been reiterated by a number of authors (e.g., Bobko et al., 1999; Hough, Oswald, & Ployhart, 2001; Hunter & Hunter, 1984). Often, a given construct can be measured by a variety of methods, and different methods may influence the distributions and co-variances found in the data (e.g., see the personality literature for self versus other assessments). To the extent that meta-analysis averages studies with unspecified constructs, the lack of understanding will be repeated at the aggregate level. Thus, there are a number of issues within meta-analysis related to the constructs and methods distinction in selection research.

As one issue, note that researchers have often meta-analyzed methods of measurement rather than constructs. For example, there are meta-analyses of employment interview validity (e.g., Huffcutt & Arthur, 1994; McDaniel, Whetzel, Schmidt, & Maurer, 1994) and employment interview standardized ethnic group differences (Huffcutt & Roth, 1998). Such studies report meta-analytic results as moderated by degrees of structure in the interview. However, such studies typically do not incorporate the analysis of constructs measured in the interview. Similarly, biodata studies (e.g., Gandy, Dye, & McLain, 1994) do not typically formally incorporate constructs into their meta-analytic results. (In fairness, it is important to note that Gandy et al. followed their primary analysis with an interesting factor analysis of their biodata form to show that it measures constructs such as academic achievement, etc.) In meta-analytic matrices, biodata research is often conceptualized as a method—clouding the rational for biodata's relationships to other constructs (cf. Schmitt et al., 1997).

One recent study has begun the work of considering the constructs involved in an interview within the context of a meta-analysis (Huffcutt, Conway, Roth, & Stone, 2001). These researchers developed a taxonomy of constructs and then logically mapped knowledge, skills, and abilities measured in the interview onto this taxonomy. They analyzed 338 ratings from 47 actual interviews and showed that approximately 19% of the ratings appeared to involve the measurement of mental abilities, 12% assessed job knowledge and skills, 37% assessed personality tendencies, and 18% assessed social skills such as communication skills and interpersonal skills. Thus, there were a wide variety of constructs that may have been measured in interviews. Analyses of validity by constructs was somewhat tentative in terms of results but suggested that interview ratings of mental ability were not as high in terms of validity as certain personality related ratings of agreeableness or emotional stability ratings.

It is also important to note that some meta-analyses can mix both methods and constructs or mix constructs. For example, Schmitt, Clause, and Pulakos (1996) analyzed a variety of predictors of job performance from major journals in applied psychology. In one case, they aggregated work samples, job knowledge tests, and situational judgment into a single category labeled *job sample/job knowledge*. The authors noted that it was very hard to disentangle work sample and job knowledge measures given information in primary studies. Given our own experience with meta-analysis, we think this might also likely be a problem of not having enough information in primary studies. The introduction of situational judgment tests into the same category of analysis appears somewhat more problematic. Given that little is known about the correlates and constructs in situational judgment, adding situational judgment tests to the category of *job sample/job knowledge* may confound analysis and subsequent inferences. For example, a researcher might want to support the thought that work sample tests are associated with a *d* that is lower than traditional measures of cognitive ability. Using the *d* of .38 from the Schmitt, Clause, and Pulakos meta-analyses would be problematic as it is not known how inclusion of situational judgment tests (and the myriad underlying constructs) influenced the mean value of .38. To return to a theme previously mentioned, it would also be interesting to know the proportion of applicant versus incumbent samples used in the calculation of .38.

In other cases, constructs can be mixed and method of measurement held constant. Hough (1998) conducted a meta-analysis of personality predictors of job performance. In one analysis, it appears (from examination of table footnotes and reference lists) that the constructs of conscientiousness and integrity are mixed together. Although conscientiousness is perhaps a substantial component of integrity, other constructs such as agreeableness are also part of the domain of integrity and add extraneous variance into calculations if the construct of interest is solely conscientiousness. We note that other researchers have also used statistics relating to integrity tests to estimate the *d* for conscientiousness given the lack of a major meta-analysis for conscientiousness (Roth, Bobko, & Potosky, 2001). Thus, we include some of our own research in this criticism. The bottom line here is that meta-analysts can only combine what is available to them from the literature. To the extent there are confounds in primary studies, there are confounds in the meta-analysis.

MISCELLANEOUS BIASING ISSUES

Levels of Analysis

There are a number of other interesting issues in meta-analytic research. Perhaps one of the more interesting issues is that meta-analysts need to be careful in considering the nature of the within-job versus across-job coefficients that they include in their analysis (Ostroff & Harrison, 1999). These authors demonstrated that one has to be careful in considering extraneous sources of variance and that extraneous variance in meta-analysis can contribute to a variety of effects that obfuscates the results.

The effect of extraneous variance (that results from across-job analysis) is exemplified by the meta-analytic Black–White d for scores on the Wonderlic Personnel Test—computed to be approximately 1.0 in a recent meta-analysis (Roth, BeVier, et al., 2001). However, this analysis computed the value of 1.0 from a large pool of applicants across a wide variety of jobs associated with a variety of levels of job complexity. As noted earlier, when analyses were conducted *within jobs*, the value dropped to .73 for medium complexity jobs and .86 for low complexity jobs. This is an important distinction, as most modeling and decisions about selections systems in applied psychology have a within-job or within-job family focus. Thus, use of across-job coefficients may positively bias results in meta-analysis or validity generalization.

Dependent Samples

The issue of dependent samples is also important. Formulas used to compute percent of sampling variance in effect sizes (e.g., r or d), sampling error, confidence intervals, etcetera typically assume that samples are independent. Further, it is very difficult to determine the influence that including dependent samples will have on computing mean values of r or d. It is possible to overweight the influence of one or more samples if those samples provide multiple coefficients. If the coefficients are larger or smaller than those from independent samples, the resulting effect size will be biased.

Our own experience with meta-analysis suggests it is extremely easy to include dependent samples. After all, one should code all the coefficients from a given study in order to facilitate moderator analyses. For example, researchers looking at the influence of grade point average on salary recorded multiple coefficients from the same sample if a person's grades were available for both MBA and undergraduate education levels (Roth & Clarke, 1998). If one is not very careful to code the dependency in analyses, both samples could be included in an overall analysis of grades on salary and this would allow the sample that was "double weighted" to have undue influence on results. The issue of including multiple dependent samples is illustrated in Cortina, Goldstein, Payne, Davison, and Gilliland (2000). When they meta-analyzed the correlation between structured interviews (structure levels three and four) with measures of cognitive ability, they appeared to include dependent samples. For example, the single sample results reported by Campion, Purcell, and Brown (1998) and McHenry, Hough, Toquam, Hadson, and Ashworth (1990) are analyzed as multiple independent samples. The reported N for Cortina et al.'s analyses was over 8,000 whereas the N for completely independent samples was approximately $N = 3,200$. The influence of the dependent samples on the study's results is unknown. Although these issues are beyond the scope of this chapter, we encourage research that investigates the effect of ignoring such dependencies in meta-analysis. For example, it would be important to know if confidence intervals are too wide or too narrow, etc. and to what degree.

Composites of Multifaceted Constructs

The estimation of effect sizes for multifaceted constructs is another issue with possible misapplication. For example, one might have multiple r's (or d's) expressing the relationship between ethnicity and different facets of cognitive abilities. There might be one r for mathematical ability, one r for verbal ability, etcetera. For a number of years, some meta-analysts would simply average (using sample weighting) these values. However, if one is interested in the relationship between ethnicity and *overall* mental ability, one needs to conceptually think about a *composite* of the facets of cognitive ability and then compute the validity of that composite against some index of performance (see Roth, BeVier, et al., 2001, for an example). The resulting r, in general, will *not* be the simple average of the validities of the components. In the example above, the appropriate validity is the validity of the composite "math ability + verbal ability" and not the average of the validities for each component. In our experience, the appropriate validity is often larger than the average of the component validities. Once again, misapplication of this issue can bias results.

Unfortunately, not all researchers have taken this approach (and let us use our own work as an example). An analysis of the relationship between cognitive ability and interview ratings did not consider a composite (Huffcutt, Roth, & McDaniel, 1996). Instead, the researchers took the largest correlation between a measure of mental ability and an overall interview rating. It is possible that they underestimated the correlation between general mental ability and interview ratings because some of their coefficients only applied to a portion of general mental ability. The general principle in the prior paragraph applies to r's, d's, and other effect sizes. It also applies to multifaceted performance domains (the average validity across different domains is not the validity estimate for a performance composite).

DEGREES OF MODEL MIS-SPECIFICATION AND RECENT META-ANALYSES

Bobko and Stone-Romero (1998) suggested that the field would be better served by conducting fewer studies of more comprehensive scope than by conducting many studies of narrowly focused scope (to potentially be meta-analyzed at a later point). Those authors briefly mentioned that model mis-specification would be reduced with the former strategy. We also believe this is an important issue for the generation of knowledge in the organizational sciences (see also James, 1980). Indeed, there is nothing wrong with meta-analyzing enhanced scope studies.

Before proceeding, we note that model mis-specification occurs when analyses fail to include all relevant variables. In this sense, all studies are mis-specified to some extent. However, it is the relative degree to which they may be mis-specified that is the subject of this section, as well as ways to reduce the degree of mis-specification.

We have noticed a tendency for meta-analytic studies in human resources management and selection to be rather bivariate in their focus (with some recent exceptions). That is, a meta-analysis might focus on the validity of cognitive ability tests in predicting job performance, or on the validity of a Big Five factor, and so forth. Indeed, such a bivariate focus makes sense on the surface because of the interest in "the validity" of a selection device (hence the term *validity generalization*). To be sure, published validity generalization studies do consider moderators of a variety of types (e.g., type of sample, types of performance measure, etc.). However, much is still missing from the typical validity generalization study. That is, to develop the most effective selection measures, it is best not to just estimate the validity of the procedure, but to understand *how* and *why* the measure might be related to performance. At this point, we are implying the need for theory development, including theory about each predictor. To develop such theory, the predictor needs to be embedded in a nomological net of relationships. That net might include other indices of the same construct assessed using different methods, and would definitely need to include other measures of related constructs. As Kerlinger (1965) summarized, a theory includes "a set of interrelated constructs (concepts), definitions, and propositions" and it specifies "relations among variables" (p. 11). We find these facets missing in many "first order" meta-analyses in selection (e.g., validity generalization studies). However, more variables and their interrelationships appear to be included in some recent meta-analytic, "second-order" matrices of multiple predictors (Bobko et al., 1999; Cortina et al. 2000; Schmitt et al., 1997; Schmidt & Hunter, 1998) as noted later.

By way of example of the possibility for incorporating more theory, consider meta-analyses of the validity of the interview. Recent meta-analyses have looked at some moderators, such as degree of structure and job complexity (Huffcutt & Arthur, 1994; Huffcutt & Roth, 1998). However, the interview is best considered as a method rather than a construct. So, meta-analyses of the interview would ideally include estimates of the interview's relationship with paper and pencil measures of cognitive ability (as per Huffcutt et al., 1996), work sample measures of oral communication skills, measures of listening skills, other facets of personality (e.g., energy levels), and so forth (i.e., direct measures of other constructs that might be implicitly assessed in an interview). In our experience, it is rare to find such primary studies, let alone a sufficient number of them to meta-analytically estimate all the predictor intercorrelations implied by the prior sentence. Until the field starts rewarding such comprehensive primary studies, meta-analysts will generally have limited (often bivariate) studies to cumulate and we will gain little by way of understanding.

To obtain a sense of what has been happening, and what still needs to happen to make better use of meta-analysis as a research tool, we informally reviewed the past 10 years of the *Journal of Applied Psychology*, *Personnel Psychology*, and the *Journal of Organizational Behavior* for meta-analyses that illustrated model misspecification issues. By discussing some articles later, we do not want to imply that the named researchers were writing low quality articles. Quite the contrary—we discuss these articles because we feel they represent some of the best thinking in the field. Our motive is to move beyond the best, and not just move beyond something average. We first start with a state-of-the-art analysis in selection by way of comparison.

Hurtz and Donovan (2000)

These authors conducted a meta-analysis of the validity of the Big Five personality factors. There have been many published meta-analyses of measures related to the Big Five (with both U.S. and

European samples), but Hurtz and Donovan wanted to assess validity of measures that were explicitly designed to measure the Big Five factors. Interestingly, they found generally smaller, but positive validity, for the factor of conscientiousness than in prior work. The authors also looked at (as had previous researchers) criterion type, occupational category, and criterion dimension, and they paid particular attention to the distinction between task and contextual performance.

So, what is potentially missing? As hinted at earlier, the focus of this meta-analysis (and most such studies looking at selection tests) is quite bivariate in nature. Although there are five factors, the meta-analysis does not provide estimates of the intercorrelations of these factors (nor intercorrelations among the criterion measures). Thus, it is not clear how combinations of Big Five factors might fare. And, of course, the relationships of the Big Five factors to other possible predictors are missing. As such, it is simply not clear whether or not the Big Five factors will provide unique predictive variance when incorporated into a selection system that uses multiple indicators. (Schmidt & Hunter, 1998, partially addressed this concern. They analyze the incremental validity of alternative tests over and above cognitive ability. However, their analysis is again limited by a focus on only two predictors at a time.) Finally, Hurtz and Donovan nicely suggested yet other variables that would need to be in a model that best understood the effects of the Big Five on work performance. Such other variables included performance expectancies, self-efficacy, and goal setting. We appreciate their statements about such motivational variables and suggest that the data were not necessarily available to them to conduct such analyses.

Organ and Ryan (1995)

These authors conducted a meta-analytic review of predictors of organizational citizenship behavior (OCBs). Predictors included job satisfaction, organizational commitment, fairness, negative affectivity, and some Big Five dimensions. Further, OCBs were assessed along the dimensions of altruism and compliance. Although the meta-analysis was extensive, there is much missing. For example, the reader does not know the intercorrelations either among the predictors or the two OCB performance dimensions (let alone the relationship between OCB performance and task performance). As such, unique variation assessment and modeling is difficult. The problem of finding predictor intercorrelations is extremely difficult (Cortina et al., 2000) and has persisted for years (Hunter & Hunter,

1984). We urge primary study authors to report such data in their journal articles and technical reports.

Hom, Caranikas-Walker, Prussia, and Griffeth (1992)

These authors conducted a meta-analysis of variables related to employee turnover. The study serves as an excellent model, as the authors included a nomological net of variables that came from several different theories of employee turnover. Constructs included job satisfaction, thoughts of quitting, search intention, quit intention, and probability of alternatives. Hom et al. (1992) cumulated across all studies that measured each of the targeted variables (rather than assemble a matrix that contained different studies in each cell). The resulting matrix was subjected to a structural equations analysis and the relative degree of fit of different theories could be assessed. This is a very research-oriented and useful way of exploiting the concept of meta-analysis. Moderators were also considered—including organizational turnover rate, public versus private sector, and unemployment rate. Interestingly, the same issue of the journal in which Hom et al. appeared contains another meta-analysis looking at the relationship between absence and turnover. This second article was bivariate in nature. It is even more interesting to note that none of the theories assessed by Hom et al. included absence as an explanatory variable in their network.

Mathieu and Zajac (1990)

These authors conducted a meta-analysis of the antecedents, correlates, and consequences of organizational commitment. Antecedents included job characteristics dimensions, role states, and organizational characteristics; correlates included job involvement, stress, job satisfaction, and occupational commitment; consequences included job performance and turnover. As such, there were many more variables in their network than one typically finds in bivariate-focused validity meta-analyses. The article also included a moderator analysis by type of commitment (attitudinal or calculative). Once again, there are many variables in this OB-based meta-analysis, and we applaud the authors for incorporating all of these constructs in their model. However, estimates of key relationships are still missing—most notably relationships between constructs within category. So, for example, it is difficult to know if organizational commitment really influences turnover (bivariate r was $-.245$) over and above other correlates in the model (e.g., job satisfaction).

Lee, Carswell, and Allen (2000)

These authors reported a meta-analysis of the antecedents and consequences of occupational commitment. Antecedents included organizational commitment, job satisfaction, role ambiguity, and so forth, as well as a variety of demographic variables. Consequences included performance, turnover intention, and turnover. The authors did not provide all meta-analytic correlations between the antecedents; thus they cannot assess unique contributions or conduct any statistical modeling. However, they did report some intercorrelations between occupational commitment, organizational commitment, job satisfaction, and turnover, so that some semipartial correlations can be considered.

Donovan and Radosevich (1999)

These authors presented a meta-analysis comparing the effect of massed versus distributed practice on task performance. They cumulated effect sizes across the two modes of training and considered moderators of simplicity of the task, intertrial interval, and methodological rigor. They also distinguished between acquisition and retention of performance skills. The authors noted that other moderators might be considered in future work (e.g., motivation level and task performed during intertrial interval), but we suggest that other constructs should be considered in the net as well. There are a host of individual difference variables (some motivational, some dispositional, some cognitive) that would be expected to affect task acquisition and performance. Similarly, there are other aspects to the training environment itself (e.g., delivery of instruction via computer, via lecture, self-paced, group paced, etc.) that would also help understand how to best design practice trials during organizational learning.

Colquitt, LePine, and Noe (2000)

These authors conducted a meta-analytic path analysis also within the domain of training. They focused on the theory of training motivation. This meta-analysis is truly exemplary of the kind of theoretical power available to researchers who choose to conduct meta-analyses. Colquitt et al. had a model that included personality variables and situational variables on the front end. The model then linked those variables to self-efficacy and a host of job and career variables, and then to learning outcomes (mediated by cognitive ability and motivation to learn). Transfer of knowledge and job performance were also considered as end-state variables. These authors constructed a meta-analytic matrix of as many of the indicators of constructs as they could find. Although some estimates of relationships were not available in the literature, the authors managed to estimate effects for at least one variable in each of their model's categories. Thus, explanatory analyses (path analyses) could be constructed for the entire model (the reader is referred to Figures 3 and 4 in their paper). Indeed, as an example of how model mis-specification might be an issue for our field, remember that the Big Five factor of conscientiousness has been found to have non-zero validity that is transportable across many situations and occupations. However, Colquitt et al. found that although conscientiousness was positively related to motivation to learn, it was negatively related to skill acquisition in their full model. Indeed, a similar notion has also been discussed by Martocchio and Judge (1997—see Colquitt et al., 2000, p. 699).

SUMMARY OF MODEL
MIS-SPECIFICATION ISSUES

In thinking about the scope of the fairly recent meta-analyses noted above, it became clear that meta-analyses are capable of adding to the research knowledge base, but they are still limited in what they accomplish. Some effect sizes have been cumulated with more precision as a result of this technique, and many moderators have been assessed. However, the pictures are far from complete. As already stated, validity generalization studies naturally tend to be focused in a bivariate way—on a precise estimate of a single relationship and a focus on when the magnitude of that single value might change (i.e., possible moderators). However, some of the meta-analyses, particularly those in organizational behavior, took a more "systems" perspective and tended to include a variety of hypothetical constructs in their meta-analytic net. However, even these meta-analyses were far from theoretically complete. They typically contained some sort of primary variable (e.g., job commitment) and measures of both antecedents and consequences. However, it was rare to find meta-analyses that reported the complete matrix of correlations within the antecedent set or the consequence set. Thus, although there was relatively less mis-specification, there was still room for improvement.

Nonetheless, those interested in selection meta-analyses (and validity generalization) can garner some lessons from the organizational behavior based meta-analyses. The field should move beyond just validity generalization and specify an entire array of theoretical variables to be analyzed in their single investigations. Many of the aforementioned articles started with some sort of model or figure—very much akin to the type of figure one might see in a linear, structural relations (LISREL) based analysis. Selection based meta-analyses would benefit from such a perspective. For example:

- In assessing the validity of a particular construct (e.g., a Big Five measure or a measure of cognitive ability), it would be important to include other selection measures in the analytic system (e.g., to assess unique contribution).

- It might also be useful to model the effects of different measurement methods of the same constructs (see Sackett, Schmitt, Ellingson, & Kabin, 2001, for a recent discussion of this issue). One such notable analysis is the inclusion of methods factors in the analysis of the U.S. Army's selection system (see Campbell, McHenry, & Wise, 1990).

- Other variables relevant to selection could also be considered in a single validity generalization study—again, with the intent of understanding how and why selection measures are related to performance outcomes. Such variables could be derived from path-analytic thinking. For example, the effects of recruiting and early life experiences might appear early in the model, the typical selection variables would appear next (along with methods factors), and mediators of job knowledge and training would appear as precursors to assessments of job performance (possibly both immediate and distal).

There have been some attempts to increase the scope of meta-analyses in the selection arena. Both Schmitt et al. (1997) and Bobko et al. (1999) considered meta-analytic matrices that included cognitive ability, job performance, and a variety of "alternative" predictors. We applaud such efforts although note that the "alternatives" (e.g., biodata or interviews) mix methods with constructs. This confound would make theory development particularly difficult. Another good attempt to use meta-analysis for modeling is found in the work of Hunter (1983) and Schmidt, Hunter, and Outerbridge (1986), who looked at the role of job knowledge, job experience, and cognitive ability on job performance. The net of constructs considered in those papers was fairly complex, although no motivational variables were considered.

Viswesvaran and Ones (1995) outlined steps for incorporating meta-analytic matrices within structural equation modeling. Interestingly, most of the studies cited there as exemplary work were not published in industrial/organizational (I/O) journals. And, of course, our cursory review shows that many recent meta-analyses still suffer from a lack of conceptual completeness. We nonetheless agree with Viswesvaran and Ones' optimism and call for more comprehensive meta-analytic modeling in I/O journals.

It is important to repeat that, in a variety of cases discussed here, the failure to incorporate many of the intercorrelations may simply be due to the lack of availability of such empirical work in the literature, rather than the lack of desire to incorporate them. We have come across this issue in our own work, in which the paucity of primary studies that report predictor intercorrelations is quite evident (Roth, Bobko, & Potosky, 2001). Although such work (or reporting thereof) may not be the sexiest thing to do, it is important if we are going to move beyond bivariate validity generalization and exploit meta-analysis for the purpose of modeling and understanding. We encourage such work at the primary study level, as well.

A Statistical Issue

We note the potential danger of combining correlational estimates from different studies in a common, second-order meta-analytic matrix (which might apply to the meta-analyses advocated by Viswesvaran and Ones (1995), and might apply to some of the OB studies noted earlier). As statisticians know (cf. Bollen, 1989) the resulting matrix entries could be mutually inconsistent and cause the matrix to be negative definite. Viswesvaran and Ones dismissed this concern by indicating that there is no empirical evidence that the problem has been realized. Although their statement is consistent with the lack of data in this area, it is not strong proof because there has been no demonstration that the problem does not exist, either. Indeed, as one reviewer of this chapter noted, it was his or her experience that negative definite matrices are common, and researchers are likely to tinker with matrices to resolve the problem before submitting results to a journal. We encourage basic statistical research (that might include Monte Carlo simulation work) on this issue to determine the magnitude of the potential problem. It could be severe. For example, in our experience, many predictor intercorrelation cells in meta-analytic matrices are either empty (no studies) or have but one or two primary studies. Suppose there are two cells, each with a single primary study with sample size n. Then the estimate of r is associated with sampling variation of order $1/\sqrt{n}$. If the n in each study is 200, the standard error of the r is about .07. A swing of .07 (in opposite directions) for each of the two r's might lead to a substantial difference in results (ironically, meta-analysis cumulates effect sizes to avoid such "swings"). In any event, we call for basic statistical research into the nature and extent of this potential problem.

A Practical Issue

We have been calling for studies of more enhanced scope (to complement, and be used in, meta-analyses). Careers being of finite length, this means there would be fewer studies published in the field and fewer studies published per researcher. Although we believe this might be a good thing, Bobko and Stone-Romero (1998) noted that the reward structures in academic departments would have to change. At this point in time, numbers of "hits" is something that deans and department chairs and tenure committees look at (quite a countable criterion measure). It would be imperative to find a way to reward fewer studies of enhanced scope. That political issue is beyond the scope of this chapter—but it is a very important one, we believe, for knowledge generation in the organizational sciences.

SUMMARY

Meta-analysis and validity generalization are very useful techniques, but they have not yet solved our understanding of literature in OB or HR/selection (see also Bobko & Stone-Romero, 1998). A number of suggestions have been made for future meta-analytic work (that also have implications for primary study research in some instances).

We urge researchers to carefully consider the purposes of their analysis and the type of samples that are most relevant. If one is interested in understanding the basic characteristics of a predictor, such as validity or standardized ethnic group differences, then sample selection and study design becomes important. For example, if one wishes to compare cognitive ability tests to "alternative predictors," then all analyses should be conducted on the same type of sample. In this case, analysis of applicant samples or sample results corrected back to the applicant level would be most helpful. We urge such research to accurately compare predictors such as cognitive ability tests, interviews, biodata, and so forth. We also urge researchers to consider conducting within-job analyses and to consider potentially extraneous sources of variance (Ostroff & Harrison, 1999).

There is an assortment of other issues in meta-analysis that could use continued attention. The issue of meta-analyzing methods (interview and biodata) while aggregating across (or ignoring) constructs does not fully inform the field of how method-construct combinations influence either validity or standardized ethnic group differences. Further, researchers should be concerned about the appropriate use of composites and independent samples.

We also agree with Viswesvaran and Ones (1995) in that meta-analysis might be usefully wedded to comprehensive networks of constructs. We encourage the use of wider scope theories as underpinnings for meta-analytic investigations, in order to minimize issues of model mis-specification. Thinking through one's study in terms of structural equations is not the only way to accomplish this goal (but it is a helpful perspective). Indeed, theory generation and thinking ahead is something we all spend a lot of time in graduate school learning how to do.

We also encourage more primary research that reports intercorrelations within predictor sets and within the criterion space. Such correlations were missing from many of the meta-analyses we found, and we suspect the correlations were missing because of a lack of availability. Perhaps journal editors can and should require more full reporting of such intercorrelations, and practitioners should include more of this work in their technical reports. Cumulating literatures can be a very helpful facet to theory development and a fuller knowledge base—we encourage further use of meta-analysis but under conditions of full information and extended variable sets.

REFERENCES

Bobko, P., Roth, P., & Bobko, C. (2001). Correcting the effect size of d for range restriction and unreliability. *Organizational Research Methods, 4,* 46–61.

Bobko, P., Roth, P., & Potosky, D. (1999). Derivation and implications of a meta-analytic matrix incorporating cognitive ability, alternative predictors, and job performance. *Personnel Psychology, 52,* 561–589.

Bobko, P., & Stone-Romero, E. (1998). Meta-analysis is another useful research tool but it is not a panacea. In J. Ferris (Ed.), *Research in personnel and human resources management* (Vol. 16, pp. 359–397). Greenwich, CT: JAI Press.

Bollen, K. (1989). *Structural equations with latent variables*. New York: Wiley.

Campbell, J., McHenry, J., & Wise, L. (1990). Modeling job performance in a population of jobs. *Personnel Psychology, 43*, 313–333.

Campion, M. A., Pursell, E. D., & Brown, B. B. (1988). Structured interviewing: Raising the psychometric properties of the employment interview. *Personnel Psychology, 41*, 25–41.

Caretta, T. (1997). Group differences on US Air Force pilot selection tests. *Sex and Ethnic Group Differences, 5*, 115–126.

Colquitt, J., LePine, J., & Noe, R. (2000). Toward an integrative theory of training motivation: A meta-analytic path analysis of 20 years of research. *Journal of Applied Psychology, 85*, 678–707.

Cortina, J. M., Goldstein, N. B., Payne, S. C., Davison, H. K., & Gilliland, S. W. (2000). The incremental validity of interview scores over and above cognitive ability and conscientiousness scores. *Personnel Psychology, 53*, 325–351.

Dean, M. (1999). *On biodata construct validity, criterion validity and adverse impact*. Unpublished doctoral dissertation, Louisiana State University, Baton Rouge, LA.

Donovan, J., & Radosevich, D. (1999). A meta-analytic review of the distribution of practice effect: Now you see it, now you don't. *Journal of Applied Psychology, 85*, 795–805.

Gandy, J., Dye, D., & MacLane, C. (1994). Federal government seletion: The individual achievement record. In G. Stokes, M. Mumford, & W. Owens (Eds.), *Biodata handbook: Theory, research, and use of biographical information in selection and performance prediction* (pp. 275–310). Palo Alto, CA: CPP Books.

Herrnstein, R., & Murray, C. (1994). *The bell curve: Intelligence and class structure in American life*. New York: Free Press.

Hom, P., Caranikas-Walker, F., Prussia, G., & Griffeth, R. (1992). A meta-analytical structural equations analysis of a model of employee turnover. *Journal of Applied Psychology, 77*, 890–909.

Hough, L. (1998). Personality at work: Issues and evidence. In M. Hakel (Ed.), *Beyond multiple choice: Evaluating alternatives to traditional testing for selection* (pp. 131–159). Mahwah, NJ: Lawrence Erlbaum Associates.

Hough, L., Oswald, F., & Ployhart, R. (2001). Adverse impact and group differences in constructs, assessment tools, and personnel selection procedures: Issues and lessons learned. *International Journal of Selection and Assessment, 9*, 152–194.

Huffcutt, A., & Arthur, W. (1994). Hunter and Hunter (1984) revisited: Interview validity for entry-level jobs. *Journal of Applied Psychology, 79*, 184–190.

Huffcutt, A., Conway, J., Roth, P., & Stone, N. (2001). Identification and meta-analytic assessment of psychological constructs measured in employment interviews. *Journal of Applied Psychology, 86*, 897–913.

Huffcutt, A., & Roth, P. (1998). Racial group differences in interview evaluations. *Journal of Applied Psychology, 83*, 179–189.

Huffcutt, A., Roth, P., & McDaniel, M. (1996). A meta-analytic investigation of cognitive ability in employment interview evaluations: Moderating characteristics and implications for incremental validity. *Journal of Applied Psychology, 81*, 459–473.

Hunter, J. (1983). A causal analysis of cognitive ability, job knowledge, job performance, and supervisory ratings. In F. Landy, S. Zedeck, & J. Cleveland (Eds.), *Performance measurement and theory* (pp. 257–266). Hillsdale, NJ: Lawrence Erlbaum Associates.

Hunter, J., & Hunter, R. (1984). Validity and utility of alternative predictors of job performance. *Psychological Bulletin, 96,* 72–98.

Hurtz, G., & Donovan, J. (2000). Personality and job performance: The big five revisited. *Journal of Applied Psychology, 85,* 869–879.

James, L. (1980). The unmeasured variables problem in path analysis. *Journal of Applied Psychology, 65,* 415–421.

Kerlinger, R., (1965). *Foundations of behavioral research.* New York: Holt, Rinehart & Winston.

Lee, K., Carswell, J., & Allen, N. (2000). A meta-analytic review of occupational commitment: Relations with person- and work-related variables. *Journal of Applied Psychology, 85,* 799–811.

Martocchio, J. J., & Judge, T. A. (1997). Relationship between conscientiousness and learning in employee training; Mediating influences of self-deception and self-efficacy. *Journal of Applied Psychology, 82,* 764–773.

Mathieu, J., & Zajac, D. (1990). A review and meta-analysis of the antecedents, correlates, and consequences of organizational commitment. *Psychological Bulletin, 108,* 171–194.

McDaniel, M., Morgeson, F., Finnegan, E., Campion, M., & Braverman, E. (2001). Use of situational judgment tests to predict job performance: A clarification of the literature. *Journal of Applied Psychology, 86,* 730–740.

McDaniel, M., Whetzel, D., Schmidt, F., & Maurer, S. (1994). The validity of employment interviews: A comprehensive review and meta-analysis. *Journal of Applied Psychology, 79,* 599–616.

McHenry, J., Hough, L., Toquam, J., Hadson, M., & Ashworth, S. 1990. Project A validity results: The relationship between predictor and criterion domains. *Personnel Psychology, 43,* 335–354.

Organ, D., & Ryan, K. (1995). A meta-analytic review of attitudinal and dispositional predictors of organizational citizenship behavior. *Personnel Psychology, 48,* 775–802.

Ostroff, C., & Harrison, D. (1999). Meta-analysis: Level of analysis, and best estimates of population correlations: Cautions for interpreting meta-analytic results in organizational behavior. *Journal of Applied Psychology, 84,* 260–270.

Roth, P., BeVier, C., Bobko, P., Switzer, F., & Tyler, P. (2001). Ethnic group differences in cognitive ability in employment and educational settings: A meta-analysis. *Personnel Psychology, 54,* 297–330.

Roth, P., Bobko, P., Switzer, F., & Dean, M. (2001). Prior selection causes biased estimates of standardized ethnic group differences: Simulation and analysis. *Personnel Psychology, 54,* 591–617.

Roth, P., Bobko, P., & Potosky, D. (2001). *An applicant level meta-analytic matrix of predictors of job performance: Analysis of validity, standardized ethnic group differences, and research needs.* Manuscript submitted for publication.

Roth, P., & Clarke, R. (1998). Meta-analyzing the relationship between grades and salary. *Journal of Vocational Behavior, 53,* 386–400.

Roth, P., Van Iddekinge C., Huffcutt, A., Eidson, C., Jr., & Bobko, P. (2002). Correcting for range restriction in structured interview ethnic group differences: The values may be larger than we thought. *Journal of Applied Psychology, 87,* 369–376.

Sackett, P., & Ellingson, J. (1997). The effects of forming multi-predictor composites on group differences and adverse impact. *Personnel Psychology, 50,* 707–721.

Sackett, P., Schmitt, N., Ellingson, J., & Kabin, M. (2001). High-stakes testing in employment, credentialing, and higher education. *American Psychologist, 56,* 302–318.

Sackett, P., & Wilk, S. (1994). Within group norming and other forms of score adjustment in preemployment testing. *American Psychologist, 49,* 929–954.

Schmidt, F., & Hunter, J. (1998). The validity and utility of selection methods in personnel psychology: Practical and theoretical implications of 85 years of research findings. *Psychological Bulletin, 124,* 262–274.

Schmidt, F., Hunter, J., & Outerbridge, A. (1986). Impact of job experience and ability on job knowledge, work sample performance, and supervisory ratings of job performance. *Journal of Applied Psychology, 71,* 432–439.

Schmitt, N., Clause, C., & Pulakos, E. (1996). Subgroup differences associated with different measures of some common job relevant constructs. In C. Cooper & I. Robertson (Eds.), *International Review of Industrial and Organizational Psychology, 11,* 115–137.

Schmitt, N., Rogers, W., Chan, D., Sheppard, L., & Jennings, D. (1997). Adverse impact and predictive efficiency of various predictor combinations. *Journal of Applied Psychology, 82,* 719–730.

Spector, P., & Levine, E. (1987). Meta-analysis for integrating study outcomes: A Monte Carlo study of its susceptibility to Type I and Type II errors. *Journal of Applied Psychology, 72,* 3–9.

Viswesvaran, C., & Ones, D. (1995). Theory testing: Combining psychometric meta-analysis and structural equations modeling. *Personnel Psychology, 48,* 865–885.

Wanous, J., Sullivan, S., & Malinak, J. (1989). The role of judgment calls in meta-analysis. *Journal of Applied Psychology, 74,* 259–264.

4 The Status of Validity Generalization Research: Key Issues in Drawing Inferences From Cumulative Research Findings

Paul R. Sackett
University of Minnesota

The assigned task was to describe the current status of the validity generalization model as a method of summarizing a research literature and as a basis for drawing inferences about predictor–criterion relationships in a given applied setting, and to assess both the contributions of this model and the lingering controversies involved in drawing inferences about test validity. To describe the current status of the validity generalization model, the opening sections of this chapter examine several settings in which deliberative bodies have carefully reviewed the validity generalization concept and method. First, the 1985 document "Forty questions about validity generalization and meta analysis, with commentaries," intended as a mechanism for identifying areas of agreement and disagreement within Industrial and Organizational psychology about validity generalization, is reviewed (Schmidt, Hunter, Pearlman, & Rothstein, 1985). Second, several professional deliberative bodies have examined validity generalization. Professional standards for testing and selection research are examined to see how the treatment of validity generalization has evolved over time. Treatment of validity generalization by a National Academy of Science committee is examined. Third, this author has had the opportunity to participate in the aforementioned events, as cochair of the 1999 revision of the *Standards for Educational and Psychological Tests*, as a member of the National Academy of Sciences committee on Validity

Generalization and the General Aptitude Test Battery, and as a participant in the "Forty Questions" exchange. As someone heavily involved in considerations of validity generalization, I offer a set of observations about issues that I see as meriting further consideration.

THE "FORTY QUESTIONS" DEBATE

In 1985, a document entitled "Forty questions about validity generalization and meta-analysis" was published. Schmidt, Pearlman, Hunter, and Hirsh (1985) had compiled a list of 40 questions and concerns that had been voiced about validity generalization and prepared a reply to each. When this was submitted to Personnel Psychology for publication consideration, I proposed to the editor, Milt Hakel, that this might be an opportunity to identify areas of agreement and disagreement about validity generalization. Milt assembled a group of individuals with expertise of the topic, and each wrote independent comments on the questions. These were assembled into a consensus document, and included as a commentary, authored by Sackett, Schmitt, Tenopyr, Kehoe, and Zedeck (1985). Sackett et al. also identified additional issues not part of the original 40 questions. Schmidt et al. then wrote replies to these commentaries.

Although framed as a debate, my sense is that there really was far less controversy than some might think. First, the commentators stated explicitly that they fundamentally accept the mechanics of meta-analysis. Although there have been a number of refinements and alternative estimation models offered, the 40 Questions document did not focus on those. This chapter does not do so either; other chapters in this volume address these alternative models. The focus is on conceptual issues in the conduct and interpretation of validity generalization analyses. Second, the commentators offered no comment on 23 of the 40 questions; many of these reflected fundamental misunderstandings of validity generalization on the part of the questioner and the Schmidt et al. reply served to clarify the issue in question. Third, although the commentators did offer input on 17 of the 40 questions, and Schmidt et al. offered replies to most, my sense is that we were often talking past each other. The commentators would raise a cautionary note (e.g., be careful if the criterion is different than that in the validity generalization data base; be careful with low power to detect moderators; be careful with assumed artifact distributions). The rebuttal from Schmidt et al. would include a spirited defense of validity generalization. The rebuttal commonly included an implicit or explicit assumption that by raising a cautionary note the commentators were arguing against validity generalization and in favor of reliance on local studies or on narrative reviews. In fact, the commentators' concern was with drawing too strong a conclusion from a validity generalization analysis under some of these conditions. At the conclusion of the paper, Schmidt et al. noted that most disagreements with the commentators are on issues of fine tuning methods or applications, rather than fundamental disagreement about validity generalization as a concept and a methodology.

There are three major issues that surface repeatedly in "Forty Questions." One is the power to detect moderators. The second is the possibility of and implications of a biased data base. The third is the role of meta-analytic evidence versus local studies when the meta-analytic data base is limited. Each of these are treated in detail in a subsequent section of this chapter, which outlines key issues in the conduct and interpretation of validity generalization analyses.

VALIDITY GENERALIZATION AND PROFESSIONAL STANDARDS

Three key documents for psychologists working in the personnel selection domain are the 1978 federal *Uniform Guidelines on Employee Selection Procedures*, the *Standards for Educational and Psychological Testing* (American Education Research Association, American Psychological Association, & National Council on Measurement in Education, 1985, 1999), and the *Principles for the Validation and Use of Personnel Selection Procedures* (Society for Industrial and Organizational Psychology, Inc., 1987). The *Guidelines* were issued essentially contemporaneously with the initial development of the general theory of validity of generalization, and thus do not incorporate validity generalization. The *Guidelines* have not been revised since 1978, and validity generalization is but one of many issues on which they are not current.

The 1985 *Standards* acknowledged the use of meta-analytic techniques both as a method of drawing scientific conclusions about a body of literature and as a means of transporting validity evidence to support test use in a new situation. The introductory text accompanying the *Standards* stated that the extent to which validity generalization can be relied on in drawing inferences of validity in new situations is a function of the amount and relevance of accumulated data. One *Standard* per se addressed validity generalization (Standard 1.16, p. 16), stating: "When adequate local validity evidence is not available, criterion-related evidence of validity for a specified test may be based on validity generalization from a set of prior studies, provided that the specified test-use situation can be considered to have been drawn from the same population of situations on which validity generalization was conducted." Note the conditional status: primacy is given to local evidence, with validity generalization a strategy for use when local evidence is not available.

The 1987 SIOP *Principles* also devoted considerable attention to validity generalization. (Note that the *Principles* are in the process of being revised at press time.) Unlike the *Standards*, the *Principles* do not frame validity generalization as a supplemental strategy. The *Principles* stated that researchers can rely on validity generalization to support the use of selection instruments to the extent that adequate validity generalization data are available. They differentiate between settings in which validity generalization is universal (i.e., when evidence suggests the usefulness of a predictor for all jobs) and settings in which evidence supports use for only some jobs. In the latter case, reliance on validity generalization requires evidence that the selection procedure is indeed a measure of the construct that is the focus of the validity generalization analysis, and evidence that the job in question falls into the job domain included in the validity generalization analysis. The *Principles* also introduced the idea that validity generalization evidence may be a useful adjunct to local evidence, with similar findings between a local study and validity generalization evidence serving to strengthen the degree of confidence in the local study. This idea of validity generalization evidence supporting local evidence and thus building a stronger case for validity in the situation in question anticipates the perspective taken in the 1999 *Standards*. The 1999 *Standards* defined validity as the degree to which evidence and theory support the inferences a user wishes to draw from test scores for a particular application, and endorse drawing on multiple lines of evidence in support of intended test use.

The 1999 *Standards* did not give primacy to any particular line of validity evidence. The relative emphasis on local versus generalized evidence is seen as a function of the comparative informational value of the two in a particular situation. According to the *Standards*, there is a strong basis for using validity generalization to draw conclusions about validity in a local setting when the meta-analytic data-base is large, representative of the local setting, and consistent in the pattern of validity evidence after accounting for artifacts. Representativeness of the local settings encompasses issues of similarity in operationalization of the predictor construct, in the type of job, and in the type of criterion. Other possible issues were mentioned as well, such as the possibility of change in validity over time in settings where the data going into the meta-analysis are quite dated. Note that the *Standards* do not assert that these features do affect validity findings, but rather that an objective of a validity generalization study is to determine whether these features do or do not influence findings. Standard 1.21 notes: "If relevant research includes credible evidence that any other features of the testing application may influence the strength of the test-criterion relationship, the correspondence between those features in the local situation and in the meta-analysis should be reported." Thus the *Standards* recognize that there is a virtually unlimited set of features on which one can compare a local setting and the settings represented in the validity generalization data base, and simply identifying a feature on which the two differ is not grounds for rejecting generalization to the local setting (e.g., "none of the studies in the validity generalization data base was done here in Minnesota"). A difference between the local study and the cumulative data base only leads to questions about the viability of generalizing from the cumulative data base when there is credible evidence that the feature in question affects validity.

In sum, the *Principles* and the 1999 *Standards* view validity generalization evidence as an appropriate basis for drawing conclusions about validity in a local setting. Concerns are not with validity generalization as an approach, but with the strength and appropriateness of the cumulative data base for the local setting.

TREATMENT OF VALIDITY GENERALIZATION BY THE NATIONAL ACADEMY OF SCIENCES (NAS)

In the late 1970's, the Department of Labor (DOL) commissioned validity generalization research on the General Aptitude Test Battery (GATB; Hunter, 1980), and used this research as the basis for widespread use of the GATB to screen applicants for organizations using the DOL's Employment Service. Based on more than 500 GATB validity studies, the DOL concluded that GATB validity could be generalized to all jobs in the U.S. workforce. In addition, the DOL used within-group percentile norming as the basis for referring applicants to employers. In other words, raw scores were converted to percentile standing within one's racial or ethnic group. Thus the same raw score could produce very different percentile scores depending on subgroup membership. The reliance on validity generalization and the use of within-group percentile norming resulted in a dispute between the DOL and the Department of Justice (DOJ) over the appropriateness of the GATB testing program. The reliance on validity generalization and the use of within-group scoring were seen as linked in the mind of critics of the system, although in fact the two are completely distinct. The DOL and DOJ agreed to have a National Academy of Sciences Committee appointed to examine this issue. A multiyear study resulted in a book titled *Fairness in employment testing: Validity generalization, minority issues, and the General Aptitude Test Battery* (Hartigan & Wigdor, 1989). The focus here is on the issue of validity generalization; for a discussion of the within-group norming aspects of the issue, see Sackett and Wilk (1994).

Hartigan and Wigdor (1989) concluded that the general thesis of the theory of validity generalization was accepted by the committee. They did challenge several aspects of some specific validity generalization applications. First, validity generalization analyses are often based on assumptions about factors such as range restriction and reliability that may not be directly supported by data. While accepting range restriction corrections when there is concrete evidence of the presence and degree of range restriction, they questioned the use of assumed values for range restriction corrections.

Second, while accepting that criterion unreliability results in observed validity being an underestimate of operational validity, they questioned the reliability estimates used for the correction when the validity generalization data base in question does not contain good reliability data. Although considerable progress has been made in gathering data to examine criterion unreliability (Viswesvaran, Ones, & Schmidt, 1996), questions about the appropriateness of particular reliability estimates remain areas of current controversy (Murphy & DeShon, 2000a, 2000b; Schmidt, Viswesvaran, & Ones, 2000).

Third, they noted that a key issue for validity generalization was the relationship between the sample of studies in the validity generalization data base and the population to which one wishes to generalize. Validity generalization relies on the implicit premise that the obtained sample of studies is a random sample from the population of interest. Failing randomness, a case must be made for representativeness, which entails the determination of the relevant study features for ascertaining representativeness. In the DOL data base, jobs were sampled on an availability basis, rather than according to a sampling plan. The Hunter (1980) research focused on the cognitive complexity of jobs, indexed by the Data-People-Things scales from the *Dictionary of Occupational Titles* and documented patterns of validity findings by job complexity, showing meaningful level of GATB validity for all complexity levels. The NAS committee focused on representativeness in terms of standard occupational categories. They questioned representativeness, noting, for example, that whereas 2.0 percent of jobs in the DOT are classified as agricultural, fishery, forestry, and related, only .04% of the validity studies were from this family. Note that they do not offer any argument as to a reason why, net of cognitive complexity, one would theorize a different pattern of results for this occupational family. It is instructive to consider the perspective of the 1999 *Standards*, as previously discussed. Recall that the *Standards* call for credible evidence that a variable influences validity findings before lack of representativeness on that variable is seen as a threat to validity generalization.

Fourth, validity generalization researchers have sometimes claimed that validity is invariant across settings, basing their claim on the finding that the residual variance in validities after subtracting variance likely due to statistical artifacts is small. The NAS committee questioned the interpretation of small residual variances. Arguments that small residual variances imply that no moderators are present require that two separate conditions be met. The first is that there be adequate representation of the various relevant levels of the moderator in the sample; the second is that there be adequate statistical power to detect a moderator. The second is conditional on the first, as a total sample size that would result in adequate power to detect a moderator would only do so the various levels of the moderator are in fact present in sample.

Each of the issues emerging in the NAS analysis remains an important concern today, and each is developed in more detail in a subsequent section of this chapter.

KEY ISSUES IN INTERPRETING VALIDITY GENERALIZATION FINDINGS

In this section, a set of issues are discussed that are important for the effective use of validity generalization. The focus is on conceptual issues, rather than on validity generalization estimation models.

Issue 1: Construct and Domain Specification: Failing to Specify the Boundaries of Generalization

When one speaks of validity generalization, a fundamental question is "generalizing from what to what?" Any meaningful discussion of generalization requires (a) specifying the domain boundaries of the predictor domain, (b) specifying the domain boundaries for the criterion domain, and (c) specifying the jobs and settings for which the relationship holds.

The range of validity generalization applications is such that there are times when this is straightforward. When a test publisher reports a validity generalization analysis in which a single instrument is correlated with a standard criterion across a set of jobs within a narrow domain, there is little uncertainty about these issues. In contrast, consider a meta-analysis addressing the relationship between integrity tests and counterproductive work behaviors. This requires (a) specifying the domain boundaries for "integrity tests," (b) specifying the domain boundaries for "counterproductive work behaviors," and (c) specifying the jobs and settings for which the relationship holds. Ones, Viswesvaran, and Schmidt (1993) reported a large scale meta-analysis of this relationship.

Consider first the predictor domain, which breaks down results into two categories of integrity tests, overt and personality based. The overt test data base includes samples using data from 19 overt integrity tests. For nontheft criteria, for applicant samples, and excluding self-report criteria, the corrected mean validity was .39 and the low end of the 90% credibility interval was .23. Key questions include the following: Can we generalize to all 19 tests? To other overt tests not included in the data set? What if a test contributed a single study to the data base (which is actually the case)? What if three tests contributed a strong majority of the studies? Ones (2001, personal communication) estimated that 60% to 70% of the studies come from the London House PSI, the Reid Report, and the Stanton Survey. It is known that these three tests are highly intercorrelated (mean $r = .85$); however, the mean r among 56 correlations between various overt integrity tests is .45 (Sackett & Wanek, 1996). Thus there is evidence that the three tests contributing the preponderance of data differ from many of the other tests. So can broad conclusions be drawn about the validity of overt integrity tests? Can the use of a single specified test be supported by the meta-analytic evidence? It would appear that one key issue would be the correlation of any specific test with the three prominent tests that heavily influence the meta-analytic results.

This concern about the domain of generalization on the predictor side is particularly salient when the domain under examination reflects a data collection method, rather than a clearly specified construct. Examples would include interviews or work sample tests. The intent of interviews varies widely, with a focus ranging from job knowledge to work values to ability to withstand stress. It is certainly the case that meta-analysis of such domains has led to important insights (e.g., support for value of a structured interview); at the same time the degree to which one can generalize to new situations is unclear. The interview may be a highly effective approach to assessing some constructs and quite ineffective for assessing others. One must be able to make a strong case that interview process and content in the setting to which one intends to generalize match the interview process and content of the validity generalization data base.

Turning to the criterion side of the equation, Ones et al. (1993) categorized studies as involving theft criteria or as a catch-all term labeled *broad counterproductivity*. This included a wide variety of counterproductive behaviors, including absence, tardiness, reason for termination, disciplinary action, causing accidents, and others. What is unclear is the relationship among these various measures. Are they all manifestations of a common underlying construct, and are each of them predicted equally well by integrity tests? This appears to be a domain where the possibility of differential relationships between integrity test and various counterproductive behaviors can be posited on theoretical grounds. What the various counterproductive behaviors have in common is that they are behaviors contrary to the organization's interests. But these behaviors can have different underlying motivations: greed, retaliation, laziness, inattention, among others. Subsequent work by Ones and co-workers has reported meta-analyses of the relationships between integrity test and specific counterproductive behaviors (e.g., absence (Ones, Viswesvaran, & Schmidt, n.d.), and there is a growing body of research on the interrelationships among various forms of counterproductive behavior (Sackett & DeVore, 2001). Thus progress is being made toward understanding the boundaries of generalization in this domain; the issue merits attention in all domains.

Finally, consider the issue of generalizing across settings, which in this example would include issues such as job type and organizational features (e.g., closeness of supervision). As noted previously, this is most straightforward when there is a clear statement of the domain from which studies are sampled. When that is not the case, interpretational difficulties arise.

For example, how would one respond to an assertion like:

The setting to which we wish to generalize is one where individuals are closely supervised. While not questioning integrity test validity in settings where individuals work without close supervision, the presence of close supervision surely influences employee behavior. Thus we question the basis for inferring integrity test validity in settings with close supervision when closeness of supervision has not been measured in any study to date.

One response might be to point to the large number of studies done and the consistency of study results. This argument would posit that although firms were not sampled randomly one can reasonably assume that a wide range of organizational characteristics are included in the data base, including varying levels of closeness of supervision. If closeness of supervision affected validity, there would be a large variance in study results. The fact that this is not the case rules out the possibility that closeness of supervision is an important moderator.

The reply might be that it is not safe to assume that studies will reflect all levels of important moderators. Might it not be the case that firm interest in integrity testing is linked to closeness of supervision? Firms may worry about the risk of counterproductive behavior when individuals work without close supervision, and thus such firms explore integrity test use and contribute to the validity data base.

At this point one might conclude that closeness of supervision may merit attention as a possible moderator and work may be undertaken to examine this possibility. But a complete examination of this issue is likely to be time consuming. What about the firm attempting to justify test use in this close-supervision setting in the face of skepticism about generalizability? Possibilities include attempting to retrospectively document closeness of supervision in some portion of the studies making up the validity generalization data base. Finding studies that do involve close supervision refutes the strong version of the premise, namely that the data base consists solely of studies done in loose supervision settings. Another possibility is a search of the validity generalization data base for a study or studies done in settings extremely similar to the one to which one is attempting to generalize. In essence, a transportability argument would be made to supplement the meta-analytic argument as the basis for generalization.

The key point remains that issues about the settings sampled and the domain to which results can be generalized are pivotal issues. There will be tension as the research data base is likely to lag the needs of practice. As in the closeness of the supervision example earlier, only when a novel moderator is suggested and supported by a sufficiently compelling conceptual rationale will data collection to address the issue be initiated. There may not be an immediate and ready answer to questions about generalizability to a setting previously unexplored in the validity generalization data base.

Issue 2: Statistical Power and the Problem of Drawing Strong Inferences From Small-Scale Meta-Analyses

The power to detect moderators has long been a focal issue in validity generalization research. At issue is the magnitude of the residual variance in validity coefficients after variance expected due to statistical artifact is subtracted from observed variance. If this value is small, the inference is that there is no opportunity for substantive or methodological moderators to operate: If such moderators were present the residual variance would be much larger.

There has been extensive simulation work examining the statistical power of meta-analysis (e.g., Osburn, Callender, Greener, & Ashworth, 1983; Sackett, Harris, & Orr, 1986). Each cautions against drawing strong conclusions from small validity generalization data bases. Each simulates differing sets of conditions. For example, Osburn et al. simulated a situation in which there is a distribution of true validity with specified variance, whereas Sackett et al. simulated a dichotomous moderator in which 50% of studies come from one population and 50% from another). Power depends on the conditions simulated (e.g., the proportion of studies drawn from each population condition), the type I error rate, and the magnitude of validity difference one is concerned about detecting; thus there is no single value that can be used to represent power. But there is agreement that power to detect validity differences of .1 to .2 is low when the number of studies is small (e.g., 10–15) and when samples are typical of I/O research (e.g., $N = 100$).

Thus the question arises as to what conclusions can be drawn in a domain when the number of studies (K) in a meta-analysis is small. One key issue is the broader context in which the meta-analysis is done. Some meta-analyses are done in a context in which there are other meta-analyses in related domains that can be drawn on for support, a point emphasized by Schmidt et al. (1985) in "Forty questions." For example, consider a publisher of a cognitive ability test conducting a meta-analysis of eight studies done using that test and producing a mean and variance virtually identical to that resulting from broader meta-analyses in the cognitive ability domain. Concerns about power would in this case be quite low. The purpose of the meta-analysis is really to link the test in question to the much broader domain, and all of the information about the presence or absence of substantive or methodological moderators from the broader domain can be drawn on.

Contrast this with a publisher of a test in a novel domain (e.g., handwriting analysis), with a similar data base of eight studies. Assume a small residual variance. Is it safe to assume that there are no moderators? The answer is no, and for three separate reasons: low power, second order sampling error, and the possibility of sampling bias. In scenario one, the data base may truly be a random sample from the domain of possible studies, with equal representation of studies from each moderator condition, but the number of studies is too small for validity variance to be reliably detected. This is the classic statistical power issue, and the remedy is more studies.

In scenario two, the data base is also a random sample, but the sample of studies is not large enough for randomization to accomplish its intended purpose. Purely by luck of the draw most or all studies come from one moderator condition, with the other virtually or completely unrepresented. The result is high correspondence between observed variance and expected variance and the failure to detect the possibility of a moderator. This is referred to as second order sampling error (Hunter & Schmidt, 1990), and again the remedy is more studies.

In scenario three, the data base is systematically biased. For any of a wide variety of reasons, the observed sample of studies are drawn in a manner that systematically overrepresents some features and underrepresents others (e.g., all studies use a single operationalization of the criterion construct when the true state of affairs is that markedly different findings are found with different operationalizations). This is not linked per se to the issue of the small number of studies in the meta-analysis: Analyses with large numbers of samples may also involve biased sampling, particularly when one publisher or one research team contributes a large number of studies all sharing the same design and measures. The biased data base is treated later as a separate issue.

Thus there is considerable literature about the risks of drawing inferences about the presence or absence of moderators (and hence about the level of validity that can be expected in the setting to which one wishes to generalize) on the basis of meta-analyses with a small number of studies. Nonetheless, there remain domains where the number of available studies is low, and in larger scale meta-analyses it is often the case that small-K subanalyses are conducted within various moderator conditions. Thus small-K

meta-analyses are commonly reported, and caution must be taken to avoid mechanically comparing observed and expected variance and drawing stronger conclusions than are warranted about the degree to which validity generalizes and the degree to which moderator variables are feasible.

Note that this is not a statement in opposition to conducting and reporting small-K meta-analyses. They are useful in documenting the current state of knowledge about a predictor–criterion relationship. Comparing the set of available studies with the current state of theory in the domain of interest should help identify potential limitations or biases in the data available to date (e.g., limited variability on theoretically important moderators), and initial findings from a small-K analysis can be a source of hypotheses about issues needing resolution.

What conclusions should be dawn from an underpowered meta-analysis? Schmidt et al. (1985) argued in "Forty questions" that the meta-analytic findings should be provisionally accepted while awaiting further studies. They also noted that other lines of evidence may also be relied on to examine the hypothesis of validity in the setting to which one wishes to generalize. This call for reliance on multiple sources of evidence seems particularly important here. It is not useful to frame this as pitting an underpowered meta-analysis against reliance on local findings. An underpowered meta-analysis can contribute to building a pattern of evidence in support of one's intended test use, with meta-analytic findings integrated with many other possible sources of evidence, including local findings, the documentation of similarity of the local setting with one or more specific studies in the validity generalization data base, and patterns of relationships between the predictor in question with other predictors for which the accumulated data base is larger.

Issue 3: The Assumption of an Unbiased Sample of Studies

The possibility that the set of studies available for analysis are not representative of the domain to which one wishes to generalize has been a recurring concern. A distinction can be drawn between concerns about bias in the reporting of findings and bias in the degree to which relevant substantive (e.g., organizational characteristics) and methodological (e.g., operationalization of key constructs) features are represented in the data set.

Concerns about bias in the reporting of findings revolve around the possibility that negative findings are less likely to be included in the data set due to a variety of mechanisms, including journal biases against negative results and researcher decisions not to write up negative findings. This was addressed in "Forty questions;" Schmidt et al. (1985) offered a compelling and multifaceted response, including the documentation of the extensive reporting of nonsignificant findings, the use of file-drawer analysis to document the number of suppressed studies that would be needed to alter meta-analytic conclusions, and the observation that typical procedures include examining an array of predictors and reporting all findings, including both significant and nonsignificant results. Sackett et al. (1985) offered no commentary on this point, thus indicating concurrence.

Concerns about bias in the representation of important features that moderate validity were also addressed in "Forty questions." In response to the assertion that to the extent that some characteristics vary little across the studies that go into a validity generalization analysis, the moderator is not given a chance to reveal itself, Schmidt et al. replied that the data on which (validity generalization) studies were based came from validity studies conducted in a wide variety of organizations and settings, and that these data can therefore safely be assumed to reflect the range of variation characteristic of such potential moderators in real organizations. Sackett et al. (1985) noted that although this was probably true in the extensively studied cognitive ability domain, the possibility of such bias may be more likely in other less studied domains. Also, a reviewer of this chapter noted that even in a well-studied domain like cognitive ability, organizations too small to permit a criterion-related validity study are not included; thus organization size is a potential moderator that is not represented. Although true, it is not clear that there is a compelling reason to expect size to matter. If anything, in small organizations there is less bureaucratic control of behavior, and thus fewer constraints on the relationship between individual differences and performance.

Note that the exchange in "Forty questions" focused on bias in the representation of organizational characteristics; my concern here includes representation of methodological characteristics as well as organizational characteristics. As an example, consider once again the integrity test domain, where the following issue was raised by Sackett and Wanek (1996). Ones et al. (1993) reported a higher mean validity for overt (.39) than for personality-based (.29) tests when validated against a broad criterion category labeled *nontheft*, which includes measures such as absence, tardiness, reason for termination, disciplinary action, and causing accidents. To interpret this finding as indicating that overt tests are more validity than personality-based tests, one must assume that each of these criterion types are equally represented in the overt test data base and in the personality-based data base. If they are not, then any differences in the relationship between the two types of tests and the different criteria can confound the results. For example, subsequent research has shown that personality-based tests are more highly related to absenteeism than are overt tests. Thus the mean validity of overt and personality tests against nontheft criteria will depend on the proportion of studies with each type of test using absence as a criterion. Although data on this issue is not available in Ones et al., it is the case that virtually all studies were reported by test publishers, and most publishers in this domain have a standard validity design on which they rely heavily (e.g., one routinely uses absence as a criterion whereas another routinely uses reason for termination as a criterion). Thus bias in the set of studies available for the two types of tests is a concern that makes conclusions about the relative validity of the two types of tests unwarranted.

There is no ready solution to the issue of the potential bias in the sample of available studies. Thorough knowledge of theory and empirical research in the domain in question seems the most likely route to identifying possible sampling biases. Note that this issue harkens back to Issue 1, namely the careful specification of the domain to which one wishes to generalize. That a certain feature is not included in the validity generalization data set is not a problem when that feature is outside of the domain of generalization; when that feature is within the domain the problem is serious.

Issue 4: Comparing Findings Across Domains and the Problems of Correlated Moderators

It is not uncommon to compare validity generalization findings in order to make statements about the relative value of one predictor versus another for the prediction of a criterion construct of interest. This can be done when comparing two separate studies, or two domains can be compared within a single meta-analytic study. Several issues arise when attempting such comparisons.

The first involves the setting in which there are multiple potential moderators of interest. The ideal approach investigates the moderators in an integrative fashion, such as in a nested or hierarchical moderator examination. But it is not uncommon to independently examine moderators, at times with the explanation that the data set is too small to examine moderators jointly. Failure to carefully consider the interrelationships among moderator variables can lead to serious errors. As an example, I return yet again to the integrity testing domain. In unpublished work prior to the Ones et al. (1993) meta-analysis, Ones was interested in whether the validity of integrity tests varied by individual test. Large numbers of studies existed for three tests, and a meta-analysis using test as a moderator produced mean validity coefficients of .71 for Test A, .35 for Test B, and .27 for Test C. On the surface, this suggests a clear winner. But a second moderator was also examined, namely, study design. Concurrent studies using self-reports of wrongdoing as the criterion produced a mean r of .76, whereas predictive studies using an external nonself report measure of wrongdoing produced a mean r of .27. The key to the analysis is examining the covariance between the two moderators. Test and study design turn out to be almost perfectly confounded: Test A relied almost solely on self-report criteria, whereas B and C relied heavily on external criteria. Thus if the intercorrelation of two moderators had not been considered, a false conclusion about the relative validity of the three tests would have been reached. The message is to be wary of any meta-analysis that examines moderators independently without examining the interrelationships among them. The reality that there may too few studies for a completely integrated moderator examination to take place must be acknowledged. Under such circumstances, results can be reported with caution; care must be taken not to draw strong conclusions under such circumstances.

A second issue that may arise in comparing findings across domains is differential access to information about information about criterion reliability and range restriction. Findings in Schmidt and Hunter (1998) illustrate this point. They presented a table summarizing meta-analytic findings for a large number of predictors of overall job performance. For each predictor type, the best estimate of the population relationship is presented. However, for some predictors this best estimate comes from a data base with sound data for range restriction correction; for others, information about the extent of range restriction is lacking, and thus no corrections are made. Schmidt and Hunter clearly documented which corrections can and cannot be made for each predictor. The result, though, is a set of findings that are not directly comparable, and potentially misinterpreted by those not attending carefully to which corrections have and have not been made. The point is not that correction should not be made; in the presence of varying degrees of range restriction across predictors uncorrected mean validities are similarly inappropriate for comparing the predictive power of the various predictors. The point is that although meta-analysis gives a good account of the cumulative pattern of results to date, one must resist the urge to simply eyeball means and draw conclusions about the relative merits of different predictors. Appropriate comparison rests on a full understanding of the data and the corrections made. For example, Schmidt and Hunter report a lower mean for reference checks ($r = .26$) than for work sample tests ($r = .54$); data on range restriction in reference checks is not available. One can ask whether any plausible degree of range restriction would result in changing the conclusion about the relative predictive power of the two, and as a result draw meaningful conclusions (e.g., all studies of reference checks would have had to be done in severely truncated samples involving only the top 20% of the applicant pool for a corrected range reference check mean r to approach the work sample mean r).

A third issue in comparing findings across domains is the appropriate basis for comparative decisions. The focus tends to be on means (e.g., Schmidt & Hunter's (1998) table comparing validity across predictors presents only means as a basis for comparison). It is worth considering the value of supplementing the mean with a presentation of credibility intervals. For example, the Ones et al. (1993) integrity meta analysis reports that whereas the mean for overt tests is higher than the mean for personality-based tests in predicting nontheft criteria, the lower bound of the 90% credibility interval is higher for personality-based tests than for overt tests. Thus one firm using the meta-analytic information as a basis for choosing between the two test types might reasonably chose the test type with the higher expected value, and thus focus on the mean, whereas another might be more risk averse and choose the test type with the higher value for the bottom end of the credibility interval. Preference between the two is a judgment call based on organizational values.

Issue 5: Assumptions in Correcting for Unreliability and Range Restriction

The concept of correcting for measurement error in the criterion and for range restriction is now well accepted, as evidenced by its inclusion in the 1999 *Standards*. Thus current concerns revolve around the values used in making the corrections, rather than questioning the corrections in principle.

One key issue is the use of artifact distributions rather than study-specific values in making corrections. Artifact distributions are of two types: empirical and assumed. Empirical distributions involve collecting reliability or range restriction data from those studies in the validity generalization data set that do report these values and assuming that that distribution also represents the studies for which such values are not available. If this assumption is reasonable, this approach makes good sense. As always, knowledge of the domain in question is critical. For example, should a set of studies include both rating criteria and objective criteria, and reliability data only be available for the ratings data, the assumption would clearly not be viable.

The second type is the assumed distribution, which refers to the setting in which no studies in the validity generalization data set report reliability or range restriction values, and where the researcher constructs a distribution that is assumed to represent the reliability and range restriction parameters in the set of studies in question. There are settings where this approach is supportable. It may generally be more reasonable for reliability than for range restriction, in that a limited set of criteria are widely used in I/O psychology, and a good amount of data may be available about error in the measurement of various criterion constructs. It is in the domain of range restriction that assumed distributions become a serious problem. The practice of taking a distribution from one domain where an empirical distribution is available and applying it to another without a strong conceptual argument as to the appropriateness of the empirical distribution for the domain in question is quite common in my experience, and is a practice that should be abandoned. For example, applying a distribution of range restriction values from the cognitive ability domain to the personality domain is inappropriate. Acknowledging that there is at present no basis for ascertaining the extent to which study findings are influenced by range restriction, and thus that uncorrected validity coefficients are conservative if range restriction is present, is recommended here. Note that it is not the mere fact of an assumed distribution that is the problem, but rather the lack of a sound basis for connecting the assumed distribution to the domain in question. An assumed distribution might make good sense in some settings. For example, a publisher of a cognitive ability test may have an interest in conducting a meta-analysis of studies using that specific test to predict a certain criterion. None of the studies may report the data needed to determine the degree of range restriction present. But if a large empirical distribution of range restriction values exists that is based on a number of other comparable cognitive ability tests, the use of such an assumed distribution would be appropriate.

A second key issue in the use of corrections is the need to insure that conceptually appropriate values are used. For example, when using performance ratings as criteria, Schmidt and Hunter (1996) argued for the use of interrater reliability rather than intrarater reliability. Recently, Murphy and De Shon (2000a) questioned the use of interrater reliability, arguing that disagreements between raters cannot unequivocally be viewed as error. They suggested that variance that is specific to a rater is not error, as specific rater effects are nonrandom. They suggest a generalizability framework for systematically sorting out rater, ratee, and interaction effects. Schmidt et al. (2000) offered a spirited reply, and Murphy and De Shon (2000b) countered with an equally spirited rebuttal. The debate will continue. Much depends on whether one takes a fixed effects or a random effects perspective on raters. If one takes a random effects perspective, one is taking the classical perspective underlying correcting for interrater reliability, namely, that interrater reliability is the correlation among randomly chosen equally qualified parallel raters. If multiple raters were available, one would average their ratings, and thus rater effects average out. Interrater reliability is indeed the appropriate correction under such circumstances. In contrast, from a fixed effects perspective one could argue that rater effects reflect differing roles. For example, I am suspicious of the literature on the correlation between the ratings of two supervisors. How often are there really two equally qualified supervisors available to rate? My sense is there is commonly an immediate supervisor, and a person in a different role (e.g., boss's boss) is called in when a second set of ratings are needed for purposes of computing reliability coefficient. Here there is the possibility that there is lower agreement between these two raters than would be the case if there truly were two equally qualified raters. This ongoing debate highlights the importance of careful attention to the conceptual meaning of the estimates used in the process of correcting observed validity coefficients.

DISCUSSION

The treatment of validity generalization in the *Standards* and the *Principles*, the endorsement of the fundamental concept of validity generalization by the National Academy of Sciences Committee on the GATB, and the agreement on the fundamental underpinnings of validity generalization in the "Forty questions" document all attest to the high degree of acceptance of validity generalization as an approach to drawing inferences about predictor–criterion relationships. The issues highlighted in this chapter generally do not represent controversies as much as issues which do not receive sufficient attention and which can lead to drawing inappropriate inferences from the validity generalization data base.

If there is general agreement that inferences about validity in a new setting can be drawn from a meta-analytic data base, then questions arise as to when the validity generalization data base is enough to support an inference of validity. I offer a number of observations on this point. First, it should be clear that there is no bright line answer, a la "you can generalize if there are at least X studies with a total sample in excess of Y and with a lower bound of a credibility interval in excess of Z." This chapter is replete with examples illustrating the needed for a thorough understanding of the domain in question and for a nuanced interpretation of validity generalization findings.

Second, it is useful to differentiate between two variants of this question, one scientific and the other pragmatic. The scientific question is "do the validity generalization findings permit me, as a knowledgeable scientist-practitioner, to be able to render an opinion as to the generalizability of a predictor-criterion relationship to a specified new setting?" The pragmatic question is "can I recommend reliance on validity generalization evidence to a client organization?" Addressing the pragmatic question factors in a variety of concerns that go beyond the scientific ones, such as legal issues treated in other chapters in this volume. But it is important to be clear as to which of the two variants one is answering.

Third, I would like to discourage framing the issue as one of pitting generalized evidence against local evidence, in the sense that one must choose one or the other. Landy (1986) used the term *stamp collecting* to refer to the mindset that there are three kinds of validity and that one's task is to determine which of the three is the right one for a given setting; his argument applies equally well here. Writers on validity, including Landy (1986), Schmitt and Landy (1993), Messick (1989), have contributed toward the unified concept of validity presented in the *Standards*, namely, viewing validity as the degree to which evidence and theory support the inference one wishes to draw from scores on a measuring instrument. Thus one can draw on a meta-analysis of the domain in question, supporting data from meta-analyses of related domains, transportability arguments identifying specific studies in the cumulative data base as highly similar to the new setting in question, evidence of convergent and discriminant validity, content-oriented evidence, and local evidence, among others, in building the case for valid inference in the setting in question. The relative emphasis on the various sources may change, and there are circumstances in which a single line of evidence may be so strong as to render other sources superfluous. But when confronted with a meta-analysis of limited size and scope, the choice is much less stark than to accept it completely or reject it completely.

On one final topic, it is interesting to look back at the history of validity generalization work in I/O psychology. In its first decade, it was applied most extensively in the cognitive ability domain. In the last decade, it has been applied most extensively in the personality domain. I find myself considering this thought experiment: What if this sequence had been reversed? I wonder whether validity generalization would have emerged differently had a different topic than the cognitive ability–job performance domain been the first to be extensively studied. In the personality domain one sees much weaker intercorrelations among measures given the same label (e.g., integrity, conscientiousness) than is the case in the ability domain. One sees a wider range of criteria used (e.g., a broad range of both productive and counterproductive behaviors), with much more variability in findings. One sees much more evidence that methodological choices have large impact (e.g., differences in findings between studies using predictive vs. concurrent strategies; differences in findings when self vs. other reports of wrongdoing are used as criteria). The finding of the dominant role of sampling error (i.e., most variance is sampling error variance) and the limited role of methodological and substantive moderators in the cognitive ability domain now appears to be a function of that domain, rather than a typical finding. Summary statements about the first decade's experience with validity generalization were consequently heavily influenced by the ability findings. Statements to the effect that most variance in validity studies is sampling error variance were not explicitly restricted to the cognitive ability domain, although perhaps they were intended as such. But validity generalization is still wrongly viewed by many, not as a theory about the process of drawing inferences from cumulative data, but as a general statement that the bulk of the variability in research findings is due to statistical artifacts.

In closing, it is clear that the ideas reflected in the theory of validity generalization have revolutionized thinking in I/O psychology. I entered the field at the tail end of the prevalidity generalization period, and vividly recall reading a prepublication copy of the Schmidt-Hunter "Development of a general solution to the problem of validity generalization" paper, subsequently published in 1977. It integrated known but not previously integrated ideas about the role of sampling error, measurement error, and range restriction into a cohesive framework and offered new insights into how to cumulate findings and how to identify artifactual sources of variance. As a result of validity generalization theory and methods, the way we approach a number of issues has changed. First, we react very differently when confronting a correlation coefficient than we did in the pre-validity generalization era. We routinely ask questions like "is the correlation corrected for any artifacts?" and "what's the confidence interval around that correlation?" Second, we routinely use meta-analytic methods as a key component of our research enterprise, gathering and synthesizing information about any predictor–criterion relationship or any other bivariate relationship of interest (e.g., the relationship between different predictor measures). This serves as a base for assessing the size, scope, and consistency of a body of knowledge. At times the finding may be that we have too little information about relationships in certain settings, or about relationships under certain hypothesized moderator conditions to draw strong conclusions. But the result is often a roadmap of the research that is needed to fill is these gaps in knowledge. Third, in applied settings we can use validity generalization findings in a variety of ways. The cumulative literature gives us a stronger basis for initial hypotheses about predictor constructs to consider in initial selection system development. It can provide information about the range of likely outcomes should a decision be made that a local study is in order. And generalized evidence can contribute to establishing the validity of the inferences an employer wishes to draw from scores on a predictor. At times, generalized evidence may be the centerpiece of one's validation strategy; at other times it may augment other sources of validity evidence. In the midst of discussions and debates about refinements of the theory and method and about appropriate interpretations of validity generalization findings, we should not loose sight of the enormous value Schmidt and Hunter's monumental contribution to the field.

REFERENCES

American Educational Research Association, American Psychological Association, & National Council on Measurement in Education (1985). *Standards for Educational and Psychological Testing*. Washington, DC: American Psychological Association.

American Educational Research Association, American Psychological Association, & National Council on Measurement in Education (1999). *Standards for Educational and Psychological Testing*. Washington, DC: American Educational Research Association.

Hartigan, J., & Wigdor, A. (1989). *Fairness in Employment Testing: Validity Generalization, Minority Issues, and the General Aptitude Test Battery.* Washington, DC: National Academy Press.

Hunter, J. E. (1980). Validity generalization for 12,000 jobs: An application of synthetic validity and validity generalization to the General Aptitude Test Battery. Washington, DC: U.S. Employment Service.

Hunter, J. E., & Schmidt, F. L. (1990). *Methods of meta-analysis.* Newbury Park, CA: Sage.

Landy, F. J. (1986). Stamp collecting vs. science: Validation as hypothesis testing. *American Psychologist, 41,* 1183–1192.

Messick, S. (1989). Validity. In R. L. Linn (Ed.), *Educational measurement* (3rd ed., pp. 13–103). New York: American Council on Education.

Murphy, K. R., & De Shon, R. (2000a). Interrater correlations do not estimate the reliability of job performance ratings. *Personnel Psychology, 53,* 873–900.

Murphy, K. R., & De Shon, R. (2000b). Progress in psychometrics: Can Industrial and Organizational psychology catch up? *Personnel Psychology, 53,* 913–924.

Ones, D. S., Viswesvaran, C., & Schmidt, F. (1993). Comprehensive meta-analysis of integrity test validities: Findings and implications for personnel selection and theories of job performance. *Journal of Applied Psychology, 78,* 679–703.

Ones, D. S., Viswesvaran, C., & Schmidt, F. L. (n.d.). Personality characteristics and absence-taking behavior: The case of integrity. Unpublished manuscript.

Osburn, H. G., Callender, J. C., Greener, J. M., & Ashworth, S. (1983). Statistical power of tests of the situational specificity hypothesis in validity generalization studies: A cautionary note. *Journal of Applied Psychology, 68,* 115–122.

Sackett, P. R., Schmitt, N., Tenopyr, M., Kehoe, J., & Zedeck, S. (1985). Commentary on "Forty questions about validity generalization and meta-analysis." *Personnel Psychology, 38,* 697–798.

Sackett, P. R., Harris, M. M., & Orr, J. M. (1986). On seeking moderator variables in the meta-analysis of correlational data: A Monte Carlo investigation of statistical power and resistance to Type I error. *Journal of Applied Psychology, 71,* 302–310.

Sackett, P. R., & Wilk, S. L. (1994). Within-group norming and other forms of score adjustment in pre-employment testing. *American Psychologist, 49,* 929–954.

Sackett, P. R., & Wanek, J. E. (1996). New developments in the use of measures of honesty, integrity, conscientiousness, dependability, trustworthiness, and reliability for personnel selection. *Personnel Psychology 47,* 787–829.

Sackett, P. R., & DeVore, C. J. (2001). Counterproductive behaviors at work. In N. Anderson, D. Ones, H. Sinangil, & C. Viswesvaran (Eds.), *International Handbook of Work Psychology.* Sage.

Schmidt, F. L., & Hunter, J. E. (1977). Development of a general solution to the problem of validity generalization. *Journal of Applied Psychology, 62,* 529–540.

Schmidt, F. L., Hunter, J. E., Pearlman, K., & Rothstein, H. R. (1985). Forty questions about validity generalization and meta-analysis. *Personnel Psychology, 38,* 697–798.

Schmidt, F. L., & Hunter, J. E. (1996). Measurement error in psychological research: Lessons from 26 research scenarios. *Psychological Methods, 1,* 199–223.

Schmidt, F. L., & Hunter, J. E. (1998). The validity and utility of selection methods in personnel psychology: Practical and theoretical implications of 85 years of research findings. *Psychological Bulletin, 124,* 262–274.

Schmidt, F. L., Viswesvaran, C., & Ones, D. S. (2000). Reliability is not validity and validity is not reliability. *Personnel Psychology, 53*, 901–912.

Schmitt, N., & Landy, F. J. (1993). The concept of validity. In N. Schmitt & W. Borman (Eds.), *Personnel selection in organizations* (pp. 275–309). San Francisco: Jossey Bass.

Society for Industrial and Organizational Psychology, Inc. (1987). *Principles for the validation and use of personnel selection procedures* (3rd ed.). College Park, MD: Author.

Viswesvaran, C., Ones, D. S., & Schmidt, F. L. (1996). Comparative analysis of the reliability of job performance ratings. *Journal of Applied Psychology, 81*, 557–574.

5

Progress Is Our Most Important Product: Contributions of Validity Generalization and Meta-Analysis to the Development and Communication of Knowledge in I/O Psychology

Hannah R. Rothstein
Baruch College
and
Biostatistical Programming Associates

Although Industrial/Organizational (I/O) psychologists sometimes use them interchangeably, validity generalization and meta-analysis are not, in fact, synonymous terms. The two terms are often confused because of the genesis of meta-analysis in I/O psychology in the sphere of personnel selection validities. It is important to differentiate the two terms in order to assess the contribution each has made to I/O psychology over the past 25 years. Thus this chapter starts by providing a definition of *meta-analysis*, and following is a discussion about the unique features of the Hunter-Schmidt method of meta-analysis, and an explanation of where in this scheme of things validity generalization fits. Following this is an explanation of what are the major contributions of meta-analysis as a methodology, and noted is the distinctive contributions of psychometric (Hunter-Schmidt) meta-analysis. After a brief review of the original set of meta-analytic findings in personnel selection research, this chapter illustrates noteworthy recent programs of research in personnel selection that have been developed largely through the application of meta-analysis. The chapter's concluding section contains some suggestions for enhancing the contribution of meta-analysis to the development and communication of knowledge in I/O psychology.

Meta-analysis is the quantitative combination of information from multiple empirical studies to produce an estimate of the overall magnitude of a relationship, or impact of an intervention. Modern meta-analysis has developed during the past 25 years, but early methods go back about 100 years (Cooper & Hedges, 1994; Olkin, 1990). In 1904, Karl Pearson used techniques that were very similar to current meta-analytic methods to determine whether or not a vaccine was effective in preventing typhoid (it was). Fisher (1932) discussed how to quantitatively combine the results of multiple studies in the 1920s, and Thorndike (1933) used combinatorial methods to integrate findings in intelligence research during the 1930s. The computation of average validities for various types of predictors by Ghiselli can also be viewed as a rudimentary form of meta-analysis (Ghiselli, 1966, 1973).

Formal methods of meta-analysis were independently invented four times within a period of about 5 years in the mid-1970's. Glass (1976) coined the term *meta-analysis* (meaning "analysis of analyses") and used the method to assess the efficacy of psychotherapy (Glass, McGaw, & Smith, 1981). At the same time, Rosenthal (1978) was developing combinatorial methods to disentangle expectancy effects in social psychology. Hedges and Olkin (1980, 1983, 1984, 1985) began publishing their work on meta-analysis in the early 1980's. In the field of industrial and organizational psychology Schmidt and Hunter (1977) were devising meta-analytic procedures to investigate the apparent situational specificity of employment test validities. In other words, they applied the general research tool called meta-analysis in a particular fashion to validity coefficients to test the hypothesis about the situation-specific validity and generalizability of validity. A substantial number of meta-analyses in the field of I/O psychology have investigated the generalizability of the validity of various selection techniques, but this method is not limited to personnel selection. Numerous meta-analyses have been done in other areas of I/O psychology as well. This chapter focuses primarily on personnel selection applications of meta-analysis, but not solely on validity generalization studies. In addition, the methodological contribution of the tool will be considered separately from the substantive contribution of the studies to which it has been applied in the area of personnel selection.

META-ANALYSIS AS A RESEARCH METHOD

Meta-analytic methods currently in use share two related goals: (1) deriving the best estimate of the population effect size and (2) determining the source or sources of variance, if any, around this best estimate of the population effect size. Meta-analysis uses statistical procedures to determine the best estimate of the population effect size and to draw inferences about whether or not the effect is uniform across the set of primary studies. In the event that the effect varies across studies, meta-analytic procedures assist the researcher in determining the sources of variation. Both the Hedges-Olkin (1985) and Hunter-Schmidt (1990) methods subscribe to these goals and are best regarded as variations on a theme, although others view them as rival approaches. The differences between the two concern the following issues: What constitutes the best estimate of the effect size; what sources of variance are considered when examining effect size variability; and what approaches are used in evaluating possible sources of effect size variance.

Distinctive Features of the Hunter-Schmidt Method

The Hedges-Olkin (1985) and Hunter-Schmidt (1990) approaches both assess sampling error as the likeliest source of variance across studies in effect size, but the latter method explicitly recognizes that other statistical artifacts cause effect size variance as well. A unique feature of the psychometric, or Hunter-Schmidt approach is that it is concerned with the detection of, and correction for many correctable errors that derive from study imperfections, most notably criterion unreliability and range restriction, which they call *artifacts*. Hunter and Schmidt maintained that the elimination of such errors is a necessary precondition for the development of cumulative knowledge in the social sciences. Although some early critics of psychometric meta-analysis psychologists have disputed this point of view (cf. Schmidt, Hunter, Pearlman, & Hirsh, 1985; Sackett, Tenopyr, Schmitt, & Kehoe, J., 1986), more recent criticisms of meta-analysis within the I/O community have taken issue with specific psychometric corrections that have been applied to employment test validities, or of the specific values of the corrections recommended by Hunter and Schmidt rather than with the overall goals and methods of validity generalization. Contemporary critics do not appear to be critical of meta-analytic methodology in general or of psychometric corrections in principle.

For example, Murphy and Shiarella (1997) and Murphy and DeShon (2000a) questioned the appropriateness and accuracy of corrections for criterion unreliability. Murphy and DeShon (2000a) suggested that interrater reliabilities are not the appropriate estimates of the reliability of job performance ratings, and proposed that better estimates could be obtained by applying the methods of generalizability theory. Murphy (2000) also argued that current values of corrections for attenuation in the criterion overcorrect, and therefore overestimate, the real validities of various selection methods. However, Murphy is supportive of meta-analysis as a method and has clearly stated

> The application of meta-analysis, in particular validity generalization (VG) analysis, to the cumulative literature on the validity of selection tests has fundamentally changed the science and practice of personnel selection. VG analyses suggest that the validities of standardized tests and other structured assessments are both higher and more consistent across jobs and organizations than was previously believed. As a result, selection researchers and practitioners can draw on the research literature to make reasonably accurate forecasts about the validity and usefulness of different tests in particular applications. (Murphy, 2000, p. 194)

With the exception of a few brief comments (see Hedges & Olkin, 1985, and Rosenthal, 1984), the developers of other methods of meta-analysis outside of I/O psychology have generally not addressed psychometric issues, although they have not expressed opposition to these corrections. Recently, Aguinis and Pierce (1998) and Hall and Brannick (2002) demonstrated how to apply psychometric meta-analysis corrections to the Hedges and Olkin (1985) meta-analytic approach.

The use of psychometric corrections contributes to the accuracy of effect size estimation and calculation of true variability, and that the advocacy for these corrections by Hunter and Schmidt (1991) is a unique contribution to meta-analytic methodology. Further, the empirical literature that has examined unreliability of criterion ratings and range restriction provides sufficient justification for the use of the values suggested by Hunter and Schmidt for these corrections (see Rothstein, 1990, and Viswesvaran, Ones, & Schmidt, 1996, for empirical studies of interrater reliability and Alexander, Carson, Alliger, & Cronshaw, 1989, Hunter, 1983, and McDaniel, Whetzel, Schmidt, & Mauer, 1994, for reports of range restriction values). Nevertheless, it is important to make the point that anyone who has doubts about the specific corrections applied need not reject meta-analysis outright. As the general meta-analytic literature shows, acceptance of specific psychometric corrections is not a precondition for accepting the scientific usefulness of the meta-analytic approach.

The Critical Contribution of Meta-Analytic Methodology

The critical contribution of meta-analytic methodology is that it produces knowledge that is unavailable in primary studies. In some instances, the ability of meta-analysis to reveal information that is obscured or misinterpreted in primary studies is the direct result of the superior statistical precision of the meta-analysis. A good example of this is the set of primary studies examining the validity of personality variables for the prediction of job performance. Barrick and Mount (1991) reported that the average observed (uncorrected) validity of conscientiousness (for a single scale) was very modest—about .13—and that the average sample size for studies of conscientiousness predictors of job proficiency was 140. These studies would have an average power of .34 to detect an effect this size, and in fact Barrick and Mount found that about 70% of the studies they included in their meta-analysis found nonsignificant results. Many of these authors interpreted their nonsignificant findings as meaning that there was no relationship between conscientiousness and job performance. The Barrick-Mount meta-analysis showed these nonsignificant results were just the result of low power. In fact, for any research area in which the average observed correlation is around .20, the typical primary study will be underpowered. For this size observed effect, assuming alpha of .05, two-tailed, a sample of 95 would be needed for power to reach .50; to reach Cohen's (1988) recommended power of .80, a sample size of 191 is necessary.

In other cases, it is the meta-analyst's ability to correct for the impact of sampling error variance that has enabled the true nature of a relationship to emerge. The best example of this is the original set of validity generalization analyses, in which in nearly all studies, sampling error alone accounted for most of the variation in validities, and corrections for sampling error variance alone supported the conclusion that validity was generalizable. (Hunter & Schmidt, 1991; Pearlman, Schmidt, & Hunter, 1980).

In addition, meta-analysis allows the researcher to test hypotheses that were never examined in the original studies. Meta-analysts can compare results across studies, and test hypotheses about the causes of variation in the studies. Of course, the first hypothesis "tested" by in a meta-analysis is that the observed variation across studies is due to sampling error. In psychometric (Hunter-Schmidt) meta-analysis the next hypothesis tested is that measurement errors are responsible for the majority of nonsampling error variance. It is true that measurement error is frequently the main source of nonsampling error variance in many cases, not only in meta-analyses of validity coefficients, but also in other areas. However, in a substantial number of cases, important amounts of variation remain after artifactual sources of variation have been corrected for. Even Schmidt and Hunter (chap. 2, this volume), who strongly dispute the presence of moderators in the aptitude and ability test area, agreed that moderators do exist outside the domain of personnel selection, and should be investigated.

Nearly all of the important moderators that have been examined in I/O meta-analyses have been study-level moderators. In other words, meta-analysts looked at the relationships between features of studies and study results. This means that many important moderators could not have been detected in an individual study, because they were not varied within studies. In some cases this is due to limitations on the financial or temporal resources of the primary researchers. In other cases, such as that reported by Kanfer, Warburg, & Kantrowitz (2001), the absence of potentially important data in the primary studies is due to the fact that these variables were not of much interest to the original investigators, but were significant for the broader theory tested by the meta-analyst. This is particularly likely to be true when the meta-analytic researchers identify potential moderators based on theoretical conceptualization rather than what is readily available in the primary studies.

In a nontrivial number of cases, an important study-level moderator has to do with the way the primary study was conducted, which by definition cannot be varied within studies. In several meta-analyses, research design has been demonstrated to moderate effect sizes. For example, Kubeck, Delp, Haslett, and McDaniel (1996) found smaller age-training performance effects in field studies than in lab studies. An intriguing example from social psychology is a set of meta-analyses in which Eagly and her colleagues (Eagly & Carli, 1981; Eagly & Wood, 1991) investigated study authorship as a moderator of effect size in studies of sex differences in interpersonal situations. They found that the sex of the author was a significant moderator, with researchers finding effects that would cast their own sex in a positive light. Similarly, Russell, Settoon, McGrath, and Blanton (1994) used meta-analysis to investigate the possibility that characteristics of the researcher affected the results of criterion-related validity studies. A similar investigation of authorship moderators could provide an empirical test of a currently controversial issue in personnel selection, namely the hypothesis advanced by some researchers (e.g., Camara & Schneider, 1994) that integrity tests validities may be influenced by the fact that some of the research has been conducted by test publishers. In other words, meta-analysis can be used to provide an empirical answer to a scientifically important question for personnel selection psychology than no other method can offer.

Take the interview meta-analysis by McDaniel et al. (1994), as an example of meta-analytic investigation of study level moderators. In this meta-analysis, several study features were hypothesized as important moderators of interview validity, including level of structure of the interview, the content of the interview (as situational, non-situational but job-related, or psychological), format (board or individual interviews), and type of criterion (job performance, training performance, or tenure). All four features (structure, content, format, and criterion type) moderated interview validities, some quite substantially. For the most part, these variables had been suggested before as moderators, and a few primary studies have investigated one of these variables (i.e., structure) as a moderator (e.g., Campion, Campion, & Hudson, 1994; Latham & Saari, 1984). However none been investigated systematically in the primary literature.

The same is true for job complexity, a variable that has turned out to be a significant moderator in many areas of I/O psychology, but has not been examined very often in primary studies. It is informative to note, for example, that job complexity is one of the few moderators of cognitive ability test validities (Hunter, 1983; Hunter & Hunter, 1984). Other areas of personnel research in which job complexity has turned out to be an important moderator include the relationships between: job satisfaction and job performance (Judge, Thoresen, Bono, & Patton, 2001), job experience and performance (McDaniel, Schmidt, & Hunter, 1988), interview validity and cognitive ability (Huffcutt, Roth, & McDaniel, 1996), interview structure and validity (Huffcutt, Conway, Roth, & Stone, 2001). Job complexity also has been shown recently to moderate group differences in cognitive ability (Roth, BeVier, Bobko, Switzer, & Tyler, 2001). Because most studies look at one job, and those that study multiple jobs most often do not vary them in terms of job complexity, investigations of job complexity as a moderator using primary studies are relatively infrequent.

As research in some research domains become more developed, it is likely that researchers may want to examine interactions among moderator variables. For example, in modeling the job satisfaction–job performance relationship, Judge and his associates (Judge et al., 2001) hypothesized an interaction between core-self evaluation and job complexity, whereas Huffcutt and his associates (Huffcutt et al., 2001) proposed a model in which job complexity interacts with various aspects of interviews to affect validity. Examination of these types of effects will be possible only through meta-analysis for at least two reasons: First, the effect sizes thus identified are likely to be of small or moderate size, and therefore of insufficient magnitude to find in the typical primary study, even if one could be done. Second, it is not likely that primary studies will have investigated all the variables of interest. Judge et al. (2001) recently noted that 17 variables have been proposed as moderators of the job satisfaction–job performance relationship but that very few of them have been investigated in more than one primary study. If single moderators have not been investigated systematically in primary studies, the likelihood that multiple proposed moderators will have been investigated becomes very small.

Although in most of these illustrations, it could be argued that results similar to those found through meta-analysis could have been obtained with larger, and better designed primary studies, the fact is that those studies were never done. Furthermore, as Schmidt and Hunter (chap. 2) pointed out earlier in this volume, single large studies are unlikely to contain the kind of variation in population, measures, analysis procedures, and other variables that are necessary for identifying many moderators, or for assessing the generalizability and boundary conditions of findings.

Advantages of the Hunter-Schmidt Method

As noted earlier in this chapter, and in many other places, the primary feature that distinguishes the psychometric, or Hunter-Schmidt (1990) approach is that it is concerned with the detection of, and correction for, errors that derive from study imperfections, which in most cases means corrections for error of measurement in the criterion and range restriction in the predictor. Because this feature of the Hunter-Schmidt approach is so well-known, here attention is paid to other useful features of this method of meta-analysis that are less widely recognized.

The Hunter-Schmidt (1990) approach to meta-analysis is also distinctive in calling attention to the credibility value, which is set on the basis of the (corrected) standard deviation for the effect size $(SD\rho)$ and which provides information about the entire distribution of effect sizes, rather than just the mean. It is a powerful tool for the assessment of the impact of moderators (if any) on the distribution of true validities (Whitener, 1990), although it does not identify those moderators. Other methods of meta-analysis historically have focused exclusively on the confidence interval around the meta-analytic mean, which estimates the extent to which sampling error remains in the sample-size weighted mean effect size, and have overlooked the question of whether effects vary across studies for reasons other than sampling error. Credibility intervals provide information not conveyed by confidence intervals alone, but they are often overlooked. Of 15 meta-analyses published in *Psychological Bulletin* in 2000 and 2001, 11 reported confidence intervals but not credibility values, two reported neither confidence intervals nor credibility values, one reported only credibility values, and one reported both confidence intervals and credibility values. The two that reported credibility values both used the Hunter-Schmidt method of meta-analysis (Kuncel, Hezlett, & Ones, 2001; Judge et al., 2001); the others all employed the Hedges-Olkin approach. As a further case in point, the most prolific producers of meta-analyses in the world, the Cochrane Collaboration, which has a standard reporting format for all its published reviews, does not present information about the standard deviation of the distribution of treatment effects. The methodologists leading this group, who primarily use the Hedges-Olkin method, are just now coming to the realization that the failure to present a statistic for the distribution of treatment effects in random-effects meta-analysis produces misleading interpretations of results (Higgins & Thompson, 2001).

Credibility intervals play a particularly critical role in interpreting meta-analytic results in applied areas in which, for example, policy needs to be made or a treatment or intervention needs to be decided on. The lower bound of the credibility value is an indication whether, despite the possible operation of true moderators, the treatment or intervention under consideration is likely to have some value across the population as a whole. For example, in the meta-analysis of test validities for clerical occupations (Pearlman, Schmidt, & Hunter, 1980), the true mean validity of general mental ability for all clerical occupations (performance criterion) was .52, and the estimated true standard deviation was .24. Because only 62% of the variance was accounted for by artifacts, application of the Schmidt-Hunter 75% rule, which was an early means of assessing situational specificity, indicated that the hypothesis of situational specificity could not be rejected. The more currently popular indicator of the presence of moderators, the actual size of the true standard deviation, also reveals that validity is not homogeneous across studies. Nevertheless, the 90% credibility value, representing the validity value above which 90% of validities are found, was .21. Clearly, although there were moderators operating, even the lowest levels of validity in the entire distribution were at a useful level, and on this basis validity was demonstrated to be generalizable.

Another important advantage of the Hunter-Schmidt method is that it is based on a random-effects model. Although Hedges, Olkin, and their colleagues (Hedges & Olkin, 1985; Hedges & Vevea, 1996) produced formulas for both random and fixed effects meta-analysis, the tendency of most followers of their method is to use the fixed-effects model even when it is clear that the effects are heterogeneous. This is problematic because, as Overton (1998) recently showed fixed effects models underestimate sampling error variance and yield confidence intervals that are too narrow when true heterogeneity exists. Because the Hunter-Schmidt formulas used by most I/O psychologists are random effects models, they do not run this risk. Although there is some evidence that the misapplication of random effects models to the homogeneous case can produce inaccurate results (Overton, 1998), because heterogeneity of observed effects is the rule, not the exception, the latter misapplication will rarely occur. It is interesting to note that during the early years of validity generalization studies, it was not commonly expected that moderators would operate in most situations. One of the most important developments over the past 25 years of validity generalization research is the recognition that even in the area of personnel selection, moderators have an important impact on the validity of many predictors.

SUBSTANTIVE CONTRIBUTIONS OF META-ANALYSES TO CUMULATIVE KNOWLEDGE IN PERSONNEL SELECTION

The Hunter and Hirsh Review

Meta-analysis was introduced to the I/O research community in the late 1970s. By the time Jack Hunter and I (Hunter & Hirsh, 1987) wrote the first review of meta-analyses conducted in industrial and organizational psychology, less than 10 years after the first studies had been published, meta-analysis had been employed in many I/O areas, although it had been most frequently applied in the area of selection test validities.

This section of the chapter reviews the results of personnel selection meta-analyses as reported in Hunter and Hirsh (1987), and notes how they affected the accepted knowledge base in I/O psychology at the time. After that, briefly mentioned are subsequent meta-analyses of each predictor covered in the Hunter and Hirsh review, and the degree to which the early and later meta-analytic results converged or diverged. A detailed look is taken at meta-analyses in two areas: personality predictors of job performance and the validity of employment interviews. These areas were selected because they exemplify the benefits that can be derived from the thoughtful application of meta-analysis in personnel research.

By the time of the Hunter and Hirsh (1987) review, more than 200 meta-analyses examining the relationship between cognitive ability and validity had been completed. These studies provided overwhelming evidence that cognitive ability tests were valid predictors of job performance, and that their validity generalized across virtually all jobs and settings. Hunter and Hirsh also presented meta-analytically estimated average validities for other popular predictors of job performance, based primarily on the work of Hunter and Hunter (1984) or Schmitt, Gooding, Noe, and Kirsch (1984).[1] These included: biodata (.39), personality (.27); reference checks (.26); education (.22) the interview (.14) traditional training and experience ratings (.13), college grades (.11), interest (.10) and age (−.01). An average validity of the assessment center (approximately .35) was reported based on a meta-analysis conducted by Gaugler, Rosenthal, Thornton, and Bentson (1987). Hunter and Hirsh found that the consistency of these averages (i.e., the variability of effects around the average) varied by predictor. Although there was evidence of validity generalizability for some of these, notably biodata, the absence of situational moderation could not be established for any. Of particular note was the variability of employment interviews, in which the first evidence of interview structure as a moderator (McDaniel et al., 1988; Wiesner & Cronshaw, 1988) was noted. At that time, Hirsh and Hunter suggested that structured and unstructured interviews measured different constructs, and speculated on the basis of results reported by McDaniel et al. (1988) that structured interviews might actually be verbally administered intelligence or job knowledge tests. These speculations were later tested meta-analytically and received some support. The results are reported in the section on interviews. Early meta-analytic findings about the interview also included moderation by format (board vs. individual).

---

[1]Where only Hunter and Hirsh or Schmitt, Gooding, Noe and Kirsch reported a validity, that validity is presented here. When both reported a validity, the average of their 2 averages is presented here. Additionally, the values from Schmitt, Gooding, Noe and Kirsch are the corrected values calculated by Hunter and Hirsh, rather than those given by the original authors.

It is apparent that within the first 10 years of validity generalization, massive amounts of evidence had accrued to show that cognitive ability was a strong, consistent predictor of job performance across a wide array of jobs and settings. Also during the first decade of validity generalization, lesser amounts of evidence also offered support for the belief that other predictors also had stable and generalizable validities. The impact of this work on the field of personnel psychology was enormous. The paradigm of situational specificity was turned on its head, and practitioners re-instituted the widespread use of ability tests. Researchers primarily interested in the prediction of job performance now began to turn their energies towards the so-called alternative predictors of job performance, in order to augment the validity generalization database for these predictors. They also began moving toward the development of composite test batteries that would maximize total validity. Those who were more interested in theory now had a stable validity base from which to explore causal models of job performance, and attention began to be directed toward the development and testing theories of job performance. (Rothstein, 1993).

Results of Meta-Analyses of "Alternative" Predictors Subsequent to the Publication of Hunter and Hirsh

Grade Point Average (GPA). Subsequent to the meta-analyses of college grades reported in Hunter and Hirsh (1987), five additional meta-analyses on this topic have been reported. One (Bretz, 1989) reported that there was virtually no relation between grades and adult success. Three others (Cohen, 1987; Dye & Reck, 1989; Samson et al., 1984) reported average validities of .15 to .20, with substantial moderation of validities by a variety of factors. The most recent and comprehensive meta-analysis (Roth, BeVier, Switzer, & Shippmann, 1996) found observed validities similar to those found by the earlier studies, with an average of .16. Correction for statistical artifacts increased the estimated true correlation to about .30. Like the first four meta-analyses, Roth et al. found that there were several moderators of the grade-job performance relationship, but they were able to show that the 80% credibility value did not include zero, thus suggesting that there was some degree of validity generalizability. Consistent with earlier studies, they found that early studies (e.g., prior to 1960) had higher validities than later studies. Taken as a whole, these studies seem to indicate that college grade point average is a slightly better and more generalizable predictor of job performance than earlier studies had indicated, but that its validity is modest compared to other predictors.

Biodata. There have been two meta-analyses of biodata validities since the Hunter and Hirsh (1987) review. Rothstein, Schmidt, Erwin, Owens, and Sparks (1990) meta-analyzed biodata validities of a single instrument (the Supervisory Profile Record, or SPR) for 11,000 first line supervisors and found that validities were generalizable across organizations, age, sex, education, supervisory experience, and company tenure. Average true validity in this sample was .32 with a lower 90% credibility value of .29. In 1998, Carlson, Scullen, Schmidt, Rothstein, and Erwin demonstrated that generalizable validities can be obtained without multi-organizational development and keying. Their results, for more than 7,000 managers and professionals in 24 organizations, showed that an instrument related to the SPR, namely the Managerial Profile Record, or MPR, was a valid predictor of rate of promotional progress across all organizations. Average cross-organizational validity in this study was .53 with a lower 90% credibility value of .47. Together these studies confirm and extend the earlier findings about the generalizability and magnitude of biodata validities for appropriately constructed instruments.

Job Experience. The results of a meta-analysis by McDaniel et al. (1988) indicate that for all levels of job experience and for both low- and high-complexity jobs, the correlation between job experience and job performance is positive. Two moderators were identified: the mean level of job experience and job complexity. The correlation between experience and performance is highest for samples with low mean levels of job experience, but it declines rapidly as mean experience increases. The experience–performance correlation was found to be higher at lower levels of job complexity. Schmidt, Hunter, and Outerbridge (1986) examined the causal impact of job experience on job knowledge and job performance. Their findings indicated that for jobs of intermediate complexity job experience has a substantial direct impact on job knowledge and a smaller direct impact on performance. In addition, job experience had a substantial indirect effect on performance through its effect on job knowledge. The strongest cause of performance was job knowledge.

Age. Waldman and Avolio (1986) conducted a meta-analysis of age differences in job performance, at about the same time that Hunter and Hirsh (1987) was published. They found that the relationship of age to job performance varied as a function of the nature of the criterion used. For productivity measures, age has a positive relationship with performance, but there is a weak negative relationship between age and supervisory ratings of performance. Later meta-analyses by these authors (Avolio & Waldman, 1990) found that experience was more strongly related to performance than was age, that occupational type moderated the age-performance relationship, and that occupational type also moderated the age-cognitive ability relationship (Avolio, Waldman, & McDaniel, 1990). A more recent meta-analysis by Kubeck et al. (1996) examined the relationship between age and job-related training performance. These authors found that older adults performed more poorly in training, with an average effect for age across three criteria of .33, but found that the effects tended to be smaller in field settings than in laboratory settings. Based on this set of meta-analyses, it would seem that the relationship of age to work behavior is not simple, and that no generalizations are warranted at this time.

Applications of Meta-Analysis to the Study
of the Personality–Job Performance Relationship

Fruitful research on the predictive validity of personality began to develop in the mid-1980's because of the serendipitous conjunction of two major developments in psychology. One, of course, was meta-analytic methodology. The second was a new theoretical development in personality psychology, specifically the acceptance (the model was developed in the 1950s) of the Five-Factor model (cf. Digman, 1990). Subsequent to the early meta-analyses of Hunter and Hunter (1984) and Schmitt et al. (1986), essentially all of the research on personality predictors of job performance has been based on the Five-Factor model, or its variants.

Barrick and Mount (1991) conducted the first meta-analytic investigation of the predictive validity of the Big 5 personality factors for job performance. They found that Conscientiousness was a valid predictor across the five occupational groups they examined (professionals, police, managers, sales, and skilled/semiskilled), with a mean true validity of .22, and a lower 90% credibility value of .10. Although the other four factors all had positive mean true validities (Extraversion $\rho =. 13$, Emotional stability $= \rho.08$, Agreeableness $= .07$, Openness to experience $\rho = .04$) none had positive 90% credibility values. Extraversion was a valid predictor for two occupations involving social interaction, management ($\rho = .18$) and sales ($\rho = .15$), and the other factors were also found to be valid predictors for some occupations or criterion categories, but the magnitude of these validities was quite small. Unlike the findings in the area of cognitive abilities, moreover, many of the personality dimension/occupational category combinations showed substantial variance in validities after corrections for artifacts, thus indicating the likely operation of moderators.

Tett, Jackson, and Rothstein (1991) conducted a meta-analysis at about the same time, whose results were somewhat different but whose general conclusions pointed in the same direction, namely that personality characteristics were likely to be better predictors of job performance than previously believed. These findings of these two meta-analyses led to a systematic program of research designed to further examine the role of personality in job performance, primarily by Barrick, Mount, and their colleagues. One arm of this research program was dedicated to explication of the moderators of the relationship between personality and performance, another arm focused on the processes by which personality influences performance. Some of the subsequent research has been meta-analytic in nature; in other cases, however, existing data were not available, and new primary studies were undertaken (e.g., Barrick, Mount, & Strauss, 1993; Martocchio & Judge, 1997).

Moderators of the Personality–Job Performance Relationship

Ability. In a follow-up study examining how conscientiousness influences performance Mount, Barrick, and Strauss (1999) investigated whether ability moderates the relationship. In a study of both military and civilian employees, they found that there was no evidence of an interaction between ability and conscientiousness in the prediction of job performance.

Autonomy. Barrick and Mount (1993) found that the validity of both Conscientiousness and Extraversion was greater for managers in high-autonomy jobs than for managers in low-autonomy jobs. Additionally, the validity of Agreeableness was also higher for high-autonomy jobs than for those low in autonomy, but the correlation was negative. These findings suggest that degree of autonomy in the job is a moderator of validity for some personality predictors.

Team Performance. Barrick, Stewart, Neubert, and Mount (1998) found that for work teams performing additive and conjunctive tasks, conscientiousness was associated with higher supervisor ratings for team performance. Agreeableness, extraversion, and emotional stability were also related to team performance. With respect to conscientiousness, this study extends findings reported for individuals to teams. These findings differ from those for individual performance where agreeableness, extraversion, and emotional stability have not been found to be consistent predictors of job performance (Barrick & Mount, 1991). This raises the interesting possibility that some personality traits may be important for predicting the effectiveness of teams even when they do not predict individual work behavior.

The Process by Which Personality Influences Performance. Some of the work by Barrick and his colleagues (Barrick, Mount, & Strauss, 1993) has been dedicated to developing a theoretical model of job performance, specifically to understanding how conscientiousness affects performance. These authors proposed that the effect of conscientiousness on performance is through motivational states such as goal setting and goal commitment. They conducted primary studies to test their model, and found that conscientiousness had both direct and indirect effects (through goal setting and commitment) on performance, and interpreted their findings as evidence of the primacy of conscientiousness as a motivational contributor to performance.

Recently, Hurtz and Donovan (2000), conducted a meta-analysis of studies based directly on measures of Big 5 factors, and found an estimated true correlation of .22, which was identical to the one found 9 years earlier by Barrick and Mount (1991). However, Hurtz and Donovan argued that the perceived impact of conscientiousness on job performance needs to be reassessed in light of the relatively modest size of the effect. They suggest, as has Hough and her colleagues (1990) that the Big Five dimensions are too broad to link to specific aspects of job performance, and that narrower facets of personality, or composites of such might yield better predictive validity, particularly if narrower dimensions of job performance were used as criteria. They also add their voice to those who propose further study of the indirect effects of personality on performance thorough their effect on motivational variables (Barrick et al., 1993, Kanfer, Warburg, & Kantrowitz 2001; Martoccio & Judge, 1997). Surprisingly to me, Hurtz and Donovan downplay the potential of Conscientiousness and other personality variables to add substantial incremental validity to a selection battery (Schmidt & Hunter, 1998).

Personality Composites. Meta-analyses have also shown that several commonly used test-types that appear to be composites of several Big 5 factors also have useful and generalizable levels of validity. For example, Frei and McDaniel (1998) have provided meta-analytic evidence that customer service orientation is best understood as a composite of agreeableness, adjustment (emotional stability) and conscientiousness, and that customer service orientation predicts performance across a variety of customer service jobs (average ρ = .50, and a positive lower 90% credibility value). Furthermore, they show that customer service orientation is uncorrelated with cognitive ability.

Integrity tests, which yield validities that generalize across tests, jobs, organizations, and settings, also appear to be a composite of these same Big 5 factors. As Ones and Visveswaran (1998) demonstrated, the increased breadth of predictor construct coverage provided by Integrity tests produced better prediction of job performance than did any single Big 5 factor, including conscientiousness. They noted that the validity of .41 for integrity tests for predicting overall job performance implies that integrity tests have higher validity than some of the more accepted forms of personnel selection, including assessment center ratings, biodata, and even mainstream personality inventories (Schmidt, Ones, & Hunter, 1992).

The primary studies based on the results of Barrick and Mount (1991) are an extremely positive and important consequence of this meta-analysis. These new primary studies were carefully designed on the basis of the results of a comprehensive, quantitative summary of the accrued literature in the area, and were constructed to investigate the specific questions that emerged from this summary. Although it is the case that no primary study can fully answer any research question, they remain the building blocks of cumulative knowledge. Because of the amount of information summarized in a meta-analysis, primary studies designed as follow ups are more likely to be able to contribute new knowledge than can primary studies designed on the basis of other primary studies. In general, one sign of a meta-analysis' success is the number of primary studies that it spawns. A good meta-analysis can settle one question firmly enough so that the next set of questions can begin to be asked. Meta-analysis thus contributes to cumulative knowledge in at least two ways—by allowing us to know some things with a degree of certainty, and to use that knowledge as the foundation for new research.

Applications of Meta-Analysis to the Study of the Employment Interview

Several meta-analyses of employment interviews (Marchese & Muchinsky, 1993; McDaniel et. al., 1994; Wiesner & Cronshaw, 1988) have provided a substantial amount of information about interview validities. First, they each reported substantially higher levels of validity for interviews than had previously been demonstrated. McDaniel et al. reported a mean true validity of about .37, as did Marchese and Muchinsky whereas Wiesner and Cronshaw reported somewhat higher values. Moreover, there appears to be at least some generalizability of validity (for example, McDaniel et al. found a lower 90% credibility bound of .08). However, even when potential moderators were taken into account there seemed to be large remaining true variance in most cases.

Second, they systematically investigated features of the interview that had been previously hypothesized to moderate validities, and obtained results that were largely consistent with each other. In the largest and most comprehensive of these meta-analyses, McDaniel et al. (1994) looked at interview content and how the interview was conducted as moderators of interview validity.

Content of the Interview. McDaniel et al. (1994) examined interview validity across three types of interview content: situational, job related, and psychological, and found that for job performance criteria, situational interviews yielded a higher mean validity (.50) than did job-related interviews (.39), which yielded higher mean validity than did psychological interviews (.29).

Conduct of the Interview. Interview structure had a major impact on interview validities in all the meta-analyses that investigated this variable. McDaniel et al. (1994) reported average validities for structured interviews of .44, whereas for unstructured interviews they were .33. Results of the Wiesner and Cronshaw (1988) study showed that structured interviews yielded much higher mean corrected validities than did unstructured interviews (.63 vs. .20) and that structured board interviews using consensus ratings had the highest corrected validity (.64). Huffcutt and Arthur (1994) reanalyzed employment interview data for entry-level jobs that had originally been meta-analyzed by Hunter and Hunter (1984) and provided evidence consistent with McDaniel et al. and Wiesner and Cronshaw with regard to both the magnitude of interview validities and the moderating effects of structure. According to a recent summary of research on the employment interview (Rynes, Barber, & Varma, 2000), the meta-analytic confirmation of the effect of structure on interview validity is "one of the most significant empirical developments in interview research over the past decade" (p. 251).

As a result of these meta-analyses, scientific interest was renewed in the interview as a predictor of job performance. However, many of the resulting studies were either conceptual or review articles (Campion et al., 1997; Dipboye & Gaugler, 1993), or surveys of current practice (Rynes et al., 1999). Campion et al., for example, reviewed the research literature and identified components of structure that they hypothesized would improve either interview content or the evaluation of information provided during the interview.

Much of the empirical research to examine the contribution of features of interviews that contribute to the prediction of performance has been conducted by Huffcutt and his colleagues. A meta-analysis by Huffcutt, Roth, and McDaniel (1996) explored the extent to which employment interview evaluations reflect cognitive ability. These researchers found a corrected mean correlation of .40 between interview ratings and ability test scores, suggesting that about 16% of the variance in interview constructs is due to cognitive ability. Intriguingly, they found that the correlation with ability tended to decrease as the level of structure increased, but that that interview ratings that correlate higher with cognitive ability tend to be better predictors of job performance. They also found that the type of questions asked influenced the correlation with ability; that ability had a greater impact on interview rating when ability test scores were available to interviewers; and that the correlation between interview ratings and ability was generally higher for low-complexity jobs.

Huffcutt and Woehr (1999) meta-analyzed the relationship between four interviewer-related factors and interview validity. The results of their meta-regression suggested that interviewer training, and use of the same interviewer across interviews produced higher validities, but that panel interviews did not lead to higher validities than individual interviews. Results were inconclusive regarding the usefulness of note-taking during the interview.

As a result of the meta-analyses of interview validity, and other recent literature on the interview, a good deal is now known about interview validity and the characteristics of interviews that moderate validities. Little, however, has been discovered about the psychological constructs that are assessed during the employment interview and their characteristics. To begin to remedy this situation, Huffcutt, Conway, Roth, and Jones (2001) developed a comprehensive taxonomy of 7 types of constructs interviews potentially assessed. They then used meta-analytically based procedures to examine 47 actual interview studies. They found that basic personality and applied social skills were the constructs most frequently assessed, followed by mental capability and job knowledge and skills. They also examined the relationship between interview ratings of various constructs and performance evaluations, and found mean corrected validities that ranged from .24 to .58. Additional analyses suggested that high- and low-structure interviews tended to focus on different constructs, and that at least part of the reason why structured interviews tend to have higher validity is because they more often assess constructs that have a stronger relationship with job performance. A previous meta-analysis had established that structured interviews had higher validities because of their greater reliability (Conway, Jako, & Goodman, 1995). Clarification of the constructs underlying the validity of interviews will contribute not only to the development of maximally valid interviews, but can also play a role in developing a theory of job performance.

The greatest practical outcome of the set of personnel selection meta-analyses that have been done to date is the production of stable estimates of average validities of the most widely used selection procedures. In a review of 80 years of personnel selection meta-analyses, Schmidt and Hunter (1998) summarized these validity estimates. A further practical benefit of these applications of meta-analysis is that they enabled researchers to estimate the validities of composite test batteries using combinations of selection procedures Schmidt and Hunter examined the composite validities of various other predictors in combination with general mental ability (GMA). As they indicate, the composite validity depends not only on the validity of the measure added to GMA, but also on the correlation between the two measures. The smaller this correlation is, the larger is the increase in overall validity. Based on primarily meta-analytically derived estimate of the correlations between mental ability and other measures, they found that the three combinations with the highest multivariate validity were: GMA plus a work sample test (mean validity of .63), GMA plus an integrity test (mean validity of .65), and GMA plus a structured interview (mean validity of .63).

Two of the greatest scholarly results have been: renewed interest in the construct validity of multiconstruct methods of selection, such as biodata and the interview, and the renascence of interest and development of increasingly sophisticated theories of job performance such as those of Hunter and Schmidt (Hunter, Schmidt, Rauschenberger, & Jayne, 2000), Judge and his colleagues (Judge & Bono, 2000; Judge et al., 2001) and Kanfer and her colleagues (Kanfer et al., 2001; Kanfer & Kantrowitz, in press). All three theories are either based on, or tested with meta-analytic research. The Hunter et al. and Kanfer et al. theories integrate contributions of both cognitive and noncognitive predictors to job-related behavior, whereas the Judge et al. theory focuses on the role of dispositional (noncognitive) factors. These developments have been made possible because application of meta-analysis to research findings has provided precise and generalizable estimates of the validity of different measured constructs for predicting job performance, as well as increasingly precise estimates of the correlations among these predictors. An additional reason for theoretical and practical advances in the areas reviewed earlier is the informed interplay of meta-analytic and primary research. That is an indication of progress when meta-analytic results give rise to a primary study because it shows we have profitably used the information we already have, and that we are now moving on to what we do not yet know but need to learn. As Johnson and Eagly (2000) stated, "meta-analysis should foster a healthy interaction between primary research and research synthesis, at once summarizing old research and suggesting promising direction for new research" (pp. 526–527). A carefully planned meta-analysis can often be the starting point for a new program of research. By establishing what we know, meta-analytic estimates of true effects can provide the empirical foundation for the construction and testing of theories of human performance. In addition meta-analyses can highlight areas that we do not know much, if anything about, and thus guide where additional primary level research would be useful. This has been the case in each of the major research programs discussed in this chapter: ability, personality, and interviews.

Suggestions for Enhancing the Contribution of Meta-Analysis

Because meta-analysis is an empirical research method, it should be carefully constructed around the same set of research and reporting procedures as the ones used in primary empirical studies. Discussions of this method in I/O psychology have usually focused somewhat narrowly on technical details, with less attention given to the broader issues in performing and interpreting meta-analyses. Although there was some early debate about extra-statistical considerations (Bullock & Svyantek, 1985; Jackson, 1984; Rothstein & McDaniel, 1989; Schmidt, Hunter, Pearlman, & Hirsh 1985), discussion of issues other than data-analysis largely disappeared from the published literature in I/O psychology. Other research areas that use meta-analysis have spent considerably more time considering the nonstatistical aspects than we have, and it is my belief that meta-analyses in I/O psychology could be improved by adopting some of the best practices in other areas. Discussed in this section is Cooper's (1982) five-stage model and how adherence to it could improve meta-analytic practice in our field. When possible, his points are illustrated with examples from the I/O literature.

Cooper's (1982) model of research synthesis provides an overall strategy for conceptualizing and conducting meta-analysis. (In fields outside of I/O psychology, *research synthesis* is the term for what is called meta-analysis, whereas meta-analysis is reserved for the data-analytic stage of the synthesis).

The first stage of Cooper's model is problem formulation. In this stage, the review's purpose is elucidated, and the question being asked is defined clearly enough so that only studies that address this question will be included in the research synthesis. I/O meta-analyses are quite variable in how they approach this stage.

In the second or data collection stage, a search strategy is identified, and the literature is searched for relevant studies, including unpublished studies. Here again, I/O meta-analysis range from poor to good. In a validity generalization study of law enforcement occupations that I co-authored with Northrop and Schmidt (Hirsh, Northrop, & Schmidt, 1986), we described our search strategy as "reviewing the published literature [and] contacted numerous state and local jurisdictions and consultants and two law enforcement-related professional associations" (p. 401). Currently, this would not be considered a satisfactory search strategy description because it is not explicit enough to be replicable, although many recently published meta-analyses are no more specific than this one. An example of better practice is presented by Kubeck et al. (1996) whose description of search strategy is as follows:

> An extensive search of various computer databases and periodicals was conducted. The following databases were searched: *Psychological Abstracts (1969–1983), Dissertation Abstracts (1985–1994), Social Science Citation Index (1972–1995); PsycLIT (1983–1995), ABI/ INFO (1971–1994),* and *ERIC (1982–1994).* See *Appendix A* for a detailed list of the key search words. The manual search involved an article-by-article search of all volumes of: *Aging and Work, Training and Development Journal, Training, Journal of the American Society of Training Directors, Psychology and Aging, Experimental Aging Research, Industrial Gerontology, Journal of Applied Psychology,* and *Journals of Gerontology.* Similarly, reference lists of all materials obtained were scanned for relevant studies. (p. 93)

This conforms to the standards of good scientific reporting practice because it is explicit and may be replicated by anyone who wishes to do so. Researchers and editors would do well to consider the amount and specificity of information about the search strategy that should be required for publication.

In the third or data evaluation stage, the studies that have been retrieved are coded on critical features such as whether they contain enough information to be included in a meta-analysis (generally an effect size estimate, standard deviation or standard error, and sample size). A common lament of early meta-analysts was that many of the studies they retrieved did not contain this basic information, and so could not be included in the analysis. For example, McEvoy and Cascio (1985) had to exclude about 90% of the studies they located because the studies did not have contain the information needed to calculate an effect size. Unfortunately, this is still a common lament. In a very recent meta-analysis of the personality and motivational attributes underlying job search and employment Kanfer et al. (2001) initially identified approximately 3000 studies during their search, but only 73 met the inclusion criteria, mainly because many studies did not contain zero-order correlations, or did not provide empirical data on the variables of interest.

In addition, operational definitions of the independent and dependent variables, the methods used in conducting the studies, and sample type need to be considered. Whether a study feature is critical or not will depend on the objectives of the meta-analysis. Those studies (or effects within studies) that meet the criteria for inclusion in the meta-analysis are retained. An example of a comprehensive presentation of information of this type may be found in Judge et al.'s (2001) meta-analysis of the satisfaction-performance relationship. They stated that:

we defined the population to which we wished to generalize a priori as consisting of the general population of employed adults. Hence, satisfaction and performance in original studies had to be measured at the individual (as opposed to group) level, and performance had to occur in a natural job setting (studies involving performance on laboratory tasks were excluded). Satisfaction was measured globally (general perceptions of one's job) or with reference to specific facets of the job situation (supervision, coworkers, opportunity for advancement, etc.), although in many cases the measure was not described in sufficient detail to determine its nature. Studies focusing on a single satisfaction facet were excluded in the overall analysis. However, we did include studies measuring at least two facets in the overall analysis as these facets could be combined to form a measure of overall job satisfaction. In addition, we were interested in analyzing studies focusing on job performance per se. Thus, we excluded studies correlating job satisfaction with absenteeism, turnover, job withdrawal, and the like. (p. 378)

Such full descriptions not only enhance the replicability of meta-analyses but also reduce the likelihood that independent meta-analyses of the same domain will contradict each other, compared to narrative reviews. In addition, where the results of two meta-analytic reviews disagree, this type of information makes it easier to determine the source of the discrepancies.

The fourth stage of Cooper's (1982) model addresses data analysis and interpretation. The goals are to perform the statistical synthesis of study outcomes of included studies, to draw appropriate inferences and conclusions and to examine threats to the validity of conclusions, and to present these in a format that will be easily understandable and useful to the audience of researchers or policy makers at whom the syntheses are aimed.

As mentioned earlier, I/O psychologist are generally thorough and consistent in their attention to and description of the data analysis stage of a meta-analysis. As a group however, they have not spent much time considering threats to the validity of their conclusions. To provide some tools that would be of assistance at this stage, discussed here are three techniques that deserve consideration by meta-analysts in our discipline. These are outlier analysis, assessment of publication bias, and sensitivity analysis.

Outlier Analysis.   Although considered only occasionally by the I/O community, outlier studies in the meta-analysis can also provide important information. (See Roth, BeVier, Switzer, & Shippman, 1996, for an example of outlier analysis in a predictive validity meta-analysis). It has been suggested "careful examination of outliers can provide important understandings and generate new hypotheses that might other wise be missed" (Wachter & Straf, 1990, p. 147). On the other hand, Schmidt and Hunter (2001, personal communication) have decided to terminate their efforts to eliminate outliers in meta-analysis, because of their concern that outlier elimination could invalidate the correction for sampling error variance—which is critical to accurate estimated of SD-rho. Any apparent outlier could really be nothing but an unusually large sampling error—which is allowed for in the formula for sampling error variance. Thus they contend that if you eliminate such values, you over-correct for sampling error, and have a biased estimate of SD-rho. Outliers should be critically examined for features that may have some bearing on the hypothesis being tested, while bearing in mind the ever-present alternative hypothesis, namely, that the outlier is a result of a methodological or measurement problem. McDaniel and I (Rothstein & McDaniel, 1989) also suggested that when outliers are present, that the meta-analysis be run twice, once with the outlier, and once excluding it, as a means of assessing the impact of the outlying study on the meta-analytic results and conclusions. Huffcutt and Arthur (1994) provided a statistic that is helpful in identifying outliers. It is important to note that if a researcher wishes to examine a distribution of effects for outliers when using artifact distribution meta-analysis, the observed correlations must be used; it is not possible to conduct an outlier assessment with the corrected ones. Distributions of individually corrected rs, however can be examined for outliers either before or after they are corrected.

Consideration of Publication Bias. Some critics of meta-analysis have argued that meta-analytic results are likely to be positively biased because primary studies with significant and positive results are more likely to be published, and therefore more likely to be retrieved during meta-analytic search procedures. This phenomenon is known as publication bias (Begg, 1994). We know that there is a large unpublished literature in I/O psychology but we have little, if any, empirical data on bias. Recent empirical studies of the issue in related disciplines suggest that publication bias is an issue that meta-analytic researchers need to consider (Cooper, DeNeve, & Charlton, 1997; Dickersin, Min, & Meinert, 1992; Easterbrook, Berlin, Gopalan, & Matthews, 1991; Sterling, Rosenbaum, & Weinkam, 1995). They too found publication bias that tended to exaggerate the size of effects. It is my sense that in our field, the likelihood of bias may vary by research area, particularly by whether research is theoretical or applied. Two doctoral students and I (Rothstein, Freeman, & Brian, manuscript in progress) are currently conducting research on the presence of publication and reporting biases in published meta-analyses in industrial and organizational psychology. So far our results indicate that most meta-analysts in our discipline have not considered these issues.

Clearly, the usefulness of meta-analysis is constrained by the threat of publication bias. When the potential for severe bias exists in a given analysis, it is imperative that this fact be identified. On the other hand, when the potential for bias can be effectively ruled out, then this should also be reported because it is a key factor in establishing the validity of the results. Several tools are available to examine publication bias, but these are not in common use in our discipline. In the next few paragraphs, a variety of methods for assessing publication bias that have been employed in meta-analyses in medicine and elsewhere are outlined.

Three kinds of techniques have been developed to deal with publication bias. The first focuses on the detection, and is best represented by a graph called a funnel plot (Light & Pillemer, 1984). The second is designed to assess the sensitivity of meta-analytic conclusions to possible publication bias. This set includes Rosenthal's (1979) file drawer analysis, and its variants. These two sets of procedures are relatively simple, and are outlined here. The third set of techniques is designed to adjust effect size estimates for the possible effects of publication bias under some explicit model of publication selection, is too complex to discuss in this chapter. Readers interested in the adjustment of effect sizes are referred to Duval and Tweedie (2000), Vevea and Hedges (1995), and Iyengar and Greenhouse (1988).

The Detection of Publication Bias.   The funnel plot is a plot of effect size estimates from each individual study on the X-axis versus some measure of each study's sample size (e.g. sample size, the standard error of the effect size, or the inverse of the standard error) on the Y-axis. If there is no publication bias, the effect size estimates from the small studies will be broadly scattered across the bottom of the graph, with less scatter as the sample sizes increase. The plot will be symmetric about its central axis, with a width that decreases with the standard error, resembling an inverted funnel (see Fig. 5.1). If there is publication bias, the plot becomes asymmetric. If the bias is because smaller studies with nonsignificant results do not get published, the top two quadrants will remain symmetric around the cen-

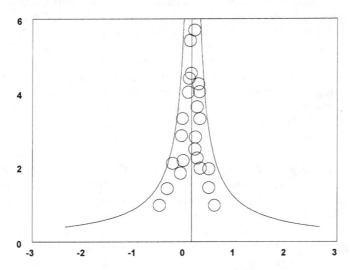

FIG. 5.1. Funnel plot of precision by effect size (symmetric).

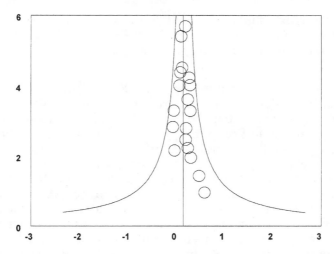

FIG. 5.2.   Funnel plot of precision by effect size (asymmetrical).

tral axis, but there will be a gap at one of the bottom corners of the plot (see Fig. 5.2).[2] Although there are reasons other than publication bias for asymmetry, including other retrieval biases and true heterogeneity of studies, the funnel plot is useful as a means of alerting the researcher that there may be a problem that needs to be considered. There are also statistical tests to assess asymmetry (Begg, 1994; Egger, Smith, Schneider, & Minder, 1997).

The Assessment of Sensitivity of Conclusions to Publication Bias.   This set of techniques are usually referred to as file-drawer analyses because they typically involve imputing the number of effect sizes estimates with zero effects (corresponding to the unpublished studies left in researchers' file drawers) that would be necessary to reduce the observed meta-analytic result to statistical insignificance (Rosenthal, 1979), zero, or to an operationally meaningless level (Hunter & Schmidt, 1990; Orwin, 1983; Pearlman et al., 1980). Meta-analyses based on small numbers of studies are particularly vulnerable to the file drawer problem. When the required number of "missing" studies is implausibly large, however, the likelihood of publication bias is effectively ruled out. For example, McNatt (2000) recently showed that it would take 367 "missing" studies (on interpersonal expectancy effects in management) that averaged a zero effect to reduce his observed effect size of d = 1.13 (a large effect) to d = .05 (a trivially small effect). Unfortunately, McNatt's study is unusual among recent I/O meta-analyses.

---

[2]Figures were created using Comprehensive Meta-Analysis (www.Meta-Analysis.com).

While several early studies included file drawer analyses, and its routine use was recommended in 1989 (Rothstein & McDaniel), most I/O meta-analyses done in the past decade have ignored it.

The Presentation of Meta-Analytic Findings.

The Presentation of Meta-Analytic Findings. Cooper's (1982) fifth and final stage is public presentation of results. Given our awareness of the potential influence of meta-analyses on personnel selection practice and on public policies in this area, we have been surprisingly casual about how are results are presented. According to Cooper, an explicit goal of every meta-analysis should be to present the findings in a way that will be easily understandable and useful to the audience at whom the meta-analysis is aimed, whether researchers or policy makers. Nearly all the meta-analyses published to date in I/O journals present results in tabular form only. Other areas in which meta-analyses have been popular have taken much fuller advantage of the information value of graphs. Graphic displays of data impose more order and structure on the results, making it easier to comprehend the overall message of the meta-analytic findings (Greenhouse & Iyengar 1994; Light, Singer, & Willet, 1994). These displays are useful not only for conveying information to the intended audience, but to the meta-analyst as well. Visually examining study outcomes facilitates the detection of both patterns and irregularities in the data. Three simple visual methods for communicating meta-analytic results, including the forest plot, stem and leaf plots, and tabular displays organized in a meaningful fashion such as by magnitude of effect size.

Stem and leaf plots, which have been around since well before the advent of meta-analysis (Tukey, 1977) are useful for displaying the shape of the distribution of effect sizes. Another method for displaying the distribution of effect sizes is the forest plot, which was developed specifically to display meta-analytic data. It is similar to a box and whiskers plot in that it shows the mean effect and the upper and lower confidence intervals or credibility values). The size of the box can be made proportional to the weight of the study. An illustration of a forest plot is provided in Table 5.1. Forest plots also make it easy to detect outlier effects (note Validity study 7 in Table 5.1). Rothstein, McDaniel, and Borenstein (2001) provided an illustration of the advantages of thoughtful tabular design by modifying data originally presented in Kubeck et al. (1996). In the original paper, Kubeck et al. followed the usual practice of displaying data sorted by author. Rothstein et al. resorted the data for correlations between age and training mastery sorted instead by magnitude of effect. This is shown in Table 5.2. The revised table includes the study name, the name of the effect size, the sample size, the correla-

TABLE 5.1
Forest Plot of Nine Hypothetical Validity Studies

Citation	Effect	NTotal	Lower	Upper					
					-1.00	-0.50	0.00	0.50	1.00
Validity study 1	.080	28	-.302	.440					
Validity study 2	.450	30	.107	.697					
Validity study 3	.250	120	.074	.411					
Validity study 4	.360	50	.091	.580					
Validity study 5	.250	25	-.161	.587					
Validity study 6	.190	150	.031	.340					
Validity study 7	-.150	100	-.337	.048					
Validity study 8	.500	80	.315	.648					
Validity study 9	.120	66	-.126	.352					
Combined (9)	**.228**	**649**	**.075**	**.370**					

Negative — Positive

143

TABLE 5.2
Training Mastery Data. Adapted from Kubeck et al. (1996)

Citation	Effect Name	NTotal	Effect
Belbin (1958)	Cloth mending (activity)	19	.372
Belbin & Serjean (1963)	Tailor Women-s (bespoke)	8	.245
Barber (1965)	Maintenance	51	.171
Belbin & Serjean (1963)	Tailor Men-s (wholesale)	24	.136
Gomez et al. (1984)	Computer text editing	40	.100
Kluge (1988)	Computer MBT errors	35	.070
Tannenbaum et al. (1963)	Blueprint reading II	17	.065
Webster et al. (1993)	Computer (work)	32	.040
Kluge (1988)	Computer IBT errors	37	.010
Hughes & McNamara (1961)	Computer (PI)	70	-.025
Tannenbaum et al. (1963)	Intro to electronics	53	-.060
Tannenbaum et al. (1963)	Oil refinery production	30	-.062
Hughes & McNamara (1961)	Computer (classroom)	42	-.070
Tannenbaum et al. (1963)	Oil refinery instrument	15	-.075
Belbin (1969)	Electrical (Discovery)	47	-.087
Tannenbaum et al. (1963)	Telephone operator errors	369	-.092
Corbin (1986)	Computer training	216	-.109
Tannenbaum et al. (1963)	Basic electronics	38	-.114
Belbin (1964)	Postal (Activity)	105	-.150
Neale et al. (1968)	Map reading (medium)	17	-.155
Barber (1965)	Spray gun	31	-.178
Belbin (1964)	Postal (Traditional)	325	-.180
Giannetto (1993)	Welfare (standard)	254	-.203
Czaja et al. (1989)	Computer (instructor)	45	-.218
Downs (1968)	Carpenters	213	-.223
Giannetto (1993)	Welfare (Self-efficacy)	25	-.230
Smith (1938)	Manual labor	155	-.234
Entwisle (1959)	Nonexperienced drivers	352	-.234
Welford (1958)	Bus driver	694	-.240
Belbin (1958)	Cloth mending (exposure)	14	-.245
Belbin & Serjean (1963)	Tailor Men-s (bespoke)	40	-.248
Barber (1965)	Scaffolding	37	-.249
Belbin (1969)	Electrical (Standard)	36	-.274
Morrow et al. (1993)	Flight simulation	28	-.298
Czaja et al. (1989)	Computer (computer)	45	-.301
Czaja (1978)	Visual inspec. (errors)	84	-.313
Tannenbaum et al. (1963)	Electronic tech	18	-.335
Gist et al. (1988)	Computer (tutorial)	75	-.389
Tannenbaum et al. (1963)	Optical tooling	46	-.396
Elias et al. (1987)	Computer	45	-.429
Gist et al. (1988)	Computer (modeling)	72	-.441
Downs (1968)	Welders	112	-.457
Czaja et al. (1989)	Computer (manual)	45	-.469
Tannenbaum et al. (1963)	Blueprint reading I	17	-.491
Egan & Gomez (1985)	Computer text editing	33	-.500
Webster et al. (1993)	Computer (play)	36	-.540
Entwisle (1959)	Experienced drivers	283	-.546
Neale et al. (1968)	Map reading (long)	18	-.552
Dodd (1967)	Gasman	13	-.747
Neale et al. (1968)	Map reading (short)	16	-.778

TABLE 5.2
(Continued)

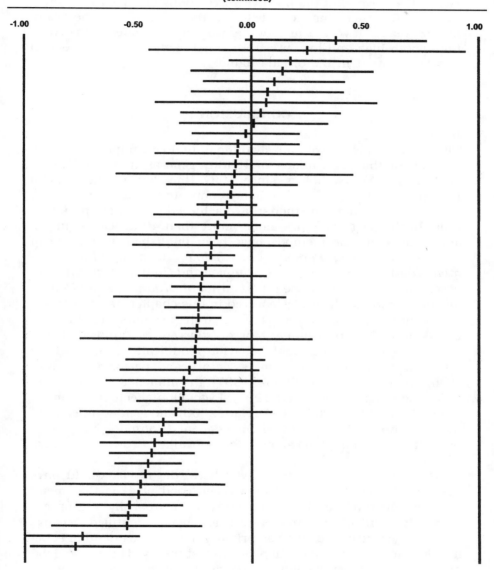

tion coefficient, and the confidence interval for each correlation co-efficient. The redesigned display makes it clear that most of the cor-relations between age and training mastery are negative. It also shows that several of the positive correlations are from very small samples. Restructuring the table to sort the effect sizes by their sam-ple size makes it very clear that many of the most aberrant correla-tions, both high and low, are from small sample studies. None of this is apparent in the original table.

CONCLUSION

The fact that it was prohibitively difficult to do a comprehensive re-view of all the applications of validity generalization and meta-analysis in I/O psychology since 1987 (the date of the original Hunter and Hirsh review) is a testimony to the acceptance and popularity that these methods have achieved in a short period of time. In the past five years alone, more than 40 articles using or about meta-analytic methods have been published in *Journal of Applied Psychology, Personnel Psychology, Academy of Manage-ment Journal, Organizational Behavior and Human Decision Proc-esses, Human Performance and Journal of Organizational Behav-ior*. In addition to the topics covered in this chapter, meta-analyses were conducted on a diverse set of research questions including: the effects and utility of training (Morrow, Jarrett, & Rupinski, 1997) the effects of organizational behavior modification (Stajkovic & Luthans, 1997), organizational structure and performance (Ket-chen, Combs, Russell, & Shook, 1997), the influence of framing on risky decisions (Kuehberger, 1998), Pygmalion effects in organiza-tions (Kirerein & Gold, 2000; McNatt, 2000) and gender differences in perceptions of both sexual harassment (Rotundo, Nguyen, & Sackett, 2001) and ethical practices (Franke, Crown, & Spake, 1997).

Had these studies been reviewed here, the report would have been much the same as it is now. The good news is that meta-analysis can reveal and pinpoint sizes of theoretically and practi-cally important effects; moderators are being identified because meta-analysis uses the study as primary data; more attention is be-ing given to the use of meta-analysis to test theory. The not-so-good news is that problems continue to exist because of poor reporting practices in primary studies (even recently conducted ones); re-ported descriptions of the decisions made by the meta-analysts vary widely in quality; the possibility of publication bias is not often considered; sensitivity analysis is generally ignored, leading to unknown robustness and generalizability of findings; and there is minimal use of visual displays to explore or communicate meta-analytic results. Clearly, the strength of the good news outweighs the other. Additionally, the weaknesses reported here are easily remedied. Considering the length of time meta-analysis has been around, it has made a remarkable contribution to knowledge in I/O Psychology, and it is still gathering speed and strength.

ACKNOWLEDGMENTS

The author is grateful to Michael Borenstein, Allen Huffcutt, Ruth Kanfer, Mike McDaniel and Frank Schmidt for their thoughtful comments on various issues discussed in this chapter.

Writing of this chapter was partially funded by SBIR/NIH grant MH 52969 to Biostatistical Programming Associates.

REFERENCES

Aguinis, H., & Pierce, C. A. (1998). Testing moderator variable hypotheses meta-analytically. *Journal of Management, 24*, 577–592.

Alexander, R. A., Carson, K. P., Alliger, G. M., & Cronshaw, S. F. (1989). Empirical distributions of range restricted SD in validity studies. *Journal of Applied Psychology, 74*, 253–258.

Avolio, B. J., & Waldman, D. A. (1990). An examination of age and cognitive test performance across job complexity and occupational types. *Journal of Applied Psychology, 75*, 43–50.

Avolio, B. J., Waldman, D. A., & McDaniel, M. A. (1990). Age and work performance in non-managerial jobs: the effects of experience and occupational type. *Academy of Management Journal, 33*, 407–422.

Barrick, M. R., & Mount, M. K. (1991). The Big Five dimensions and job performance: A meta-analysis. *Personnel Psychology, 44*, 1–26.

Barrick, M. R., & Mount, M. K. (1993). Autonomy as a moderator of the relationships between the Big Five personality dimensions and job performance. *Journal of Applied Psychology, 78*, 111–118.

Barrick, M. R., Mount, M. K., & Strauss, J. P. (1993). Conscientiousness and performance of sales representatives: Test of the mediating effects of goal setting. *Journal of Applied Psychology, 78*, 715–722.

Barrick, M. R., Stewart, G. L., Neubert, M. J., & Mount, M. K. (1998). Relating member ability and personality to work-team processes and team effectiveness. *Journal of Applied Psychology, 83*, 377–391.

Begg, C. (1994). Publication Bias. In H. Cooper & L. V. Hedges (Eds.), *The handbook of research synthesis* (pp. 399–409). New York: Russell Sage.

Bretz, R. (1989). College grade point average as a predictor of adult success: A meta-analytic review and some additional evidence. *Public Personnel Management, 18,* 11–22.

Bullock, R. J., & Svyantek, D. J. (1985). Analyzing meta-analysis: Potential problems, an unsuccessful replication, and evaluation criteria. *Journal of Applied Psychology, 70,* 108–115.

Camara, W. J., & Schneider, D. L. (1994). Integrity tests: Facts and unresolved issues. *American Psychologist, 49,* 112—119.

Campion, M. A., Campion, J. E., & Hudson, J. P. (1994). Structured interviewing: a note on incremental validity and alternative question types. *Journal of Applied Psychology, 79,* 998–1002.

Campion, M. A., Palmer, J. E., & Campion, H. J. (1997). A review of structure in the selection interview. *Journal of Applied Psychology, 50,* 655–702.

Carlson, K. D., Scullen, S. E., Schmidt, F. L., Rothstein, H. R., & Erwin, F. W. (1998). Generalizable biographical data: Is multi-organizational development and keying necessary? *Personnel Psychology, 52,* 731–755.

Cohen, J. (1988). *Statistical power analysis for the behavioral sciences* (2nd ed.). Hillsdale, NJ: Lawrence Erlbaum Associates.

Conway, J. M., Jako, D. A., & Goodman, R. F. (1995). A meta-analysis of inter-rater and internal consistency reliability of selection interviews. *Journal of Applied Psychology, 80,* 565–579.

Cooper, H. (1982). Scientific guidelines for conducting integrative research reviews. *Review of Educational Research, 52,* 291–302.

Cooper, H., DeNeve, K., & Charlton, K. (1997). Finding the missing science: The fate of studies submitted for review by a human subjects committee. *Psychological Methods, 2,* 447–452.

Cooper, H., & Hedges, L. V. (1994). Research synthesis as a scientific enterprise. In H. Cooper & L. V. Hedges (Eds.), *The handbook of research synthesis* (pp. 3–14). New York: Russell Sage.

Dickersin, K., Min, Y., & Meinert, C. (1992). Factors influencing the publication of research results: Follow-up of applications submitted to two institutional review boards. *Journal of the American Medical Association, 267,* 374–378.

Digman, J. M. (1990). Personality structure: Emergence of the five-factor model. *Annual Review of Psychology, 41,* 417–440.

Dipboye, R. L., & Gaugler, B. B. (1993). Cognitive and behavioral processes in the selection process. In N. Schmitt & W. C. Borman (Eds.), *Personnel Selection in Organizations* (pp. 135–170). San Francisco: Jossey-Bass.

Duval, S., & Tweedie, R. (2000). Trim and fill: A simple funnel plot based method of testing and adjusting for publication bias in meta-analysis. *Biometrics, 56,* 276–284.

Dye, D. A., & Reck, M. (1989). College grade point average as a predictor of adult success. *Public Personnel Management, 18,* 235–241.

Dye, D. A., Reck, M., & McDaniel, M. A. (1993). The validity of job knowledge measures. *International Journal of Selection and Assessment, 1,* 153—157.

Eagly, A., & Carli, L. L. (1981). Sex of researchers and sex-typed communications as determinants of sex differences in influenceability: A meta-analysis of social influence estudies. *Psychological Bulletin, 90,* 1–20.

Eagly, A., & Wood, W. (1991). Explaining sex differences in social behavior: A meta-analytic perspective. *Personality & Social Psychology Bulletin, 17,* 306–315.

Egger, M., Smith, G., Schneider, M., & Minder, C. (1997). Bias in meta-analysis detected by a simple graphical test. *British Medical Journal, 315,* 629–634.

Easterbrook, P., Berlin, J., Gopalan, R., & Matthews, D. (1991). Publication bias in clinical research. *Lancet, 337,* 867–882.

Fisher, R. A. (1932). *Statistical methods for research workers* (4th ed.). Edinburgh, Scotland: Oliver & Boyd.

Franke, G., Crown, D., & Spake, D. (1997). Gender differences in ethical perceptions of business practices: A social role theory perspective. *Journal of Applied Psychology, 82,* 920–934.

Frei, R., & McDaniel, M. (1998). Validity of customer service measures in personnel selection: a review of criterion and construct evidence. *Human Performance, 11,* 1–27.

Gaugler, B. B., Rosenthal, D. B., Thornton, G. C., & Bentson, C. (1987). Meta-analysis of assessment center validity. *Journal of Applied Psychology, 72,* 493–511.

Ghiselli, E. E. (1966). *The validity of occupational aptitude tests.* New York: Wiley.

Ghiselli, E. E. (1973). The validity of aptitude tests in personnel selection. *Personnel Psychology, 26,* 461–477.

Glass, G. V. (1976). Primary, secondary and meta-analysis of research. *Educational Researcher, 5,* 3–8.

Glass, G. V., McGraw, B., & Smith, M. (1981). *Meta-analysis in social research.* Thousand Oaks, CA: Sage.

Greenhouse, J., & Iyengar, S. (1994). Sensitivity analysis and diagnostics. In H. Cooper & L. Hedges (Eds.), *The Handbook of Research Synthesis* (pp.). New York: Russell-Sage.

Hall, S., & Brannick, M. (2002). Comparison of two random-effects methods of meta-analysis. *Journal of Applied Psychology, 87,* 377–389.

Hedges, L., & Olkin, I. (1980). Vote-counting methods in research synthesis. *Psychological Bulletin, 88,* 359–369.

Hedges, L., & Olkin, I. (1983). Clustering estimates of effect magnitude from independent studies. *Psychological Bulletin, 93,* 563–573.

Hedges, L., & Olkin, I. (1984). Nonparametric estimators of effect size in meta-analysis. *Psychological Bulletin,* 573–580.

Hedges, L., & Olkin, I. (1985). *Statistical methods for meta-analysis.* Orlando, FL: Academic Press.

Hedges, L. V., & Vevea, J. L. (1996). Estimating effect size under publication bias: Small sample properties and robustness of a random effects selection model. *Journal of Educational and Behavioral Sciences, 21,* 299–332.

Higgins, J. P. T., & Thompson, S. G. (2001, October 9–13). Presenting random-effects meta-analyses: where are we going wrong? Paper presented at the 9th International Cochrance Colloquium, Lyon, France.

Hirsh, H. R., Northrop, L., & Schmidt, F. L. (1986). Validity generalization results for law enforcement occupations. *Personnel Psychology, 39,* 399–420.

Hough, L., Eaton, N., Dunnette, M., Kamp, J., & McCloy, R. (1990). Criterion-related validities of personality constructs and the effect of response distortion on those validities. *Journal of Applied Psychology, 75,* 581–585.

Huffcutt, A. I., & Arthur, W. (1994). Hunter and Hunter (1984) revisited: Interview validity for entry-level jobs. *Journal of Applied Psychology, 79,* 184–190.

Huffcutt, A. I., Conway, J. M., Roth, P. L., & Jones, N. J. (2001). Identification and meta-analytic assessment of psychological constructs measured in employment interviews. *Journal of Applied Psychology, 86*, 897–913.

Huffcutt, A. I., Roth, P. L., & McDaniel, M. A. (1996). A meta-analytic investigation of cognitive ability in employment interview evaluations: Moderating characteristics and implications for incremental validity. *Journal of Applied Psychology, 81*, 459–473.

Huffcutt, A. I., Weekley, J. A., Wiesner, W. H., Degroot, T. G., & Jones, C. (2001). Comparison of situational and behavior description interview questions for higher-level positions. *Personnel Psychology, 54*, 619–644.

Huffcutt, A. I., & Woehr, D. (1999). Further analysis of employment interview validity: A quantitative evaluation of interviewer-related structuring methods. *Journal of Organizational Behavior, 20*, 549–560.

Hunter, J. E. (1983). *Test validation for 12,000 jobs: An application of job classification and validity generalization analysis to the General Aptitude Test Battery.* Washington, DC: US Employment Service, USDOL. USES Test Research Report No. 45.

Hunter, J. E., & Hirsh, H. R. (1987). Applications of meta-analysis. In C. L. Cooper & I. T. Robertson (Eds.), *International review of industrial and organizational psychology* (pp. 321–357). New York: Wiley.

Hunter, J. E., & Hunter, R. F. (1984). Validity and utility of alternative predictors of job performance. *Psychological Bulletin, 96*, 72–98.

Hunter, J. E., & Schmidt, F. L. (1990). *Methods of meta-analysis: Correcting error and bias in research findings.* Beverly Hills, CA: Sage.

Hunter, J. E., & Schmidt, F. L. (1991). Meta-analysis. In R. K. Hambleton & J. N. Zaal (Eds.), *Advances in educational and psychological testing: Theory and applications* (pp. 157–183). Norwell, MA: Kluwer Academic Publishers.

Hunter, J. E., Schmidt, F. L., Rauschenberger, J. M., & Jayne, M. E. A. (2000). Intelligence, motivation and job performance. In C. L. Cooper & E. A. Locke (Eds.), *Industrial and Organizational Psychology: Linking theory with practice* (pp. 278–303). Oxford, UK: Blackwell.

Hurtz, G. M., & Donovan, J. J. (2000). Personality and job performance: The Big Five revisited. *Journal of Applied Psychology, 85*, 869–879.

Iyengar, S., & Greenhouse, J. (1988). Selection models and the file drawer problem. *Statistical Science, 3*, 109–135.

Jackson, S. E. (1984, August). *Can meta-analysis be used for theory development in organizational psychology?* Paper presented at the meeting of the American Psychological Association, Toronto, Canada.

Johnson, B., & Eagly, A. (2000). Quantitative syntheses of social psychological research. In H. Reis & C. Judd (Eds.), *Handbook of research methods in social and personality psychology* (pp. 496–528). New York: Cambridge.

Judge, T. A., & Bono, J. E. (2000). Relationship of core self-evaluations traits—self-esteem, generalized self-efficacy, locus of control, and emotional stability—with job satisfaction and job performance: A meta-analysis. *Journal of Applied Psychology, 86*, 80–92.

Judge, T., Thoresen, G., Bono, J., & Patton, K. (2001). The Job Satisfaction—Job Performance Relationship: A Qualitative and Quantitative Review. *Journal of Applied Psychology, 86*, 326–407.

Kanfer, R., & Kantrowitz, T. M. (in press). Ability and non-ability predictors of performance. In S. Sonnentag (Ed.), *Psychological Management of Individual Performance*. London: Wiley.

Kanfer, R., Warburg, C. R., & Kantrowitz, T. M. (2001). Job search and employment: A personality motivational analysis and meta-analytic review. *Journal of Applied Psychology, 86,* 837–855.

Ketchen, D., Combs, J., Russell, C., & Shook, C. (1997). Organizational configurations and performance. *Academy of Management Journal, 40,* 223–240.

Kierein, N. M., & Gold, M. A. (2000). Pygmalion in work organizations: A meta-analysis. *Journal of Organizational Behavior, 21,* 913–928.

Kubeck, J., Delp, N., Haslett, T., & McDaniel, M. (1996). Does job-related training performance decline with age? *Psychology & Aging, 11,* 92–107.

Kuehberger, A. (1998). The influence of framing on risky decisions. *Organizational Behavior and Human Decision Processes, 75,* 23–55.

Kuncel, N., Hezlett, S., & Ones, D. (2001). A comprehensive meta-analysis of the predictive validity of the graduate record examinations: Implications for graduate student selection and performance. *Psychological Bulletin, 127,* 162–181.

Latham, G. P., & Saari, L. M. (1984). Do people do what they say? Further studies on the situational interview. *Journal of Applied Psychology, 69,* 569–573.

Light, R., & Pillemer, D. (1984). *Summing up: The science of reviewing research.* Cambridge, MA: Harvard.

Light, R. J., Singer, J. D., & Wilett, J. B. (1994). The visual presentation and interpretation of meta-analysis. In H. Cooper & L. V. Hedges (Eds.), *Handbook of research synthesis* (pp. 439–453). New York: Russell Sage Foundation.

Marchese, M., & Muchinsky, P. (1993). The validity of the employment interview: A meta-analysis. *International Journal of Selection and Assessment, 1,* 18–26.

Martocchio, J. J., & Judge, T. A. (1997). Relationship between conscientiousness and employee learning in employee training: Mediating of self-perception and self-efficacy. *Journal of Applied Psychology, 84,* 764–773.

McDaniel, M. A., Schmidt, F. L., & Hunter, J. E. (1988). Job experience correlates of job performance. *Journal of Applied Psychology, 73,* 327–330.

McDaniel, M. A., Whetzel, D. L., Schmidt, F. L., & Mauer, S. D. (1994). The validity of employment interviews: A comprehensive review and meta-analysis. *Journal of Applied Psychology, 79,* 599–616.

McEvoy, G. M., & Cascio, W. F. (1985). Strategies for reducing employee turnover: A meta-analysis. *Journal of Applied Psychology, 70,* 342–353.

McNatt, D. (2000). Ancient Pygmalion joins contemporary management: A meta-analysis of the result. *Journal of Applied Psychology, 85,* 314–322.

Morrow, C., Jarrett, M., & Rupinski, M. (1997). An investigation of the effect and economic utility of corporate-wide training. *Personnel Psychology, 50,* 91–119.

Mount, M. K., & Barrick, M. R. (1995). The Big Five personality dimensions: Implications for research and practice in human resources management. In G. R. Ferris (Ed.), *Research in personnel and human resources management* (Vol. 13, pp. 153–200). JAI Press.

Mount, M. K., Barrick, M. R., & Strauss, J. P. (1999). The joint relationship conscientiousness and ability with performance: Test of the interaction hypothesis. *Journal of Management, 25,* 707–721.

Murphy, K. R., & DeShon, R. (2000a). Interrater correlations do not estimate the reliability of job performance ratings. *Personnel Psychology, 5*, 873–900.

Murphy, K. R., & DeShon, R. (2000b). Progress in psychometrics: Can industrial and organizational psychology catch up? *Personnel Psychology, 53*(4), 913–924.

Murphy, K. R., & Shiarella, A. H. (1997). Implications of the multidimensional nature of job performance for the validity of selection tests: Multivariate frameworks for studying test validity. *Personnel Psychology, 50*, 823–854.

Murphy, K. R. (2000). Impact of assessments of validity generalization and situational specificity on the science and practice of personnel selection. *International Journal of Selection & Assessment, 8*, 194–206.

Olkin, I. (1990). History and goals. In K. W. Watcher & M. L. Straf (Eds.), *The future of meta-analysis* (pp. 3–10). New York: Russell Sage Foundation.

Ones, D. S., & Viswesvaran, C. (1998). Gender, age, and race differences on overt integrity tests: Results across four large-scale job applicant datasets. *Journal of Applied Psychology, 83*, 35–42.

Ones, D. S., Viswesvaran, C., & Schmidt, F. L. (1993). Comprehensive meta-analysis of integrity test validities: Findings and implications for personnel selection and theories of job performance. *Journal of Applied Psychology Monograph, 78*, 679–703.

Orwin, R. (1983). A fail-safe N for effect size in meta-analysis. *Journal of Educational Statistics, 8*, 157–159.

Overton, R. C. (1998). A Comparison of Fixed-Effects and Mixed (Random-Effects) Models for Meta-Analysis Tests of Moderator Variable Effects. *Psychological Methods, 3*, 354–379.

Pearlman, K., Schmidt, F. L., & Hunter, J. E. (1980). Validity generalization results for tests used to predict job proficiency and training success in clerical occupations. *Journal of Applied Psychology, 65*, 373–406.

Rosenthal, R. (1978). Combining results of independent studies. *Psychological Bulletin, 85*, 185–193.

Rosenthal, R. (1979). The "file drawer problem" and tolerance for null results. *Psychological Bulletin, 86*, 638–641.

Rosenthal, R. (1984). *Meta-analysis procedures for social research*. Beverly Hills, CA: Sage.

Roth, P. L., BeVier, C. A., Switzer, F. S., & Shippmann, J. S. (1996). Meta-analyzing the relationship between grades and job performance. *Journal of Applied Psychology, 81*, 548–556.

Roth, P. L., BeVier, C., Bobko, P., Switzer, F. S., & Tyler, P. (2001). Ethnic group differences in cognitive ability in employment and educational settings: A meta-analysis. *Personnel Psychology, 54*, 297–330.

Rothstein, H. R. (1990). Interrater reliability of job performance ratings: Growth to asymptote level with increasing opportunity to observe. *Journal of Applied Psychology, 75*, 322–327.

Rothstein, H. R. (1993). Meta-Analysis and construct validity. *Human Performance, 5*, 71–80.

Rothstein, H. R., Freeman, S., & Brian, J. (2001). Publication and reporting biases in meta-analyses in Industrial and Organizational psychology. Research in progress.

Rothstein, H. R., & McDaniel, M. A. (1989). Guidelines for conducting and reporting meta-analyses. *Psychological Reports, 65*, 759–770.

Rothstein, H. R., McDaniel, M. A., & Borenstein, M. (2001). Meta-Analysis: A Review of Quantitative Cumulation Methods. In N. Schmitt & F. Drasgow (Eds.), *Measuring and Analyzing Behavior in Organizations: Advances in Measurement and Data Analysis*. San Francisco: Jossey-Bass.

Rothstein, H. R., Schmidt, F. L., Erwin, F. W., Owens, W. A., & Sparks, C. P. (1990). Biographical data in employment selection: Can validities be made generalizable? *Journal of Applied Psychology, 75*, 175–184.

Rotundo, M., Nguyen, D., & Sackett, P. (2001). A meta-analytic review of gender differences in perceptions of sexual harassment. *Journal of Applied Psychology, 86*, 914–922.

Russell, C. J., Settoon, R. P., McGrath, R. N., & Blanton, A. E. (1994). Investigator characteristics as moderators of personnel selection research: A meta-analysis. *Journal of Applied Psychology, 79*, 163–170.

Rynes, S. L., Barber, A. E., & Varma, G. H. (2000). Research on the Employment Interview: Usefulness for Practice and Recommendations for Future Research. In C. L. Cooper & E. A. Locke (Eds.), *I/O Psychology: What We Know about Theory and Practice* (pp. 250–277). Oxford.

Rynes, S. L., Orlitzky, M. O., & Bretz, R. D. (1999). Experienced hiring versus college recruiting: Practices and emerging trends. *Personnel Psychology, 50*, 309–339.

Sackett, P. R., Tenopyr, M. L., Schmitt, N., & Kehoe, J. (1986). Commentary on Forty questions about validity generalization and meta-analysis. *Personnel Psychology, 38*, 697–798.

Samson, G. E., Gaue, M. E., Weinstein, T., & Walberg, H. (1984). Academic and occupational performance : A quantitative synthesis. *Journal of Research & Development in Education, 17*, 52–56.

Schmitt, N., Gooding, R., Noe, R., & Kirsch, M. (1984). Meta-analyses of validity studies published between 1964 and 1982 and the investigation of study characteristics. *Personnel Psychology, 37*, 407–422.

Schmidt, F. L., & Hunter, J. E. (1977). Development of a general solution to the problem of validity generalization. *Journal of Applied Psychology, 68*, 529–540.

Schmidt, F. L., & Hunter, J. E. (1998). The validity and utility of selection methods in personnel psychology: Practical and theoretical implications of 85 years of research findings. *Psychological Bulletin, 124*, 262–274.

Schmidt, F. L., Hunter, J. E., & Outerbridge, A. N. (1986, August). Impact of job experience and ability on job knowledge, work sample performance, and supervisory ratings of job performance. *Journal of Applied Psychology, 71*(3), 432–439.

Schmidt, F. L., Hunter, J. E., Pearlman, K., & Hirsh, H. R. (1985). Forty questions about validity generalization and meta-analysis. *Personnel Psychology, 38*, 697–798.

Schmidt, F. L., Ones, D., & Hunter, J. E. (1992). Personnel selection. *Annual Review of Psychology, 43*, 627–670.

Stajkovic, A., & Luthans, F. (1997). A meta-analysis of the effects of organizational behavior modification on task performance. *Academy of Management Journal, 40*, 1122–1149.

Sterling, T., Rosenbaum, W., & Weinkam, J. (1995). Publication decisions revisited: The effect of the outcome of statistical tests on the decision to publish and vice versa. *American Statistician, 49*, 108–112.

Tett, R. P., Jackson, D. N., & Rothstein, M. (1991). Personality measures as predictors of job performance: A meta-analytic review. *Personnel Psychology, 44*, 703–742.

Thorndike, E. L. (1933). The effect of the interval between test and re-test on the consistencey of the IQ. *Journal of Educational Psychology, 25*, 543–549.

Tukey, J. (1977). *Exploratory Data Analysis*. Reading, MA: Addison-Wesley.

Vevea, J. L., & Hedges, L. V. (1995). A general linear model for estimating effect size in the presence of publication bias. *Psychometrika, 60*, 419–435.

Viswesvaran, C., Ones, D. S., & Schmidt, F. L. (1996). Comparative analysis of the reliability of job performance ratings. *Journal of Applied Psychology, 81*, 557–560.

Wachter, K., & Straf, M. (Eds.). (1990). *The Future of Meta-Analysis*. New York: Russell Sage.

Waldman, D. A., & Avolio, B. J. (1986). A meta-analysis of age differences in job performance. *Journal of Applied Psychology, 72*, 33–38.

Whitener, E. M. (1990). Confusion of confidence intervals and credibility intervals in meta-analysis. *Journal of Applied Psychology, 75*, 315–321.

Wiesner, W. H., & Cronshaw, S. F. (1988). The moderating impact of interview format and degree of structure on the validity of the employment interview. *Journal of Occupational Psychology, 61*, 275—290.

6

Validity Generalization: Then and Now

Frank J. Landy
SHL

INTRODUCTION

I was asked to prepare a chapter dealing with the way in which validity generalization has changed the landscape for the personnel psychologist. Having been actively engaged in personnel psychology since 1964, this is a task for which I am well suited (at least by virtue of "being there" and being "here"). Because I was asked to contrast "then" with "now," I take, of necessity, a historical perspective. I am also comfortable with the role of the historiographer, particularly of the deconstructionist ilk. Further, I take a somewhat broader view than many of the other chapter authors. I pay scant attention to microanalytic and statistical detail. I do not (unduly) concern myself with controversies surrounding general mental ability (*g*), or the most recent findings with respect to the parameters of assessment (e.g., personality characteristics such as conscientiousness) or the process of assessment (e.g., the structured interview). Instead, I attempt to describe the evolution of the concept of validity generalization as well as the uneven role it plays today in research, theory, practice, and public policy formulation.

AN OVERVIEW

The goal of psychology, like all sciences, is to uncover general laws. This was the vision of Wundt, James and most of the conceptual architects of the "new" science in 1880. So validity generalization (VG), at least as a concept, is perfectly compatible with such a goal. But not everyone is convinced that the current versions of VG meet the overarching goal of uncovering laws of behavior. This reluctance stems from two sources. The first of these is epistemological—the fact that personnel psychology derives from the marriage of differential psychology and psychometrics. The epistemological question is whether or not we can ever come to *understand* behavior from a largely analytic and quantitative perspective. The second source is much less elegant—validity generalization has been steeped in controversy from the beginning.

VG involves the application of a larger body of analytic procedures known as meta-analysis. In its simplest form, meta-analysis is the aggregation of cumulative research on a topic in an attempt to make sense out of apparent conflicting results from individual studies. Further, meta-analysis statistically controls for certain sample characteristics (e.g., sample size) that may obscure underlying relationships. The techniques of meta-analysis are well described and accepted and accompanied by little controversy (Glass, 1976; Hedges, 1988; Hunter, Schmidt, & Jackson, 1982; Wortman, 1983). VG adds a number of corrections to observed statistical values, most of which are drawn from standard psychometric texts, and in principle, VG is nothing other than a variation on the theme laid out by other meta-analytic methods. Things have not turned out this way; VG has been the subject of controversy, often intense. Although this controversy has abated substantially in recent years, it is still an important part of the development and legacy of VG, and there is much that might be learned from analyzing the nature and the source of this controversy.

Why did VG generate such controversy? There are several answers to this question. The first has to do with the sheer number and complexity of corrections applied to effect sizes in the form of validity coefficients. In addition, many of the studies which form the basis for the VG inference are missing information necessary for the application of various "corrections." For example, many validity studies published even as recently as 20 years ago are missing reliability data for the criterion variable, or unrestricted variance data for the predictor variable. As a result, these missing values are often estimated rather than calculated. There is disagreement about the way in which these values should be estimated. Finally, there is the inherent promise of high validity coefficients—increased effectiveness or productivity. Personnel psychology has a history of promising more than it can deliver, or at least promising results more quickly than they can be delivered. Yerkes (1921) used the WWI intelligence testing juggernaut to capture the interest of employers in the rewards of selection testing. Cattell (1923) promised much the same benefit from the newly formed Psychological Corporation in 1921 (Landy, 1993). But the reality fell well short of the promise. The explosion of psychometric devices in the 50's did not fill the predictive gap.

When VG burst on the scene in the 1970's, the promise seemed to be that with some relatively straightforward, low cost, cognitive tests, employers could hire effective employees for virtually any job with the expectation of high levels of productivity and profitability (i.e., cognitive ability tests had high utility). The icing on the cake was that the employer would no longer need to do time consuming, expensive, and often disappointing criterion related validity studies to support the use of a particular test. This part of the promise was particularly important at the time because of the increasing application of the Civil Rights Act of 1964 to issues of employment. Up to that point, it was unlikely that an employer would have been successful in defending a charge of unfair discrimination in hiring without a validity study, preferably a criterion-related study. In some senses, it might be fair to say that the heightened sensitivity of the psychometric and public policy community to VG resulted from the fact that it promised so much at such a small cost. It was the psychometric equivalent of alchemy. Lead was turned into gold—a collection of disappointing and contradictory validity studies were unraveled to show that we had been doing the right thing all along.

There is little doubt that VG is a powerful instrument for inference. Virtually every I/O and personnel testing textbook published since 1985 has included coverage of VG. Each year the Annual Review of Psychology presents a synopsis of important research and theory related to various areas of psychology. The Annual Review presents a chapter dealing with personnel psychology every other year. For almost 20 years, VG earned its own heading in every chapter dealing with personnel psychology.

From this sampling of professional sources, it is fair to say that most I/O psychologists expected that VG would have a profound effect on research, theory, practice, and public policy related to personnel decisions. The reality is a bit less dramatic. Certainly, the meaning and inferences from research has changed substantially from the pre-VG days. Practice has also changed somewhat in that the choice of predictors is better informed by virtue of meta-analytic studies and VG inferences. The changes in theory have been a good deal less substantial. The one attempt at major public policy modification—the wide spread use of the General Aptitude Test Battery (GATB) for job families—was largely mooted by the 1991 Civil Rights Act (CRA), which forbade race norming. Had the GATB been adopted as the universal test of general mental ability, adverse impact would have been massive. To bypass this difficulty, it was proposed that separate norms be used for White and Black applicants (i.e., the establishment of dual lists). Such a practice was forbidden by the revision of the Civil Rights Act adopted in 1991. Employers have been reticent to invoke VG in the defense of test batteries so it has had little significant impact on case law. In summary, it is clear that the VG concept is universally recognized by personnel psychologists but it is equally clear that its early promise has yet to be recognized in many arenas. The sections that follows describes the somewhat fitful track of VG in the time since its introduction.

THE LIMITS OF INFERENCE

A popular axiom of experimental design and inference is that one can only generalize to what one samples. That simple truism is at the heart of all debates about the likelihood of deriving general laws of behavior—whether they are laws seeking to explain social aggression, autistic behavior, or the relationship of ability to job performance.

Like their colleagues in other areas of psychology, personnel psychologists most often conduct single studies of limited variables with small sample sizes. In addition, these studies were most often conducted in the field with little hope of experimental control. Data were not gathered regarding potentially relevant other variables (i.e., covariates) that might permit statistical control. Thus, not only were their inferences weak, but they were also narrow. As an example, a practitioner might develop a novel application blank for the selection of operators of an esoteric piece of production equipment. The application blank might then be validated on a sample of convenience (incumbents who appeared for work on a given day at one designated plant location and who could be made available to complete the application blank during working hours). To make matters worse, unlike the physical sciences, the behavioral sciences were (and are) loathe to publish replications. (It has been said that in the physical sciences, progress is made by standing on the shoulders of those who go before you, in the social and behavioral sciences, progress is made by stepping in the faces of those who go before you). As a result, the research literature in personnel psychology might be characterized as a collection of one-shot studies whose meaning and contribution are unclear.

Thus, when Ghiselli (1955) did his first review of the validity of various psychometric devices it should not be surprising to find that there was wide variability in published results of validity coefficients. Nor should it be surprising to find that similar variability appeared in his second and third reviews (Ghiselli, 1966; 1973). To say that he had discovered the doctrine of situational validity is less to explain than to label. Consider the studies that represented his data base. They varied along at least the following parameters:

- predictor psychometric characteristics (including but not limited to reliability)
- criterion psychometric characteristics (including but not limited to reliability)
- the construct measured by the predictor
- the construct measured by the criterion
- sample size
- interval between the collection of the predictor and criterion scores
- sample demographics
- range restriction on the predictor variable
- range restriction on the criterion variable

Nevertheless, the general conclusion drawn from the Ghiselli reviews (and to a lesser extent from the Validity Information Exchange that had been published between 1954 and 1963 in *Personnel Psychology*) was that there was sufficient variability among validity coefficients representing putatively similar predictor constructs to caution against assuming that a predictor that was valid in one situation would be valid in another. It is instructive to digress here briefly to consider the usage (if not the *meaning*) of the term *valid*. Personnel psychologists have dug themselves into a hole by assuming a binary state for validity—a test is either valid or not valid from that perspective. To make matters worse, employment law has followed the same path. But tests can vary in how well they represent the latent constructs they were designed to measure or how well they predict relevant criteria. It was this binary view of the world that provided a backdrop for notions of situational validity. Consider these quotes from Guion's 1965 text on the topic of situational validity:

> In spite of generalizations, therefore, it continues to be essential that every situation use its own validity study, because we do not know the essential variables well enough to say in advance how effective any given predictor will be. (p. 455)

> Situational thinking should precede situational validation. Validation should be more than merely a check on tests to see if they will work in this situation. (p. 455)

This variability in study outcomes was a source of great frustration for the personnel psychologist at the time. It was well recognized that until and unless some form of generalization of validity results was possible, personnel psychology would lack the legitimacy of other branches of psychology (e.g., as compared to learning theory or theories of sensation and perception) but would also fall far short of the goal of all scientific endeavor—the discovery of general laws.

The notion that there must be some way to transport partial or limited validity findings by combining them with other partial findings was suggested in the work of Lawshe (1952), and later in the writings of Guion (1965) in the concept of synthetic validity. The notion was that one could synthesize validity by aggregating bits and pieces that would fit together. In its simplest form, this meant decomposing many jobs into what we might now call "essential duties." By doing this, we might find that a substantial number of jobs, each with but a few incumbents, all included a particular essential duty, thus permitting a statistical examination of the correlation between a predictor and criterion scores on that essential duty with a much larger sample. In applications and extensions of the same basic logic, test batteries were constructed to predict success in visual job families (Tiffin & McCormick, 1958) and jobs requiring perceptual motor skills (Drewes, 1961). It is interesting, however, to note that even while looking for bridges of generalization, Guion (1965) still cautioned: "Where the number of cases permit, there is still no substitute for carrying out situational validities" (p. 286).

So for all intents and purposes, in 1965, personnel psychology was mired in the accepted doctrine of situational validity. At first glance, it might seem we were there because we had disappointing data. To some extent, that is true. But there were other larger forces that brought us to that point.

A SHORT PSYCHOMETRIC TOUR

Although it is true that the founders of psychology were desperate for general laws of behavior as a source of legitimacy, there were other forces at work as well. The most dramatic of these forces was James McKeen Cattell. Although Cattell had studied under Wundt, he was more interested in exceptions to Wundt's psychophysical rules than the rules themselves. It was this fascination with the exceptions that presented the platform for differential psychology—the study of individual differences. In order to study these differences, Cattell had developed measurement procedures, several of which he later he termed *mental tests* (Cattell, 1890).

After leaving Wundt's laboratory in Leipzig to pursue a medical degree at Cambridge, he became enamored with the work and the personality of Sir Francis Galton. Galton was a cousin of Charles Darwin and was busily engaged in gathering anthropometric data that would further bolster Darwin's theory of evolution. The possibility of demonstrating that mental abilities were inherited in much the same way as other human characteristics was appealing so he asked Cattell to lend his tests to the project. Cattell was pleased to cooperate and eventually took the same mental tests to the University of Pennsylvania, then to Columbia in order to test all incoming freshmen with respect to their mental abilities. This could be considered a genuine psychometric enterprise. There were two purposes to be served by this testing. First, it might aid in the selection and placement of students into curricula or lines of study. More importantly, however, Cattell hoped to develop a theory of intelligence from an analysis of the mass of data he had collected at Penn and Columbia.

Cattell had no real theory but having been classically trained in the philosophy of Francis Bacon and the methods of induction, he firmly believed a theory of intelligence would emerge if he collected enough data. It didn't. But it is testimony to the force and stature of Cattell, that what could only be considered a research disaster (almost 20 years of data gathering and no pleasing conclusions), left his reputation, and the vitality of differential psychology undiminished. There were other figures who contributed to the rising popularity of the new field of psychometrics, in particular Hugo Munsterberg and his student Harold Burtt. But it was Clark Hull who added luster to the psychometric movement with his 1928 book called *Aptitude Testing*. This book was a *tour de force* in the new practice of psychometrics. Not only did it describe the variety of aptitude tests available, but also the application of these tests to industrial selection. Although Hull never used the term *situational validity*, his writings make it clear that he believed that each vocation required specialized abilities, both cognitive and noncognitive. He had little patience for his colleagues who touted the notion of *g* or general intelligence.

> It has been and still is the custom to a very large extent, even among trained psychologists, to call nearly all psychological tests, tests of intelligence. Sometimes they are spoken of as tests of *general* intelligence.
>
> The recognition that if a test is to be of any particular value, it must enable us to forecast a *particular* aptitude or group of aptitudes rather than some hypothetical or semi-metaphysical faculty, constitutes a great advance. During the period now happily drawing to a close, psychologists dominated by an essentially metaphysical notion of intelligence and consequently having no definite concrete criterion against which to test the validity of their tests, frequently moved in a circle in their scientific efforts. With the abandonment of this paralyzing idea of measuring *general* intelligence as the goal of the testing activity, there is now appearing a vigorous and healthy concentration upon the development of tests for the greatest variety of particular concrete aptitudes. (Hull, 1928, pp. 19–20)

Hull went on to describe research into the unique aptitudes necessary for successful performance of such jobs as telephone operator, free hand draftsman, sewing machine operator, and traveling salesman. He adopted what we would now call the predictive validity study as a reasonable method for establishing the value of an aptitude test. The sole alternative available at the time was what he and his contemporaries referred to as "armchair theorizing" and they had no tolerance for that approach. (I often wonder what the Viteles and Hull's of the world would have thought of content or construct oriented validation procedures).

It is tempting to tie the positivism of the Hull's criterion related study to the emerging behaviorist paradigm of Watson in looking for precursors of the situationism of Ghiselli and Guion. There was every reason for the personnel psychologist at the mid-point of the 20th century to see validity coefficients as surrogates for a theory linking aptitude with performance (much like the Law of Effect was to stand for a theory of learning). Further, the deep tradition of differential psychology that spawned psychometrics and personnel testing was perfectly compatible with the notion of situational validity.

The point of this historical excursion has been to set the stage for the appearance of VG, but more importantly, to point to the roots of personnel psychology in looking for epistemological explanations of why VG is controversial, or represents a problem. Until the late-1970s, whether they knew it or not, most classically trained personnel psychologists were Baconians, well versed in the psychometrics and positivism of Cattell and Hull. Situational validities, as evidenced by variations in validity coefficients, were not seen as remarkable. The more practical minded (or cynical) of them might have seen the doctrine of situationism as a guarantee of full employment.

PRE- META-ANALYSIS LITERATURE REVIEWS

In the preceding sections, I have described the trek from Wundt's laboratory to Bob Guion's (1965) landmark book in personnel testing. Prior to meta-analysis and VG, one of the most substantial inferential tools for the personnel psychologist was the traditional literature review. A well-done literature review on a topic of general interest was a daunting task. It involved weeks, and often months, in the bowels of libraries. Completed index cards were arrayed, and re-arrayed, in an attempt to find some general laws that governed the phenomenon under consideration. But if the review was a good (persuasive) one, it had a long shelf life. Consider two such reviews published in the same year. The first was done by Ulrich and Trumbo (1965), which covered 14 years of research on the employment interview. The second was done by Guion and Gottier (1965) and examined the use of personality tests for employee selection. Ulrich and Trumbo provided ample and persuasive argument that the employment interview deserved a role in the employee selection process. Guion and Gottier (1965) were equally persuasive in arguing against any role for personality testing in employee selection. Both of these reviews played a role in graduate education and professional practice for the next 15 to 20 years and both were eventually replaced by meta-analytic research. In the case of the interview, its role was affirmed (Wiesner & Cronshaw, 1988). In the case of personality testing, recent developments in theory and practice have largely muted the concerns of Guion and Gottier about any role for personality testing in employee selection.

But even well-done literature reviews were not always universally accepted. A case in point deals with the possible relationship between job satisfaction and performance. In 1955, Brayfield and Crockett published an extensive review of the satisfaction and performance literature and concluded that there was little or no relationship. In 1957, Herzberg, Mausner, and Snyderman published a book coming to exactly the opposite conclusion. Katzell (1957) suggested the reasons for the discrepancies: (a) they covered different literatures, (b) they used different statistical standards for determining what constituted support for their positions, and (c) they used different criterion variables to measure job performance. The interesting thing about the Herzberg–Brayfield controversy was that it occurred at all. It was completely accidental that two literature reviews on the same topic appeared at the same time. No one bothered to re-examine the Guion and Gottier (1965) or Ulrich and Trumbo (1965) literature. This was the psychological equivalent to the law of motion—literature once reviewed, tends to stay reviewed. In the case of the Guion and Gottier review, this was particularly unfortunate because the most important conclusions of that review were largely ignored. Guion and Gottier are largely credited with putting a stop to personality testing by showing that personality tests were not valid. Their actual conclusions were very different. They concluded that off-the-shelf personality measures available at that time (pre-1965) and applied mindlessly to selection situations and validated with flawed criterion measures were poor candidates for inclusion in a test battery. They further suggested that the same careful research that would support the use of any predictor be conducted for a proposed personality test. To be sure, they were still firmly advocating a situational view of validity, but they were not proposing a moratorium to personality testing. The point is that the daunting nature of traditional literature reviews discouraged replications, re-analyses, or reconsiderations. For the most part, readers tended to skim through reviews looking for (and occasionally inferring) simple summary conclusions.

THE ADVENT OF META-ANALYSIS
AS A TOOL OF INFERENCE

From an inferential point of view, however, the problem with the classical literature review was not that it was labor intensive, it was that the conclusions depended heavily on the scholarship and decision strategies of the authors. The Brayfield–Herzberg disagreement was a perfect example of the problem, and seldom were these limits to inference considered. This seemed to change with the introduction of meta-analysis (Glass, 1976; Hunter et al., 1982). As Wortman (1983) noted, meta-analytic procedures took the research community by storm, and for good reason. It promised to remove the subjectivity from inference through statistical methods (Glass, 1977). "These techniques can often burn through the haze of uncertainty that surrounds any one study and clearly reveal effects only dimly perceived before" (Wortman, 1983, p. 245). But there was another, equally important, characteristic of meta-analyses that would immediately appeal to the personnel psychologist: ". . . the resulting effect size estimate has both direction and magnitude" (Wortman, 1983, p. 236). Now one could burn through the haze of the Ghiselli reviews and come to a conclusion about the value of various assessment devices for personnel selection. Personnel psychologists enthusiastically climbed aboard the meta-analysis wagon with their colleagues from the other subdisciplines of psychology.

A HARBINGER OF THINGS TO COME:
DIFFERENTIAL VALIDITY

The Civil Rights Act of 1964, and in particular, Title VII, led to a new development in personnel psychology. The concept of validity moved from the scientific community to the courtroom. The doctrine of situational validity suggested that tests which might be valid for one use (e.g., job, location, subgroup), might not be for another. In the context of employment litigation, the implications were clear: A test that was valid for Whites might not be valid for Blacks. In fact, this was not an uncommon finding in comparing the test or performance correlations for White and Black subgroups within a given study. There was a great deal of emotion that surrounded this debate since the issue was no longer simply psychometric; it had assumed social-political importance. It was common then (as it is now) for Black applicants to score more poorly on standardized tests of cognitive ability than White applicants. If candidates were selected from the top of an eligibility list down in rank order (the standard of the time), it was axiomatic that Blacks would be hired less frequently than Whites. One line of argument from the plaintiff class was that although Blacks might have scored more poorly on the test, it was of no consequence because the test in question did not predict as accurately for Blacks as for Whites. Given the fact that research literature could be found to support that assertion, it could be a powerful argument in court proceedings.

In a series of increasingly sophisticated statistical analyses conducted by Boehm (1977), Hunter, Schmidt, and Hunter (1979), and Schmidt, Berner, and Hunter (1973), the "myth" (Landy, 1985) of single group validity was put to rest. All of the apparent differences between the validity coefficients for White and Black subgroups disappeared when controls for various statistical artifacts were applied. This was the first serious assault on the doctrine of situational validity. Further, it was a simple and largely axiomatic assault from the statistical flank. It did not require any "theory" of abilities in Whites and Blacks, any tortured examination of three way interactions including race, test content, and other situational variables. This research demonstrated in a very direct manner that at least with respect to racial subgroups, the doctrine of situational validity did not seem tenable. The clearest statement of these principles can be found in Schmidt and Hunter's (1978) treatment of *Moderator Research and the Law of Small Numbers*. This is a must read for those interested in the emergence of the VG juggernaut. It succinctly lays out the statistical argument, and at the same time questions the devotion of personnel psychologists to the ever-hypothesized moderator variables. In psychometric lore, a moderator variable was a mystical element that changed the size or direction of a relationship between two variables without being correlated with either of those variables. Moderator variables were often invoked to explain situational validity. It was often more convenient to propose some unknown moderator as the reason for variability of validity coefficients than to actually identify what that moderator variable might be. This was simply intellectual laziness. Schmidt and Hunter exposed this brand of laziness and showed that implied moderator variables could be seen as little more than magical thinking. Note that they were not denying the *possibility* of moderator variables in particular settings; rather, they were pointing out the inappropriate use of the *concept* of a moderator to explain variability among validity coefficients. At least with respect to observed validity coefficients, race was certainly not a moderator variable.

By this time, the Glass (1976) work on meta-analysis was becoming widely known and applied. In 1982, Hunter et al. produced their own book on meta-analytic techniques with a clear emphasis on personnel selection applications. From an examination of the contemporaneous writings, it seems clear that the power of meta-analysis was recognized almost simultaneously by Schmidt and Hunter, on the one hand, and Glass on the other. Having put the myth of differential validity to rest, it was a short step to the larger topic of VG and the final assault on the doctrine of situational validity.

UTILITY, *G*, AND MODERATOR VARIABLES

During exactly the same period when Schmidt and Hunter (1978) were addressing the issue of differential validity, they embarked on two additional lines of research, both of which were important from a scientific as well as a practical and legal perspective. These lines of research can be characterized as the elevation of general mental ability or *g* to primary (or possibly even exclusive) status in test batteries and the examination of utility or cost benefit analysis in personnel selection. Inevitably, the three lines of research became blurred, often as a direct result of links forged by Schmidt and Hunter. Schmidt and Hunter had access to enormous data sets generated over decades that examined the validity of cognitive ability tests (principally the General Aptitude Test Battery or GATB used by the United States Employment Service). They were able to apply VG principles to these data sets, correcting for artifacts directly when necessary data were available, and making corrections by estimates when the necessary data were not available. Having made all of their corrections (direct and estimated), Schmidt and Hunter concluded that there was simply not enough variance remaining in the validity coefficients to allow for any substantial contribution to criterion prediction from a noncognitive predictor or from a moderator variable. Of course, this begged lots of questions (most of which are covered in some detail and with some enthusiasm in other chapters) but it did permit the killing of four birds with one stone: Not only was validity generalizable in an abstract sense, but it was the validity of *cognitive* tests in particular that was not only generalizable, but also sufficient for any employer's purpose. They were able to kill the third bird by introducing the concept of utility of these cognitive tests. The fourth bird was the fact that these tests seemed to be just as fair for Whites as for Blacks. Once again, Schmidt and Hunter used a combination of direct calculations and estimates or inferences to conclude that most employers could save millions of dollars in personnel costs by using nothing more than tests of cognitive ability for selection.

From the legal perspective, this hat trick presented another problem for plaintiffs. In 1978, the Uniform Guidelines on Employee Selection Procedures was published and became the primary administrative authority in employment litigation. These guidelines stated that if adverse impact were demonstrated by plaintiffs, then defendant employers needed to demonstrate the job relatedness (validity) and business necessity (e.g., utility) of the challenged practice. Even if the defendant employer was able to demonstrate the job relatedness and business necessity of the practice, the plaintiffs were permitted to show that another practice, that would serve the employer's interest equally well (i.e., had equal job relatedness and equal business necessity evidence) but that had a lesser adverse impact was available to the employer at the time the challenged practice had been adopted. The Schmidt and Hunter advocacy of tests of general mental ability, their demonstrations of generalizable nature of these tests, and their demonstrations of utility of these tests had the potential of supporting not only the job relatedness and business necessity of the tests, but also had the potential for destroying any argument that there was another type of test that would serve the employer's interests equally well. The employer could argue that no other type of device had demonstrated this high level of validity and utility, thus any search for alternatives was doomed to failure. It is no surprise, then, that by the early 1980's, Schmidt and Hunter were not likely to win any popularity contests with minority plaintiffs or their lawyers in class action employment litigation. One example of the status of the Schmidt Hunter analyses among plaintiff's lawyers will suffice. Richard Seymour is a well known and trial-hardened plaintiff's attorney who has been on the staff of the Lawyer's Committee on Civil Rights for many years. He was well aware of the danger posed by the VG doctrine being proposed by Schmidt and Hunter. He also recognized that the various corrections that were part of the VG model could weaken any arguments about differential validity, or alternative practices. In an article that Seymour published in 1988, he described the Schmidt Hunter corrections as "hydraulics functions":

> Hydraulics functions are mathematical operations which have the effect of increasing the size and significance of any observed correlation, based on assumptions the accuracy of which in the case at hand is seldom examined. They are so called because they have the effect of any hydraulic system: they push to the sky things which properly belong on the ground. (p. 351)

Although Seymour was most animated about the Schmidt Hunter notion of corrections, he was also concerned about the whole meta-analytic approach, which he artfully dubbed the "Theory of Universal Validity":

> It is worth remembering that a "meta-analysis" of published findings of natural scientists in the mid-18th century would have produced a striking uniformity of that opinion that fire was caused by a substance called phlogiston and that a meta-analysis of the findings of physi-

cians in the last two centuries would have produced an equally strik-ing uniformity of opinion that disease was caused by an imbalance of the humors or of bile of various hues. (p. 361)

Although Seymour's comparison of VG to phlogiston and hu-mors might seem a bit strained, in a way he was right on target. Much of the early enthusiasm for VG was based on the GATB data base. This data base was a heterogeneous mixture of good and bad studies. When researchers began to broaden the data base, many of the early (and characteristically confident) conclusions of Schmidt and Hunter turned out to be wrong. As an example, it is now generally accepted that job complexity is a moderator variable even though Schmidt and Hunter had claimed that there was no possibility of moderators of cognitive ability because all of the vari-ation among validity coefficients could be accounted for by statisti-cal artifacts. It is not that difficult to appreciate Seymour's disdain for the psychometric revolution manifest in VG. Although more statistically sophisticated than many of his colleagues, he fairly represents the mixture of terror and contempt that surrounded the introduction of VG into the courtroom. So the Schmidt and Hunter planets of VG, Utility and *g* were all aligned by the mid 1980's, and battle was to be joined.

ANOTHER BRIEF DIVERSION: THE PSYCHOMETRIC SMACKDOWN

As indicated in the introduction to this chapter, I am a bit like Chance, the Gardener (a.k.a. Chauncey Gardner) in the classic Pe-ter Seller's movie "Being There." I can remember with some clarity and confidence (the two do not always co-exist) the feeling I had reading the latest Schmidt and Hunter paper. I was always pre-pared for bombast and unbridled arrogance. I was seldom disap-pointed. It was not so much that I was opposed to the substance of whatever their latest publication was, but I was predisposed to ar-gue with whatever they were saying. That was the effect they had on me. I know I was not alone (see Q&A # 9 in the "Forty Questions" article, Schmidt et al., 1985).

Schmidt, Hunter, et al. (1985) made a strategic decision to make strong and sweeping claims in many of their papers. In the "Forty Questions" article, Schmidt and Hunter argued that: (a) when you are right, you can make strong statements, (b) unless psychologists make strong statements, their work will be trivialized by socio-political bodies, and (c) their form of expression is protected by the first amendment and they don't plan to change it anytime soon. There is evidence that Schmidt and Hunter continue to exercise their constitutional right of unrestrained expression. Consider two quotes, one 10 years ago and one 2 years ago. When describing the likely impact of meta-analysis of research in I/O psychology, Schmidt (1992) opined as follows: "Traditional procedures for data analysis and interpretation in individual studies and in research literatures have hampered the development of cumulative knowledge" (p. 1180). One is left to wonder if he meant all, some, or the occasional "traditional procedure"—and what he meant by "traditional procedures." But he went on: "There will be the traditional researchers and the meta-analysts, and the *meta-analysts will make the scientific discoveries*" (p. 1180).

More recently, Schmidt and Hunter (1998) published a review of 85 years worth of validity and utility research. Interestingly, they conclude that there is life beyond general mental ability and that increments in validity (and presumably utility) can be realized from including additional predictors in your tool bag. Never mind the fact that this seems a bit of a retreat from their earlier position regarding *g* as the only tool one might need in a bag. What is interesting is their position on *g* from an analytic perspective. They demonstrated that the validity of a test battery can be enhanced by adding assessment supplements, in the form of other tests or procedures. They use multiple regression techniques to show the validity increments. But *g* is always considered the core or primary element. They said: "Because of its special status, GMA can be considered the primary personnel measure for hiring decisions, and one can consider the remaining 18 personnel measures as supplements to GMA measures" (p. 271). This is a "strong statement" given the results of other meta-analyses directed toward these "supplements," some of which have shown levels of validity comparable to or higher than that achieved by cognitive ability tests. It also ignores completely the elephant in the room: the criterion problem. Suppose you did not want to predict whatever the rater had in mind when he or she was rating "overall job performance." What would happen to the "primary personnel measure" if one was more interested in contextual performance? Would GMA still be at the top of the scale?

It is this unwillingness to acknowledge even the possibility that they may be wrong or incomplete that has fueled much of the controversy surrounding VG. To be sure, even without the Schmidt and Hunter style, VG would have been a new and uncomfortable doctrine for many to grasp, after so many years of situationism. And VG would also have been threatening to plaintiff lawyers versed in attacks on single validation studies. But perhaps all of this would have played itself out somewhat differently if it had been approached as a complex and powerful paradigm, a paradigm to be studied and understood rather than as test of wills and intellect.

1985: 40 QUESTIONS AND 17 ANSWERS

By the mid-1980s, there were few personnel psychologists who were not aware of the concept of VG or the controversy surrounding it. Personnel Psychology agreed to publish a series of questions and answers that captured the confusion and controversy at the time (1985). A total of 40 questions were posed to the team of Schmidt, Hunter, Pearlman, and Hirsch. Each answer was then considered by the team of Sackett, Schmitt, Tenopyr, Kehoe, and Zedeck (1985). The Schmidt team was then permitted a rebuttal.

This was a good idea and did much to clarify the issues as well as come to some understanding of where were agreements and disagreements. Of the 40 questions and answers, a total of 17 received commentary from the Sackett team, and several of those commentaries were in agreement with the answer but extended the answer or raised a previously unconsidered question. Thus, the Schmidt team answers to 23 or more of those questions were considered adequate. This high level of agreement would seem to belie any controversy, but that does not capture the essence of this published debate. Also, it ignores the fact that most of the 40 questions were actually posed by Schmidt and Hunter, so in one sense, it was a bit like putting a bullet hole in a wall then drawing a bull's eye around it. This may also account for the fact that none of the Schmidt and Hunter answers were "We don't know."

In the debate format, Schmidt and Hunter were required to state more clearly than ever before exactly what VG was all about. In doing so, some things became obvious that had not been obvious before. First and foremost, it was clear that VG was understood differently by different people. It became clear that there were a number of hypotheses that were encompassed in the VG paradigm, some embraced by Schmidt and Hunter, and others simply (and often, wrongly) attributed to Schmidt and Hunter. The first, and possibly most important hypothesis addressed the population estimate for the validity of cognitive ability tests for a wide range of occupations. Was it .00 or positive and significant? Schmidt and Hunter considered this to one of the central hypotheses addressed by meta-analytic techniques. The data showed that the null hypothesis (i.e.,

p = .00) could be confidently rejected. Keep in mind that, at least in part, by rejecting this hypothesis, one could also reject the situational validity implication that in some instances, cognitive ability tests were not valid predictors of job performance. But again, only if we think of validity as a binary state. If the population correlation coefficient between a test and some acceptable performance measure is .02 after all of the corrections are made, and we have collected enough data to reliably distinguish between .00 and .02, the test can be seen as valid in the binary sense. But this is a far cry from the suggestion that an employer might save millions of dollars in personnel costs by using this test of cognitive ability.

The second hypothesis was another variation on the situational validity doctrine. It might be stated as follows: Cognitive ability tests are *equally* valid for all jobs. Schmidt and Hunter (Schmidt et al., 1985) explicitly disowned this hypothesis and reminded their audience that what they *could* conclude was that ". . . all cognitive abilities have some (substantial) degree of validity for all job families" (p. 713). There was a related hypothesis that readers and listeners inferred from the work of Schmidt and Hunter. It was the hypothesis that no predictors *other than* cognitive ability test would prove useful (i.e., valid) for personnel selection. Schmidt et al. disowned this hypothesis as well: "While it is our conclusion that further validation research for certain test-job combinations would be of limited usefulness, we have actually encouraged the search for 'additional valid predictors of job performance' " (Schmidt et al., 1985, p. 734).

In fact, Schmidt and Hunter (1998) have continued to affirm this position by examining the validity of integrity tests and a broad range of additional potential predictors. Nevertheless, Schmidt and Hunter continue to assert primary status for cognitive ability tests. It is also noteworthy that Schmidt et al. used the phrase ". . . for certain test-job combinations. . . ." This was an acknowledgment that there might be a world beyond the GATB, or the job of computer programmer or clerk that could benefit from more traditional (albeit better designed) validity studies.

So, at least in part, some members of the scientist and practitioner audience were disagreeing with propositions that Schmidt and Hunter had never explicitly endorsed. To be fair, a less than careful reader of previous work of Schmidt and his colleagues might have inferred such strong positions with respect to cognitive ability tests, but the "40 Questions" more clearly framed the various hypotheses. In all fairness to the "reader" however, Schmidt and Hunter were not always precise in what was intended when they used the term *valid*. This was a side effect of their decision to take "strong" positions.

In summary, the effect of the 40 questions and answers was to re-place some heat with some light. Both protagonists and antagonists got a lot of their chests, stepped back and took a breath. More im-portantly, the debate identified areas that all concerned agreed needed some attention. Many of those areas are covered in great de-tail in other chapters of this book.

In the preceding pages, I present an admittedly idiosyncratic and personal recounting of the forces at play between the beginnings of personnel psychology and the publication of the 1985 debate on VG. In the sections that will follow, I present what I see as the impact of VG on three different domains—science, public policy and litigation, and practice.

SCIENCE

The scientific potential for meta-analysis, generally and VG applica-tions specifically was recognized almost immediately. Most text-books written after the publications of the Schmidt et al. (1973), Boehm (1977), and Schmidt and Hunter (1978) research on the concept of differential validity had sections addressing the effect of statistical artifacts on observed validity coefficients. The general theme of the coverage was positive, suggesting that validity results seemed unaffected by subgroup membership. An example can be seen in a text I authored in 1980 with Don Trumbo (Landy & Trumbo, 1980):

> In the late 1960's and early 1970's, there were many articles pur-porting to demonstrate "differential validity," i.e., situations in which a test was valid for one group (usually a majority group) but not for another group (usually a minority group). . . . Schmidt and his colleagues (Schmidt, Berner, & Hunter, 1973; Hunter & Schmidt, 1978) have been able to demonstrate that these differ-ences in validity can be just as easily attributed to statistical arti-facts as to real differences between majority and minority groups . . . it is safe to say that substantially different validities for majority and minority samples is probably a lot less common than we thought. (pp. 93–95)

By 1985, I had identified meta-analysis as a major conceptual and analytic breakthrough:

> The second analytic technique to receive attention is called meta-analysis. If you read the research literature, you will find dozens,

sometimes hundreds of studies on the same general topic. Each study is done with a different subject sample, a different sample size, and often a different observational or experimental environment. . . . How are all of those studies to be considered? Should each study be considered by itself, should the 'best' study be identified and used for explanatory purposes, or can studies somehow be averaged to yield a general conclusion? Meta-analysis is a specific technique for averaging the results of many studies on the same topic. There are several good sources which describe the techniques of meta-analysis (Glass, 1976; Hunter, Schmidt and Jackson, 1982). . . . In the next few years, meta-analysis will become a more common technique for inference and theory building. (Landy, 1985, pp. 38–39)

By 1989, I had narrowed the discussion of meta-analysis to applications involving VG.

A very specific application of meta-analysis that is becoming quite important in personnel testing is called *validity generalization*. In this application, a statistical analysis is done to determine if there differences between patterns of associations noticed in several different studies mean that the actual relationship changes from one location to another, or that there are other variables (e.g., sample size) that could account for these differences. As you can see, meta-analysis permits us to exercise statistical control over third variables that might be obscuring a relationship. (Landy, 1989, p. 44)

I then followed that introduction with an extensive review of the current status, indicating that there was disagreement between the "strong" advocates of VG and those who were more cautious, and concluded by pointing out what the next decade might look like:

It is clear that validity generalization is a concept that will be with us for some time to come. There is sufficient confirmation in studies conducted by Schmidt and his colleagues to warrant acceptance of the basic propositions. Further, it is clear that it has clear and important policy implications. As an example, the National Research Council (the operational unit of the National Academy of Sciences) has just begun a substantial evaluation of the General Aptitude Test Battery (GATB), a test used widely for public sector employment decisions, to determine the extent to which validity information currently available for 400 job titles can be generalized to a full range of 12,000 job titles.
    . . . Thus, within a few years, there should be a definitive answer to the questions raised in the VG debate. Keep in mind, however, that the issue is not whether the basic propositions of VG are reason-

able—they are. The issue is how far these propositions can be stretched and what the implications will be for the conduct of validity studies. (Landy, 1993, p. 83)

Had I done another revision of my textbook in 1993 or 1994, I am not sure what I might have said to the undergraduate audience, but I did publish an Annual Review Chapter in 1994 (Landy, Shankster, & Kohler, 1994) that addressed the issue. Because this publication was devoted to a more statistically sophisticated audience, I could be more detailed in my comments about meta-analysis, generally, and about VG specifically.

Further, we see meta-analysis, if suitably grounded in constructs, as *a* method for theory development not *the* method. Meta-analysis and traditional empirical research should be complementary and not competitors. In some situations, meta-analysis can illuminate where traditional single study research cannot, but meta-analysis depends heavily on the topics researchers choose to study, the designs employed to study those phenomena, the operations chosen to define the variables, etc. (p. 286)

As a final note, it might be helpful to consider an assumption implicit in much of the validity generalization discussion—that jobs and roles within organizations are crystallized rather than dynamic. Ilgen (1993) suggests that this may no longer be true (if it ever was), which means that even if we accept the viability of validity generalization as a post dictive device, its potential for predictive accuracy may be limited by the nature of work. (p. 287)

A second challenge is understanding the limits of meta-analytic approaches to theory building and testing. The meta-analytic approach cannot and should not be deified. It is a powerful and illuminating procedure but will always be an aid and never a substitute for logic. Regardless of the claims of the meta-analysis proponents, traditional researchers and theoreticians should stay the course and collaborate, rather than compete or accept second-tier status. (p. 289)

In reviewing my contemporaneous views of VG from a scientific perspective through my published comments and comparing and contrasting my views with those held by other text authors and Annual Review authors, it is relatively easy to trace the trajectory of VG from the late 70's to the mid 90's. Early on, there was a rather immediate recognition of the value of meta-analytic techniques for addressing some vexing issues in validity analyses (e.g., differential prediction). The length of the honeymoon was extended when VG was applied to the GATB data base by Schmidt and his colleagues (Schmidt & Hunter, 1978). But by the mid-1980s, the honeymoon was over. Serious reservations were expressed in various Annual Review Chapters (e.g., Zedeck & Cascio, 1984) and by the late 1980s, even undergraduate texts were sending the message that the jury was still out on the extent to which VG might be applied to issues of personnel selection. It is interesting to note that since the early 90's, there has been a trend toward separating VG from the early claims and propositions of Schmidt and Hunter (1978) (e.g., no moderators of cognitive ability, no attributes of any predictive value beyond g, etc.) VG research has shown that test validities are larger and more stable than I/O psychologists had previously thought and that testing is likely to have a meaningful and positive impact on organizations. If there are any cautions expressed now, they are cautions about the early claims of Schmidt and Hunter rather than about the contribution of meta-analysis and VG conceptually.

Meta-analytic procedures are now being widely applied to many different areas of research, both in I/O and in other areas of psychology. Hardly a month goes by when one or another I/O journal does not publish a meta-analytic study. As an example, in 2001, the Journal of Applied Psychology published meta-analytic studies of the following phenomena:

- Risk propensity differences between entrepreneurs and managers
- The relationship of core self evaluation traits
- Organizational justice research
- The Guilty Knowledge Test
- Job Search and Employment
- The Employment Interview
- Gender Differences in Perceptions of Sexual Harassment

From the scientific perspective the wide and broad use of meta-analysis generate concerns that are paralleled in the VG area. The first of these concerns is that analytic techniques may seduce researchers and make original research less attractive. It is clear that if no original research is done, there is a point of diminishing returns. There are only so many extant pieces of research to review. There is also the temporal problem. The studies (and more importantly the work situations they examine) have a half-life. Until the mid-1980s, most jobs were solitary rather than social. That has changed. Until the mid-1980s, computers were tools used by specialists. That has changed. Until the mid-1980s, most client contact occurred between sales reps and customers. That has changed. In short, work has changed, often dramatically. No matter how many or what variety of meta-analytic studies are conducted on work as it existed 30 years ago, it is unlikely that such an analysis will tell us all we need to know about work of today (or more importantly, tomorrow). An additional concern is that VG and other meta-analytic results may be viewed as theory. This would be a serious problem. In the beginning of the century, psychometricians such as Cattell were often the butt of ridicule by social observers who likened intelligence testing to a man who had lost his wallet on a dark street and gone to an adjacent street with overhead lights to look for it. The criticism was that testing was done simply because tests were available. The same may be feared of meta-analysis. Bobko and Stone-Romero (1998) painted a bleak picture of a research world dominated by meta-analyses, very different from that envisioned by Schmidt (1992) when he proclaimed that, ". . . meta-analysts will make the scientific discoveries." In some senses, Schmidt's view is similar to Cattell's earlier faith in the data he gathered from incoming freshmen at Penn and Columbia—a theory of intelligence would somehow emerge from the mass of data. Data and their analysis are certainly part of inductive reasoning (and theory building), but not the definition of induction. The 40's and 50's have been characterized as the period of dust bowl empiricism for I/O psychology. We must be cautious that we do not fall into dust bowl empiricism *redux* as a result of the current enchantment with meta-analysis. Campbell (1990) expressed this caution elegantly, and very early in the VG and meta-analytic debate:

> It should be obvious that validity generalization is much more than a meta-analysis of existing data, or simply a refutation of the situational specificity hypothesis. It forces us to confront our operative theories of predictors and models of performance, or at least it should. To conduct validity generalization meta-analyses without this kind of conceptual specification is to practice blind dust bowl empiricism. (p. 722)

Bobko and Stone-Romero (1998) noted that as a result of the proliferation of meta-analytic studies, it is not uncommon to find two meta-analyses on the same subject matter that disagree on conclusions. This is ironic given that the goal of meta-analysis was to eliminate the subjectivity and bias that often arose in drawing inferences from more traditional literature reviews. These differences are often attributed to factors such as differing research covered, statistical treatments, and different (or largely undefined) dependent or criterion variables. The similarity of these explanations for discrepant conclusions to those proposed by Katzell (1957) to settle the Brayfield–Herzberg controversy regarding the satisfaction–performance relationship is startling. It is tempting to conclude we have come full circle. One could make the case that there is as much subjectivity and bias in meta-analyses as there was in traditional literature reviews. But with meta-analysis, at least there is the appearance of precision. Bobko and Stone-Romero concluded with the apocalyptic vision of "meta-analyses of meta-analyses" to examine differences across meta-analyses. Well, the apocalypse is upon us. As an example, Hermelin and Robertson (2001) did just that. They conducted a meta-analysis of various population validity estimates in the personnel selection research. In addition they use a set of standardizing procedures for assessing the likelihood that there are possible moderator variables present in the data (which would re-introduce at least some modest version of situational validity). Like Schmidt and Hunter, Hermelin and Roberston concluded that most well developed modern assessment procedures and devices are valid (i.e., do not include an r value of .00 in the confidence interval). Contrary to the fears of Bobko and Stone-Romero, this super meta-analysis is quite helpful, generating some exciting hints at possible moderators, while still affirming the most basic proposition of VG—the significant and positive population validity estimate for many commonly used selection procedures.

In summary, there is reason for both optimism and pessimism with respect to the current status of VG in the scientific community. The optimistic view is that some very powerful analytic tools are now widely understood and applied. These tools are helping researchers to understand heretofore confusing phenomena and data sets. It seems clear, as expressed by Guion (1998), that there is room for both general laws and situational theories in the personnel decision making arena. The pessimism is rooted in the fear that (well conducted) original research will be seen as less valuable than meta-analyses of less well conducted research or that meta-analytic results are substitutes for theory. It appears that there is still a great deal more potential energy in the VG arena now than there is kinetic energy.

VG AND PROFESSIONAL AND LEGAL STANDARDS

As should be obvious by now, VG is not simply or solely a scientific issue. By the mid-1980s, VG had entered the mainstream of public policy discussions in the form of initiatives being contemplated federal agencies as well as in employment discrimination litigation. The federal initiative revolved around the pairing of VG and the GATB for applicants processed through the United States Employment Service. Discussions of VG in the employment litigation arena usually involved the application of sets of standards, guidelines, or "authorities".

There were two sets of guidelines promulgated by scientific bodies. One set was published by a coalition including the American Psychological Association (APA), The American Educational Research Association, and the National Council on Measurement in Education and was intended to be a broad set of principles governing the use of psychological and educational tests in a wide variety of settings, including settings involving personnel selection. This document is known by the name "Standards for Educational and Psychological Testing." These standards were first published in 1954 but given the recency of the VG phenomenon, we need only be concerned with editions of the Standards that have appeared since 1974. The other set of professional guidelines was first published by the Division of Industrial and Organizational Psychology of the APA in 1975. These guidelines were titled "Principles for the Validation and Use of Personnel Selection Procedures" and have been revised three times since their initial appearance. The third edition of these principles was published by the Society for Industrial and Organizational Psychology (SIOP) and in recent history have been referred to as the SIOP Principles, a convention adopted for the current discussion.

A third set of guidelines was published by a coalition of Federal agencies to cover topics related to employee selection. These guidelines were titled the "Uniform Guidelines on Employee Selection Procedures" and were published in 1978. These are usually referred to as the "Uniform Guidelines" They have never been revised. The simplest way to examine the evolving understanding of VG viewed through these standards is to track the changes in the treatment of VG by the subsequent revisions of the APA Standards and the SIOP Principles.

The Uniform Guidelines

With respect to the Uniform Guidelines, the task is a simple one. Because the Guidelines have never been revised, we simply need to examine what they said about VG. The Uniform Guidelines, of course, are at a disadvantage since most of the serious work and modifications of VG occurred after these guidelines were published. The Guidelines say nothing *directly* about VG. Instead, they refer to the situation in which one wants to use "Evidence from Validity of Other Studies" (Section 15E of the Guidelines). It seems clear from a reading of that section that the authors of the Guidelines had not contemplated VG in its final form. Instead, this section of the Guidelines really addresses the narrower issue of "Validity Transport," a method for demonstrating that two situations are sufficiently similar such that validity documented in one situation can be inferred for the other situation. The described procedures for accomplishing this transport are daunting and seem to contemplate a one-off application of the test used in Situation A for Situation B. This includes a careful matching of selection instruments, job duties, etcetera. Hardly the "job families" and tests of g that formed the foundation for the initial articulation of VG. Further, in the questions and answers that followed the publication of the Uniform Guidelines (1978), it seems clear that the doctrine of situational validity was alive and well in the minds of those who would enforce these guidelines.

> 43. Q. Can a selection procedure be a valid predictor of performance on a job in a certain location and be invalid for predicting success on a different job or the same job in a different location?

> A. Yes. Because of differences in work behaviors, criterion measures, study samples of other factors, a selection procedure found to have validity in one situation does not necessarily have validity in different circumstances. Conversely . . .

As is true in most of life, timing is everything. The Guidelines were simply published before most of the conceptual, statistical, and operational issues surrounding VG had been articulated. You can be sure that if the Uniform Guidelines are ever revised, VG will get a good deal of attention.

The APA Standards

Although the APA Standards of 1974 did not specifically refer to the analytic practices that have come to be known as validity generalization, they did inadvertently adopt a standard that was in direct contradiction to what would become accepted practice in VG. The 1974 Standards cautioned against the correction of observed validity coefficients for criterion unreliability and range restriction. These two artifacts, along with sample size, define the principle analytic tools of VG. So, to the extent to which they said anything about VG, the

1974 Standards would have been opposed to the concept. As was the case with the Uniform Guidelines, the development of the data base, logic and operational postdated the 1974 Standards so the fact that VG is not mentioned is hardly noteworthy.

When the APA Standards were revised in 1985, however, VG was explicitly recognized. A section was devoted to VG (p. 12) that allows for the possibility that "if generalization is extensive, then situation specific evidence of validity may not be required." Standard 1.16 allows for the use of VG, but in a reluctant manner. It states that when "Adequate local validation evidence is not available . . . test use may be based on validity generalization. . . ." The implication is that if local validity evidence *is available*, then the local validation is preferred. This standard also implies that if VG has already been accomplished for a class of tests, you should not conduct a local study because it really will not help you, and it might lead you to disregard the VG evidence. In fact, if meta-analysis and VG show anything, it is that when VG evidence and local validation evidence are both available (and conflict), the VG evidence may be the preferred data set. (Brannick & Hall, chap. 12, this volume, present Bayesian methods for combining evidence from VG with local evidence to reach conclusions about how well a test is likely to work in a given situation). In Standard 1.17, there is an endorsement of corrections for statistical artifacts which states that if corrections are made, both corrected and uncorrected values must be reported. It would be fair to conclude that the revision of corrections stance was a direct result of VG research and debate.

The latest revision of the APA Standards was published in 1999. There is a dramatic change in tone on the topic of VG. It is no longer suggested that local validation studies are to be preferred. In fact, the standards clearly recognize the potential limitations of single studies. They simply allow for the conduct of a single study if adequate data are available. They suggest that the relative value of local validation studies versus meta-analytic studies be considered when choosing a basis for inferring validity or job relatedness. Standards 1.20 and 1.21 are sophisticated treatments of the strength and limitations of meta-analysis and VG. As an aside, in Standard 1.18, it is now acknowledged that "Statistical methods . . . for adjusting the correlation . . ." for range restriction and criterion unreliability are ". . . often appropriate, as when comparing results across various situations." One can only imagine Richard Seymour's reaction to the fact that hydraulic corrections are now accepted by APA.

It is fair to conclude that the current APA Standards provide support without undue reservation to the principles embodied by VG.

The SIOP Principles

By 1975, Title VII of the Civil Rights Act of 1964 had resulted in substantial employment litigation and there was confusion and disagreement about almost all issues related to "professionally accepted" standards for establishing job relatedness. Although the APA Standards could be examined, they were more general and in some cases, at odds with accepted practice in the I/O community. As a result, in 1975, the Division of Industrial-Organizational Psychology of the APA (Division 14) published a set of principles that might be used to examine the adequacy of personnel selection procedures. Division 14 incorporated some years later as the Society for Industrial and Organizational Psychology (SIOP) and later revisions of these Principles have come to be known as the SIOP Principles (Principles). The Principles have been revised twice (1980 and 1987) and the 4th edition is currently in draft form, to appear by 2003. By tracking the treatment of VG across the various editions of the Principles, we can get some sense of the evolution of the concept.

In the 1975 Principles, VG was addressed from the narrower perspective of validity transport. The Principles stated that, "Validity evidence obtained in one unit of a multi-unit organization may be applied in other units where jobs and job settings are essentially similar." But then the Principles go on to state that, "Validity coefficients are obtained in specific situation. *They apply only to those situations*" (p. 13, ital added). This latter position simply reflects the vestiges of prior situational validity thinking. Further evidence of the tenuous position of VG in 1975 comes from a section of the Principles dealing with criterion-related validity evidence. "Where traditional criterion-related validation is not feasible, the psychologist should consider alternative strategies . . . examples include "synthetic" validation, or cooperative research plans such as industry wide validation, consortia of small users, or generalization of validity. Such activities call for some pioneering research, and they are not to be undertaken lightly" (p. 6). In a later section, the principles revisit the situational validity doctrine in discussing "moderator variables." They direct that "the analysis should, when reasonable and feasible, investigate the possibility of moderating effects . . . such . . . as . . . ethnic group, socio-economic status, age, sex, cognitive styles, etc." (p. 8). They qualify this suggestion by stating that, ". . . this approach has not been found to improve validity appreciably." In the Glossary section of the 1975 Principles, there is no entry for VG.

It seems clear from the 1975 Principles that what was contemplated by VG was prospective research with multiunit organizations or consortia. There is no guidance with respect to the retrospective re-analyses that were part of meta-analytic procedures. In contrast to the 1974 APA Standards, however, the Principles did acknowledge the need and propriety for correcting observed validity coefficients for statistical influences in the form of criterion unreliability and range restriction.

By 1980, VG had moved onto most radar screens and was afforded a more detailed treatment in the Principles revision published that year. An expanded section entitled "Generality of Validation Efforts" included a subsection titled "Validity Generalization." In this section, the Principles acknowledge that, ". . . empirical data (find) . . . that much of the difference in observed outcomes of validation research is due to statistical artifacts" (pp. 15–16). Nevertheless, the Principles still seem to envision generalization built primarily on prospective research rather than meta-analysis of existing data: "Cooperative validation efforts being carried on by a number of trade and industry associations will provide the data necessary for evaluation. Such cooperative efforts are to be applauded and encouraged" (p. 16). There was also an entry in the glossary section of the 1980 Principles for VG but it also seems to lean heavily toward the narrower issue of validity transport between highly similar settings.

Validity Generalization: the transportability of validity evidence; the application of validity evidence obtained in one or more situations to other situations.

The 1980 Principles repeat the statement that "Where traditional Criterion-Related Validation is Not Feasible . . ." that the researcher consider alternative methodologies, including ". . . gathering data for validity generalization." But warn that, ". . . most non-traditional approaches require considerable research and development effort." One might infer from these statements that VG is an alternative only when "traditional criterion related strategy is not feasible."

There was a substantial increase in the sophistication of the treatment of VG in the 1987 Principles. The 1987 Principles no longer considered the traditional criterion-related design to be primary and VG as an alternative to the traditional design. The Principles now stated that, "The researcher may consider alternative criterion-related research methods that offer a sound rational . . . including . . . gathering data for validity generalization" but caution the researcher to exercise ". . . care in ascertaining the appropriateness of the data included from different sources" (p. 14).

VG was given the status of a major heading in a later lengthy section of the Principles. In this section, the Principles largely abandon the classic situational validity doctrine, but point out that most of the VG efforts have been devoted to cognitive ability tests and that explorations of other test-job combinations were becoming more common. In a very important departure from earlier treatments, the 1987 Principles describe two conditions for invoking VG for a particular predictor or predictor type:

> a) that situational differences have little or no effect on operational (or true) validities *or* [italics added] b)that true validities of measures of the construct or of the predictor type have acceptably low probabilities of falling below specified values in new settings.

There are a number of important implications of these two conditions. Notice that VG is acceptable if either of the two conditions are met, both conditions are not required. These conditions implicitly recognize the two different aspects of VG research. The first is the demonstration of the absence of moderator variables. The second is the affirmation that the operational (or true) validity coefficient not include the value of .00 in the confidence interval. The glossary entry for VG in the 1987 Principles was slightly broadened but largely unchanged from the earlier edition.

The newest (draft) version of the SIOP Principles is by far the most sophisticated treatment to date. VG is addressed in a section entitled "Meta-Analysis" but the tone and the acceptance of the principles of VG are largely unchanged from earlier editions. Nevertheless, the draft Principles added two very important points for consideration. The first is that there is little meta-analytic data available for helping draw inferences about the optimal *combination* of procedures or devices. In addition, researchers accessing meta-analytic data are cautioned not to confuse a meta-analysis of a procedure (e.g., the structured interview) with a meta-analysis related to a construct (e.g., conscientiousness or cognitive ability). Both of these points are addressed in the concluding section of this chapter.

In summary, the SIOP Principles, in various revisions, can be seen to accurately mirror the growing understanding of the strengths and weaknesses of meta-analysis applied to observed validity coefficients. Both the 1987 and the current draft Principles provide perhaps the best guidance of any existing authority for purposes of evaluating a given VG application. The most recent APA Standards, although somewhat less detailed, also express support for VG. As demonstrated in some representative court cases, the Uniform Guidelines are largely out of touch with modern VG, although some of the underlying principles are addressed (e.g., validity transport, correction for statistical artifacts, etc.). Nevertheless, any attempts to find direction in the guidelines with respect to VG is doomed to failure. They were issued before the most serious and illuminating work on this concept was available.

CASE LAW

Compared to the attention VG has received in the scientific community, it has received scant treatment in court cases. In part, of course, this is because few employers have raised VG as a defense for particular tests or test types. Meta-analysis is becoming a more common case phenomenon and in some respects, is emerging as a legal or statistical tool in much the way that multiple regression did several decades ago. Nevertheless, VG has been invoked directly in several cases, and indirectly in others.

In a 1977 case involving the Richmond, Virginia fire Department (*Friend et al. v. Leidinger et al.*), a major issue related to the extent to which a validity study conducted in one setting could be used to support the use of a test in another setting (i.e., the doctrine of situational validity). The trial judge offered the opinion that:

> . . . the job of a fireman in Richmond is very similar to the job of a fireman in certain California cities . . . the Court concludes that the City of Richmond carried its burden of showing the Firefighters B1(m) test to be job related by proof that the test had been validated . . . in a validation study in California, and that proof that the job for which the test was validated was substantially the same as the job for which the test was being used in Richmond. (p. 369)

The following year, the Court of Appeals upheld that conclusion and stated that:

> A part of the validation study was done in California and plaintiffs objected to a study not conducted in Richmond. However, plaintiffs have shown no difference in the duties of a fireman in the 55 areas of California where the test was validated, from the duties of a Richmond fireman. To require local validation in every city, village and hamlet would be ludicrous. (p. 65)

So it appears that both the trial Judge and the Appeals Court endorsed the concept of validity transportability if the test were identical and the jobs demonstrably similar.

In 1982, a reverse discrimination case was brought by White firefighter applicants who were rejected by the City of Detroit fire department (*Van Aken et al. v. Young et al.*). They were claiming that the written examination scores should have been used in a strict rank-ordered fashion to make academy appointments rather than the out-of-rank appointment process used by the city. Jack Hunter was the expert witness for the White firefighters and used VG arguments as the foundation for his opinion that the written test score should have been used in a top down appointment manner. Hunter also invoked utility principles as a show of business necessity and opined that the City of Detroit would save approximately $39 million in 30 years by using the test in the way he suggested. The Court ruled against the White applicants and noted that:

> Hunter was completely destroyed on cross examination. He admitted he knew nothing specific about the Detroit Fire Department and its curriculum. . . . He was unable to explain how a person in a wheelchair, who could get the highest grade on the examination, could be an active firefighter. He further testified that there was a high correlation between cognitive ability and the ability to be a good lemon picker. Most of Hunter's testimony lacked credibility, and the Court is completely disregarding it. (p. 454)

In this case, a major issue for the court was the seeming unfamiliarity of the expert with the job in question. The point seemed to be that at a minimum, VG would require that someone be able to make the link between the VG data base and the job in question. Hunter did not do that to the satisfaction of the Court. It was also obvious from the Court's comparison of lemon pickers to firefighters, that the broader applications of VG seemed implausible. From Hunter's perspective, the Court had completely missed the point of VG. Because he believed that he had shown that cognitive ability was important for all jobs, it was unnecessary to demonstrate that it was "valid" for a particular job. As a result, detailed hands-on knowledge of a particular job was largely irrelevant.

In 1983, in a case titled *Pegues v. Mississippi State Employment Service*, the trial Judge referred to the testimony of Jack Hunter for the defendants in that case and concluded that:

> Empirical research has demonstrated that validity is not perceptibly changed by differences in location, differences in specific job duties

or applicant populations. Valid tests do not become invalid when these circumstances change. Plaintiff's allegation that validity is specific to a particular location, a particular set of tasks, and to a specific applicant population, or in other words, that a valid test in one set of circumstances is not valid in another, is not true. . . . According to research, even gross changes in Job duties did not destroy validity. It follows that small and/or hypothesized differences have little or no effect on validity. Plaintiffs have not shown that the USES tests (in this case the GATB), were invalid because the tasks of the jobs in the research setting may have been different from those in Bolivar County. (p. 1136)

These conclusions widen the reach of transportability considerably, and they were based on Hunter's testimony about the GATB VG research. Once again, situational specificity was rejected by the judge.

In another case begun in 1983 and concluded in 1987 against the Consolidated Rail Corporation (*Cox v. Consolidated Rail Corporation*), a claim was made that the engineering training program (ETP) discriminated against Black trainees. The court found the training program to be content valid and mentioned VG in passing. In fact, this was a straightforward transportability study in which results from the study of the locomotive engineer position at another rail company (Burlington Northern) was shown to be relevant for the Conrail position.

In a case brought by the Equal Employment Opportunity Commission (EEOC) against the Atlas Paper Box Company in 1987, Jack Hunter testified about the validity of the Wonderlic test, offering the opinion that it was a standard cognitive ability test, and as such, could be assumed (through the VG research) to have validity in its application by Atlas. The trial judge was also of the opinion that the sample sizes available for a criterion-related validation study at Atlas would have been too small to provide any meaningful results, again suggesting the value of the VG support for the Wonderlic. Two years later, the Sixth Circuit Court of Appeals firmly rejected the VG argument:

The expert witness offered by the defendant, John Hunter, failed to visit and inspect the Atlas office and never studied the nature and the content of the Atlas clerical and office jobs involved. The validity of the generalization theory utilized by Atlas with respect to this expert testimony under these circumstances is not appropriate. Linkage or similarity of jobs in dispute in this case must be shown by such on site investigation to justify application of such a theory.

In a concurring but separate opinion, one of the judges offered the following thoughts:

> The first major problem with a validity generalization approach is that it is radically at odds with Albemarle Paper Co v. Moody . . . and Griggs v. Duke Power and the EEOC Guidelines, all of which require as showing that a test is actually predictive of performance at a specific job. (1989, p. 1499)

> As a matter of law, Hunter's validity generalization theory is totally unacceptable under relevant case law and professional standards. (p. 1501)

It is important to note here that there is a "pecking order" with regard to the importance of judicial decisions. In the federal judicial system, the trial court is where the case is actually heard. If the case is appealed on a procedural issue, it goes to a Circuit Court of Appeals. It may also be appealed on constitutional grounds to the Supreme Court. A Circuit Court of Appeals opinion carries a great deal more weight (i.e., it establishes broader application of law) than a trial court opinion. It is binding within the particular Circuit and influential in other Circuits. Similarly, a Supreme Court decision is binding across all circuits and trial courts. This makes the Sixth Circuit Atlas decision particularly daunting for VG application. Thus, in this case, the doctrine of situational validation was accepted and VG rejected.

In 1989, a case alleging racial discrimination in promotions was brought against the James River Corporation (*Taylor v. James River Corporation*). The court accepted the job relatedness evidence provided by the defendant, and simply mentioned in passing that "The principles of the American Psychological Association endorse the validity generalization strategy used by Dr. Nowlin." In this case, the use of the term *validity generalization* was a stretch. In fact, the defendants had provided a combination of content and construct information as support for the test battery.

We can conclude several things from the review of this sampling of cases. The most telling conclusion is that VG is not often introduced. The chilling language of the Atlas decision is certainly one reason. When a Circuit Court of Appeals concludes that *as a matter of law* practice is unacceptable, lawyers tend to listen. Although judges do seem to grasp the narrower concept of validity transport, and allow for its application, there seems to be a strong desire to see direct links between the jobs under consideration and the data base from which the transport will occur. In the few instances in which

VG was actually addressed (as opposed to validity transport), it has not fared well.

In summary, it appears that VG has been largely a nonevent in influencing case law. Further, it appears that anyone considering the possibility of invoking VG as the sole defense for a test or test type might want to seriously consider including additional defenses (e.g., transportability analyses) and would be well advised to know the essential duties of the job in question, and in its local manifestation, well. Persuasive expert testimony will be required to bridge the gap between VG and a specific practice.

VG AND THE PRACTICE OF PERSONNEL SELECTION

As described in earlier sections of the chapter, in the early 1980's, VG promised a new era for personnel selection. For many job titles (e.g., clerical, computer programmer), there was the possibility of using an off-the-shelf test of cognitive ability without the need for local validation. In its grandest form, VG might not even require a job analysis because Schmidt and his colleagues asserted that *g* was important for virtually every job and job family. In this idealized world, one might simply refer to a tabled value as the reported validity coefficient for that application. A slightly more sophisticated treatment would be to report the confidence interval for that value and allow the user to determine the utility at various points along that interval. Taking an expansive view, one might extend the application to include similar tabled values for noncognitive predictors, although for certain attributes (e.g., personality characteristics), one might need separate tables for specific jobs or job families.

The fact is that every employer, and the I/O practitioner who was retained by an employer, was wary of any larger scale application of VG. The debate surrounding VG was a very public one. In addition, one attempt at large scale application of VG by the United States Employment Service (see chap. 2 for a more detailed description of this initiative), was caught up in a political maelstrom resulting from the use of separate norms for White and Black GATB test takers but this political debate had virtually nothing to do with VG itself. Had it not been for the issue of separate norming, it is likely that the political roles in the debate would have been reversed, with broad support for GATB referrals from the right, and concern from the left. Thus, although a trial court had ruled in 1983 that VG was an acceptable foundation for documenting job relatedness, other trial courts and one circuit court were more skeptical. Which practitioner would have the courage to suggest a VG approach to an employer in the face of a ruling that stated in unequivocal terms that, ". . . as a matter of law, VG is inappropriate?" (p. 1501).

Nevertheless, the body of VG research did have a number of enduring effects on practice. The most obvious was the conclusion that virtually every job and job family depended, at least to some statistically significant amount, on cognitive ability for successful performance. As a result, most practitioners are now quite confident in recommending that a test battery for selection include a test of cognitive ability. It is ironic, however, that this recommendation is made *after* a job analysis has been completed. Although the practitioner could have recommended the cognitive ability test without the job analysis, in an abundance of caution, the job analysis is still completed. But it is not uncommon for the practitioner to simply document that there are cognitive tasks and then use the accumulated VG research base as the foundation or showing of job relatedness for the inclusion of the cognitive ability test. In practice, it would appear, at least with respect to the recommendation for a cognitive test, that the job analysis is simply cosmetic. So what we are seeing is a hybrid of VG and the narrower version of validity transport. In a traditional transportability study, the practitioner would establish a link between the job under consideration and a job for which a given test had demonstrated validity. In the traditional transport study, the predictor variable (e.g., the cognitive ability test) being recommended would be identical to that one that demonstrated validity in the earlier study. But in the current hybrid model, there is neither a direct job to job comparison on essential duties, nor would there be any requirement that the test being recommended be anything other than a test of cognitive ability or general mental ability.

Similar extensions of this hybrid model are beginning to appear in other, noncognitive, areas. Ones and her colleagues (Ones, Viswesvaran, & Schmidt, 1993) demonstrated the generalizability of the personality characteristic of integrity. This research is compatible with the recent meta-analyses of conscientiousness (e.g., Barrick & Mount, 1991). Although integrity and conscientiousness are clearly different (yet related) constructs, they both represent generalizable attributes derived from VG analyses. Once again, however, practitioners are careful to show that the job or job family in question actually includes tasks or challenges that would benefit from integrity or conscientiousness.

Practitioners are also learning to depend heavily on meta-analyses of procedures, as well as attributes. As an example, in recent years various meta-analyses (McDaniel, Whetzel, Schmidt, & Maurer, 1994; Schmidt & Hunter, 1998; Wright, Lichtenfels, & Pursell, 1989) have demonstrated the value of the structured interview. Thus, most practitioners are more likely now to recommend a structured interview than they might have been 20 years ago. These meta-analyses report estimates of "validity" for the device. But this is not really VG in the sense that there is an attribute (e.g., g or conscientiousness) that is being addressed by the analysis. A structured interview might assess communication skills, interpersonal skills, cognitive ability, values, technical knowledge, and so forth. So although the practitioner might have renewed confidence in the interview as a medium (like the standardized paper and pencil test), without further guidance or research, we cannot be sure what exactly is being generalized. If the interview was structured around the investigation of cognitive ability, what would be the advantage of gathering possibly redundant information (i.e., information already assessed by a paper and pencil test) in an expensive and time consuming manner. So I am skeptical of claims of generalized validity for a device (e.g., a paper and pencil test regardless of content) or a medium (oral interview regardless of content). When a device or a medium is being considered, some consideration of job content would seem to be required (most often through a job analysis).

Practitioners will continue to depend heavily on the meta-analytic research of their colleagues for guidance. Absent of any dramatic ruling of a Circuit Court of Appeals or the Supreme Court, practitioners will continue to use the hybrid model described earlier with respect to VG. It is also possible (though highly unlikely) that the Uniform Guidelines will be brought up to date with respect to VG and meta-analysis. This would also encourage practitioners to depend more heavily on VG data bases. But even if the guidelines were revised to acknowledge VG, it is likely that such a revision would lead to a constitutional challenge because they would then be at odds with established law—in particular the Sixth Circuit Atlas case that dismisses VG as inconsistent with Albemarle and impermissible *as a matter of law*.

CONCLUSION

The turbulence that once characterized the VG phenomenon has abated somewhat. The advocates have become more thoughtful and sober in their evaluations of the potential contribution of VG.

The enemies of VG (lawyers who commonly represent plaintiff groups) have seen that their apocalyptic fears may have been overstated. Scientific skeptics have become more accepting as conventions for conducting meta-analyses have emerged. And those who were raised on the bible of situational validity are accepting new truths. Meta-analysis and VG will continue to evolve and address the increasing complex questions of moderators, noncognitive predictors, and predictor combinations. This will be productive, but *only* if well designed traditional validation research remains alive and well. We may have already gone beyond the valuable half-life of many of the studies that form the foundation for the VG findings on cognitive ability. Cognitive ability will remain essential for virtually all jobs. It is not likely that memory or reasoning will not be part of any job one can imagine for the next century. Nevertheless, the *relative* contribution of cognitive ability to job success has probably already changed dramatically from what it was in 1970, and will continue to change. Meta-analyses and VG applications will need to grapple with these dynamic forces.

ACKNOWLEDGMENTS

I gratefully acknowledge the help of Barbara Nett in both the background research and the production of this chapter. In addition, I am grateful for the assistance of Meredith Ramsey, Danielle Pare, and Lauren Havighurst in the literature review. Earlier drafts of the manuscript were reviewed by Bob Guion, Kevin Murphy, Shelly Zedeck, and Rick Jacobs. Their insights were invaluable in producing the final draft and I am pleased to acknowledge their assistance.

REFERENCES

American Educational Research Association, American Psychological Association, & National Council on Measurement in Education (1999). *Standards for educational and psychological testing.* Washington, DC: American Educational Research Association.

American Psychological Association, American Educational Research Association, & National Council on Measurement in Education (1974). *Standards for educational & psychological tests.* Washington, DC: American Psychological Association.

Barrick, M. R., & Mount, M. K. (1991). The big five personality dimensions and job performance: A meta-analysis. *Personnel Psychology, 44,* 1–26.

Bobko, P., & Stone-Romero, E. F. (1998). Meta-analysis may be another useful research tool, but it is not a panacea. *Research in Personnel and Human Resources Management, 16,* 359–397.

Boehm, V. R. (1977). Differential prediction: A methodological artifact? *Journal of Applied Psychology, 62,* 146–154.

Brayfield, A. H., & Crockett, W. H. (1955). Employee attitudes and employee performance. *Psychological Bulletin, 52,* 396–424.

Campbell, J. P. (1990). Modeling the performance prediction problem in industrial and organizational psychology. In M. D. Dunnette & L. M. Hough (Eds.), *Handbook of Industrial and Organizational Psychology: Second Edition* (pp. 687–732). Palo Alto: Consulting Psychologists Press.

Cattell, J. M. (1890). Mental tests and measurements. *Mind, 15,* 373–380.

Cattell, J. M. (1923). The Psychological Corporation. In C. King (Ed.), *Psychology and business: The annals* (Vol. CX, pp. 165–171). New York: Academy of Sciences.

Cox v. Consolidated Rail Corporation, LEXIS 14299 (US Dist. 1987).

Division of Industrial-Organizational Psychology, American Psychological Association (1975). *Principles for the validation and use of personnel selection procedures.* Dayton, OH: Industrial-Organizational Psychologist.

Division of Industrial-Organizational Psychology, American Psychological Association (1980). *Principles for the validation and use of personnel selection procedures: Second edition.* Berkeley, CA: Industrial-Organizational Psychologist.

Drewes, D. W. (1961). Development and validation of synthetic dexterity tests based on elemental motion analysis. *Journal of Applied Psychology, 45,* 179–185.

Equal Employment Opportunity Commission v. Atlas Paper Box Company, 680 F. Supp. 1184 (U. S. Dist. 1987).

Friend et al. v. City of Richmond et al., 588 F.2d 61 (4th Cir. 1978).

Friend et al. v. Leidinger et al., 446 F. Supp. 361 (U.S. Dist. 1977).

Ghiselli, E. E. (1955). The measurement of occupational aptitude. *University of California Publications in Psychology, 8,* 101–216.

Ghiselli, E. E. (1966). *The validity of occupational aptitude tests.* New York: Wiley.

Ghiselli, E. E. (1973). The validity of aptitude tests in personnel selection. *Personnel Psychology, 26,* 461–477.

Glass, G. V. (1976). Primary, secondary and meta-analysis of research. *Educational Researcher, 5,* 3–8.

Glass, G. V. (1977). Integrating findings: The meta-analysis of research. In L. S. Shulman, *Review of Research in Education* (Vol. 5, pp. 351–379). Itasca, IL: Peacock.

Guion, R. M. (1965). *Personnel testing.* New York: McGraw-Hill.

Guion, R. M. (1998). *Assessment, measurement, and prediction for personnel decisions.* Mahwah, NJ: Lawrence Erlbaum Associates.

Guion, R. M., & Gottier, R. F. (1965). Validity of personality measures in personnel selection. *Personnel Psychology, 18,* 135–164.

Hedges, L. V. (1988). The meta-analysis of test validity studies: Some new approaches. In H. Wainer & H. I. Braun (Eds.), *Test validity* (pp. 191–212). Hillsdale, NJ: Erlbaum.

Hermelin, E., & Robertson, I. T. (2001). A critique and standardization of meta-analytic validity coefficients in personnel selection. *Journal of Occupational and Organizational Psychology, 74,* 253–277.

Herzberg, F., Mausner, B., & Snyderman, B. B. (1957). *The motivation to work*. New York: Wiley.

Hull, C. L. (1928). *Aptitude testing*. Yonkers-on-Hudson, NY: World Book Company.

Hunter, J. E., Schmidt, F. L., & Hunter, R. (1979). Differential validity of employment tests by race: A comprehensive review and analysis. *Psychological Bulletin, 86*, 721–735.

Hunter, J. E., Schmidt, F. L., & Jackson, G. B. (1982). *Meta-analysis: Cumulating research findings across studies*. Beverly Hills, CA: Sage.

Katzell, R. A. (1957). Industrial psychology. *Annual Review of Psychology, 8*, 237–268.

Landy, F. J. (1985). *Psychology of work behavior* (3rd ed.). Chicago, IL: Dorsey Press.

Landy, F. J. (1989). *Psychology of work behavior* (4th ed.). Pacific Grove, CA: Brooks/Cole.

Landy, F. J. (1993). Early influences on the development of industrial/organizational psychology. In T. K. Fagan & G. R. VandenBos (Eds.), *Exploring applied psychology: Origins and critical analyses* (pp. 83–118). Washington, DC: American Psychological Association.

Landy, F. J., Shankster, L. J., & Kohler, S. S. (1994). Personnel selection and placement. *Annual Review of Psychology, 45*, 261–296.

Landy, F. J., & Trumbo, D. A. (1980). *Psychology of work behavior (revised edition)*. Homewood, IL: Dorsey Press.

Lawshe, C. H. (1952). What can industrial psychology do for small business (a symposium): 2. Employee selection. *Personnel Psychology, 5*, 31–34.

McDaniel, M. A., Whetzel, D. L., Schmidt, F. L., & Maurer, S. D. (1994). The validity of employment interviews: A comprehensive review and meta-analysis. *Journal of Applied Psychology, 79*, 599–616.

Ones, D. S., Viswesvaran, C., & Schmidt, F. L. (1993). Comprehensive meta-analysis of integrity test validities: Findings and implications for personnel selection and theories of job performance. *Journal of Applied Psychology, 78*, 679–703.

Pegues v. Mississippi State Employment Service, 488 F. Supp. 239 (N.D. Miss. 1980), aff'd, 699 F.2d 760 (5th Cir. 1983), cert. denied, 464 U.S. 991, 78 L. Ed. 2d 679, 104 S. Ct. 482, (1983).

Sackett, P. R., Schmitt, N., Tenopyr, M. L., Kehoe, J., & Zedeck, S. (1985). Commentary on forty questions about validity generalization and meta-analysis. *Personnel Psychology, 38*, 697–798.

Schmidt, F. L. (1992). What do data really mean? Research findings, meta-analysis, and cumulative knowledge in psychology. *American Psychologist, 47*, 1173–1181.

Schmidt, F. L., Berner, J. G., & Hunter, J. E. (1973). Racial differences in validity of employment tests: Reality or illusion? *Journal of Applied Psychology, 58*, 5–9.

Schmidt, F. L., & Hunter, J. E. (1978). Moderator research and the law of small numbers. *Personnel Psychology, 31*, 215–231.

Schmidt, F. L., & Hunter, J. E. (1998). The validity and utility of selection methods in personnel psychology: Practical and theoretical implications of 85 years of research findings. *Psychological Bulletin, 124*, 262–274.

Schmidt, F. L., Hunter, J. E., Pearlman, K., & Hirsh, H. R. (1985). Forty questions about validity generalization and meta-analysis. *Personnel Psychology, 38*, 697–798.

Seymour, R. T. (1988). Why plaintiffs' counsel challenge tests, and how they can successfully challenge the theory of "validity generalization." *Journal of Vocational Behavior, 33*, 331–364.

Society for Industrial and Organizational Psychology, Inc. (1987). *Principles for the validation and use of personnel selection procedures (Third Edition)*. College Park, MD: Author.

Society for Industrial and Organizational Psychology, Inc. (Draft: 2001/2002). *Principles for the validation and use of personnel selection procedures* (4th Ed.).

Standards for educational and psychological testing. (1985). Washington, DC: American Psychological Association.

Taylor v. James River Corporation, LEXIS 16101 (U.S. Dist. 1989).

Tiffin, J., & McCormick, E. J. (1958). *Industrial psychology* (4th ed.). New York: Prentice-Hall.

Ulrich, L., & Trumbo, D. (1965). The selection interview since 1949. *Psychological Bulletin, 63*, 100–116.

Uniform guidelines on employee selection procedures (1978). *Federal Register, 43*, 38290–38315.

Van Aken et al. v. Young and City of Detroit et al., 541 F. Supp. 448 (U.S. Dist. 1982).

Wiesner, W. H., & Cronshaw, S. F. (1988). A meta-analytic investigation of the impact of interview format and degree of structure on the validity of the employment interview. *Journal of Occupational Psychology, 61*, 275–290.

Wortman, P. M. (1983). Evaluation research: A methodological perspective. *Annual Review of Psychology, 34*, 223–260.

Wright, P. M., Lichtenfels, P. A., & Pursell, E. D. (1989). The structured interview: Additional studies and a meta-analysis. *Journal of Occupational Psychology, 62*, 191–199.

Yerkes, R. M. (Ed.). (1921). Psychological examining in the United States Army. *Memoirs of the National Academy of Sciences, 15*.

Zedeck, S., & Cascio, W. F. (1984). Psychological issues in personnel decisions. *Annual Review of Psychology, 35*, 461–518.

7

Impact of Meta-Analysis Methods on Understanding Personality– Performance Relations

Murray R. Barrick
Michael K. Mount
University of Iowa

Understanding the relations among personality dimensions and job performance is a fundamental concern of industrial–organizational (I/O) psychologists. This chapter discusses the impact that meta-analysis has had on furthering our knowledge in this area. First discussed are the results and conclusions from research conducted prior to 1990, which was based largely on narrative reviews of personality performance relations and did not utilize a taxonomy for classifying personality traits. Then examined are the results and conclusions derived from the literature based on studies conducted between 1990 and 2000 that used both meta-analysis and the Five Factor Model (FFM) to classify personality traits. Next discussed is the overall impact that meta-analysis has had on understanding personality performance relations. Finally, suggestions are provided for the role that meta-analysis can play in the future in furthering our understanding of personality–performance relations.

In order to understand the impact that meta-analysis has had on understanding personality–performance relations, it is useful to review the methods and conclusions of studies conducted prior to the meta-analytic studies, as well as the reasons for the conclusions. Literally hundreds of studies have investigated this topic over the past 25 years, which attests to its importance to the I/O field. One of the first major reviews of personality tests was conducted by Ellis and Conrad (1948). The purpose of their study was to examine the validity of personality inventories used in the military compared to those used in civilian settings. Although the validities were higher overall for inventories used in the military, this conclusion must be qualified by several factors. First, the review did not provide precise quantitative estimates of validity, making the comparisons tentative at best. Further, many of the favorable conclusions arrived at in the military setting were based on predicting psychiatric criteria such as neuropsychiatric unfitness for military duty. Also, according to the authors there were spurious factors that may have accounted for the higher correlations in the military setting. Examples of these included criterion contamination, whereby those who had knowledge of the criterion also had some knowledge of predictor scores. And, in some cases there was criterion overlap, in which there was duplication of questions in the predictor and criterion measures.

A few years later, Ghiselli and Bartol (1953) conducted the first major review of the validity of personality measures for selection purposes. Their research examined only those studies for which the personality traits had relevance to the job in question. In general their findings were positive, but they argued for caution in the use of personality measures as selection instruments, largely because results varied widely across job category and by study. Locke and Hulin (1962) examined 18 studies that had used The Activity Vector Analysis and reported generally low validities and also pointed out that there were numerous methodological problems in some of the validation studies. Shortly after that, Guion and Gottier (1965) published their influential study, which was a qualitative review of 12 years of research in the *Journal of Applied Psychology* and *Personnel Psychology* pertaining to personality–performance relations. They concluded that personality measures and job performance were not related in any meaningful way across traits and across situations.

Schmitt, Gooding, Noe, and Kirsch (1984) conducted the first meta-analytic review of personality–performance relations. They examined criterion-related validity studies published in *Personnel Psychology* and the *Journal of Applied Psychology* between 1964 and 1982. They did not examine the validity of specific personality constructs or attempt to analyze the data according to conditions of the studies (e.g., whether job analysis was used or whether researchers tested specific hypotheses). They reported the average uncorrected correlation between personality measures and measures of job success (across criteria and occupations) was $r = .149$. They also reported uncorrected mean correlations between personality and five different criteria: performance ratings, $r = .206$; turnover, $r = .121$;

achievement/grades, $r = .152$; status change, $r = .126$; and wages, $r = .268$. Their conclusions were similar to those of previous researchers: "Results concerning different types of predictors are consistent with previous literature reviews (Ghiselli, 1973; Guion and Gottier, 1965) which conclude that personality tests have low validity" (p. 420). Interestingly, the average observed correlation of .149 reported by Schmitt et al. over all criteria is larger than that obtained by Barrick and Mount (1991) for conscientiousness ($r = .13$ across occupations). Yet, Schmitt et al.'s conclusion about the usefulness of personality measures for selection purposes are more pessimistic than Barrick and Mount's. One reason for Barrick and Mount's more optimistic view pertains to the purpose of their study and the methodology used, which focused on understanding personality–performance linkages. Thus, the finding that the validity of one personality dimension, conscientiousness, generalized across occupations was more important than the magnitude of the validities obtained.

Needless to say the pessimistic conclusions by Guion and Gottier (1965) and Schmitt et al. (1984) led to a decline in the use of personality measures for selection purposes. Subsequently, however, researchers began to explore several reasons for these pessimistic conclusions, and began to examine alternative ways to examine personality–performance relations. For example, there are thousands of personality traits that pertain to specific aspects of human behavior, yet prior to the late 1980's, no accepted classification system was available. Prior reviews drew broad conclusions about the predictive validity of personality as if personality were a unitary construct. Thus, one explanation for these findings was that personality is not a good predictor of job performance when dealt with as one concept. In contrast, it was believed that understanding could only be achieved if we examined the relationship of specific personality traits with performance.

During the 1980s and 1990s researchers intensely searched for the dimensionality of personality in order to identify a parsimonious, yet comprehensive taxonomy of human behavior. Without the capability to reduce the number of personality traits into a smaller, more manageable number, the process of studying personality–performance linkages was unwieldy and resulted in ambiguity about which personality traits were being measured. In some cases researchers were using the same name to refer to traits with different meanings and in others were using different names for traits with the same meaning. A related problem was that researchers did not distinguish between the measurement of personality at the construct level and measurement at the inventory scale level. Researchers implicitly treated each individual personality scale as if it measured a distinct construct, rather than recognizing that each scale from a personality inventory assessed only one aspect or facet of a higher-order construct. Furthermore, many researchers simply correlated all of the scales on the personality inventories with the criteria without regard to the relevance of the relations. This approach was problematic because in the absence of theory driven hypotheses, it is difficult to interpret the results meaningfully. Finally, the reviews of the literature at this time were largely narrative (with the exception of Schmitt et al., 1984), rather than quantitative meta-analytic reviews. Because study artifacts were not corrected across studies, the validity estimates were downwardly biased. Given these problems, it was difficult if not impossible to identify consistent relationships among personality traits and criteria. It is understandable that little advancement was made in understanding personality–performance relationships.

In the past decade significant progress has been made due largely to the convergence of two developments in the psychology literature. The first is the emergence of a widely accepted taxonomy, the FFM, which could be used to classify the thousands of personality traits into a manageable number of personality dimensions. Each personality dimension from the FFM pertains to a specific aspect of human behavior, one that is relatively independent of others. These five traits generally can be defined as follows. Extraversion consists of sociability, dominance, ambition, positive emotionality, and excitement seeking. Cooperation, trustfulness, compliance, and affability define Agreeableness. Emotional Stability is defined by the lack of anxiety, hostility, depression, and personal insecurity. Conscientiousness is associated with dependability, achievement striving, and planfulness. Finally, intellectance, creativity, unconventionality, and broad-mindedness define Openness to Experience. Taken together, the FFM has provided a comprehensive yet parsimonious framework to systematically examine the relationship between specific personality traits and job performance.

The second development was the formulation and refinement of meta-analytic methods (e.g., Hunter & Schmidt, 1990). As discussed earlier, numerous problems characterized personality research that hindered the ability to draw meaningful conclusions. Some reviews were largely qualitative in nature, whereas others computed mean validities for personality traits or sets of traits but did not correct for statistical artifacts across studies such as sampling error, range restriction, and differences in reliabilities for predictors and criteria. The use of meta-analysis to investigate these relations has led to more positive conclusions. In fact, Guion (1998) recently noted that, "Meta-analyses have provided grounds for optimism" (p. 145).

Meta-analysis has had a positive impact on our knowledge in this area. Nonetheless, it is important to point out that it was not meta-analysis alone that led to these advancements. For example, the Schmitt et al. (1984) study was a meta-analysis and was helpful in understanding the magnitude of the validity of personality measures. However, because they did not use a taxonomy like the FFM to categorize personality traits, their findings did not enhance understanding of how well specific, meaningful personality constructs predicted performance. Subsequently, when the literature was examined using the FFM taxonomy coupled with meta-analytic methods, the resulting conclusions were more positive than before. The results were useful not so much because they shed light on the magnitude of the validities but because they increased understanding at the construct level. Prediction that does not enhance understanding is not theoretically meaningful.

Armed with an understanding about the predictive validity of different personality constructs from meta-analytic research, researchers can develop, test and refine theories of job performance. One example comes from the study by Barrick, Mount, and Strauss (1993), who used structural equations modeling to test the theory that distal motivational processes associated with conscientiousness were related to proximal motivational variables such as goal setting behaviors, which in turn, were linked with higher performance. Their results confirmed the hypothesis that proximal goal-setting behaviors mediated the relations between distal personality traits and performance. Thus meta-analysis provided the initial, broad level of understanding about the predictive validity of conscientiousness, which was then used as the basis for developing and testing a more specific set of hypotheses about the way Conscientiousness relates to performance.

Thus, the recent optimism about the usefulness of personality measures for personnel selection purposes is due equally to the use of the FFM to classify personality traits and to methods of meta-analysis to cumulate results across studies. It is difficult to imagine how understanding in this area could have advanced by using only one and not the other. This underscores the need for any meta-analytic study to use a well-defined taxonomy for classifying both predictors and criteria. Having said this, it is important to point out that very few meta-analyses have actually met this standard. That is, although most recent meta-analyses of personality–performance relations have used the FFM taxonomy, there has been little consensus regarding the classification of criterion measures. Further, considering the issue more broadly, most selection-oriented meta-analyses have focused on the validity of various methods of selection such as interviews, integrity tests, and ability tests, rather than on the validity of the constructs measured by the methods.

META-ANALYTIC STUDIES OF
PERSONALITY–PERFORMANCE RELATIONS

Since 1990, at least 16 meta-analytic studies investigated relations between personality traits using the FFM of personality (or some variant of it) and job performance. This statement is both striking and provocative in its implications. On one hand it is striking because of the sheer number of studies: 16 meta-analytic studies investigating the same topic in the short time span of a decade is remarkable. (Prior to 1990 only one meta-analytic study had investigated these relations (Schmitt et al., 1984) and it did not use the FFM taxonomy.) To our knowledge, there is no other topic in the I/O Psychology literature that has been the focus of so many meta-analyses in such a short period of time.

The aforementioned statement is also provocative in several ways. The purpose of meta-analysis is to cumulate the results across studies to establish facts (Hunter & Schmidt, 1990). Because a meta-analysis necessarily summarizes results across large numbers of studies while correcting for study artifacts, it would be expected that the conclusions would be very robust. Hence, if a meta-analytic study were comprehensive and well executed, it would seem that additional meta-analyses on the same topic would be unnecessary. In light of this, it begs the question: Why have so many researchers conducted meta-analyses on essentially the same topic over the past decade? And, why have editors of major journals continued to publish them?

There are several possible explanations. One reason is that emergence of meta-analysis and the FFM occurred at about the same time, and were viewed as natural partners in the study of personality–performance linkages, which stimulated further research using both of them. A second reason is that relations between personality and performance are complex, which means that they can be difficult to discover and that they can be investigated in several ways. Further, meta-analysis involves formulating numerous decision rules about which studies to include, how to classify measures, how to code data, and so on. Although there are numerous judgment calls that must be made in any meta-analysis, this is especially true in personality research given the countless number of personality traits that exist and the ambiguity regarding their labels and definitions. Similarly, judgment calls also are made on the criterion side, where little consensus exists regarding a taxonomy of performance dimensions. Because these decision rules obviously have a bearing on the outcome of the meta-analysis, subsequent researchers may believe that different conclusions would be reached if different decision rules were used. Another reason that it may be fruitful to conduct a new meta-analysis on the same topic is that over time, new primary studies are conducted and when a sufficient number have become available, researchers recognize that re-analyses could alter the conclusions of the original meta-analysis.

But what have the additional meta-analyses of personality-performance relations shown? Have they resulted in different conclusions? Are additional meta-analyses needed? By coincidence there were three meta-analyses of personality and performance relations that appeared in published journals in the I/O Psychology field at about the same time (Barrick & Mount, 1991; Hough, 1992; Tett, Jackson, & Rothstein, 1991). Each of these studies examined personality–performance linkages using the FFM framework (or some variant of it) and covered much of the same literature; yet, conclusions regarding the validity of the personality constructs differed somewhat across these studies. For example, Barrick and Mount (1991) found that Conscientiousness was the only FFM trait to display non-zero correlations with job performance across different occupational groups and criterion types. In contrast, Tett et al. (1991) found that only Emotional Stability displayed nonzero correlations with performance, and two other Big Five traits—Agreeableness and Openness to Experience—displayed higher correlations with performance than Conscientiousness. Goldberg (1993) described these differences in findings based on a similar body of knowledge as "befuddling" (p. 31).

The methodological differences between the Barrick and Mount (1991) and Tett et al. (1991) studies that might have accounted for the disparities in the FFM results have been discussed at length elsewhere (Ones, Mount, Barrick, & Hunter, 1994; Tett, Jackson, Rothstein, & Reddon, 1994), so it is not reiterated here. The important point is that although both the Barrick and Mount (1991) and the Tett et al. (1991) meta-analyses were designed to enhance understanding of personality and performance relations, the studies had quite different purposes and examined fundamentally different questions. The primary purpose of the Barrick and Mount (1991) meta-analysis was to enhance understanding at the *construct* level. That is, we used a construct-oriented approach to examine whether there were generalizable relationships between FFM dimensions and job performance. Based on both theory and common sense, we reasoned that there should be generalizable relations between two personality dimensions, Conscientiousness and Emotional Stability, with job performance. That is people who are hard working, organized, prudent, persistent, dependable, and achievement oriented (Conscientiousness) should be better performers in about any job. Similarly, those who are insecure, lack confidence, are stress-prone, and are moody (low in Emotional Stability or Neuroticism), are likely to be poor performers in about any job. The availability of the FFM enabled us to classify personality traits into the appropriate categories to examine whether these hypotheses were true.

On the other hand, the Tett et al. (1991) meta-analysis was designed to enhance understanding of the *conditions* under which personality best predicts performance. Although their study summarized results at the FFM level, these analyses were actually secondary in importance. Tett et al. were primarily interested in the magnitude of the validities that could be obtained when the authors of primary studies had formulated hypotheses or had used a job analysis to choose personality measures, irrespective of which construct the personality measure assessed. In the 1994 re-analysis of this data (Tett et al., 1994),[1] they showed that in those situations when researchers had formulated hypotheses about personality–performance relationships (a confirmatory strategy), the estimated mean true score correlation was higher (.24) than when an exploratory strategy was used (.04). And when job analysis was used explicitly to choose predictors, the corrected mean validity was slightly higher (.25).[2]

---

[1]The results reported here are from Tett, Jackson, Rothstein, and Reddon (1994). This meta-analysis is a re-analysis of Tett et al.'s (1991) non-FFM data, and is based on a number of revisions to address the statistical concerns raised by Ones, Mount, Barrick, and Hunter (1994).

[2]The re-analysis from Tett et al. (1994) resulted in different magnitudes than those reported in Tett et al. (1991). For example, across the two analyses, the mean correlation when a confirmatory strategy was used was .29 in 1991 and .24 in 1994, when an exploratory strategy was used the estimate was .12 in 1991 and .04 in 1994. Finally when job analysis was used, the estimate was .38 in 1991 and .25 in 1994. The latter estimate was not significantly higher than the "no job analysis" estimate (.24) in the 1994 re-analysis. In 1991, this distinction had been found to significantly differ. The 1994 estimate is reported here because they are likely to be more accurate.

The point of the preceding discussion is not that one of these meta-analyses is superior to the other (methodological differences notwithstanding). Rather, the point is that two meta-analyses that examined the same body of literature, and that were conducted independently and at about the same time, can appropriately yield different results because they investigated quite different questions. In fact, our view is that these two meta-analyses should be viewed as complimentary, in that each provides information that the other does not. Barrick and Mount (1991) did not try to identify the optimal circumstances or conditions that might yield higher validities for Conscientiousness (or other personality constructs). And in their analyses, Tett et al. (1991) did not examine which personality constructs accounted for the higher validities in the confirmatory or job analysis based studies.

But the preceding discussion does not explain why at least 13 other meta-analyses were conducted on this same topic after 1992. Most of these meta-analyses seemed to follow the construct-oriented approach taken by Barrick and Mount (1991), which focused on increasing understanding of which personality constructs were related to performance constructs. One possible reason why the additional meta-analytic studies were conducted was to clarify some apparent conflicting findings in the Barrick and Mount (1991) and Tett et al. (1991) studies with respect to the FFM dimensions. For example, some of these discrepancies may have occurred because of different decision rules used in the studies (e.g., which scales from personality inventories were assigned to FFM dimensions). Other meta-analyses were conducted because they used different populations (international rather than U.S. participants) or because they used only inventories that measured personality at the FFM level rather than individual scales from personality inventories.

It is especially useful to examine three of these meta-analytic studies (Barrick & Mount, 1991; Hurtz & Donovan, 2000; Salgado, 1997) because they had a similar purpose (i.e., they examined personality and performance relations using the FFM framework), but the meta-analyses were operationalized differently (i.e. different decision rules and nonoverlapping samples). Comparison of the results of these studies provides a unique opportunity to determine the convergent validity of three meta-analyses where samples and decision rules differ in important ways. For example, Salgado's (1997) study used a similar methodology as Barrick and Mount (1991), but used only participants in the European community. Hurtz and Donovan (2000) also used a similar methodology as

Barrick and Mount but considered only studies where personality was measured at the FFM level.

Table 7.1 presents the results from these three meta-analyses as well as the sample-weighted mean estimates of these prior meta-analytic results (i.e., average estimates). For each study, there are five columns, which contain respectively, the total sample size for each trait (N), the mean observed correlation ($\overline{r}$ and $\overline{r}^{sw}$), the estimated true score correlation (ρ or $\overline{\rho}^{sw}$), the estimated true residual standard deviation (SD_ρ or $SD\overline{\rho}^{sw}$), and the percentage of observed variance that was accounted for by statistical artifacts (%V and %$\overline{V}^{sw}$; where the four artifacts are sampling error and between-study differences in predictor and criterion unreliability, and degree of range restriction).

The best estimate of the true population parameters is provided by the average estimates reported in the last five columns of Table 7.1. Inspection of these results reveals that among the Five Factor Model constructs, Conscientiousness and to a lesser extent, Emotional Stability have produced consistent, acceptable validities against various job performance criteria across numerous jobs. Consequently, these two personality traits appear to be universal predictors across many, if not all jobs. Although the results are not reported here, a meta-analysis of meta-analyses (Barrick, Mount, & Judge, 2001) has shown that the other three personality traits, Agreeableness, Extraversion, and Openness to Experience, are also valuable predictors of performance, but only in some jobs and in some situations. Thus, these three traits are contingent predictors, as they will be relevant only in some situations.

These findings are important and would not have been discovered without meta-analysis and the FFM. However, meta-analysis yields important information other than the magnitude of the estimated true score correlation, namely the variability in the estimates of the true score correlation. This is a critical area that needs to be scrutinized in more detail. As shown in Table 7.1, the estimated true score correlations across these three meta-analyses are strikingly similar. For example, the estimated true score correlations for Conscientiousness are .20, .22, and .25 (Barrick & Mount, 1991; Hurtz & Donovan, 2000; Salgado, 1997; respectively). Thus, the meta-analytic estimates were remarkably stable across these three studies, despite the inclusion of different primary studies, different decision rules, and even different operationalizations of personality traits (one study only included FFM level measures (Hurtz & Donovan, 2000), whereas the other two studies averaged the validities

TABLE 7.1

Meta-Analytic Results for Personality Factors Pooled Across Criteria and Occupations

Personality Trait	Barrick & Mount					Salgado					Hurtz & Donovan					Average Estimates				
	N	$\bar{r}$	ρ	SD_ρ	%V	N	$\bar{r}$	ρ	SD_ρ	%V	N	$\bar{r}$	ρ	SD_ρ	%V	N	$\bar{r}^{sw}$	ρ^{sw}	SD_ρ^{sw}	$\%\bar{V}^{sw}$
Conscientiousness	19,721	.13	.22*	.09	.70	3,295	.10	.25*	.09	.66	8,083	.14	.20*	.14	.44	31,099	.13	.22*	.10	.63
Emotional Stability	18,719	.05	.08	.10	.63	3,877	.09	.19 *	.07	.78	5,671	.09	.13 *	.05	.85	28,267	.07 *	.12	.08	.69
Agreeableness	17,520	.04	.07	.09	.54	3,466	.01	.02	.07	.79	6,447	.07	.11	.09	.62	27,433	.04	.07	.09	.59
Extraversion	19,511	.08	.13	.11	.69	3,806	.05	.12	.16	.42	6,453	.06	.09	.10	.57	29,770	.07	.12	.11	.63
Openness to Experience	14,326	.03	.04	.13	.59	2,722	.04	.09	.06	.81	5,525	.04	.06	.08	.70	22,573	.03	.05	.11	.64

Note. N = sample size; $\bar{r}$ = Mean Observed Correlation; ρ = Mean True Score Correlation; SD_ρ = True Score Residual Standard Deviation; %V = Percentage of Variance Explained By Artifactual Errors; $\bar{r}^{sw}$ = Estimated Sample Weighted Mean Observed Correlation; $\bar{\rho}^{sw}$ = Estimated Sample Weighted Mean True Score Correlation; SD_ρ^{sw} = Estimated Sample Weighted True Score Standard Deviation; And $\%\bar{V}^{sw}$ = Estimated Sample Weighted Percentage Of Variance Explained By Artifactual Errors.

across components of the constructs). These results reveal the robustness of conclusions drawn from large-scale meta-analyses.

The obvious conclusion from Table 7.1 is that a comprehensive meta-analysis, in combination with a meaningful taxonomy to classify personality traits, has allowed researchers to determine the magnitude of the relationship between personality and performance that is more accurate, credible, and stable than can be derived in any one primary study. Another important conclusion that can be drawn from these results is that the point now has been reached where there is no need for future meta-analyses of this type, as they are likely to result in quite similar findings and conclusions.

FUTURE ROLE OF META-ANALYSIS EXAMINING PERSONALITY–PERFORMANCE RELATIONS

Before the future role of meta-analysis in this area is discussed, we would like to offer several recommendations for conducting meta-analyses of personality–performance relations. These recommendations are based on our review of 16 previous meta-analyses in this area and are aimed specifically at meta-analyses of personality traits, rather than at meta-analyses of other topics (e.g., whether unpublished studies are included, how to treat multiple correlations from the same sample). The first recommendation pertains to the classification schemes used. Researchers should clearly define their predictor and criterion taxonomies. If the FFM taxonomy was used to assign personality traits, the definitions for the FFM dimensions should be provided (or made available), as there is not universal agreement on their meaning. If a different personality taxonomy is adopted, there should also be some discussion regarding the theoretical support and comprehensiveness of the taxonomy, in addition to providing definitions of the various dimensions in that taxonomy. If multiple criterion categories (e.g., contextual vs. task performance; objective vs. subjective criteria; organizational citizenship and counterproductive behaviors) are used, the rationale for using them and their definitions should be provided. In addition, researchers should provide (or make available) which specific personality traits or criteria were assigned to each category. Researchers should also clearly describe the jobs that are studied, and if they are assigned to occupational categories, the classification scheme should be explicit.

The second recommendation pertains to the conditions under which the correlations were obtained in the primary studies. We recommend that the following study conditions be coded so that potential moderator analyses can be conducted. Was the correlation hypothesized? Was the personality dimension selected by primary researchers based on a job analysis? Were correlations obtained from a study that reported only significant correlations or from a study that reported all correlations? Was the personality trait a lower-level facet from a scale on a personality inventory, or was it a higher-level personality construct measured at the FFM level? Was the study obtained from a refereed journal article or was it unpublished?

The third recommendation pertains to the way researchers code and analyze signed correlations. This is a particularly relevant issue for personality traits because of the potential ambiguity regarding the meaning of certain traits. We recommend that the sign of the correlation always should be coded, provided it is done in a consistent way. For example, if in a sample Conscientiousness is found to have a negative correlation with the criterion of number of accidents, this relation is actually in the expected direction and should be coded as a positive correlation. On the other hand, if in a particular sample Conscientiousness has a negative correlation with supervisor ratings of amount of effort exerted, this is in the opposite direction expected and should be coded negatively. These are a few of the practices that if implemented, might lead to greater consistency in conducting and interpreting meta-analytic studies.

It has been argued that meta-analysis is a very powerful technique that researchers (e.g., Barrick & Mount, 1991; Hurtz & Donovan, 2000; Salgado, 1997; Tett et al., 1991) have applied to reverse the longstanding belief that personality measures do not contribute to individual differences in work performance. Given that conclusions about the usefulness of personality in work situations are now more optimistic than they were 25 to 30 years ago, we believe research attention should shift to other questions. Two critical questions are how personality traits are converted into behaviors, and what factors may moderate these relationships. Although these issues have been examined in some previous primary studies (e.g., Barrick et al., 1993; Barrick, Stewart, & Piotrowski, 2002; Borman, White, Pulakos, & Oppler, 1991; Gellatly, 1996), there is very little research that has systematically examined potential mediator and moderator variables. This is not surprising because we only recently have been able to conclude "personality matters." Thus, it can be expected that a large number of primary studies will be conducted over the next decade to examine the effect of mediators and moderators of the relationship between personality and performance.

Does this mean there is no future role for meta-analysis in this area of research? Although there may be a reduction in the number of meta-analyses conducted in the next few years, we do believe meta-analysis will play as pivotal a role during the next decade as was true of the past decade. However, we expect the purposes of those meta-analyses to change dramatically. The following section discusses the role meta-analysis should play in future research.

Clearly, meta-analyses have played a crucial role in advancing our theoretical understanding of the nature of the relationship between specific personality constructs and success at work. However, relatively little attention has been paid to the magnitude of these relationships, which are modest at best. The estimated true score correlations for specific traits rarely exceed .30, which is relatively modest compared with the estimated true score correlation for cognitive ability. Meta-analysis can play a key role in trying to understand the conditions that produce higher predictive validities, especially in the search for moderator variables. A critical outcome in any meta-analysis of selection studies is the amount of variation in the predictive validities that is attributed to different work settings. Inspection of the results reported in Table 7.1 (%V and %$\overline{V}^{sw}$ columns) suggests that differences in correlations may exist across subpopulations. The sample-weighted mean estimate of the percentage of variance explained by the four artifactual errors (%$\overline{V}^{sw}$) fails to exceed the 75% rule (Hunter & Schmidt, 1990) for all five of the FFM personality traits. Stated another way, the estimated true residual standard deviation (SD_ρ) values are large in comparison to the estimated true scores (ρ). These findings point to the urgent need to further search for moderators of these relationships.

A number of meta-analyses have examined the nature of these relationships across different job types and criteria. For example, the three meta-analyses reviewed in Table 7.1 examine estimated true score correlations across different jobs (managers, sales, skilled and semiskilled, etc.) as well as across different criteria (job proficiency, training proficiency, and personnel data, etc.). Differences in job content and criteria serve as important potential moderators and warrant further examination. Tett et al. (1991) examined the effects of these same moderators, including those found across types of criteria (objective vs. subjective); across different jobs (professional vs. nonprofessional; managerial vs. nonmanagerial; civilian vs. military); and across applicant samples versus incumbent samples. They also examined differences across studies in which researchers developed a priori hypotheses (confirmatory approach) or did not (exploratory approach); and by source of data (researchers vs. company; articles vs. dissertations). These are also important types of moderators that future research should examine. We are particularly intrigued by Tett et al.'s (1994) finding that when researchers follow a confirmatory approach rather than just an exploratory approach, the magnitude of the effects for personality are substantially larger (ρ = .24 vs. .04). Specifically, what attributes are researchers focusing on when deriving a priori hypotheses? Robertson and Kinder (1993) found that when asked to generate hypotheses linking a specific personality test or scale to job performance on the basis of written descriptions, practitioner's predictions were supported by empirical data less than 45% of the time. Thus, the usefulness of a priori judgments about the traits relevance to a particular criteria will have to be examined carefully. Nevertheless, the findings by Tett et al. (1994) suggest there is merit in such an approach, particularly when researchers examine theoretically meaningful factors that influence personality–performance relations. Below, we discuss a few of the moderating factors researchers should consider.

Researchers have long been interested in personality as a means to explain a person's behavior. This is one of the primary reasons personality is of such interest to researchers in the field of I/O psychology. Yet, there is very little research that accounts for the effects of personality on behavior at work. Instead, much of this research relies on outcomes (sales, turnover, promotions, etc.) and supervisory ratings of performance. These measures are certainly influenced by the actions people take (behavior), but they also include, to an unknown extent, factors outside the individual's control. To the extent these performance measures include variance that is due to factors the individual cannot control, the correlates are likely to underestimate how well personality predicts behavior.

Thus, we suggest that future research should focus on behavior rather than outcomes. Although job analysts have devoted considerable effort to describing behavior at work (Harvey, 1991), there has been inadequate theoretical and empirical work to link the domain of individual differences (e.g., cognitive abilities, personality traits, and interests) with the domain of job behavior constructs (e.g., delegating and coordinating, exchanging information, operating machines, etc.). We believe that our understanding of the relationship between personality and behavior will be enhanced if we develop and apply theories of the structure and content of work behavior.

There is also considerable recognition that situations are important determinants of the nature of the relationship between personality and performance. To date, there have only been a few papers (e.g., Barrick, Mitchell, & Stewart, in press; Murtha, Kanfer, & Ac-

kerman, 1996; Stewart & Barrick, in press) that attempt to concep-
tualize the basic kinds of situations and links those situations to
personality traits. One fundamental situational variable that must
be accounted for in personality research is the level of autonomy.
Autonomy captures the extent to which the external environment
constrains a person's freedom to choose how to behave (Barrick &
Mount, 1993). In *strong situations* (low in autonomy), the organization exerts considerable pressure to induce behavioral conformity.
These controlling forces press the individual to behave in a specific
way or exhibit a very narrow range of behaviors. In such circumstances, personality has at best, a weak effect on behavior. In contrast, *weak situations* (high in autonomy) present few demands or
presses to conform. In such settings, the individual's free will determines which behaviors, if any, to undertake. The magnitude of the
relation between personality traits and behavior is likely to be
greater in weak situations, in which people have greater discretion
or choice in how they will perform their job. Thus, an important
moderator researchers must consider involves the influence autonomy has on the relationships between personality and behavior.

In research on cognitive ability, a theory has been developed and
tested that focuses on the complexity of the job to explain the relationship between ability and performance (Hunter, 1986; Schmidt,
Hunter, Outerbridge, & Trattner, 1986). This research shows that
cognitive ability relates to job performance indirectly through its relation to job knowledge, which in turn relates to performance. These
results also demonstrate that cognitive ability relates directly to performance, although the effects are smaller than the indirect effects.
This theory shows that more complex jobs require even more job
knowledge and learning, which in turn leads to higher performance.
Thus, job complexity is an important situational variable. Is job
complexity likely to be an important moderator for personality? It is
unknown. However, if it is, it may be because complexity is associated with greater discretion or autonomy, in addition to a need for
more knowledge.

There are also a number of methodological issues researchers
should consider as potential moderators. Mount, Barrick, and
Strauss (1994) found that job-relevant personality constructs were
valid predictors of performance when based on ratings from observers (e.g., supervisor, co-workers, and customers). Further, they
showed observer ratings of sales representatives on Conscientiousness (corrected r ranged from .32 to .42) and Extraversion (corrected
r ranged from .28 to .38) were correlated with ratings of performance, and that these correlations accounted for additional variance

beyond that due to self-ratings alone. This distinction is important because observer ratings capture the social reputation of the individual (Hogan, 1991). Further, these reputational effects are primarily derived from work settings for these raters (supervisors, co-workers, customers). In contrast, self-ratings tend to capture what people are like "way down deep." Ratings from the individual's perspective are influenced by an individual's perceptions of himself or herself in numerous situations, incorporate less observable information about motives, intentions, feelings, and past behavior, and also includes the effects of one's attempt at impression management, that is to consciously manage the impression one conveys to others. Taken together, it may well be that observer ratings capture more valid variance from work behaviors, particularly if those ratings are obtained almost exclusively in the work environment. Thus, one methodological moderator researchers should consider is rating source (self vs. observer).

There is considerable debate in the field about the appropriate level of analysis for assessing relationships between personality and performance. Schneider, Hough, and Dunnette (1996) argued that FFM traits are too broad and that prediction will improve if you rely on more precise facets of these traits, whereas Ones and Viswesvaran (1996) argued for greater breadth in the use of personality traits. The appropriate level of analysis depends on the purpose. If the purpose is to make a selection decision, a broader, more comprehensive measure is appropriate for predicting an equally broad measure of overall success at work. Support for this position can be found in two recent meta-analyses, one pertaining to integrity (Ones, Viswesvaran, & Schmidt, 1993) and the other to Customer Service (Frei & McDaniel, 1998). The estimated true score validity for integrity measures and customer service measures was .41 and .50 when predicting supervisory ratings of overall job performance, respectively. In both cases, construct validity evidence suggests these measures were positively and strongly related to Conscientiousness, Emotional Stability, and Agreeableness. Thus, broad measures of personality have very high predictive validities of overall performance, higher even than those typically reported for specific FFM personality traits. More importantly, these broad measures of success at work are the appropriate criteria to consider when making selection decisions.

In contrast, if the purpose is to enhance understanding, linking specific, lower level facets of FFM constructs to specific, lower level criteria may result in stronger correlations. For example, Mount and Barrick (1995) found that lower level personality traits predicted specific performance criteria better when they were conceptually related to the criterion. In this meta-analysis, they examined the strength of relations for Conscientiousness and two lower level facets, dependability and achievement. As hypothesized, they found dependability was a better predictor of employee reliability ($\rho = .47$) and quality ($\rho = .48$) than was conscientiousness ($\rho = .41$ and .44, respectively) or achievement ($\rho = .33$ and .22, respectively). In contrast, achievement was a better predictor of effort ($\rho = .58$) and creativity ($\rho = .19$) than was Conscientiousness ($\rho = .51$ and .13, respectively) or dependability ($\rho = .43$ and $-.04$, respectively). Although the estimates for conscientiousness were not larger than the relevant lower level component, they were always larger than the nonrelevant lower level component. Researchers can examine the influence of this moderator by using meta-analysis to generate a more accurate and more credible estimate of the predictive validity of higher level or lower level personality traits across these various purposes.

Past research has focused on differences among individuals on single traits (e.g., Conscientiousness, Emotional Stability, etc.). Although this was the appropriate step when initially trying to establish the effectiveness of personality in selection settings, it is time to examine the multivariate relation among personality traits when predicting performance. Can meta-analysis play a role in examining indexes of multivariate predictability? Meta-analysis used in combination with structural equation modeling could be used to establish the estimated true score correlation between multiple personality dimensions and performance measures (Viswesvaran & Ones, 1995). Researchers should apply structural equation modeling to the matrix of estimated true score correlations derived from two separate meta-analyses; one assessing the relation between personality traits, the other assessing the relation between personality and performance. Such research will enable researchers and practitioners to begin talking about the multivariate validity of multiple personality traits.

A second multivariate role for meta-analysis, in combination with structural equations modeling would be to find whether FFM personality traits accounted for incremental variance over that accounted for by cognitive ability, the interview, biodata, and other selection predictors. Some recent evidence (Goffin, Rothstein, & Johnston, 1996; McHenry, Hough, Toquam, Hanson, & Ashworth, 1999; McManus & Kelly, 1999; Mount, Witt, & Barrick, 2000) demonstrates that increments for Conscientiousness and Emotional Stability over these predictors typically range between 0.05 and 0.15, which may seem small when contrasted with cognitive ability constructs. Nevertheless, it should be noted that such gains in incremental validity yield large economic and social gains. For example, personality measures typically result in minimal disparate impact compared to cognitive ability measures (Mount & Barrick, 1995). Moreover, a practical issue is that it often is quite inexpensive to obtain information from personality measures. More importantly, personality traits also predict many other outcomes organizations value, including whether the person shows up for work on time (Judge, Martocchio, & Thoresen, 1997), remains with the firm (voluntary turnover; Barrick & Mount, 1996), contributes to the firm beyond that which is required by the job (organizational citizenship behavior; Organ & Ryan, 1995), and avoids harmful behaviors, including theft, sabotage, and breaking the rules (counterproductive behaviors; Hough, Eaton, Dunnette, Kamp, & McCloy, 1990). Meta-analysis along with structural equations modeling could play a substantial role in determining the likely effects firms would realize by using personality traits along with other predictors during selection.

Two recent examples illustrate the integration and application of these two methods when exploring incremental validity. Cortina and associates (Cortina, Goldstein, Payne, Davison, & Gilliand, 2000) formed a "meta-correlation matrix" representing the relations between cognitive ability, Conscientiousness, interviews, and job performance to examine the incremental validity of 3 levels of structured interviews on job performance. Although this study did not report whether Conscientiousness predicts job performance above and beyond cognitive ability and interviews, it could have. Schmidt and Hunter (1998) did use this methodology to illustrate that for most jobs, Conscientiousness combined with an intelligence test is 18% more valid than an intelligence test alone. Combining meta-analysis with structural equation modeling will enable researchers and practitioners to begin talking about the incremental validity of personality, across multiple dimensions of personality.

Another multivariate role for meta-analysis is to account for the effect of impression management on these validities. There has been concern raised that the factor structure of personality scales differs for applicant responses, due to the demands to manage ones impressions in an applicant setting (Ellingson, Sackett, & Hough, 1999; Montag & Comrey, 1990; Schmit & Ryan, 1993). Recent evidence suggests that social desirability in responses can erode the dimensionality of personality (Ellingson et al., 1999) or results in an additional "halo/good impression" factor (Montag & Comrey, 1990; Schmit & Ryan, 1993). In either case, one implication is the FFM factors become more highly intercorrelated, due to the influence of impression management.

To test this, one could apply meta-analysis to explore the relations found between personality traits from applicant studies and compare that matrix to one found from incumbent samples. The resulting estimated true score correlation matrixes for the two sets of analyses should differ substantially, with much higher intercorrelations found in the applicant sample, if factor structures do indeed differ across applicant and incumbent settings. If this is so, the predictive validity of a structural equations model including all FFM traits should be significantly lower when using applicant samples instead of incumbent samples. Ironically, Tett et al. (1994) found just the opposite in their meta-analysis of individual personality scales (although not a multivariate analysis), as the estimated true score validity was significantly higher for recruits ($\rho = .27$) than for incumbents ($\rho = .12$).

Finally, another multivariate approach to personality assessment focuses on the patterning and organization of traits within a person. This approach recognizes we are each characterized by a unique constellation of personality traits that defines who we are and how we behave. This *profile configural* approach aims to discover the basic categories of human nature and emphasizes how various personality dimensions may interact to predict behavior. For example, Simonton's (1999; 2000) work suggests that eminence will only emerge when a number of traits all are present in high levels. This theory specifies a complex interaction among multiple personality variables and stands in sharp contrast to past attempts to predict job performance with specific personality traits. Given configural data would not be available in studies focusing on the main effects of personality, researchers must first conduct a number of primary studies. Consequently, in contrast to the other moderators explored here, the role for meta-analysis is likely to be a number of years away, however, as there is a dearth of primary studies assessing this effect in the literature.

Taken together, it can be argued that meta-analysis should play a meaningful role in future theory development, as it provides the promise of clarifying the magnitude and establishing the importance of a number of theoretically oriented moderator variables. The second way meta-analysis can contribute to theory development is to facilitate the discovery of the effects of various mediators on this body of research. Prior meta-analyses have not examined the mediating effect of other variables on the personality–performance relation. This type of application of meta-analysis will become particularly important to researchers during the next decade.

Although there is clear evidence that specific personality constructs are important determinants of work performance, very little is known about the mechanisms through which these distal traits affect job performance. The primary way personality is thought to affect performance is through a person's motivation (Barrick et al., 2002; Kanfer, 1991; Mount & Barrick, 1995; Murray, 1938). To date, research has been significantly hindered because an accepted framework does not exist for studying motivational constructs. Nevertheless, with the development of a theoretically relevant motivational taxonomy, meta-analysis can effectively be used to explore the nature and magnitude of the relations between specific motivational variables and personality traits. The next decade will witness an explosion of interest in the structure of motivation. Through this research, a meaningful taxonomy will emerge that will enable researchers to examine the process through which personality affects motivation, and motivation in turn, affects job performance.

To illustrate, one could study how Conscientiousness affects performance. Conscientious individuals are achievement oriented, hard working, persistent, decisive, responsible, dependable, reliable, careful, organized, and planful. These traits are fundamentally linked to motivation at work. Motivation is defined by Campbell (1991) as: "[it is] a combined effect from three choice behaviors—choice to expend effort, choice of level of effort to expend, and choice to persist in that level of effort" (p. 706). A researcher could use these three choice behaviors to develop a motivational taxonomy, and than apply meta-analytic procedures to examine how Conscientiousness affects these three motivational variables, and in turn, how these motivational variables influence performance.

In conclusion, meta-analysis combined with the FFM has enabled researchers to further our understanding of the true nature of the relationship between specific personality traits and success at work in the past decade. Meta-analysis will continue to play a critical role in the development of our theoretical understanding of these relations. However, the focus of future meta-analyses should shift from explaining the relationship between personality traits and performance toward explaining the motivational process through which personality affects performance (mediation) as well as clarifying the influence of situational and methodological factors on those relations (moderators). Such work will be crucial both theoretically in the continued development of models of job performance, and practically, as it will clarify the value of using personality-based tests during the selection or promotion of employees.

REFERENCES

Barrick, M. R., Mitchell, T. R., & Stewart, G. L. I. (in press). Situational and motivational influences on trait—behavior relationships. In M. R. Barrick & A. M. Ryan (Eds.), *Personality and Work*. San Francisco: Jossey-Bass.

Barrick, M. R., & Mount, M. K. (1991). The Big Five personality dimensions and job performance: A meta-analysis. *Personnel Psychology, 44*, 1–26.

Barrick, M. R., & Mount, M. K. (1996). Effects of impression management and self-deception on the predictive validity of personality constructs. *Journal of Applied Psychology, 81*, 261–272.

Barrick, M. R., Mount, M. K., & Judge, T. A. (2001). The FFM personality dimensions and Job Performance: Meta-Analysis of Meta-Analyses. Invited submission to a special "selection" issue of *International Journal of Selection and Assessment, 9*, 9–30.

Barrick, M. R., Mount, M. K., & Strauss, J. P. (1993). Conscientiousness and performance of sales representatives: Test of the mediating effects of goal setting. *Journal of Applied Psychology, 78*, 715–722.

Barrick, M. R., Stewart, G. L., & Piotrowski, M. (2002). Personality and job performance: Test of the mediating effects of motivation among sales representatives. *Journal of Applied Psychology, 87*, 43–51.

Borman, W. C., White, L. A., Pulakos, E. D., & Oppler, S. H. (1991). Models of supervisor job performance ratings. *Journal of Applied Psychology, 76*, 863–872.

Campbell, J. P. (1991). Modeling the performance prediction problem in industrial and organizational psychology. In M. D. Dunnette & L. M. Hough (Eds.), *Handbook of Industrial and Organizational Psychology* (pp. 687–732). Palo Alto, CA: Consulting Psychologists.

Cortina, J. M., Goldstein, N. B., Payne, S. C., Davison, H. K., & Gilliland, S. W. (2000). The incremental validity of interview scores over and above cognitive ability and conscientiousness scores. *Personnel Psychology, 53*, 325–352.

Ellingson, J. E., Sackett, P. R., & Hough, L. M. (1999). Social desirability corrections in personality measurement: Issues of applicant comparison and construct validity. *Journal of Applied Psychology, 84*, 155–166.

Ellis, A., & Conrad, H. S. (1948). The validity of personality inventories in military practice. *Psychological Bulletin, 45*, 385–426.

Frei, R. L., & McDaniel, M. A. (1998). Validity of customer service measures in personnel selection: A review of criterion and construct evidence. *Human Performance, 11*, 1–27.

Gellatly, I. R. (1996). Conscientiousness and task performance: Test of a cognitive process model. *Journal of Applied Psychology, 81*, 474–482.

Ghiselli, E. E. (1973). The validity of aptitude tests in personnel selection. *Personnel Psychology, 26*, 461–477.

Ghiselli, E. E., & Bartoll, R. P. (1953). The validity of personality inventories in selecting employees. *Journal of Applied Psychology, 37*, 18–20.

Goffin, R. D., Rothstein, M. G., & Johnston, N. G. (1996). Personality testing and the assessment center: incremental validity for managerial selection. *Journal of Applied Psychology, 81*, 746–756.

Goldberg, L. R. (1993). The structure of phenotypic personality traits. *American Psychologist, 48*, 26–34.

Guion, R. M. (1998). *Assessment, measurement, and prediction for personnel decisions.* Mahwah, NJ: Lawrence Erlbaum Associates.

Guion, R. M., & Gottier, R. F. (1965). Validity of personality measures in personnel selection. *Personnel Psychology, 18*, 135–164.

Harvey, R. J. (1991). Job analysis. In M. D. Dunnette & L. M. Hough (Eds.), *Handbook of Industrial and Organizational Psychology* (Vol. 2, pp. 71–164). Palo Alto, CA: Consulting Psychologists.

Hogan, R. T. (1991). Personality and personality measurement. In M. D. Dunnette & L. M. Hough (Eds.), *Handbook of industrial and organizational psychology* (Vol. 2, 2nd ed., pp. 873–919). Palo Alto, CA: Consulting Psychologists.

Hough, L. M. (1992). The "Big Five" personality variables–construct confusion: Description versus prediction. *Human Performance, 5*, 139–155.

Hough, L. M., Eaton, N. K., Dunnette, M. D., Kamp, J. D., & McCloy, R. A. (1990). Criterion-related validities of personality constructs and the effect of response distortion on those validities [Monograph]. *Journal of Applied Psychology, 75*, 581–595.

Hunter, J. E. (1986). Cognitive ability, cognitive aptitudes, job knowledge, and job performance. *Journal of Vocational Behavior, 29*, 340–362.

Hunter, J. E., & Schmidt, F. L. (1990). *Methods of meta-analysis.* Newbury Park, CA: Sage.

Hurtz, G. M., & Donovan, J. J. (2000). Personality and job performance: The Big Five revisited. *Journal of Applied Psychology, 85*, 869–879.

Judge, T. A., Martocchio, J. J., & Thoresen, C. J. (1997). Five-factor model of personality and employee absence. *Journal of Applied Psychology, 82*, 745–755.

Kanfer, R. (1991). Motivation theory and industrial and organizational psychology. In M. D. Dunnette & L. M. Hough (Eds.), *Handbook of Industrial and Organizational Psychology* (pp. 75–170). Palo Alto, CA: Consulting Psychologists.

Locke, E. A., & Hulin, C. L. (1962). A review and evaluation of the activity vector analysis. *Personnel Psychology, 15*, 25–42.

McHenry, J. J., Hough, L. M., Toquam, J. L., Hanson, M. A., & Ashworth, S. (1990). Project A validity results: The relationship between predictor and criterion domains. *Personnel Psychology, 43*, 335–354.

McMannus, M. A., & Kelly, M. L. (1999). Personality measures and biodata: Evidence regarding their incremental predictive validity in the life insurance industry. *Personnel Psychology, 52*, 137–148.

Montag, I., & Comrey, A. L. (1990). Stability of major personality factors under changing motivational conditions. In J. W. Neuliep (Ed.), *Replication research in the social sciences* (pp. 253–262). Newbury Park, CA: Sage.

Mount, M. K., & Barrick, M. R. (1995). The Big Five personality dimensions: Implications for research and practice in human resource management. *Research in Personnel and Human Resources Management, 13*, 153–200.

Mount, M. K., Barrick, M. R., & Strauss, J. P. (1994). Validity of observer ratings of the Big Five personality factors. *Journal of Applied Psychology, 79,* 272–280.

Mount, M. K., Witt, A., & Barrick, M. R. (2000). Incremental validity of empirically-keyed biographical scales over GMA and the Big Five personality constructs. *Personnel Psychology, 53,* 299–323.

Murray, H. A. (1938). *Explorations in personality.* New York: Oxford University Press.

Murtha, T. C., Kanfer, R., & Ackerman, P. L. (1996). Toward an interactionist taxonomy of personality and situations: An integrative situational—dispositional representation of personality traits. *Journal of Personality & Social Psychology, 71,* 193–207.

Ones, D. S., Mount, M. K., Barrick, M. R., & Hunter, J. E. (1994). Personality and job performance: A critique of the Tett, Jackson, & Rothstein (1991) meta-analysis. *Personnel Psychology, 47,* 147–156.

Ones, D. S., & Viswesvaran, C. (1996). Bandwidth-fidelity dilemma in personality measurement for personnel selection. *Journal of Organizational Behavior, 17,* 609–626.

Ones, D. S., Viswesvaran, C., & Schmidt, F. L. (1993). Comprehensive meta-analysis of integrity test validities: Findings and implications for personnel selection and theories of job performance. *Journal of Applied Psychology, 78,* 679–703.

Organ, D. W., & Ryan, K. (1995). A meta-analytic review of attitudinal and dispositional predictors of organizational citizenship behavior. *Personnel Psychology, 48,* 775–802.

Robertson, I. T., & Kinder, A. (1993). Personality and job competencies: The criterion-related validity of some personality variables. *Journal of Occupational and Organizational Psychology, 66,* 226–244.

Salgado, J. F. (1997). The five factor model of personality and job performance in the European community. *Journal of Applied Psychology, 82,* 30–43.

Schmidt, F. L., & Hunter, J. E. (1998). The validity and utility of selection methods in personnel psychology: Practical and theoretical implications of 85 years of research findings. *Psychological Bulletin, 124,* 262–274.

Schmidt, F. L., Hunter, J. E., Outerbridge, A. N., & Trattner, M. H. (1986). The economic impact of job selection methods on the size, productivity, and payroll costs of the Federal workforce: An empirical demonstration. *Personnel Psychology, 39,* 1–29.

Schmit, M. J., & Ryan, A. M. (1993). The Big Five in personnel selection: Factor structure in applicant and nonapplicant populations. *Journal of Applied Psychology, 78,* 966–974.

Schmitt, N., Gooding, R. Z., Noe, R. A., & Kirsch, M. (1984). Meta-analysis of validity studies published between 1964 and 1982 and the investigation of study characteristics. *Personnel Psychology, 37,* 407–422.

Schneider, R. J., Hough, L. M., & Dunnette, M. D. (1996). Broadsided by broad traits: How to sink science in five dimensions or less. *Journal of Organizational Behavior, 17,* 639–655.

Simonton, D. K. (1999). Talent and its development: An emergenic and epigenetic model. *Psychological Review, 106,* 433–457.

Simonton, D. K. (2000). Creativity–cognitive, personal, developmental, and social aspects. *American Psychologist, 55,* 151–158.

Stewart, G. L., & Barrick, M. R. (in press). Lessons learned from the person-situation debate: A review and research agenda. In B. Smith & B. Schneider (Eds.), *Personality and Organizations*. Lawrence Erlbaum Associates.

Tett, R. P., Jackson, D. N., & Rothstein, M. (1991). Personality measures as predictors of job performance: A meta-analytic review. *Personnel Psychology, 44,* 703–742.

Tett, R. P., Jackson, D. N., Rothstein, M., & Reddon, J. R. (1994). Meta-analysis of personality–job performance relations: A reply to Ones, Mount, Barrick, and Hunter (1994). *Personnel Psychology, 47,* 147–156.

Viswesvaran, C., & Ones, D. S. (1995). Theory testing: Combining psychometric meta-analysis and structural equations modeling. *Personnel Psychology, 48,* 865–886.

8

The Challenge of Aggregating Studies of Personality

Mitchell G. Rothstein
R. Blake Jelley
The University of Western Ontario

Individual differences are generally recognized as central concerns to many industrial/organizational (I/O) psychologists (Goffin & Helmes, 2000; Mount & Barrick, 1998; Murphy, 1996). In the past decade, there has been a dramatic resurgence of research interest in personality–job performance relations and increased consideration of other noncognitive individual difference variables (Murphy, 1996). Meta-analytic studies are often considered fundamental catalysts of this revival (e.g., Goffin, Rothstein, & Johnston, 2000; Hogan, 1998; Hogan, Hogan, & Roberts, 1996; Hough, 1997; Hough & Oswald, 2000; Irving, 1993; Mount & Barrick, 1995; Murphy, 1996, 2000). Indeed, Barrick and Mount's (1991) meta-analysis was *Personnel Psychology's* most highly cited article of the 1990s (Mount & Barrick, 1998). A decade after its publication the influence of this work does not appear to be diminishing, as citations to this article have accumulated to almost 400 (Institute for Scientific Information, 2001).

Other personality–job performance meta-analyses published in the early 1990s (i.e., Hough, 1992; Hough, Eaton, Dunnette, Kamp, & McCloy, 1990; Tett, Jackson, & Rothstein, 1991) have received interest and stimulated discussion that has "illustrated that there are complex methodological and theoretical issues that must be considered when conducting research in this area" (Mount & Barrick, 1998, p. 853). In this chapter, discussed are the key challenges and limitations inherent in applying meta-analytic methods both to summarize the personality–job performance research literature and to make inferences of validity generalization from the cumulated research. Also discussed are some of the important contributions that have been made by meta-analytic researchers in the personality–job performance domain.

Meta-analytic methods provide tools with which to summarize, in a quantitative way, a body of research such that making sense of that literature is facilitated (Hunter & Schmidt, 1990; Murphy, 1997; Rosenthal & DiMatteo, 2001). Various methods of meta-analysis exist (Murphy, 1997, 2000; Rosenthal & DiMatteo, 2001), but the procedures pioneered by Schmidt and Hunter (1977; Hunter & Schmidt, 1990) are most common in I/O psychology. Meta-analysis cumulates results across a set of studies that all bear on the same relation to establish basic facts (Hunter & Schmidt, 1990). Those facts include point estimates of the general effect size and estimates of how much a given effect varies across studies. The Hunter-Schmidt procedures are unique among meta-analytic methods in that they specifically seek to estimate and correct for several artifactual sources of variation (e.g., sampling error, error of measurement) that attenuate point estimates and inflate variance estimates (Hunter & Schmidt, 1990). Applications of meta-analysis have shown that effects are generally larger and more consistent than is evident by perusing a number of individual studies (Murphy, 1997). Although controversies exist and procedures continue to be refined, the basic methods, assumptions, and findings are increasingly accepted and applied in research and practice (Murphy, 1997, 2000).

Meta-analysis has had major influences on the science and practice of I/O psychology (Hough & Oswald, 2000; Murphy, 1996, 1997, 2000; Schmidt, 1992) and on a number of other fields (Rosenthal & DiMatteo, 2001). It has influenced the way researchers think about data and its decryption (Schmidt, 1992). Substantively, meta-analysis has been applied in many areas of I/O psychology and organizational behavior (OB), but its most frequent application has been in personnel selection research where it has had important consequences both for applied practice and for theoretical advances (Hunter & Schmidt, 1990; Murphy, 1997, 2000; Schmidt, 1992).

The application of meta-analytic techniques to examine and extend research on the validity of employment predictor data, traditionally but not exclusively involving tests of ability and aptitude, is often termed validity generalization research (Hartigan & Wigdor, 1989; Hunter & Schmidt, 1990; Murphy, 1997, 2000; Schmidt,

1992; Schmidt & Hunter, 1977). It was from their initial research on validity generalization (Schmidt & Hunter, 1977) that generally applicable methods of psychometric meta-analysis evolved (Hunter & Schmidt, 1990).

In applying their validity generalization procedures, Schmidt and Hunter (1977) challenged the doctrine of situational specificity and they and their colleagues conducted a number of other studies throughout the 1980s to test if validity might actually be generalizable (Schmidt, 1992). However, demonstration that (after appropriate artifact corrections have been made) a test, for example, is at least *minimally valid* in all settings in which it has been applied and is therefore likely to be valid in other, similar settings (i.e., validity generalizes) is not identical to finding that the level of validity is *constant* across settings (i.e., no situational specificity exists) (Murphy, 1997, 2000). Although the term *validity generalization* is sometimes used to describe a particular set of meta-analytic procedures, it is also a process of interpreting and making inferences from meta-analytic results (Murphy, 1997, 2000). It is therefore important to be aware of the limitations of meta-analysis, as well as its strengths, as a basis for making valid inferences (e.g., Bobko & Stone-Romero, 1998; Hartigan & Wigdor, 1989; Murphy, 1997, 2000). This is particularly important to the meta-analysis of personality–job performance relations.

Murphy (2000) outlined key considerations with respect to making justified inferences from meta-analyses of employment assessment procedures. These considerations include: (a) the quality of the database and the quality of the primary studies it contains; (b) whether the studies included in the meta-analysis are representative of the population of potential applications of the predictor; (c) whether a particular test being considered for use is a member of the population of instruments examined in the meta-analysis; and (d) whether the situation intended for test use is similar to the situations sampled in the quantitative review. Unfortunately, meta-analyses often omit essential information from which to answer key questions (Murphy, 2000).

Tests of cognitive ability are generally recognized as being valid predictors of job performance, with validities being generalizable across virtually all jobs and organizations, although moderated to some degree by job complexity (Hunter & Hunter, 1984). Success in the cognitive domain has been accompanied by applications of validity generalization procedures to many other predictors (Schmidt, 1992). Can validity generalization apply to the personality domain? At first glance, it would certainly appear so as a number of meta-analyses have been conducted with personality variables as predictors of job performance and other organizationally relevant outcomes. However, there are fundamental differences between the cognitive domain and personality variables and these differences present additional challenges both for cumulating results in a meaningful way and for drawing valid inferences from personality–job performance research.

CURRENT STATUS:
CONTRIBUTIONS AND CONTROVERSIES

The meta-analyses of personality–job performance relations conducted in the early 1990s (i.e., Barrick & Mount, 1991; Hough, 1992; Hough et al., 1990; Tett et al., 1991) have been visible and influential. This research has been used in defense of dispositional approaches in organizational behavior (House, Shane, & Herold, 1996) and to support the use of personality assessment for personnel selection (Jackson & Rothstein, 1996). Primary researchers have started to consider issues beyond the basic question of whether personality can predict job performance. For example, researchers have investigated goal setting and other cognitive-motivational processes as mediators of the Conscientiousness–job performance relation (e.g., Barrick, Mount, & Strauss, 1993; Gellatly, 1996). Barrick and Mount (1993) considered a boundary condition of personality–job performance relations by examining the degree to which autonomy, or the discretion accorded to an incumbent in the selection of appropriate work behaviors, acted as a moderator. Stewart, Carson, and Cardy (1996) considered the effects of Conscientiousness in combination with self-leadership training on employee self-direction. In short, these meta-analyses have helped put personality back into research and practice. Personality psychology has never been more active nor had contributions from such a diverse array of researchers (Funder, 2001). "The relevance of personality to I/O psychology is no myth; it is an undeniable and scientifically exciting reality" (Hough & Schneider, 1996, p. 76). Meta-analytic research seems to have played an instrumental role in revitalizing interest in personality among researchers in I/O psychology. However, the early 1990s work represents only a subset of the meta-analyses that have been conducted in this area.

Earlier reviews of personality job–performance relations, both quantitative and qualitative, did not necessarily indicate that personality had no potential in personnel psychology, but they were generally cautionary and pessimistic about the accumulated validity evidence (Ghiselli & Barthol, 1953; Guion & Gottier, 1965; Weiss & Adler, 1984). The pessimism continued in the organizational research community, with respect to personality, as applications of psychometric meta-analysis became more popular. Hunter and Hunter (1984) did not include measures of personality variables in their influential meta-analysis of alternative predictors of job performance. Schmitt, Gooding, Noe, and Kirsh (1984) compared various predictors of organizationally relevant criteria and concluded that "personality measures were clearly less valid" (p. 407). Based on their meta-analysis, Ford, Walker, Churchill, and Hartley (1987) contended that, despite the popularity of personality variables in sales validation studies, they were generally not very successful predictors of sales performance. Conversely, Lord, De Vader, and Alliger (1986) were more optimistic about the potential of personality variables. They applied validity generalization procedures to personality–leadership perception data. Both corrected and uncorrected mean correlations were higher than the effects reported in classic leadership literature and most between study variance could be attributed to artifacts. Although Lord and colleagues dealt with leadership perceptions rather than performance, they foreshadowed subsequent developments when they wrote "the validity generalization approach, along with other conceptual . . . and methodological improvements . . . may well yield a more optimistic conclusion concerning the ability of personality traits to predict behaviors" (p. 408).

In an effort to understand the hundreds of personality traits and measures in the literature, many personality–job performance meta-analysts have sought a meaningful taxonomy with which to organize their reviews. The choice of taxonomy is an issue of ongoing controversy. The Five Factor Model (FFM) of personality or "Big Five" (cf. Hough & Schneider, 1996; John & Srivastava, 1999; Mount & Barrick, 1995) has, despite some persistent opposition, become prevalent in the personality literature (Funder, 2001). A number of personality–job performance meta-analysts have examined the criterion-related validity of the Big Five personality dimensions (Barrick & Mount, 1991; Hurtz & Donovan, 2000; Mount, Barrick, & Stewart, 1998; Salgado, 1997, 1998). In other meta-analyses (e.g., Frei & McDaniel, 1998; Mount & Barrick, 1995; Organ & Ryan, 1995; Tett et al., 1991; Vinchur, Schippmann, Switzer, & Roth, 1998) Big Five dimensions have played a role, even if they were not the primary or exclusive focus. Indeed, a good number of researchers have regarded the emergence of the Big Five as a major achievement because it can serve as a common framework for research integration. They have argued that it has helped to reveal the true predictive validity of personality that was obscured in previous research (Barrick & Mount, 1991, 1993; Frei & McDaniel, 1998; Hurtz & Donovan, 2000; Mount & Barrick, 1995, 1998; Mount et al., 1998; Ones, Mount, Barrick, & Hunter, 1994; Ones & Viswesvaran, 1996; Salgado, 1997, 1998). Generally, the criterion-related validities reported in these reviews have been in the low to moderate range (i.e., mean, corrected validities rarely exceeding 0.30). Conscientiousness typically shows the highest and most consistently generalizable criterion-related validity in these studies. Emotional Stability also generalizes its validity quite well in some analyses, although its validity is of lower magnitude. Other dimensions have also shown useful relations in particular areas. These meta-analyses have demonstrated that personality validities, at least for some constructs, may generalize more readily than previously believed. Moreover, the Conscientiousness construct does have intuitive appeal as a predictor of job performance and this may well have helped garner interest in personality–job performance linkages (Hurtz & Donovan, 2000; Mount & Barrick, 1998). Overall, Mount and Barrick (1995) contend that there are many reasons for optimism about personality measures in our field, and that much of the optimism can be attributed to the widespread acceptance of the Big Five. "The importance of this taxonomy cannot be overstated as the availability of such a classification scheme provides the long missing conceptual foundation necessary for scientific advancement in the field" (Mount & Barrick, 1995, p. 190).

However, other researchers are more cautious regarding the Big Five and its potential to benefit the science and practice of I/O psychology. Barrick and Mount's (1991) results have been met with considerable enthusiasm (e.g., they have led "us out of the empirical darkness," Hogan, 1998, p. 126) despite the fact that even their best (i.e., Conscientiousness) effect size (in this study, the estimated value of rho = 0.22) was similar to the pessimistic validity of personality (estimated rho = 0.21, with performance ratings as the criterion) reported by Schmitt et al. (1984). Hurtz and Donovan (2000) recognized this and, in their meta-analysis, offered more temperate interpretations of the validity of explicit Big Five measures. Although the FFM is useful as a global, descriptive taxonomy it has important limitations and may be inadequate for the prediction of important life outcomes (Hough, 1992, 1997). "The FFM yields information about the higher-order factor structure of personality; however, it ignores, confounds, or otherwise obscures understanding of variables combined into five broad factors" (Hough & Oswald, 2000, p. 637). It is possible that the importance of the Big Five has been overstated.

The Big Five is not the only conceptual framework from which personality–job performance meta-analyses have been and can be conducted. For example, Hough and colleagues (Hough, 1992; Hough et al., 1990) employed a taxonomy which differentiates subdimensions of Big Five factors and includes other constructs (e.g., Rugged Individualism) that are not considered within the Big Five. Recently, Judge and Bono (2001) conducted a meta-analysis of some of the most pervasive personality constructs in personality and applied psychology. The four constructs (Self-Esteem, Generalized Self-Efficacy, Locus of Control, & Emotional Stability—a Big Five dimension) were theoretically linked through a higher order construct called *Core Self-Evaluations* or *Positive Self-Concept*. In this more focused meta-analysis the traits examined compared favorably, in terms of predictive validity, to Conscientiousness results from Big Five studies. The limitations of the Big Five are discussed in more detail later, but it is evident that meta-analysis of personality need not necessarily adopt the Big Five framework.

A closely related controversy that has implications for the validity generalization of personality concerns the bandwidth of personality constructs and measures. Some researchers contend that the Big Five dimensions are too broad in that predictive and interpretive benefits arise from the use of traits at lower levels of the personality hierarchy (e.g., Hough, 1992; Paunonen, Rothstein, & Jackson, 1999; Schneider, Hough, & Dunnette, 1996). The other perspective dictates that the Big Five or even broader variables are desirable for job performance prediction and theoretical development (Mount & Barrick, 1995; Ones & Viswesvaran, 1996; Ones, Viswesvaran, & Schmidt, 1993). These issues impact the ability to use validity generalization with personality and will be explored more fully in this chapter.

Using the Big Five, or any taxonomy, to integrate findings can create some complexities. For example, scales that measure narrower personality constructs have been classified, post hoc, into relevant Big Five dimensions. This can be a difficult and contentious process (Hogan et al., 1996; Hurtz & Donovan, 2000; Judge & Bono, 2001; Ones et al., 1994; Salgado, 1997; Tett, Jackson, Rothstein, & Reddon, 1994). More recent studies have tried to overcome such problems by using more explicit measures of the Big Five (e.g., Hurtz & Donovan, 2000). Mount et al. (1998) meta-analyzed one particular Big Five instrument, their Personal Characteristics Inventory (PCI), in jobs involving interpersonal interaction. Although sample sizes are reduced in such studies and second-order sampling error may be a concern (cf. Hunter & Schmidt, 1990), this strategy has some important benefits. For those wishing to use meta-analytic results as a basis for inferring validity generalization, it becomes a simple process to determine if the test (or scale) being considered is a member of the population of tests included in the meta-analysis. Moreover, Mount et al. (1998) described predictive validities as a function of the nature of interpersonal interactions. This information could prove useful to help determine whether the situation intended for test use is similar to the situations in which particular scales exhibited meaningful validities.

Of course, meta-analyses of particular instruments need not be limited to those designed to assess the Big Five. Robertson and Kinder (1993; Salgado, 1996) meta-analyzed research conducted with the work-related scales (e.g., Persuasive, Socially confident, Data rational, Innovative, Critical, Decisive) contained in the Occupational Personality Questionnaire (OPQ). They convened a panel of practitioners and psychologists who generated predictions for 12 criterion areas (e.g., Planning and organizing, Managing staff, Communication, Resilience). Robertson and Kinder concluded that the use of a priori hypotheses may explain why they found higher validities than had been reported in previous meta-analyses of personality variables. The use of confirmatory versus exploratory research strategies was also a primary focus of the Tett et al. (1991) meta-analysis and demonstrated the benefits of the former strategy (cf. Tett et al., 1994; Tett, Jackson, Rothstein, & Reddon, 1999a).

Ones et al. (1994) argued that it is inappropriate to exclude exploratory studies when using meta-analysis in combination with a personality taxonomy. However, Tett et al. (1994) maintained that the use of a personality taxonomy to organize meta-analytic research does not necessarily mitigate the problem of averaging meaningful predicted validity coefficients with those obtained from exploratory studies. Tett et al. (1994) argued that greater specificity in linking personality and job performance can be achieved through confirmatory approaches than through broad predictor and criterion categories. Mount and Barrick (1995) also determined, from a meta-analysis of Conscientiousness and its facets, that the lower level traits predict more specific performance measures better than the broad factor "only when they are conceptually related to the criterion" (p. 174). However, the majority of meta-analyses of personality–job performance research have lumped together coefficients where a predictor-criterion relation is expected with coefficients where there is no particular reason to expect a relation. When estimating the overall validity of personality variables, this can result in underestimates (Schneider et al., 1996; Tett et al., 1991, 1994, 1999a). Validities are higher when a trait is chosen to predict criteria on the basis of some conceptual or theoretical foundation.

The use of job-related compound personality variables (constellations of narrow traits, Schneider et al., 1996) is another method of obtaining higher predictive validities (e.g., Frei & McDaniel, 1998; Robertson & Kinder, 1993). However, Paunonen et al. (1999) have recommended the use of multiple, nonredundant, unidimensional predictors to maximize prediction and interpretation. That is, rather than building factorial complexity into a particular test (e.g., a customer service orientation inventory), it is best to meet criterion multidimensionality with a battery of tests purposely selected to match criterion facets (e.g., scales for friendliness, reliability, responsibility, & courteousness). For predictive purposes, unidimensional predictors can be optimally combined with a multiple regression equation (Nunnally, 1978; Paunonen et al., 1999). Moreover, the use of construct valid unidimensional personality measures is superior to a linear composite of heterogeneous measures for behavior explanation (Paunonen et al., 1999). That is, it is more informative to know that successful customer service representatives are, for example, friendly and reliable (as measured by scales with solid construct definitions and evidence for construct validity) than it is to know that they tend to receive high scores on customer service orientation.

Another important development in personality–job performance meta-analytic research involves methodological developments in meta-analytic procedures that evolved from consideration of the substantive domain. When a positive relation is expected between variables, traditional meta-analysis expects some negative correlations due to sampling error. Tett et al. (1991, 1994, 1999a) challenged the assumption of unidirectional relations and argued that there are reasons to believe that true bidirectional relations can and do exist between personality predictors and job performance. For example, friendliness and responsiveness to customers' needs may positively predict the job performance of customer service representatives. However, these same traits may detract from effective performance in jobs like border patrol officer or foot solider where national security interests are a top priority (Tett et al., 1999a). It is theoretically possible to use traditional meta-analysis and moderator identification procedures to investigate bidirectional relations if the key characteristics of work environments were known (Tett et al., 1999a). However, the required information is rarely available in source studies. Alternative procedures, beginning with Tett et al. (1991), have evolved during the 1990s (Ones et al., 1994; Tett et al., 1994, 1999a, 1999b). These developments highlight that methodological and statistical procedures need to be carefully examined when applied to new substantive domains, and such extensions may lead to revised procedures that could be adopted in other meta-analytic research.

In summary, meta-analyses of personality–job performance relations have been instrumental in the revival of personality research in I/O psychology. Nevertheless, the differences between measures of personality and general mental ability, the controversies surrounding the use of an appropriate taxonomy and relevant bandwidth of personality constructs, and the problems inherent in using meta-analysis with personality data, all present limitations to the use of validity generalization with personality measures.

Limitations to the Use of Validity
Generalization with Personality Measures:
Differences Between Measures of Personality
and Measures of General Mental Ability

Validity generalization researchers have been highly successful in demonstrating that in virtually all jobs across all organizations measures of general mental ability will, to some extent, predict job performance. The work of Schmidt and Hunter and their colleagues (Schmidt & Hunter, 1977, 1981; Schmidt, Hunter, & Caplan, 1981; Schmidt, Hunter, & Pearlman, 1981; Pearlman, Schmidt, & Hunter, 1980) provided compelling evidence for the proposition that general mental ability contributes to the performance of all jobs. The parsimony of the validity generalization model is extremely attractive to I/O and personnel psychologists. The ability to use a measure of g to select employees also has the potential to enhance productivity in organizations to a considerable extent (Schmidt & Hunter, 1983; Schmidt, Hunter, McKenzie, & Muldrow, 1979). Although there have been critiques and limitations proposed to meta-analysis and the validity generalization model (e.g., Bobko & Stone-Romero, 1998; Hartigan & Wigdor, 1989; Murphy, 1997, 2000), including cautions to conduct appropriately sensitive tests of situational specificity (Hartigan & Wigdor, 1989; Murphy, 1997, 2000), the validity generalization model has been widely accepted with respect to general mental ability and job performance.

It is argued here that the validity generalization model may be more limited in its application with personality measures than it has been with measures of general mental ability. The first of these limitations is based on the substantial differences between measures of personality and *g*. Although the validity generalization model may certainly apply to personality measures under some circumstances, differences between personality measures and *g* complicate the use of validity generalization with personality measures to a far greater degree than has been the case with measures of *g*. These complications become evident immediately as we begin to consider the differences between the psychological constructs of general mental ability versus personality.

General mental ability has perhaps been the most widely researched individual difference variable in the history of psychological testing. Although there is considerable disagreement among the major theorists concerning the structure of general mental ability, or intelligence, or *g* (all these terms have been used synonymously in the research literature although general mental ability has more recently become the preferred expression), most researchers would concede that individual differences in the performance of cognitive tasks are systematic and highly correlated (Eysenck, 1979; Humphreys, 1979; Jensen, 1980). Spearman (1927) was the first to posit that correlations between all cognitive measures demonstrate the existence of a general intellectual factor or *g*. Thurstone (1938) and Vernon (1965) both argued for the existence of what they called group factors that were related to *g* but not identical. Subsequent researchers have suggested different ways of conceptualizing the structure of general mental ability (e.g., Cattell, 1963) and argued for the existence of more complex and multidimensional structures of general mental ability (e.g., Guilford, 1988; Sternberg, 1977, 1985). Generally, however, the concept of *g* is widely accepted among psychologists. From a practical perspective, the use of *g* in personnel testing is pervasive. Certainly group factors and other more specific abilities have been used in personnel selection (e.g., Hartigan & Wigdor, 1989), but measures of *g* remain the most widely acceptable and practical form of assessment in personnel selection (Murphy & Davidshofer, 1991; Schmidt & Hunter, 1998). Murphy (1996) noted that this has led to oversimplifications regarding the nature of *g* and that lower levels of the ability hierarchy could potentially increase our understanding of the nature of ability in the prediction of overall job performance, as well as its relation to other important work-related criteria. Researchers in validity generalization, however, have embraced the concept of *g* wholeheartedly in that, from both a methodological and conceptual standpoint, g represents an appealing and parsimonious view of the role of general mental ability in job performance. Because almost every reliable measure of cognitive processing may be used to assess g, these measures reflect a homogeneous construct domain that is relatively easy to interpret when accumulated in a meta-analytic study.

Psychologists use personality constructs and theories "to account for individuals' characteristic patterns of thought, emotion, and behavior together with the psychological mechanisms—hidden or not—behind those patterns" (Funder, 2001, p. 198). Personality measures differ in a number of ways from measures of general mental ability and these differences may have a substantial effect on meta-analytic studies and the argument for validity generalization. First, personality measures are based on distinctly different theories of personality, or in some cases on no theory at all (Block, 1995). Although theories of general mental ability have also varied to a substantial degree, as discussed previously, all of the prominent theories of general mental ability are based on the fundamental premise that this ability involves cognitive activity requiring mental processing, retrieval, or manipulation of information (Murphy & Davidshofer, 1991). In the realm of personality, however, the prominent theoretical formulations are so fundamentally different that measures derived from these theories have little in common theoretically, methodologically, or empirically (Lanyon & Goodstein, 1997). These fundamental differences have created considerable discussion on the importance of construct validity in personality assessment (e.g., Goffin & Helmes, 2000; Weiss & Adler, 1984). The core purpose of construct validity is to demonstrate the relations between the personality measure and the theoretical system from which it was derived. Construct validity evidence requires the use of convergent and discriminant validity techniques to develop a nomological network of relations that demonstrate that the measure of interest is theoretically and empirically distinct from measures of other personality constructs and is related to other measures of the same construct or criterion measures that represent observable manifestations of the construct (Jackson, 1971; Weiss & Adler, 1984). The importance of construct validity to the development of personality measures has long been emphasized and has remained a critical component of the evaluation of personality measures (Cronbach, 1989; Cronbach & Meehl, 1955; Jackson, 1971; Wiggins, 1973).

Measures of general mental ability are rarely scrutinized with respect to their construct validity. The reason for this is that the characteristics of a good test of general mental ability are straightforward and relatively easily attained (Murphy & Davidshofer, 1991). The often-cited observation that most measures of general mental ability are correlated stems, to a considerable extent, from the common content domain that the tests are attempting to measure. Personality measures are fundamentally different in this regard in that there is no common content domain for personality measures.

A second fundamental difference between measures of general mental ability and personality concerns differences in test construction methodology. Reviews of personality assessment methods (e.g., Anastasi, 1982; Cronbach, 1970; Hopkins, Stanley, & Hopkins, 1990; Murphy & Davidshofer, 1991) and numerous other influential pieces written on this topic (e.g., Jackson, 1971; Guion, 1991; Hogan, 1991; Wiggins, 1973) have discussed the variety of test construction methods used in the development of personality measures and the difficulties many measures have had in demonstrating adequate levels of reliability and meaningful criterion-related validity. In a review of this problem with respect to employment decisions, Hogan et al. (1996) observed that of the many measures of personality, only a small subset meet the essential criteria of temporal stability and criterion-related validity. Clearly not all personality measures are created equal. An explicit example of the implications of this inequality was recently demonstrated by Goffin et al. (2000) who compared the criterion-related validity of Dominance and Extraversion as measured by two different inventories in which quite different scale development techniques were employed. The two personality measures were selected for comparison on the basis of their apparent construct similarity, but significant differences were found in the prediction of performance criteria between the two different types of measures. Unlike general mental ability therefore, it cannot be assumed, that personality measures, even those with the same name, are actually measuring the same content domain. Therefore there is little basis for the expectation that these measures assess a homogeneous construct.

A third basic difference between measures of general mental ability and personality concerns the problem of social desirability, which again is particular to personality measures. Edwards (1964) was among the first of many researchers to investigate this problem. He demonstrated that for a large number of personality measures, individuals responded to items on personality tests on the basis of their socially desirable scale values as opposed to the trait that the measure was designed to assess. He concluded that individuals tend not to respond to the trait being measured but rather the social acceptability of the statement. For many years, this problem in the measurement of personality has been debated and there is still no widespread agreement concerning the severity of this problem (Murphy & Davidshofer, 1991). The many complexities of this debate cannot be reviewed here, but it is safe to say that this problem does not apply to cognitive ability assessment whereas it is an issue that must be taken into account in personality assessment. Recently, some researchers have suggested that although individuals can distort their responses to personality items in a socially desirable direction, this distortion of their responses does not affect criterion-related validity (Hough & Schneider, 1996). However, one study that is often cited to support this contention (Christiansen, Goffin, Johnston, & Rothstein, 1994) demonstrated that although criterion-related validity may not be negatively affected in a personnel selection context, different individuals would be hired as a result of applying a correction formula to correct for the distorting effect of social desirability. More research on the problem of social desirability with personality measures used in personnel selection is required, but it is clear that this problem provides unique challenges to the validity generalization of personality measures in employee selection. To the degree that some of these measures are confounded with social desirability, accumulating them in a meta-analysis will obscure validity generalization arguments. Bobko and Stone-Romero (1998) observed that many meta-analysts give insufficient attention to contamination and construct validity issues and this can lead to erroneous meta-analytic conclusions. Moreover, they remind us that because construct validity is a component of external validity, lack of construct validity can render suspect meta-analytic conclusions regarding external validity (i.e., generalizability).

These differences between personality measures and measures of general mental ability have significant implications for the use of meta-analysis to demonstrate validity generalization. Unlike measures of general mental ability, personality measures are considerable more diverse, they are more difficult to develop, they have considerably more problems demonstrating reliability and validity, and measures with the same name often measure different constructs whereas measures with different names may assess the same constructs. As we shall see below, this creates considerable difficulties both in conducting meta-analyses of personality measures and in interpreting the results.

The Dimensionality of General Mental Ability Versus Personality. As discussed earlier, Schmidt and Hunter (1977, 1981) and their colleagues (e.g., Schmidt, Gaast-Rosenberg, & Hunter, 1980;

Schmidt, Hunter, & Caplan, 1981; Schmidt, Hunter, & Pearlman, 1981, 1982) have provided compelling evidence for the validity generalization of general mental ability or g. Although this program of research has generated considerable debate and controversy, the general findings of validity generalization research with respect to general mental ability measures have been accepted, although not without a caution to generalize validities only to appropriately similar jobs (Hartigan & Wigdor, 1989). The Schmidt–Hunter program of research is indeed compelling, but it must be noted that the meta-analytic research methodology used to demonstrate validity generalization benefited from a one-factor model of ability, which allowed the accumulation of source studies in the meta-analysis to be undertaken efficiently and with limited concern for measurement differences. Can we use meta-analysis in the same way with measures of personality? We will be discussing meta-analytic procedures with personality data in some detail in a later section, but here we must first explore the fundamental differences in structure between measures of general mental ability and measures of personality.

Although several researchers have suggested that there may be a "functional personality" at work (Mount & Barrick, 1995) or that the Big Five may be aggregated into a higher level trait, such as Integrity, which would be more useful for selection than traits at a lower level of aggregation (Ones & Viswesvaran, 1996), no compelling evidence has accumulated from other researchers to support these contentions. On the contrary, in a review of the use of personality measures in personnel selection, Irving (1993) concluded that "personality is not like cognitive ability with its large underlying g factor. It involves a substantial number of largely uncorrelated traits that serve to make the generalizability of traits across jobs improbable" (p. 209). Ashton (1998) submitted 21 personality scales to principal components analysis to determine if a large general Integrity factor would emerge. The first unrotated principal component accounted for 20.7% of the scales' variance, did not show high loadings for Integrity-related scales (i.e., Responsibility, Risk Taking, Conscientiousness, & Agreeableness), and exhibited a near-zero correlation with a measure of overall workplace delinquency. This pattern of evidence is not consistent with what one would expect of a broad Integrity factor (Ashton, 1998). Similarly Murphy (1996), in a discussion of individual difference variables in general, concluded that the simple structure obtained in the ability domain is unlikely to be obtained in other areas of individual difference research. Discussing personality specifically, Murphy concluded that no meaningful general factors accounting for large proportions of variance underlie the personality domain. Hough and Schneider (1996) also argued that it is premature to suggest that Integrity functions in the personality domain in a manner similar to how g functions in the cognitive ability domain.

A meaningful and valid taxonomy of personality would unquestionably provide a basis for integrating the results of diverse research and would facilitate more systematic research on personality–job performance relations (Hough, 1997; Mount & Barrick, 1995), but the enthusiasm for embracing a particular taxonomy should be anchored in the necessary conditions for demonstrating a valid taxonomy. These conditions have been articulated by Eysenck (1991) and Hough and Schneider (1996) and are critical to evaluate the validity of any personality taxonomy. According to these authors, the essential evaluation criteria for a valid personality taxonomy are replicability across a variety of contexts, comprehensiveness, the existence of external correlates, identification of underlying source traits, and inclusion of multiple levels of specificity. It is not possible to review all of the personality taxonomies documented in the research literature, although it is worthwhile to examine one of these taxonomies—the Big Five—in some detail because this taxonomy has clearly been the most prominent in recent years (Funder, 2001; Hough, 1997; Mount & Barrick, 1995; Tokar, Fischer, & Subich, 1998).

Although some researchers have expressed confidence that the Big Five describe the basic dimensions of normal personality (e.g., Mount & Barrick, 1995), many researchers disagree that the Big Five taxonomy is adequate as a comprehensive taxonomy of the structure of personality. The most thorough review and critique has been provided by Block (1995, 2001). Block (1995) began his critique with a fundamental problem: that no theory of personality structure had been articulated that would provide a basis for deriving or interpreting five factors of personality. Although there have been, more recently, attempts to develop a theoretical basis for the Big Five (e.g., McCrae & Costa, 1999), these were not available when the Big Five factors were derived. Without a coherent and falsifiable explanation for the Big Five (Briggs, 1989) it is difficult to argue that these particular five factors provide the best underlying structure of personality. It is generally possible to find, in a variety of data sets, the Big Five when one hopes to uncover the Big Five. "However, finding the Big Five is *not* the same as failing to find additional factors" (Jackson, Paunonen, Fraboni, & Goffin, 1996, p. 33). Jackson and colleagues found that a 6-factor solution provided a significantly better fit to Personality Research Form (PRF) variables than did a

FFM. Evidence for the Big Five taxonomy has relied on factor analytic studies and numerous other taxonomies have been derived and proposed as alternatives to the Big Five. This has occurred because no consistent basis for determining the number of factors to extract, or the particular rotation method to apply, has been employed by the various researchers using factor analysis to find a meaningful taxonomy underlying the structure of personality (Block, 1995). Researchers have employed different assumptions, preferences, and unstated decision rules in undertaking factor analysis of a particular set of personality measures. Thus, both Block (1995) and Goldberg (1993) observed that there is wide disagreement on the number of factors underlying the structure of personality. Rothstein and Goffin (2000) pointed out that there is evidence to suggest that this structure may in fact be the "Big Two" (Wiggins, 1968), the "Big Three" (Eysenck, 1991), the "Big Six" (Hogan, 1986), the "Big Seven" (Jackson, 1984), the "Big Eight" (Hough, 1998), or the "Big Nine" (Hough, 1992). Thus, one of the key criteria for evaluating the validity of a personality taxonomy, replicability, cannot be unequivocally demonstrated with the Big Five. Block concluded that none of the personality taxonomies in the research literature provide a better or worse theoretical explanation or empirical justification for an underlying structure of personality. Ultimately, the usefulness of any particular number of factors must be decided based on their differential utility in predicting important criteria, not solely on their prominence in a factor space (Jackson et al., 1996).

An additional problem concerning replicability has been that when data from heterogeneous samples are factored or when personality variables other than a select set are included in the analysis, different five factor structures often emerge (Block, 1995; Costa & McCrae, 1992; Goldberg, 1992; Paunonen & Jackson, 2000; Peabody & Goldberg, 1989; Schmit & Ryan, 1993). For example, the facet of Achievement is included in Conscientiousness for Costa and McCrae (1988) but not so for Peabody and Goldberg (1989) or Hogan (1991). A number of other differences in Big Five factor structures have been noted. For example, Extroversion may confound Sociability and Ambition, and Achievement is confounded with both Extroversion and Conscientiousness (Hough, 1997). Hough (1992) regarded Achievement as a factor by itself. Hough (1997) commented on the difficulty of understanding the nature of Conscientiousness, when both Achievement and Dependability are included in this factor. Paunonen and Jackson (1996) identified three distinguishable "dimensions related to being (a) methodical and orderly, (b) dependable and reliable, and (c) ambitious and driven to succeed" (p. 55) that may not overlap sufficiently to justify a single Conscientiousness variable. Moreover, the aggregation of facets into broad, confounded factors can mask predictor-criterion relations (Hough, 1992, 1997; Hough & Oswald, 2000).

The criterion of comprehensiveness for a valid personality taxonomy is also problematic for the Big Five. Block (1995) has stated that there had been a considerable amount of prestructuring of the variables used in the factor analyses to demonstrate the Big Five taxonomy. According to Block, personality variables were preselected for inclusion in the analyses and other variables were specifically excluded, thrown out of the analysis if they did not fit, or simply ignored. Numerous other researchers have found that certain prominent personality characteristics that have well demonstrated construct validity do not fit into the Big Five taxonomy (Hough, 1992; Judge & Bono, 2001; Paunonen & Jackson, 1996, 2000). Clearly, no personality taxonomy can claim to comprehensively represent the fundamental structure of personality when theoretically important personality constructs do not fit into the taxonomy.

The problems with the Big Five cannot be ignored. It has been suggested that, at best, the Big Five represents a valuable tool for organizing personality measures at a descriptive level, but that the Big Five constructs are too broad for understanding and predicting behavior (Hough, 1992, 1997). The implications for validity generalization should be clear. Unlike the case for general mental ability in which one underlying factor, g, has been used to accumulate evidence in meta-analytic studies to demonstrate validity generalization, there is no one underlying factor in personality and the evidence reviewed earlier suggests that the number of underlying factors of personality is not currently known to an adequate degree. A taxonomy of personality measures (however many dimensions exist in this taxonomy) must demonstrate adequate levels of comprehensiveness and replicability as a prerequisite to any attempt to assess validity generalization because a lack of comprehensiveness or replicability casts doubts on the construct validity of the taxonomic dimensions. An absence of construct validity at the predictor level is unlikely to contribute to the understanding of job performance criteria. Moreover, if a personality factor cannot demonstrate adequate levels of reliability and validity or is confounded with other measures, meta-analysis cannot be used effectively to accumulate findings across studies. The ability to generalize the validity of a personality predictor across jobs and organizations requires strong empirical support, such as that provided in the case of general mental ability. Hurtz and Donovan (2000) concluded from their meta-analytic study of explicit Big Five measures, that personality measures should not be accorded the same status as general mental abilities. This is not to say that certain measures of personality, either facet traits or broad dimensions, may not demonstrate limited validity generalization. Clearly the numerous meta-analyses of personality measures have demonstrated the potential for validity generalization, however, it must be conceded that validity generalization of personality measures is much more limited or restricted than is the case with general mental ability. In addition, as will be discussed in a subsequent section, the meta-analytic studies of personality–job performance relations have contributed to some of these limitations.

Trait Bandwidth: The "Broad–Narrow" Debate

Meta-analyses that restrict their focus to a small set of well-defined and appropriately measured constructs are, in general, more likely to be informative than are those that attempt to pull together disparate measures and constructs (Hunter & Schmidt, 1990). Unfortunately, "the question of how varied the independent and dependent variable measures included in a meta-analysis should be is a more complex and subtle one than it appears to be at first glance" (p. 498). In the personality–job performance area there have been spirited exchanges concerning the relative merits of measuring personality at various bandwidths. Aspects of this debate are pertinent to the present discussion of validity generalization of personality–job performance relations because meta-analytic evidence is sometimes cited as supporting the position that broad measures are better (e.g., Ones & Viswesvaran, 1996). It is argued here that such meta-analytic evidence does not necessarily provide unequivocal support to such a position. Several critiques and limitations are outlined here of meta-analysis and the validity generalization model that have led us to question whether researchers can appropriately conclude that there is no situationally specific variance in need of explanation, hence no room for narrow traits to offer incremental prediction in a particular situation. In addition, to the extent that narrow personality measures, especially if the criteria are also narrow and specific, are better predictors of job performance criteria, this presents another potential limitation to the use of validity generalization with personality. Further, the breadth of measurement used in primary research has important implications for the future meta-analytic research that can be conducted and for the theoretical advances that can be made.

Ones and Viswesvaran (1996), although not the only advocates of broad measures (e.g., Mount & Barrick, 1995), provoked a number of responses (Ashton, 1998; Hogan & Roberts, 1996; Paunonen et al., 1999; Schneider et al., 1996) by asserting that the use of broader personality traits in personnel selection research is preferable to the use of narrower traits both for prediction and for explanation. A number of other researchers have specified exactly the opposite to be true. That is, it has been argued that the use of relatively narrow personality traits can provide predictive benefits and explanatory and interpretability benefits over the use of broader traits (Ashton, 1998; Ashton, Jackson, Paunonen, Helmes, & Rothstein, 1995; Hough, 1992, 1997; Hough et al., 1990; Moon, 2001; Paunonen, 1998; Paunonen & Ashton, 2001; Paunonen et al., 1999; Paunonen & Nicol, 2001; Schneider et al., 1996).

A point that is likely of mutual agreement is that narrow traits will have higher predictive and explanatory power only to the extent that trait-specific variance is related to criteria of interest. However, some researchers believe that the common variance among a set of traits (reflected in a broad measure of that dimension; e.g., Extraversion) contains all the information that is predictive and meaningful. The alternative view posits that the nonerror variance that is unique to a narrow trait (e.g., that which distinguishes Dominance from other Extraversion traits like Affiliation and Exhibition) can also be important and useful. A second point of agreement is that measures of job performance are complex and multidimensional. Whether this necessitates the use of broad traits to maximize prediction (e.g., Ones & Viswesvaran, 1996; e.g., Paunonen & Nicol, 2001; Paunonen et al., 1999; Schneider et al., 1996) has been the subject of considerable debate.

A clear definition of what constitutes a broad trait and a narrow trait can be elusive (cf. Hogan & Roberts, 1996; Schneider et al., 1996). The choice between *broad* and *narrow* personality measurement may actually be a choice between broad and broader assessments (Hogan & Roberts, 1996). A hierarchical organization of personality, although a simplified representation of its structure (Hough & Schneider, 1996; Paunonen, 1998), has long held intuitive and theoretical appeal (Paunonen, 1998; Paunonen & Nicol, 2001). For example, at the lowest level of the hierarchy exist a variety of specific behavioral responses, several of which define a habitual response pattern at the next level. Several habitual response patterns, together, form a (facet-level or "narrow") personality trait. Several of these traits (e.g., Responsibility, Orderliness, Ambition, Endurance, Methodicalness) define a factor-level variable (i.e. Conscientiousness; Paunonen, 1998; Paunonen & Nicol, 2001). The organization of the personality hierarchy has, in recent years, centered on the Big Five as defining the factor level. Although complete consensus does not yet exist on the hierarchy's exact organization, it is far closer to being resolved than are the issues of the number of levels in the hierarchy or the relative utilities of different components of the hierarchy (Paunonen, 1998). It is the relative utility of different trait bandwidths that is of interest in this section.

Ones and Viswesvaran (1996) based their arguments for broad measures, in part, on their interpretation of meta-analytic results. In the personality domain, they argued that Conscientiousness measures (Barrick & Mount, 1991) and Integrity tests (Ones et al., 1993) generalize their criterion-related validities across situations. Taking personality meta-analyses in combination with evidence from the ability domain, Ones and Viswesvaran (1996) drew the following conclusion:

> We now know there is no situationally specific variance in job performance in need of explanation. . . . Thus, the question of whether the specific variance associated with a narrower trait will be related to valid variance specific to a situation, has already been answered in the negative in the literature. (p. 615)

A more cautious interpretation of meta-analytic results is suggested here. This is based, in part, on various limitations and critiques of meta-analysis and the validity generalization model (e.g., Bobko & Stone-Romero, 1998; Hartigan & Wigdor, 1989; Murphy, 1997, 2000). Examples of these problems include (a) it is difficult to conduct appropriately sensitive tests of the situational specificity hypothesis with meta-analysis; (b) the meta-analytic database may not be representative of the population of workers; (c) a database may not contain sufficient studies in a particular category (e.g., situation) to detect the operation of a true moderator; (d) psychometric meta-analytic procedures may treat meaningful situational differences, and other theoretically appropriate moderators, as statistical artifacts; and, (e) omnibus (i.e., overall) moderator tests often have insufficient power to detect a moderator effect. These and other problems lead Murphy (1997) to conclude that, although strong support for the hypothesis of situational specificity has not been generated, "the available body of evidence and research is not sufficient to support the conclusion that there is *no* true variability in validity coefficients" (p. 335). Therefore, it seems premature to conclude that narrow traits can not contribute valid variance specific to a particular job or performance criterion.

Evidence that narrower facets can have predictive advantages over factor variables also questions whether broader traits are truly superior. To support the view that broad personality variables are preferable, Ones and Viswesvaran (1996) cited Barrick and Mount's (1994) findings that Conscientiousness was more predictive of a variety of criteria than its components. However, Schneider et al. (1996) argued that these results, in particular those pertaining to more specific criteria, underestimate the criterion-related validity of the narrow traits by aggregating validity coefficients where a predictor-criterion relation is expected with coefficients where there is no expected relation (cf. Tett et al., 1991, 1994, 1999a; with respect to the importance of confirmatory research strategies). Moreover, Mount and Barrick (1995) published meta-analytic data that cast doubt on the conclusion that Conscientiousness is more predictive than its facets. Mount and Barrick updated their Conscientiousness results (Barrick & Mount, 1991) and compared the validities of Conscientiousness to scales classified as representing either Achievement or Dependability. Mount and Barrick also classified criteria as representing overall job performance or specific performance measures (e.g., effort, quality, creativity). Mount and Barrick concluded that the factor level was not too broad to predict overall job proficiency but specific criteria may be better predicted with a conceptually related predictor.

Results reported by Mount and Barrick (1995) demonstrated that the narrow trait of Achievement was the best predictor of overall job proficiency and certain specific performance measures (i.e., effort, creativity). Another narrow trait, Dependability, was largely uncorrelated (−.04, corrected) with the creativity performance dimension. However, Dependability was the best predictor of other specific performance dimensions (e.g., employee reliability, quality). Similarly, in their meta-analysis of predictors of sales performance, Vinchur et al. (1998) found that the facets of Achievement (Conscientiousness) and Potency (Extraversion) were particularly strong predictors of sales success. Hough (1992) demonstrated that Achievement predicted performance positively for managers and executives but negatively for health care workers. For health care workers, Dependability was most predictive of performance but this trait did not predict the performance of managers and executives. A number of primary studies also provide evidence of incremental prediction and explanatory power through the use of narrow personality traits (e.g., Ashton, 1998; Ashton et al., 1995; Moon, 2001; Paunonen, 1998; Paunonen & Ashton, 2001; Paunonen & Nicol, 2001; Stewart, 1999). These findings provide support for the view that narrow traits may be better predictors of at least certain job performance criteria compared with broader factors of personality.

The predictive and interpretive benefits that can arise through the consideration of facet traits leads us to urge caution in examining only broad factors in meta-analytic or primary research. There appear to be a number of studies in the current literature where the only personality variables measured are the Big Five (Paunonen, 1998). We are concerned that a variation of the *shotgun* ("broadside") approach to personality research, which has long plagued this area (Irving, 1993; Schneider et al., 1996; Tett et al., 1991, 1994, 1999a; Weiss & Adler, 1984), will become increasingly common if the perception is created that all important variation is contained within measures of the Big Five or other broad variables. The Big Five does provide an organizing framework from which to choose personality variables for use in selection research, and it is not desirable to return to the days when a disorganized plethora of (seemingly) unrelated traits beset the personality domain (Hough, 1997). However, if a researcher uses only broad, explicit measures of the similarities among traits (e.g., Big Five), it will be impossible to (a) investigate the unique, nonerror variance that distinguishes one trait from others, and (b) consider attributes that do not fit neatly within the Big Five. The taxonomic structure of personality requires more than five factors to be complete and lower levels of the personality hierarchy must be considered (Hough, 1997). An approach where responses are collected on a number of personality scales (e.g., one or more inventories) and correlated with criteria to explore potential relations is not an optimal strategy for revealing the true potential of personality for predicting job performance (Tett et al., 1991, 1994, 1999a) or any other criteria. The use of short measures (e.g., 44 items; John & Srivastava, 1999) of broad factors can be included in research without any clear, a priori explication of the nomological network but will likely substantially underestimate the true validity (Tett et al., 1991, 1994, 1999a). Future meta-analyses may yield even worse estimates of the validity of personality if this approach to primary research dominates, particularly if meta-analysts do not differentiate confirmatory from exploratory approaches. Moreover, if measurements are taken only at the broadest (e.g., Big Five) level, whether or not a priori conceptual work is involved, it will be impossible for future meta-analysts to evaluate the relative utility of different components of the personality hierarchy. Like Paunonen and Ashton (2001), we do not profess that broad measures are always ill advised for predictive purposes. However, measuring personality exclusively at a broad level sacrifices information, whereas nothing is sacrificed when measurements are made at the facet level (Paunonen & Ashton, 2001). Even the creators of some popular Big Five measures recognize the importance of facet scales (Paunonen & Nicol, 2001).

For predictive purposes, broad measures should not be assumed to be optimal and alternative prescriptions for better prediction are available (e.g., Paunonen & Nicol, 2001; Paunonen et al., 1999; Schneider et al., 1996). Moreover, the nature of the taxonomy that defines the highest level of the personality hierarchy is important (Hough & Schneider, 1996). If it confounds variables or otherwise obscures relations, as has been suggested in the case of the Big Five (Hough, 1992, 1997; Hough & Oswald, 2000), then exclusive use of broad measures may yield unrealistically low estimates of the true potential of personality. For theory development (as well as for selection in particular domains), narrow traits provide unique information about job performance that may be obscured by broader measures (Hough, 1992; Hough et al., 1990; Mount & Barrick, 1995; Vinchur et al., 1998).

The preceding discussion has important implications for validity generalization in the personality domain. There is no compelling evidence that either broad or narrow personality measures are preferable for predicting job performance. Indeed, the evidence reviewed suggests both may be useful under certain circumstances. It is these circumstances that limit the use of validity generalization with personality measures. If both broad and narrow personality measures predict job performance criteria in different circumstances, it is much more difficult to support validity generalization with personality measures without carefully limiting its use to similar predictor measures and criteria.

Multidimensional Criteria

The implications of the differences between the predictor measures of general mental ability and personality for validity generalization extend to the criterion measures of job performance used in validation research. Meta-analyses are most informative when there is construct similarity in both predictors and criteria (Hunter & Schmidt, 1990). In the case of general mental ability almost all measures of intelligence are heavily g loaded (Murphy & Davidshofer, 1991) and thus can be easily accumulated on the predictor side. The most common criterion measure available across hundreds of these validation studies is overall job performance. It seems that the contribution of general mental ability to job performance is so pervasive that criterion specificity is unnecessary to demonstrate the validity of measures of g in predicting job performance. However, the power of general mental ability to contribute to overall job performance and the arguments for validity generalization with respect to measures of g can not be used to support the contention that job performance is unidimensional. Measures of overall job performance are most readily available and have been used to organize personality-based meta-analyses. However, this does not indicate that overall job performance represents the gold standard in validation research (Hogan & Roberts, 1996). Just as there has been considerable research investigating the dimensionality of general mental ability and personality, the dimensionality of job performance criteria has also been the subject of much research. Many researchers have commented on the importance of the dimensionality and dynamic nature of job performance criteria (e.g., Borman & Motowidlo, 1993, 1997; Campbell, 1990; Campbell, McCloy, Oppler, & Sager, 1993; Campbell, McHenry, & Wise, 1990; Hogan & Roberts, 1996; Hough & Oswald, 2000; Hunt, 1996; Murphy, 1996; Tett, Guterman, Bleier, & Murphy, 2000). As yet there is no consensus that there is one taxonomy of job performance that generalizes across all jobs, just as there is no consensus on an adequate taxonomy of personality measures. However, it is clear that job performance is complex and multidimensional.

The dimensionality of job performance criteria in conjunction with the dimensionality of personality measures contributes substantial complexity to attempts to determine validity generalization of personality measures. As we have seen, there is no g of personality. Taxonomies of personality measures and job performance criteria clearly require a matching between predictors and criteria at both the individual validity study level as well as in attempts to demonstrate validity generalization with meta-analytic studies, a process that is very different from that used with general mental ability. There is considerable research that demonstrates the variable relations between personality predictors and job performance criteria. For example, Hough (1998) found that in the Project A research program, each of the personality dimensions derived was significantly related to different criteria. In some cases the criterion-related validity of a personality construct is in opposite directions for different types of criteria (Hough, 1998). These problems create substantial difficulties for conducting meta-analyses to support the use of validity generalization, a problem that is discussed in more detail in the following section.

What can be reasonably concluded from this discussion of the differences between measures of personality and measures of general mental ability? Whereas meta-analytic studies of general mental ability provide compelling evidence for validity generalization, in the personality domain it is necessary to carefully match a personality construct with an appropriate criterion measure. At a minimum, meta-analytic studies of personality–job performance relations that ignore the importance of matching predictor and criterion measures in a meaningful way will underestimate the degree of validity generalization possible with personality data. Considerable research (Ford et al., 1987; Ghiselli & Barthol, 1953; Guion & Gottier, 1965; Hogan & Roberts, 1996; Hogan et al., 1996; Hough, 1998; Hough & Schneider, 1996; Hurtz & Donovan, 2000; Irving, 1993; Mount et al., 1998; Robertson & Kinder, 1993; Schneider et al., 1996; Tett et al., 1991, 1994, 1999a; Tokar et al., 1998; Weiss & Adler, 1984) supports the contention that personality measures in selection research should be chosen on the basis of a priori hypothesis regarding their potential relations with appropriate constructs in the job performance domain, and that meta-analytic studies of these relations would benefit from these situational-specific relations to demonstrate more limited applications of validity generalization.

Using Meta-Analysis to Support Validity Generalization with Personality Measures: Conceptual and Methodological Problems

In the case of general mental ability, meta-analysis has clearly provided support for validity generalization. In the case of personality measures however, meta-analytic research has succeeded in demonstrating the potential value of personality measures as predictors of job performance (e.g., Mount et al., 1998), but support for validity generalization is ambiguous and complicated by a number of limitations that do not apply to meta-analytic studies of general mental ability measures. Researchers and practitioners examining evidence for validity generalization of personality measures find meta-analytic studies that report substantially different findings (e.g., Barrick & Mount, 1991; Tett et al., 1991). Even meta-analytic studies organized around the Big Five taxonomy have produced results that are somewhat different with respect to their ability to support a validity generalization argument for any given dimension of the Big Five across jobs and performance criteria (Barrick & Mount, 1991; Hurtz & Donovan, 2000; Mount & Barrick, 1995; Salgado, 1997; Vinchur et al., 1998). To understand the limitations of validity generalization with respect to personality measures and job performance it is useful to examine the conceptual and methodological problems inherent in meta-analytic studies of personality–job performance relations.

Although the basic concept and procedures are clear (Hunter & Schmidt, 1990; Murphy, 1997, 2000; Rosenthal & DiMatteo, 2001), meta-analysis is not a straightforward application of a standard methodology. Each individual meta-analysis presents unique complexities (Hunter & Schmidt, 1990). There are a number of important judgment calls and choices that researchers must make in the course of undertaking a meta-analytic study and these judgments and choices may have a significant impact on the results of the meta-analysis (Wanous, Sullivan, & Malinik, 1989). Wanous et al. identified 11 steps in a meta-analysis procedure, 8 of which require a judgment call on the part of a researcher. Wanous et al. found that, as a function of these judgment calls, considerable differences were observed between sets of meta-analyses in four different areas of research. A number of these judgment calls apply directly to the meta-analytic studies of personality–job performance relations and help to understand the differences in results obtained by the various studies to a considerable degree.

Interestingly, Wanous et al. (1989) did not clearly articulate what is certainly the first judgment call or decision made by researchers undertaking a meta-analysis, a decision that may be one of the most important in determining the final results. This decision concerns the basic research question that the researchers are attempting to answer. Examples of some of the different research questions asked in the published meta-analytic studies of personality–job performance relations are: (1) what is the overall validity of the Big Five taxonomy (e.g., Barrick & Mount, 1991; Hurtz & Donovan, 2000); (2) what is the difference in overall validity between confirmatory versus exploratory research strategies (Tett et al., 1991, 1994, 1999a); (3) what is the difference in personality–job performance validity between military and civilian occupations in Europe (Salgado, 1998); (4) what are the validities of personality measures in a particular inventory (Mount et al., 1998; Robertson & Kinder, 1993; Salgado, 1996), and (5) what is the validity of personality predictors for a specific occupation (Ford et al., 1987; Vinchur et al., 1998). The nature of the research question addressed by the meta-analytic study has a significant impact on the results and conclusions of the study. Different research questions may produce results that are simply not comparable. This was certainly one of the biggest factors underlying the debate between Ones et al. (1994) and Tett et al., (1994) with respect to the meta-analyses reported by Barrick and Mount (1991) and Tett et al. (1991). Although there were numerous issues debated in this exchange of views, fundamentally the purposes of the two meta-analyses were quite different. Barrick and Mount were interested in determining the overall validity of each of the Big Five personality dimensions in predicting three types of job performance criteria across five occupational groups. Tett et al. (1991) had two research objectives. First, they were interested in determining the overall validity of personality predictors in source studies that developed a predictive hypothesis and used a confirmatory research strategy versus those studies that simply used personality measures in an exploratory fashion to determine if they contributed to job performance. Secondly, Tett et al. were concerned that potential bidirectional validity coefficients with personality measures were being ignored in previous meta-analytic studies which, if true, would result in averaging positive and negative correlations and an underestimate of the true validity of personality measures for predicting job performance. The implication for validity generalization from these two meta-analytic studies are quite different. Results from the Barrick and Mount study suggest which Big Five personality dimension may be best for predicting certain job performance criteria in a specific occupational group. Results from the Tett et al. study on the other hand, indicate that validity generalization should be based on construct similarity between predictors and criteria, regardless of the specific nature of the personality trait or taxonomic dimension. Both sets of conclusions have implications for validity generalization and these implications, stemming from the original research questions, suggest some limitations to the use of validity generalization with personality measures. It is quite clear for example, from Barrick and Mount (1991), that several Big Five dimensions predict job performance with different criteria and occupational groups. A reasonable conclusion from the Tett et al. (1991) study is that validity generalization must be focused on construct similarity between personality predictors and performance criteria.

A second judgment call of concern involves the criteria for including studies in the meta-analysis. For example, interest in the Big Five taxonomy has focused most meta-analytic researchers on using this taxonomy as an organizing framework for meta-analysis. Unfortunately, using the Big Five taxonomy to organize data for the meta-analysis creates a significant problem. As previously discussed, there are a substantial number of important (i.e., well validated) personality constructs that do not fit into the Big Five taxonomy. Meta-analytic research organized around the Big Five taxonomy must exclude personality characteristics that do not fit into the Big Five taxonomy. The impact of excluding certain personality constructs on these allegedly comprehensive meta-analytic studies may be significant. Hough (1992) demonstrated that the highest criterion-related validities in her meta-analytic research were for personality scales that could not be classified with the Big Five taxonomy. Hough (1998) described preliminary meta-analytic results based on five factors similar to the results reported by Barrick and Mount (1991). Hough and her colleagues found the results disappointing, so they modified the taxonomy to include nine factors and obtained substantially better validity coefficients.

A third judgment call in a meta-analysis that may impact results concerns decisions on what type of data should be extracted from the selected studies. Wanous et al. (1989) pointed out that potential problems arise when a decision is made to use only a subset of data available in the source study. This is particularly relevant of meta-analytic studies of personality–job performance relations when researchers extract correlations relevant only to the Big Five taxonomy when a larger set of personality measures may be available for inclusion in the meta-analysis. An additional problem concerns extracting only significant correlations from a larger set of potential personality predictors. Tett et al. (1991) identified this procedure in some meta-analytic reviews prior to their own and point out how this could potentially inflate the results of the meta-analysis.

A fourth important judgment call in meta-analysis procedures according to Wanous et al. (1989) concerns the decision on whether or not to group measures of interest for some theoretical or operational reason and if so, should they be grouped a priori or not. This type of judgment is also particularly relevant to meta-analytic studies of personality and job performance and the potential impact on these meta-analytic studies is still undetermined. The most important grouping judgment that has been made in the meta-analytic studies of personality has been whether or not to use the Big Five taxonomy to group personality measures. The problems with the Big Five have been discussed previously and the advantages and disadvantages of using the Big Five to group personality measures in meta-analysis have been debated vigorously (e.g., Hough, 1992; Ones et al., 1994; Tett et al., 1994). However, despite the conceptual and methodological problems identified by critics of the Big Five taxonomy, there is no question that the use of the Big Five to group personality variables in meta-analysis has contributed significantly to progress in understanding the extent of validity generalization, as well as its limitations, with personality measures. As John and Srivastava (1999) and others have discussed, there are hundreds of personality measures in the research literature, many with the same name that, clearly on scrutiny, measure different constructs, and many with different names that turn out to actually measure the same construct. However flawed the Big Five taxonomy, it has brought some coherence to researchers' efforts to investigate the potential for validity generalization with personality measures in employee selection. It should be noted however, that the use of the Big Five taxonomy to group personality measures increases the need to make several other judgment calls that may impact results in addition to the problem of grouping nonequivalent personality measures previously discussed. For example, Hough (1992) argued that when validity coefficients are summarized across personality measures within a Big Five construct, the true underlying predictor-criterion construct relation may be obscured. In addition, a number of researchers have pointed to the problem of misclassifying personality measures into the Big Five taxonomy due to differences of opinion on the nature of the Big Five constructs, as discussed previously, as well as inherent ambiguities in the Big Five classification system (Hogan et al., 1996; Hurtz & Donovan, 2000; Judge & Bono, 2001; Ones et al., 1994; Salgado, 1997; Tett et al., 1994). A final problem regarding the grouping of variables in the meta-analysis of personality measures, concerns decisions made on using job type as a moderator variable. Many nonequivalent jobs may be grouped together (Hogan et al., 1996) and an insufficient number of studies within a job category may lead to unwarranted conclusions (Bobko & Stone-Romero, 1998). Clearly all of these grouping and classification judgments provide the basis for differences in results in meta-analytic studies of personality measures.

The final judgment call suggested by Wanous et al. (1989) as having an important impact on meta-analysis results that is also pertinent to the meta-analysis of personality measures is the selection of potential moderators. Barrick and Mount (1991) examined job performance criteria and job classification as potential moderators in their study. Tett et al. (1991) were primarily interested the difference between confirmatory and exploratory research strategies. As discussed previously, these differences make comparisons between the two studies tenuous. Clearly there are advantages and disadvantages to both meta-analytic studies. Barrick and Mount were interested in how personality measures may vary in their ability to predict different performance criteria in different types of jobs, an objective that clearly facilitates the use of validity generalization within each level of the moderator. The disadvantages to their study, as discussed previously, stem from the controversies surrounding the Big Five taxonomy as well as the problem of being unable to identify significant moderators due to insufficient primary studies (Bobko & Stone-Romero, 1998). Tett et al. (1994) believed that it was critical to distinguish between confirmatory and exploratory research findings in source studies because "confirmatory findings are more likely to capture the realistic potential of personality measures for use in selection, as exploratory efforts yield numerous spurious and meaningless validities owing to lack of theoretical rationales guiding trait selection" (p. 159). The problems of blind empirical approaches to the study of personality and job performance relations has been noted by numerous researchers (e.g., Guion & Gottier, 1965; Irving, 1993; Schneider et al., 1996; Weiss & Adler, 1984) and the Tett et al. (1991, 1994, 1999a) results clearly demonstrated that confirmatory research strategies were far superior for using personality measures in employee selection. On the other hand, validity generalization conclusions from the Tett et al. study provide less guidance to personnel researchers on the specific personality traits that may be useful in a particular selection context. The selection of moderators therefore, is an excellent example of how judgment calls in meta-analyses of personality–job performance relations has a significant impact on the results and conclusions obtained in these studies.

Finally, one other problem unique to meta-analyses with personality measures must be recognized due to its detrimental effect on the ability of meta-analysis to determine the true validity of personality measures in personnel selection. This problem may potentially undermine arguments for validity generalization with personality measures. Tett et al. (1991) argued that due to the bidirectional nature of most personality measures that, unlike the situation with measures of general mental ability, there would be expected and naturally occurring negative correlations between some personality measures and criterion measures. For example, Agreeableness and its facets may predict cooperative behavior positively, but correlate negatively with change-oriented, constructive communications (LePine & Van Dyne, 2001). Similarly, although it is generally desirable to be planful, there may be times when being high on this trait interferes with productivity (e.g., analysis paralysis; Tett et al., 1999a). It is also important to realize that facets of a given dimension may not all correlate in the same direction with a given criterion (Paunonen & Ashton, 2001). In confirmatory studies these negative correlations could be identified and taken into account for the meta-analysis. However, in exploratory research strategies with personality measures, it was not possible to determine which negative correlations were expected and which were simply due to sampling fluctuations. Therefore, as Tett et al. (1994) argued:

When averaging signed correlations, negative correlations will reduce the mean correlation obtained. When these negative values are statistically significant and meaningful (i.e., they cannot be considered error), and are averaged with positive values, the mean correlation will underestimate the value of personality in predicting job performance. (p. 163)

Tett et al. demonstrated that the number of negative correlations in their data set outnumber those expected by chance by a ratio of 28 to 1. Tett et al. (1991) devised a method of using the absolute value of the correlation in their meta-analysis and correcting for the upward bias in mean validity that the use of absolute values would create. This correction formula was later revised by Tett et al. (1994) and has recently been revised again (Tett et al., 1999a, 1999b) in an effort to ensure that estimates of true validity between personality measures and job performance criteria are as accurate as possible. Tett et al. (1991, 1994, 1999a, 1999b) argued that it is absolutely essential to take into account the effect of bidirectional relations between personality and job performance, because without doing so in the appropriate manner the effect of averaging positive and negative correlations in a meta-analysis will be to underestimate the true validity in personality measures in employee selection. This would also undermine the case significantly for validity generalization with personality measures.

CONCLUSION

This discussion is not intended to lead to a conclusion that meta-analytic studies of personality–job performance relations are plagued with so many problems that validity generalization is not possible. On the contrary, meta-analytic research has enhanced our understanding of the contribution of personality to job performance to a significant degree. It is true, however, that the problems and differences in results from the various meta-analyses of personality measures limit the use of validity generalization with respect to personality in a way that is not the case with measures of general mental ability. The judgment calls and unique problems associated with personality measures have led to meta-analytic results that vary considerably, a problem that does not exist in the domain of general mental ability. Researchers and personnel practitioners therefore must take these issues into account in developing a validity generalization argument for the particular context of interest. Unlike the case of general mental ability, it is simply not possible to use meta-analytic results from personality studies to develop validity generalization arguments to justify the selection of a particular personality measure across all or most jobs. Clearly, personality measures compared to measures of general mental ability are relatively more situationally specific and there appears to be a broad consensus developing that this is the case, even among Big Five enthusiasts (Hurtz & Donovan, 2000; Mount & Barrick, 1998; Mount et al., 1998). This is, it must be emphasized, a *relative* difference. This is not to advocate that criterion-related validity studies must be conducted in each and every setting to support test use. Validity generalization is still possible with personality measures on the basis of meta-analytic results, but the key is to ensure alignment of personality and criterion constructs. Simply stated, the relative ease of using one predictor and one criterion such as the case with general mental ability measures in personnel selection is unfortunately not possible in the domain of personality measures.

REFERENCES

Anastasi, A. (1982). *Psychological testing*. New York: Macmillan.

Ashton, M. C. (1998). Personality and job performance: The importance of narrow traits. *Journal of Organizational Behavior, 19*, 289–303.

Ashton, M. C. Jackson, D. N., Paunonen, S. V., Helmes, E., & Rothstein, M. G. (1995). The criterion-related validity of broad factor scales versus specific facet scales. *Journal of Research in Personality, 29*, 432–442.

Barrick, M. R., & Mount, M. K. (1991). The Big Five personality dimensions and job performance: A meta-analysis. *Personnel Psychology, 44*, 1–26.

Barrick, M. R., & Mount, M. K. (1993). Autonomy as a moderator of the relationship between the Big Five personality dimensions and job performance. *Journal of Applied Psychology, 78*, 111–118.

Barrick, M. R., & Mount, M. K. (1994, April). *Do specific components of conscientiousness predict better than the overall construct?* Paper presented at the symposium, Personality and Job Performance: Big Five versus Specific Traits, conducted at the meeting of the Society for Industrial and Organizational Psychology, Nashville, TN.

Barrick, M. R., & Mount, M. K., & Strauss, J. P. (1993). Conscientiousness and performance of sales representatives: Test of the mediating effects of goal setting. *Journal of Applied Psychology, 78*, 715–722.

Block, J. (1995). A contrarian view of the five-factor approach to personality description. *Psychological Bulletin, 177*, 187–215.

Block, J. (2001). Millennial contrarianism: The five-factor approach to personality description 5 years later. *Journal of Research in Personality, 35*, 98–107.

Bobko, P., & Stone-Romero, E. F. (1998). Meta-analysis may be another useful research tool, but it is not a panacea. In G. R. Ferris (Ed.), *Research in Personnel and Human Resources Management* (Vol. 16, pp. 359–397). Stamford, CT: JAI.

Borman, W. C., & Motowidlo, S. J. (1993). Expanding the criterion domain to include elements of contextual performance. In N. Schmitt & W. C. Borman (Eds.), *Personnel selection in organizations* (pp. 71–98). San Francisco: Jossey-Bass.

Borman, W. C., & Motowidlo, S. J. (1997). Task performance and contextual performance: The meaning for personnel selection research. *Human Performance*, *10*, 99–109.

Briggs, S. R. (1989). The optimal level of measurement for personality constructs. In D. M. Buss & N. Cantor (Eds.), *Personality psychology: Recent trends and emerging directions* (pp. 246–260). New York: Springer.

Campbell, J. P. (1990). Modeling the performance prediction problem in industrial and organizational psychology. In M. D. Dunnette & L. M. Hough (Eds.), *Handbook of industrial and organizational psychology* (Vol. 1, 2nd ed., pp. 687–732). Palo Alto, CA: Consulting Psychologists.

Campbell, J. P., McCloy, R. A., Oppler, S. H., & Sager, C. E. (1993). A theory of performance. In N. Schmitt & W. C. Borman (Eds.), *Personnel selection in organizations* (pp. 35–70). San Francisco: Jossey-Bass.

Campbell, J. P., McHenry, J. J., & Wise, L. L. (1990). Analyses of criterion measures: The modeling of performance. *Personnel Psychology*, *43*, 313–333.

Cattell, R. B. (1963). Theory of fluid and crystallized intelligence: A critical experiment. *Journal of Educational Psychology*, *54*, 1–22.

Christiansen, N. D., Goffin, R. D., Johnston, N. G., & Rothstein, M. G. (1994). Correcting the 16PF for faking: Effects on criterion-related validity and individual hiring decisions. *Personnel Psychology*, *47*, 847–860.

Costa, P. T., & McCrae, R. R. (1988). From catalog to classification: Murray's needs and the five-factor model. *Journal of Personality and Social Psychology*, *54*, 258–265.

Costa, P. T., & McCrae, R. R. (1992). *Revised NEO Personality Inventory (NEO-PI-R) and NEO Five-Factor Inventory (NEO-FFI) professional manual*. Odessa, FL: Psychological Assessment Resources.

Cronbach, L. J. (1970). *Essentials of psychological testing* (3rd ed.). New York: Harper & Row.

Cronbach, L. J. (1989). Construct validation after thirty years. In R. Linn (Ed.), *Intelligence: Measurement, theory, and public policy* (pp. 147–171). Urbana, IL: University of Illinois Press.

Cronbach, L. J., & Meehl, P. E. (1955). Construct validity in psychological tests. *Psychological Bulletin*, *52*, 281–302.

Edwards, A. J. (1964). Social desirability and performance on the MMPI. *Psychometrika*, *29*, 295–308.

Eysenck, H. J. (1979). *The structure and measurement of intelligence*. New York: Springer-Verlag.

Eysenck, H. J. (1991). Dimensions of personality: 16, 5, or 3? Criteria for a taxonomy paradigm. *Personality and Individual Differences*, *12*, 773–790.

Ford, N. M., Walker, O. C., Churchill, G. A., & Hartley, S. W. (1987). Selecting successful salespeople: A meta-analysis of biographical and psychological selection criteria. In M. J. Houston (Ed.), *Review of marketing* (pp. 90–131). Chicago: American Marketing Association.

Frei, R. L., & McDaniel, M. A. (1998). Validity of customer service measures in personnel selection: A review of criterion and construct evidence. *Human Performance, 11*, 1–27.

Funder, D. C. (2001). Personality. *Annual Review of Psychology, 52*, 197–221.

Gellatly, I. R. (1996). Conscientiousness and task performance: Test of cognitive process model. *Journal of Applied Psychology, 81*, 474–482.

Ghiselli, E. E., & Barthol, R. P. (1953). The validity of personality inventories in the selection of employees. *Journal of Applied Psychology, 37*, 18–20.

Goffin, R. D., & Helmes, E. (2000). *Problems and solutions in human assessment: Honoring Douglas N. Jackson at seventy.* Boston: Kluwer Academic Publishers.

Goffin, R. D., Rothstein, M. G., & Johnston, N. G. (2000). Predicting job performance using personality constructs: Are personality tests created equal? In R. D. Goffin & E. Helmes (Eds.), *Problems and solutions in human assessment: Honoring Douglas N. Jackson at seventy* (pp. 249–264). Boston: Kluwer Academic Publishers.

Goldberg, L. R. (1992). The development of marker variables for the Big-Five factor structure. *Psychological Assessment, 4*, 26–42.

Goldberg, L. R. (1993). The structure of phenotypic personality traits. *American Psychologist, 48*, 26–34.

Guilford, J. P. (1988). Some changes in the Structure-of-Intellect model. *Educational and Psychological Measurement, 48*, 1–4.

Guion, R. B. (1991). Personnel assessment, selection, and placement. In M. D. Dunnette & L. M. Hough (Eds.), *Handbook of industrial and organizational psychology* (Vol. 2, 2nd ed., pp. 327–397). Palo Alto, CA: Consulting Psychologists.

Guion, R. M., & Gottier, R. F. (1965). Validity of personality measures in personnel selection. *Personnel Psychology, 18*, 135–164.

Hartigan, J. A., & Wigdor, A. K. (Eds.). (1989). *Fairness in employment testing: Validity generalization, minority issues, and the General Aptitude Test Battery.* Washington, DC: National Academy Press.

Hogan, R. (1986). *Hogan Personality Inventory manual.* Minneapolis, MN: National Computer Systems.

Hogan, R. (1991). Personality and personality measurement. In M. D. Dunnette & L. M. Hough (Eds.), *Handbook of industrial and organizational psychology* (Vol. 2, pp. 873–919). Palo Alto, CA: Consulting Psychologists.

Hogan, J. (1998). Introduction: Personality and job performance [Special Issue]. *Human Performance, 11*, 125–127.

Hogan, R., Hogan, J., & Roberts, B. W. (1996). Personality measurement and employment decisions: Questions and answers. *American Psychologist, 51*, 469–477.

Hogan, R., & Roberts, B. W. (1996). Issues and non-issues in the fidelity-bandwidth trade-off. *Journal of Organizational Behavior, 17*, 627–637.

Hopkins, K. D., Stanley, J. C., & Hopkins, B. R. (1990). *Educational and psychological measurement and evaluation.* Englewood Cliffs, NJ: Prentice Hall.

Hough, L. M. (1992). The "Big Five" personality variables-construct confusion: Description versus prediction. *Human Performance, 5*, 139–155.

Hough, L. M. (1997). The millennium for personality psychology: New horizons or good old daze. *Applied Psychology: An International Review, 47,* 233–261.

Hough, L. M. (1998). Personality at work: Issues and evidence. In M. D. Hakel (Ed.), *Beyond multiple choice: Evaluating alternatives to traditional testing for selection* (pp. 131–166). Mahwah, NJ: Lawrence Erlbaum Associates.

Hough, L. M., Eaton, N. K., Dunnette, M. D., Kamp, J. D., & McCloy, R. A. (1990). Criterion-related validities of personality constructs and the effect of response distortion on those validities [Monograph]. *Journal of Applied Psychology, 75,* 581–595.

Hough, L. M., & Oswald, F. L. (2000). Personnel selection: Looking toward the future—remembering the past. *Annual Review of Psychology, 51,* 631–664.

Hough, L. M., & Schneider, R. J. (1996). Personality traits, taxonomies, and applications in organizations. In K. R. Murphy (Ed.), *Individual differences and behavior in organizations* (pp. 31–88). San Francisco: Jossey-Bass.

House, R. J., Shane, S. A., & Herold, D. M. (1996). Rumors of the death of dispositional research are vastly exaggerated. *Academy of Management Review, 21,* 203–224.

Humphreys, L. G. (1979). The construct of general intelligence. *Intelligence, 3,* 105–120.

Hunt, S. T. (1996). Generic work behavior: An investigation into the dimensions of entry-level, hourly job performance. *Personnel Psychology, 49,* 51–83.

Hunter, J. E., & Hunter, R. F. (1984). Validity and utility of alternative predictors of job performance. *Psychological Bulletin, 96,* 72–98.

Hunter, J. E., & Schmidt, F. L. (1990). *Methods of meta-analysis: Correcting error and bias in research findings.* Newbury Park, CA: Sage.

Hurtz, G. M., & Donovan, J. J. (2000). Personality and job performance: The Big Five revisited. *Journal of Applied Psychology, 85,* 869–879.

Institute for Scientific Information (2001). Web of Science [electronic resource: <*http://wsocanada.isihost.com*> accessed July, 2001]: Social Sciences Citation Index.

Irving, P. G. (1993). On the use of personality measures in personnel selection. *Canadian Psychology, 34,* 208–214.

Jackson, D. N. (1971). The dynamics of structured personality tests: 1971. *Psychological Review, 78,* 229–248.

Jackson, D. N. (1984). *Personality Research Form manual* (3rd ed.). Port Huron, MI: Research Psychologists.

Jackson, D. N., Paunonen, S. V., Fraboni, M., & Goffin, R. D. (1996). A five-factor versus six-factor model of personality structure. *Personality and Individual Differences, 20,* 33–45.

Jackson, D. N., & Rothstein, M. G. (1996). The circumnavigation of personality. *International Journal of Selection and Assessment, 4,* 159–163.

Jensen, A. R. (1980). *Bias in mental testing.* New York: Free Press.

John, O. P., & Srivastava, S. (1999). The Big Five trait taxonomy: History, measurement, and theoretical perspectives. In L. A. Pervin & O. P. John (Eds.), *Handbook of personality: Theory and research* (2nd ed., pp. 102–138). New York: The Guilford Press.

Judge, T. A., & Bono, J. E. (2001). Relationship of core self-evaluation traits—self-esteem, generalized self-efficacy, locus of control, and emotional stability—with job satisfaction and job performance: A meta-analysis. *Journal of Applied Psychology*, *86*, 80–92.

Lanyon, R. I., & Goodstein, L. D. (1997). *Personality assessment* (3rd ed.). New York: Wiley.

Lord, R. G., De Vader, C. L., & Alliger, G. M. (1986). A meta-analysis of the relation between personality traits and leadership perceptions: An application of validity generalization procedures. *Journal of Applied Psychology*, *71*, 402–410.

McCrae, R. R., & Costa, P, T., Jr. (1999). A Five-Factor theory of personality. In L. A. Pervin & O. P. John (Eds.), *Handbook of personality: Theory and research* (2nd ed., pp. 139–153). New York: The Guilford Press.

Moon, H. (2001). The two faces of conscientiousness: Duty and achievement striving in escalation of commitment dilemmas. *Journal of Applied Psychology*, *86*, 533–540.

Mount, M. K., & Barrick, M. R. (1995). The Big Five personality dimensions: Implications for research and practice in human resource management. In G. Ferris (Ed.), *Research in Personnel and Human Resource Management* (Vol. 13, pp. 153–200). Stamford, CT: JAI.

Mount, M. K., & Barrick, M. R. (1998). Five reasons why the "Big Five" article has been frequently cited. *Personnel Psychology*, *51*, 849–857.

Mount, M. K., Barrick, M. R., & Stewart, G. L. (1998). Personality predictors of performance in jobs involving interaction with others. *Human Performance*, *11*, 145–166.

Murphy, K. R. (1996). Individual differences and behavior in organizations: Much more than g. In K. R. Murphy (Ed.), *Individual differences and behavior in organizations* (pp. 3–30). San Francisco: Jossey-Bass.

Murphy, K. R. (1997). Meta-analysis and validity generalization. In N. Anderson & P. Herriot (Eds.), *International Handbook of Selection and Assessment* (Vol. 13; pp. 323–342). Chichester, UK: Wiley.

Murphy, K. R. (2000). Impact of assessments of validity generalization and situational specificity on the science and practice of personnel selection. *International Journal of Selection and Assessment*, *8*, 194–206.

Murphy, K. R., & Davidshofer, C. O. (1991). *Psychological testing: Principles and applications* (2nd ed.). Englewood Cliffs, NJ: Prentice Hall.

Nunnally, J. C. (1978). *Psychometric theory*. New York: McGraw Hill.

Ones, D. S., Mount, M. K., Barrick, M. R., & Hunter, J. E. (1994). Personality and job performance: A critique of the Tett, Jackson, and Rothstein (1991) meta-analysis. *Personnel Psychology*, *47*, 147–156.

Ones, D. S., & Viswesvaran, C. (1996). Bandwidth-fidelity dilemma in personality measurement for personnel selection. *Journal of Organizational Behavior*, *17*, 609–626.

Ones, D. S., Viswesvaran, C., & Schmidt, F. L. (1993). Comprehensive meta-analysis of integrity test validities: Findings and implications for personnel selection and theories of job performance [Monograph]. *Journal of Applied Psychology*, *78*, 679–703.

Organ D. W., & Ryan, K. A. (1995). A meta-analytic review of attitudinal and dispositional predictors of organizational citizenship behavior. *Personnel Psychology*, *48*, 775–802.

Paunonen, S. V. (1998). Hierarchical organization of personality and prediction of behavior. *Journal of Personality and Social Psychology*, *74*, 538–556.

Paunonen, S. V., & Ashton, M. C. (2001). Big Five predictors of academic achievement. *Journal of Research in Personality*, *35*, 78–90.

Paunonen, S. V., & Jackson, D. N. (1996). The Jackson Personality Inventory and the Five-Factor Model of personality. *Journal of Research in Personality*, *30*, 42–59.

Paunonen, S. V., & Jackson, D. N. (2000). What is beyond the Big Five? Plenty! *Journal of Personality*, *68*, 821–835.

Paunonen, S. V., & Nicol, A. A. M. (2001). The personality hierarchy and the prediction of work behaviors. In R. Hogan & B. W. Roberts (Eds.), *Personality psychology in the workplace* (pp. 161–191). Washington, DC: APA.

Paunonen, S. V., Rothstein, M. G., & Jackson, D. N. (1999). Narrow reasoning about the use of broad personality measures for personnel selection. *Journal of Organizational Behavior*, *20*, 389–405.

Peabody, D., & Goldberg, L. R. (1989). Some determinants of factor structure from personality-trait descriptors. *Journal of Personality and Social Psychology*, *57*, 552–567.

Pearlman, K., Schmidt, F. L., & Hunter, J. E. (1980). Validity generalization results for tests used to predict job proficiency and training success in clerical occupations. *Journal of Applied Psychology*, *65*, 373–406.

Robertson, I. T., & Kinder, A. (1993). Personality and job competences: The criterion-related validity of some personality variables. *Journal of Occupational and Organizational Psychology*, *66*, 225–244.

Rosenthal, R., & DiMatteo, M. R. (2001). Meta-analysis: Recent developments in quantitative methods for literature reviews. *Annual Review of Psychology*, *52*, 59–82.

Rothstein, M. G., & Goffin, R. D. (2000). The assessment of personality constructs in industrial-organizational psychology. In R. D. Goffin & E. Helmes (Eds.), *Problems and solutions in human assessment: Honoring Douglas N. Jackson at seventy* (pp. 215–248). Boston: Kluwer.

Salgado, J. F. (1996). Personality and job competences: A comment on the Robertson and Kinder (1993) study. *Journal of Occupational and Organizational Psychology*, *69*, 373–375.

Salgado, J. F. (1997). The Five Factor Model of personality and job performance in the European community. *Journal of Applied Psychology*, *82*, 30–43.

Salgado, J. F. (1998). Big Five personality dimensions and job performance in army and civil occupations: A European perspective. *Human Performance*, *11*, 271–288.

Schmidt, F. L. (1992). What do data really mean? Research findings, meta-analysis, and cumulative knowledge in psychology. *American Psychologist*, *47*, 1173–1181.

Schmidt, F. L., Gaast-Rosenberg, I., & Hunter, J. E. (1980). Validity generalization results for computer programmers. *Journal of Applied Psychology*, *65*, 643–661.

Schmidt, F. L., & Hunter, J. E. (1977). Development of a general solution to the problem of validity generalization. *Journal of Applied Psychology*, *62*, 529–540.

Schmidt, F. L., & Hunter, J. E. (1981). Employment testing: Old theories and new research findings. *American Psychologist, 36*, 1128–1137.

Schmidt, F. L, & Hunter, J. E. (1983). Individual differences in productivity: An empirical test of estimates derived from studies of selection procedure utility. *Journal of Applied Psychology, 68*, 407–414.

Schmidt, F. L., & Hunter, J. E. (1998). The validity and utility of selection methods in personnel psychology: Practical and theoretical implications of 85 years of research findings. *Psychological Bulletin, 124*, 262–274.

Schmidt, F. L., Hunter, J. E., & Caplan, J. R. (1981). Validity generalization results for two jobs in the petroleum industry. *Journal of Applied Psychology, 66*, 261–273.

Schmidt, F. L., Hunter, J. E., McKenzie, R. C., & Muldrow, T. W. (1979). Impact of valid selection procedures on work-force productivity. *Journal of Applied Psychology, 64*, 609–626.

Schmidt, F. L., Hunter, J. E., & Pearlman, K. (1981). Task differences as moderators of aptitude test validity in selection: A red herring. *Journal of Applied Psychology, 66*, 166–185.

Schmidt, F. L., Hunter, J. E., & Pearlman, K. (1982). Assessing the economic impact of personnel programs on work force productivity. *Personnel Psychology, 35*, 333–347.

Schmit, M. J., & Ryan, A. M. (1993). The Big-Five in personnel selection: Factor structure in applicant and non-applicant populations. *Journal of Applied Psychology, 78*, 966–974.

Schmitt, N., Gooding, R. Z., Noe, R. A., & Kirsch, M. (1984). Meta-analysis of validity studies published between 1964 and 1982 and the investigation of study characteristics. *Personnel Psychology, 37*, 407–422.

Schneider, R. J., Hough, L. M., & Dunnette, M. D. (1996). Broadsided by broad traits: How to sink science in five dimensions or less. *Journal of Organizational Behavior, 17*, 639–655.

Spearman, C. (1927). *The abilities of man.* New York: Macmillan.

Sternberg, R. J. (1977). *Intelligence, information processing, and analogical reasoning: The componential analysis of human abilities.* Hillsdale, NJ: Lawrence Erlbaum Associates.

Sternberg, R. J. (1985). *Beyond IQ: A triarchic theory of human intelligence.* New York: Cambridge University Press.

Stewart, G. L. (1999). Trait bandwidth and stages of job performance: Assessing differential effects for Conscientiousness and its subtraits. *Journal of Applied Psychology, 84*, 959–968.

Stewart, G. L., Carson, K. P., & Cardy, R. L. (1996). The joint effects of conscientiousness and self-leadership training on employee self-directed behavior in a service setting. *Personnel Psychology, 49*, 143–164.

Tett, R. P., Guterman, H. A., Bleier, A., & Murphy, P. J. (2000). Development and content validation of a "hyperdimensional" taxonomy of managerial competence. *Human Performance, 13*, 205–251.

Tett, R. P., Jackson, D. N., & Rothstein, M. (1991). Personality measures as predictors of job performance: A meta-analytic review. *Personnel Psychology, 44*, 703–742.

Tett, R. P., Jackson, D. N., Rothstein, M., & Reddon, J. R. (1994). Meta-analysis of personality—job performance relations: A reply to Ones, Mount, Barrick, and Hunter (1994). *Personnel Psychology, 47*, 157–172.

Tett, R. P., Jackson, D. N., Rothstein, M., & Reddon, J. R. (1999a). Meta-analysis of bidirectional relations in personality—job performance research. *Human Performance, 12*, 1–29.

Tett, R. P., Jackson, D. N., Rothstein, M., & Reddon, J. R. (1999b). Meta-analysis of bidirectional relations in personality—job performance research: Errata. *Human Performance, 12*, 177–181.

Thurstone, L. L. (1938). *Primary mental abilities*. Psychometric Monographs, No. 1. Chicago, IL: University of Chicago.

Tokar, D. M., Fischer, A. R., & Subich, L. M. (1998). Personality and vocational behavior: A selective review of the literature, 1993–1997. *Journal of Vocational Behavior, 53*, 115–153.

Vernon, P. E. (1965). Ability factors and environmental influences. *American Psychologist, 20*, 723–733.

Vinchur, A. J., Schippmann, J. S., Switzer III, F. S., & Roth, P. L. (1998). A meta-analytic review of predictors of job performance for salespeople. *Journal of Applied Psychology, 83*, 586–597.

Wanous, J. P., Sullivan, S. E., & Malinak, J. (1989). The role of judgment calls in meta-analysis. *Journal of Applied Psychology, 74*, 259–264.

Weiss, H. M., & Adler, S. (1984). Personality and organizational behavior. In B. M. Staw & L. L. Cummings (Eds.), *Research in organizational behavior* (Vol. 6, pp. 1–50). Greenwich, CT: JAI.

Wiggins, J. S. (1968). Personality structure. *Annual Review of Psychology, 19*, 293–350.

Wiggins, J. S. (1973). *Personality and prediction: Principles of personality assessment*. Reading, MA: Addison-Wesley.

9
Maximum Likelihood Estimation in Validity Generalization

Nambury S. Raju
Illinois Institute of Technology

Fritz Drasgow
University of Illinois–Urbana/Champaign

Since Schmidt and Hunter's seminal publication in 1977 (Schmidt & Hunter, 1977) on situational specificity, the assessment of the generalizability of organizational interventions has received a great deal of attention among researchers and practitioners, especially among industrial/organizational (I/O) psychologists concerning the generalizability of the validity of predictors across organizations. The art and science of validity generalization (VG) revolves around the estimation of the mean and variance of population validities. That is, given a set of k validity coefficients (correlations between the same or similar predictors and criteria in the same or similar jobs) obtained from samples drawn from k different populations, one is interested in obtaining an estimate of the mean and variance of population validities in order to establish whether the validity in question is (a) significant and substantial and (b) generalizable across populations. An estimate of the mean of population validities is used to answer the first question and an estimate of the variance of population validities is used to answer the second question. The estimation of the mean and variance of population validities and the resulting substantive interpretations is the crux of VG research and practice.

There are currently several VG models and procedures for estimating the mean and variance of population validities. Some models and procedures are designed for use with observed correlations corrected for unreliability and range restriction, whereas others are not. Some models and procedures are couched in observed correlations, whereas others use transformations of such correlations to estimate the mean and variance of population validities. The statistical estimation methods employed also vary across procedures. For example, the early estimation procedures relied mostly on the method of moments, but some of the newer procedures use estimation methods based on the maximum likelihood principle. Recently, Bayesian estimation techniques have been used by VG researchers (Brannick, 2001). Statistical estimation procedures (e.g., the method of moments, maximum likelihood estimation, method of least squares, and Bayesian estimation) are described in standard texts on mathematical statistics (e.g., Lehmann, 1983; Mood & Graybill, 1963; Rao, 1973).

The use of different statistical estimation methods has, at times, led to some confusion and controversy among VG researchers and practitioners. Although the choice among the different statistical estimation methods may not be an easy one, especially for practitioners, the availability of procedures for estimating the VG parameters (mean and variance of population correlations) based on different statistical estimation methods would be very desirable. The choice of estimation method is usually based on a consideration of optimality. For example, unbiased estimators are usually preferred over biased estimators. The early VG estimation procedures were based on the method of moments. Unfortunately, the statistical properties of estimates based on the method of moments are not necessarily optimal. Maximum likelihood estimation is optimal in several important respects. For example, as shown by Kendall and Stuart (1977, 1979, pp. 38–81), under quite general conditions, maximum likelihood (ML) estimates are consistent and asymptotically efficient. These properties are briefly described in the following paragraphs.

ML estimators are not necessarily unbiased. However, as sample size becomes large, they have the property of *consistency*. This means that an ML estimate is sure to approach the parameter it estimates as sample size becomes large. In general, one estimator should be preferred to another if it has a smaller standard error of estimate. An *efficient* estimator has the smallest standard error of all unbiased estimators of a parameter. As sample size becomes large (i.e., asymptotically), ML estimators are efficient. Thus, in large samples, no other estimator has a smaller standard error of estimate than an ML estimator.

In addition to being consistent and asymptotically efficient, the sampling distribution of ML estimators is normal in large samples.

An estimator with this combination of consistency, asymptotic efficiency, and asymptotic normality is called a best asymptotically normal (BAN) estimator (Kendall & Stuart, 1979). Another property that is important for this chapter is that ML estimators are invariant in the following sense: Let $f(\theta)$ be a function of θ with a single-valued inverse and let $\hat{\theta}$ be an ML estimator of θ, then $f(\hat{\theta})$ is the ML estimator of $f(\theta)$. For example, if sigma-hat-squared is the ML estimator of the variance, then sigma-hat is the ML estimator of the standard deviation. As demonstrated next, this property will be very helpful in estimating the necessary VG parameters when correlations are corrected for unreliability and range restriction using hypothetical distributions of predictor and criterion unreliability and range restriction. This is because the corrections for unreliability and range restriction can be viewed as the function f. Thus, we can derive the ML estimator for the uncorrected correlations (a simpler task), and then use this property to obtain the ML estimator for corrected correlations.

Although the ML estimation method has received substantial attention lately among VG researchers (Brannick, 2001; Erez, Bloom, & Wells, 1996; Hedges & Olkin, 1985), much of it is confined to Fisher's z-transformation of an observed correlation or validity coefficient. ML estimation procedures for VG parameters, when correlations are corrected for unreliability and range restriction, have not been previously derived. Given the many statistically optimal properties that ML estimators enjoy, it is natural and desirable to extend the ML estimation technique to VG situations in which correlations are corrected for unreliability in the predictor and criterion and direct range restriction on the predictor. Therefore, it is the purpose of this chapter to fill this void in the VG estimation methodology. It should be noted that for the purposes of the flow of presentation and comprehensiveness, ML estimation methods are presented for both corrected and uncorrected correlations. Moreover, in this presentation we will only deal with correlation coefficients, not Fisher's z-transformations of such correlations. Readers interested in the use of Fisher's z-transformation in VG analysis are referred to Erez et al. (1996) and Hedges and Olkin (1985).

SOME PRELIMINARIES

In this section, presented are some well known results about correlations and a brief description of the fixed-effects and random-effects models. These models are receiving a great deal of attention lately, especially with respect to which VG parameters are estimated.

Single Population

Let the r_{xy} represent the correlation between a predictor (x) and a criterion (y) in a sample of size n drawn from a population. Let the correlation between x and y in the population be denoted as ρ_{xy}. Let the hypothesized relationship between r_{xy} and ρ_{xy} be expressed as:

$$r_{xy} = \rho_{xy} + e, \tag{1}$$

where e represents the sampling error. Let us further assume that r_{xy} is an unbiased estimate of ρ_{xy} and is normally distributed. Strictly speaking, r_{xy} is not an unbiased estimate of ρ_{xy}; in fact, it underestimates ρ_{xy} (Hedges & Olkin, 1985; Stuart & Kendall, 1977). According to Hedges (1989) and Hedges and Olkin (1985), this bias is seldom of practical significance if the sample size is not too small. Therefore, the current assumption may be restated as that the asymptotic (or large sample) distribution of r_{xy} is approximately normal with a mean of ρ_{xy} and an asymptotic variance of $\sigma^2_{r_{xy}}$. According to Kendall and Stuart (1977), the asymptotic mean/expectation and variance of r_{xy} can be expressed as:

$$E(r_{xy}) = \rho_{xy}, \tag{2}$$

$$\sigma^2_{r_{xy}} = \frac{(1 - \rho^2_{xy})^2}{n}. \tag{3}$$

When r_{xy} is substituted for ρ_{xy} in Equation 3, this equation may be rewritten as:

$$\hat{\sigma}^2_{r_{xy}} = \frac{(1 - r^2_{xy})^2}{n - 1}. \tag{4}$$

Prior to discussing the distribution of correlations in several populations, it should be noted that Fisher's z-transformation of an observed correlation is known to be much less biased and its sampling distribution approaches normality much more quickly (as the sample size increases) than the sampling distribution of r_{xy} (Kendall & Stuart, 1977). Fisher's z-transformation and its sampling variance can be expressed, respectively, as:

$$z \equiv z(r_{xy}) = \frac{1}{2}\ln\frac{1 + r_{xy}}{1 - r_{xy}} \, , \tag{5}$$

$$\sigma_z^2 = \frac{1}{n - 3} \, . \tag{6}$$

While Fisher's z has many desirable statistical properties, its use in VG, when the observed correlations are corrected for unreliability and range restriction as it is commonly done, appears to be rather complicated. The sampling variance of z when the observed correlations are corrected for both unreliability and range restriction is unknown. Mendoza (1993) and Shohoji, Yamashita, and Tarumi (1981) provided formulas for the sampling variance of z when the observed correlation is corrected for range restriction. These sampling variance formulas, however, do not involve corrections for unreliability. For these reasons, only observed correlations and their asymptotic means and variances are used in this chapter.

Several Populations

Let us now consider k different populations drawn at random from a universe of populations and denote the observed correlation, based on a sample (of size n_i) drawn from population i, be denoted as $r_{x_i y_i}$ and the population correlation as $\rho_{x_i y_i}$. A major goal of VG methods is to estimate the mean and variance of population validities or correlations ($\rho_{x_i y_i}$). Another equally important goal is to develop appropriate confidence intervals for estimates of the mean. With this information at hand, researchers and practitioners can assess the degree to which validity is generalizable across organizations, provided that we continue to sample from the same universe of populations. Procedures for estimating the mean and variance of population validities are presented next using the well known maximum likelihood approach. Prior to presenting these procedures, the fixed-effects and random-effects models are briefly described.

Fixed- and Random-Effects Models

In the meta-analysis and VG literature, a model is said to be fixed (or homogeneous) if $\rho_{x_i y_i}$ values are considered identical across the k populations (drawn at random from a universe of populations with a constant correlation) so that the variance of $\rho_{x_i y_i}$ values is zero. That is,

$$\rho_{x_1 y_1} = \rho_{x_2 y_2} = \ldots = \rho_{x_k y_k} = \rho. \tag{7}$$

In view of Equation 7, the fixed-effects model may be written as:

$$r_{x_i y_i} = \rho + e_i. \tag{8}$$

In Equations 7 and 8, ρ refers to the common population validity across the universe of populations. In the random-effects model, $\rho_{x_i y_i}$ values may not be equal across populations. That is,

$$r_{x_i y_i} = \mu_\rho + \tau_i + e_i, \tag{9}$$

where μ_ρ is the grand mean in the sense of the analysis of variance (ANOVA) terminology and $\tau_i = \rho_{x_i y_i} - \mu_\rho$. In the fixed-effects model, $\tau_i = 0$ for all i. In the random-effects model, $\sigma_\tau^2 = \sigma_\rho^2$, which is typically not equal to zero. Moreover, the magnitude of $\sigma_\tau^2 = \sigma_\rho^2$ is of critical importance in answering the question of whether validity is generalizable.

MAXIMUM LIKELIHOOD ESTIMATION
WITH UNCORRECTED CORRELATIONS

In this section, described are procedures for estimating the relevant VG parameters when the observed correlations are not corrected for unreliability or range restriction. For ease of presentation, this scenario is referred to as the *bare-bones* VG model.

Fixed-Effects Model

In view of the fixed-effects VG model given in Equation 8, the (asymptotic) mean and variance of an observed correlation or validity coefficient may be expressed as:

$$E(r_{x_i y_i}) = \rho, \tag{10}$$

$$\sigma_{r_{x_i y_i}}^2 = \sigma_{e_i}^2. \tag{11}$$

Using Equations 10 and 11, the likelihood function, under the assumption that the sample validities are normally distributed, may be written as:

$$L(\rho) = (2\pi)^{-\frac{k}{2}} (\prod_{i=1}^{k} \sigma_{e_i}^{-1}) \exp(-\frac{1}{2} \sum_{i=1}^{k} \frac{(r_{x_i y_i} - \rho)^2}{\sigma_{e_i}^2}) \qquad (12)$$

The log of this likelihood function may be expressed as:

$$\ln L(\rho) = \frac{-k}{2} \ln(2\pi) - \sum_{i=1}^{k} \ln(\sigma_{e_i}) - \frac{1}{2} \sum_{i=1}^{k} \frac{(r_{x_i y_i} - \rho)^2}{\sigma_{e_i}^2} . \qquad (13)$$

The derivative of Equation 13 with respect to ρ may be written as:

$$\frac{d \ln L(\rho)}{d\rho} = \sum_{i=1}^{k} \frac{(r_{x_i y_i} - \rho)}{\sigma_{e_i}^2} . \qquad (14)$$

Setting this equation to zero and solving for ρ leads to

$$\rho = \frac{\sum_{i=1}^{k} w_i r_{x_i y_i}}{\sum_{i=1}^{k} w_i} , \qquad (15)$$

where

$$w_i = \frac{1}{\sigma_{e_i}^2} . \qquad (16)$$

Equation 15 can be used to solve for ρ. According to Equation 15, the maximum likelihood estimate of ρ is a weighted average of the observed correlations from k different populations. It should be noted that in a fixed-effects model, ρs do nor vary from population to population and, hence, there is no need to estimate their variance.

The weight for each validity coefficient is the reciprocal of its error variance. Typically, the bigger the sample size, the smaller the error variance and hence the bigger the weight. That is, validity coefficients based on bigger samples will receive bigger weights than validities based on smaller samples. In view of Equation 4, an estimate of each weight may be written as

$$\hat{w}_i = \frac{n_i - 1}{(1 - r_{x_i y_i}^2)^2} \tag{17}$$

and used in Equation 15 to solve for ρ. It should be noted that Equations 15 and 16 are not new and were previously presented by Hedges and Olkin (1985); Erez et al. (1996) provided similar equations for Fisher's z transformation of an uncorrected correlation. According to Kendall and Stuart (1977), the maximum likelihood estimate $\hat{\rho}$ is (asymptotically) normally distributed with mean equal to ρ and sampling variance equal to

$$\sigma_{\hat{\rho}}^2 = \frac{-1}{E\left\{\dfrac{d^2 (\ln L(\rho))}{d\rho^2}\right\}}, \tag{18}$$

where the denominator in Equation 17 is the expectation (E) of the second derivative of the log of the likelihood function with respect to ρ. In view of Equations 14 and 16, Equation 18 can be rewritten as:

$$\sigma_{\hat{\rho}}^2 = \frac{1}{(\sum\limits_{i=1}^{k} w_i)}. \tag{19}$$

Using Equation 17, Equation 19 can be rewritten as:

$$\hat{\sigma}_{\hat{\rho}}^2 = \frac{1}{\sum\limits_{i=1}^{k} \dfrac{(n_i - 1)}{(1 - r_{x_i y_i})^2}}. \tag{20}$$

A confidence interval for ρ may be written as:

$$\hat{\rho} - a\hat{\sigma}_{\hat{\rho}} < \rho_{xy} < \hat{\rho} - a\hat{\sigma}_{\hat{\rho}}, \tag{21}$$

where a is a constant and depends on the alpha level specified by the investigator. In practice, the population validity is assumed to be zero if this confidence interval contains the zero point. It should be noted that this error variance formula for $\hat{\rho}$ is only valid when the validity is the same across populations. Strictly speaking, one should first check to see if the hypothesis of equal population validities is valid, given the observed validities. Hedges and Olkin (1985) and Hunter and Schmidt (1990) offered statistical procedures (based on the chi-square statistic) for testing this null hypothesis.

Random-Effects Model

In view of Equation 9, the (asymptotic) mean and variance of an observed correlation may be written as:

$$E(r_{x_i y_i}) = \mu_\rho,$$

(22)

$$\sigma^2_{r_i y_i} = \sigma^2_\rho + \sigma^2_{e_i}.$$

(23)

A comparison of Equation 22 with Equation 10 shows an important distinction between the fixed-effects model and the random-effects model. The variance of population validities is included in the sampling variance of an observed correlation in the random-effects model, but not in the fixed-effects model. Therefore, the fixed-effects sampling variance of an observed correlation is smaller than or equal to the sampling variance in the random-effects model. This distinction is not always well understood by practitioners and has received a great deal of attention lately (Erez at al., 1996; Hedges & Vevea, 1998; Hunter & Schmidt, 2000; Overton, 1998).

Prior to presenting the maximum likelihood estimates, it should be noted that, in the method of moments, an estimate of μ_ρ may be defined as the simple average or the sample-size weighted average of the observed correlations. Similarly, an estimate of σ^2_ρ may be defined as the difference between the variance of observed correlations and the average of sampling variances. A justification for the mean and variance estimates in the method of moments may be seen from the following equations for the random-effects model:

$$E(\bar{r}) = E(\frac{r_{x_1 y_1} + r_{x_2 y_2} + \ldots + r_{x_k y_k}}{k}) = \mu_\rho.$$

(24)

$$\sigma^2_{r_{x_i y_i}} = \sigma^2_\rho + \frac{\sum_{i=1}^{k} \sigma^2_{e_i}}{k}.$$

(25)

Finally, an estimate of the sampling variance of $\bar{r}$ (or $\hat{\mu}_\rho$) is obtained by dividing Equation 25 by k, the number of validity studies included in a VG study. This method of estimating the VG parameters is equally popular in VG procedures that correct for unreliability and restriction of range.

Assuming that the sample validities are normally distributed, the likelihood function for the random-effects model may be expressed as:

$$L(\mu_\rho, \sigma_\rho^2) = (2\pi)^{\frac{-k}{2}} (\prod_{i=1}^{k} (\sigma_{e_i}^2 + \sigma_\rho^2)^{-\frac{1}{2}} \exp(-\frac{1}{2} \sum_{i=1}^{k} \left\{ \frac{(r_{x_i y_i} - \mu_\rho)^2}{(\sigma_{e_i}^2 + \sigma_\rho^2)} \right\}). \quad (26)$$

Partial derivates of the log (ln) of the aforementioned likelihood function with respect to μ_ρ and σ_ρ^2 may be written, respectively, as:

$$\frac{\delta \ln L(\mu_\rho, \sigma_\rho^2)}{\delta \mu_\rho} = \sum_{i=1}^{k} \frac{(r_{x_i y_i} - \mu_\rho)}{\sigma_\rho^2 + \sigma_{e_i}^2}, \quad (27)$$

$$\frac{\delta \ln L(\mu_\rho, \sigma_\rho^2)}{\delta \sigma_\rho^2} = -\frac{1}{2} \sum_{i=1}^{k} \frac{1}{\sigma_\rho^2 + \sigma_{e_i}^2} + \frac{1}{2} \sum_{i=1}^{k} \frac{(r_{x_i y_i} - \mu_\rho)^2}{(\sigma_\rho^2 + \sigma_{e_i}^2)^2}. \quad (28)$$

Setting these two equations to zero and solving for μ_ρ and σ_ρ^2 results in:

$$\mu_\rho = \frac{\sum_{i=1}^{k} w_i r_{x_i y_i}}{\sum_{i=1}^{k} w_i}, \quad (29)$$

$$\sigma_\rho^2 = \frac{\sum_{i=1}^{k} w_i^2 [(r_{x_i y_i} - \mu_\rho)^2 - \sigma_{e_i}^2]}{\sum_{i=1}^{k} w_i^2}, \quad (30)$$

where

$$w_i = \frac{1}{\sigma_\rho^2 + \sigma_{e_i}^2}. \quad (31)$$

In view of Equation 4, an estimate of w_i ($\hat{w}_i$) can be written as:

$$\hat{w}_i = \frac{1}{\sigma_\rho^2 + \dfrac{(1 - r_{x_i y_i}^2)^2}{n - 1}} . \tag{32}$$

These weights ($\hat{w}_i$) can then be used in solving Equations 29 and 30 simultaneously to obtain estimates for the mean and variance of population validities. It is not a difficult task, but numerical procedures are needed to successfully accomplish this estimation. It should also be noted that Equation 29 is similar in format to Equation 15, except that weights (the w_i) in Equations 15 and 29 are differently defined. Furthermore, in the fixed-effects model, there was only one parameter to be estimated and, hence, there was only equation to be solved. Erez et al. (1996) presented equations similar to Equations 27 and 28 for Fisher's z transformed correlations. Again, the sampling variance of $\hat{\mu}_\rho$ within the ML framework may be expressed as:

$$\hat{\sigma}_{\hat{\mu}_\rho}^2 = \frac{1}{(\sum_{i=1}^{k} \hat{w}_i)} . \tag{33}$$

Using Equation 33, appropriate confidence intervals for μ_ρ can be developed using an equation similar to the one given in Equation 21.

MAXIMUM LIKELIHOOD ESTIMATION WITH CORRECTED CORRELATIONS

Up to this point, we have only looked at the relation between observed validities and their population parameters. In validity generalization research, it is a common practice to correct observed validities for unreliability in the criterion or predictor reliability and range restriction on the predictor. Standard psychometric and statistical procedures (Lord & Novick, 1968) are used in making these corrections. Two well known procedures for making such corrections to observed validity coefficients are as follows: (a) Correcting correlations using hypothetical distributions of predictor reliability, criterion reliability and range restriction (or corrections based on hypothetical artifact distributions) and (b) correcting correlations at the study level (i.e., using sample-based reliability and range restriction values). The currently available VG procedures for corrected correlations are based on one of these types of corrections. For ease of presentation, the psychometric model with corrections based on hypothetical artifact distributions will be hereafter referred to as VG with artifact distributions and the one based on study-level corrections as VG with direct corrections. Each of these models is described later, along with procedures for obtaining the maximum likelihood estimates of the mean and variance of population validities. Because the random-effects model is considered by many to be a much more realistic model in practice, we describe the ML estimation only for the random-effects model. Readers interested only in the fixed-effects model may ignore the estimation of the variance of population validities. For this group of researchers and practitioners, the estimation task is rather straightforward and does not require any iterative algorithms.

VG With Artifact Distributions

Prior to defining this model, let $\rho_{x_i x_i}$ represent the unrestricted population reliability of x, $\rho_{y_i y_i}$ represent the unrestricted population reliability of y, and u_i represent the attenuated population range restriction factor or simply the ratio of attenuated, restricted population standard deviation to the attenuated, unrestricted population standard deviation. This model may be expressed as:

$$r_{x_i y_i} = \rho_{x_i y_i} \sqrt{\rho_{x_i x_i}} \sqrt{\rho_{y_i y_i}} \frac{u_i}{\sqrt{(1 + (u_i^2 - 1)\rho_{x_i y_i}^2 \, \rho_{x_i x_i} \, \rho_{y_i y_i}}} + e_i \qquad (34)$$

for study i. It should be noted that $\rho_{x_i y_i}$ is the unattenuated, unrestricted population validity (or correlation between x and y) in population i. For ease of presentation, the above equation may be rewritten as:

$$r_{x_i y_i} = h(\rho_{x_i y_i}, \rho_{x_i x_i}, \rho_{y_i y_i}, u_i) + e_i = h_i + e_i, \qquad (35)$$

where

$$h_i \equiv h(\rho_{x_i y_i}, \rho_{x_i x_i}, \rho_{y_i y_i}, u_i) =$$
$$\rho_{x_i y_i} \sqrt{\rho_{x_i x_i}} \sqrt{\rho_{y_i y_i}} \frac{u_i}{\sqrt{(1 + (u_i^2 - 1)\rho_{x_i y_i}^2 \, \rho_{x_i x_i} \, \rho_{y_i y_i}}} . \qquad (36)$$

Using the ANOVA notation in Equation 9, Equation 35 may be rewritten as

$$r_{x_i y_i} = \mu_h + \tau_i + e_i, \tag{37}$$

where μ_h is the grand mean and $\tau_i = h_i - \mu_h$. In the fixed-effects model, $\tau_i = 0$ for all i. In the random-effects model, $\sigma_\tau^2 = \sigma_h^2$. In view of Equation 35, at an individual study level, the mean (or expectation) and variance of $r_{x_i y_i}$ may be written, respectively, as:

$$E(r_{x_i y_i}) = \mu_h, \tag{38}$$

$$\sigma_{r_i y_i}^2 = \sigma_h^2 + \sigma_{e_i}^2. \tag{39}$$

As before, the maximum likelihood estimates of μ_h and σ_h^2 can be obtained by solving the following two equations simultaneously.

$$\mu_h = \frac{\sum_{i=1}^{k} w_i r_{x_i y_i}}{\sum_{i=1}^{k} w_i}, \tag{40}$$

$$\sigma_h^2 = \frac{\sum_{i=1}^{k} w_i^2 [(r_{x_i y_i} - \mu_h)^2 - \sigma_{e_i}^2]}{\sum_{i=1}^{2} w_i^2}. \tag{41}$$

As in the previous scenarios and in view of Equation 4, an estimate of w_i ($\hat{w}_i$) can be written as:

$$\hat{w}_i = \frac{1}{\sigma_h^2 + \dfrac{(1 - r_{x_i y_i}^2)^2}{n - 1}}. \tag{42}$$

Equations 40 and 41 form the basis for iteratively solving for the maximum likelihood estimates of the mean and variance of h. The difference between these two equations and Equations 29 and 30 is that ρ is replaced with h. Finally, the sampling variance of $\hat{\mu}_h$ within the ML framework may be expressed as:

$$\hat{\sigma}^2_{\hat{\mu}_h} = \frac{1}{(\sum\limits_{i=1}^{k} \hat{w}_i)} . \tag{43}$$

Although solving Equations 40 and 41 will yield maximum likelihood estimates of μ_h and σ^2_h, these are not the parameters of interest in a VG analysis because they refer to the restricted, attenuated relationship. The parameters of interest are μ_ρ and σ^2_ρ. Due to the invariance property of ML estimators, it is possible to obtain the ML estimators for μ_ρ and σ^2_ρ. Using Equation 36 and the Taylor series approximations, μ_h and σ^2_h may be expressed, respectively, as (Kendall & Stuart, 1977):

$$\mu_h = \frac{\mu_\rho \sqrt{\mu_{\rho_{xx}}} \sqrt{\mu_{\rho_{yy}}} \mu_u}{\sqrt{1 + (\mu^2_u - 1)\mu^2_\rho \mu_{\rho_{xx}} \mu_{\rho_{yy}}}} , \tag{44}$$

$$\sigma^2_h = A^2\sigma^2_\rho + B^2\sigma^2_{\rho_{xx}} + C^2\sigma^2_{\rho_{yy}} + D^2\mu^2_u. \tag{45}$$

In Equation 45, the terms A, B, C, and D are the partial derivatives of h (Equation 36) with respective to $\rho_{x_i y_i}$, $\rho_{x_i x_i}$, $\rho_{y_i y_i}$, and u_i, respectively. The exact expressions for A, B, C, and D are provided below. In Equations 44 and 45, $\mu_{\rho_{xx}}$ and $\sigma^2_{\rho_{xx}}$ refer, respectively, to the mean and variance of unrestricted population reliability of x, $\mu_{\rho_{yy}}$ and $\sigma^2_{\rho_{yy}}$ refer, respectively, to the mean and variance of unrestricted population reliability of y, and μ_u and σ^2_u represent the mean and variance of u in the attenuated populations. It should be noted that Equation 45 assumes that $\rho_{x_i y_i}$, $\rho_{x_i x_i}$, $\rho_{y_i y_i}$, and u_i are uncorrelated. The same assumption was also made by Callender and Osborn (1980), Pearlman, Schmidt, and Hunter (1980), Raju and Burke (1983), Schmidt, Gast-Rosenberg, and Hunter (1980), and Law, Schmidt, and Hunter (1994) in providing estimates for μ_ρ and σ^2_ρ.

Solving Equations 44 and 45 for μ_ρ and σ^2_ρ, respectively, one obtains

$$\mu_\rho = t(\mu_h) = \frac{\mu_h}{\sqrt{\mu_{\rho_{xx}} \mu_{\rho_{yy}} (\mu^2_u + \mu^2_h(1 - \mu^2_u))}} , \tag{46}$$

$$\sigma^2_\rho = \frac{\sigma^2_h - (B^2\sigma^2_{\rho_{xx}} + C^2\sigma^2_{\rho_{yy}} + D^2\sigma^2_u)}{A^2} . \tag{47}$$

In view of the invariance property of the ML estimators, ML estimates of μ_ρ and σ_ρ^2 may now be expressed, respectively, as:

$$\hat{\mu}_\rho = \frac{\hat{\mu}_h}{\sqrt{\mu_{\rho_{xx}}\mu_{\rho_{yy}}(\hat{\mu}_u^2 + \hat{\mu}_h^2(1-\mu_u^2))}} , \tag{48}$$

$$\hat{\sigma}_\rho^2 = \frac{\hat{\sigma}_h^2 - (B^2\sigma_{\rho_{xx}}^2 + C^2\sigma_{\rho_{yy}}^2 + D^2\sigma_u^2)}{A^2} . \tag{49}$$

It should be recalled that $\hat{\mu}_h$ and $\hat{\sigma}_h^2$ are the ML estimators of μ_h and σ_h^2, respectively, derived from Equations 40 and 41. Estimates of A, B, C, and D may be written as:

$$A = \frac{\hat{\mu}_h}{\hat{\mu}_\rho} + \frac{\hat{\mu}_h(1-\mu_u^2)}{\hat{\mu}_\rho\mu_u^2} , \tag{50}$$

$$B = \frac{1}{2}\left(\frac{\hat{\mu}_h}{\mu_{\rho_{yy}}} + \frac{\hat{\mu}_h^3(1-\mu_u^2)}{\mu_{\rho_{yy}}\mu_u^2}\right) , \tag{51}$$

$$C = \frac{1}{2}\left(\frac{\hat{\mu}_h}{\mu_{\rho_{xx}}} + \frac{\hat{\mu}_h^3(1-\mu_u^2)}{\mu_{\rho_{xx}}\mu_u^2}\right) , \tag{52}$$

$$D = \frac{\hat{\mu}_h - \hat{\mu}_h^3}{\mu_u} . \tag{53}$$

Finally, an estimate of the variance of $\hat{\mu}_\rho$ within the ML framework may be expressed as (Kendall & Stuart, 1977; Wilks, 1962):

$$\hat{\sigma}_{\hat{\mu}_\rho}^2 = (t'(\mu_h))^2\left(\frac{-1}{E\left\{\frac{\delta^2(\ln L(\mu_h,\sigma_h^2))}{\delta^2\mu_h}\right\}}\right) . \tag{54}$$

In view of Equations 18 and 19, Equation 54 can be written as:

$$\hat{\sigma}_{\hat{\mu}_\rho}^2 = (t'(\mu_h))^2\hat{\sigma}_{\hat{\mu}_h}^2 , \tag{55}$$

where t' is the derivative of t (Equation 46) with respect to μ_h which can be expressed as:

$$t'(\mu_h) = \frac{dt(\mu_h)}{d\mu_h} = \frac{\mu_{\rho_{xx}}\mu_{\rho_{yy}} + (\mu_h - 1)(1 - \mu_u^2)(\mu_{\rho_{xx}}\mu_{\rho_{yy}}\mu_h)}{\left(\mu_{\rho_{xx}}\mu_{\rho_{yy}}(\mu_u^2 + \mu_h^2(1 - \mu_u^2))\right)^{\frac{3}{2}}} . \tag{56}$$

Using Equation 43 and 54 through 56 and substituting sample-based estimates, an estimate of the variance of $\hat{\mu}_\rho$ may be expressed as:

$$\hat{\sigma}^2_{\hat{\mu}_\rho} = \frac{\left(\mu_{\rho_{xx}}\mu_{\rho_{yy}} + (\hat{\mu}_h - 1)(1 - \mu_u^2)(\mu_{\rho_{xx}}\mu_{\rho_{yy}}\hat{\mu}_h)\right)^2}{\left(\mu_{\rho_{xx}}\mu_{\rho_{yy}}(\mu_u^2 + \hat{\mu}_h^2(1 - \mu_u^2))\right)^3} \frac{1}{(\sum\limits_{i=1}^{k} \hat{w}_i)} , \tag{57}$$

where $\hat{w}_i$ are as defined in Equation 42.

The statistical rationale used here for estimating the mean and variance of ρ is similar to the one used by Raju and Burke (1983) in developing their TSA procedures. It may be possible to use any one of the six currently available procedures (Callender & Osborn, 1980; Law et al., 1994; Pearlman et al., 1980; Raju & Burke, 1983; Schmidt et al., 1980) for this purpose. Among the six procedures, the TSA1 and TSA 2 procedures of Raju and Burke (1983) made direct use of the mean and variance of hypothetical range restriction values while the other four procedures use the mean and variance of a function of range restriction values. Given this relative simplicity associated with the TSA procedures, we have decided to use some of the same techniques used in one of the TSA procedures (TSA 1) to estimate the mean and variance of ρ from the maximum likelihood estimates of the mean and variance of h. As the acronym implies, this procedure uses the Taylor series approximation (TSA) to estimate the mean and variance of a function of several variables. These are asymptotic estimates (Kendall & Stuart, 1977); that is, as the sample size increases, these estimates converge to their population parameters.

The reliabilities and range restriction values appearing in Equations 34 through 36 are commonly referred to as artifacts. Their means and variances in Equations 44 and 45 are assumed known at the population level. Furthermore, these reliabilities are for the unattenuated and unrestricted populations, whereas the range restriction values are for the attenuated (adjusted for unreliability) populations. The prevailing practice (Callender & Osborn, 1980;

Law et al., 1994; Pearlman et al., 1980; Raju & Burke, 1983; Schmidt et al., 1980) is to use hypothetical distributions (means and variances) of artifacts in estimating the mean and variance of unattenuated and unrestricted population validities. The question of the degree to which the use of hypothetical artifact distributions affects the accuracy of true validity estimates has been addressed by Raju, Pappas, and Williams (1989), Raju, Anselmi, Goodman, and Thomas (1998), and Thomas and Raju (1998), among others. It appears that this effect is much more severe for estimating the variance of ρs than it is for estimating the mean of ρs.

Within the framework of VG with artifact distributions, the use of hypothetical artifact distributions gets around the frequently faced problem of not having access to sample-based reliability and range restriction values. In practice, one should be careful, however, in accepting the validity of hypothetical artifact distributions across all conditions. Hypothetical distributions of artifacts are probably justifiable in some situations, but may not be in others. Practitioners need to pay careful attention to the degree to which hypothetical distributions match the true distributions of artifacts.

In addition to the assumption about the validity of artifact distributions, the currently available procedures for VG with artifact distributions assume that the hypothetical distributions are uncorrelated across populations. Several investigators have commented on the meaning and tenability of this assumption. For this assumption to be true, according to James, Demaree, Mulaik, and Ladd (1992), the situational moderators that underlie situational specificity must be independent from the statistical artifacts. If the two are not independent, then the current procedures remove part of the actual variance attributable to the situational moderators when they subtract the artifactual variance. In two recent Monte Carlo studies, Raju et al. (1998) and Thomas and Raju (1998) have shown that if this assumption is violated, then the σ_ρ^2 estimates derived from the procedures based on VG with artifact distributions are not always accurate. In response to the problems associated with the use of hypothetical artifact distributions and the uncorrelatedness of these distributions, Raju, Burke, Normand, and Langlois (1991) proposed a different model (VG with direct corrections), which assumes that the study-level range restriction and reliability values are available. Then they go on show that this model may still be useful when only partial (study-level) artifact data are available. A description of this model is presented below along with its maximum likelihood estimates of the mean and variance of unrestricted and unattenuated population validities.

VG with Direct Corrections

As before, let $r_{x_i y_i}$ represent the observed correlation between x and y in a sample drawn from population i. Let $r_{x_i x_i}$ and $r_{y_i y_i}$ represent the sample-based (restricted) reliabilities for x and y, respectively. Finally, let u_i represent the unattenuated, but sample-based range restriction value. Then, using classical test theory (Lord & Novick, 1968), a sample-based estimate of the unrestricted and unattenuated population validity (ρ_i) may be written as:

$$r_i = \frac{g_i r_{x_i y_i}}{\sqrt{r_{x_i x_i} r_{y_i y_i} - r_{x_i y_i}^2 + g_i^2 r_{x_i y_i}^2}} , \tag{58}$$

where $g_i = 1/u_i$. In view of this equation, the model for VG with direct corrections (within the random-effects framework) may be expressed as:

$$r_i = \mu_\rho + \tau_i + e_i. \tag{59}$$

As previously defined, μ_ρ is the grand mean and $\tau_i = \rho_i - \mu_\rho$. In the fixed-effects model, $\tau_i = 0$ for all i; in the random-effects model, $\sigma_\tau^2 = \sigma_\rho^2$. In view of Equation 59, at an individual study level, the mean (or expectation) and variance of r_i may be written, respectively, as:

$$E(r_i) = \mu_\rho, \tag{60}$$

$$\sigma_{r_i}^2 = \sigma_\rho^2 + \sigma_{e_i}^2 . \tag{61}$$

According to Raju et al. (1991), an asymptotic variance of e_i may be written as:

$$\hat{\sigma}_{e_i}^2 = \frac{g_i^2 r_{x_i x_i} r_{y_i y_i} (r_{x_i x_i} - r_{x_i y_i}^2)(r_{y_i y_i} - r_{x_i y_i}^2)}{(n_i - 1)\hat{V}_i^3} , \tag{62}$$

where

$$\hat{V}_i = r_{x_i x_i} r_{y_i y_i} - r_{x_i y_i}^2 + g_i^2 r_{x_i y_i}^2 . \tag{63}$$

Given this model, the necessary maximum likelihood equations for VG with direction corrections may be expressed as:

$$\mu_\rho = \frac{\sum\limits_{i=1}^{k} w_i r_i}{\sum\limits_{i=1}^{k} w_i}, \tag{64}$$

$$\sigma_\rho^2 = \frac{\sum\limits_{i=1}^{k} w_i^2 [(r_i - \mu_\rho)^2 - \sigma_{e_i}^2]}{\sum\limits_{i=1}^{k} w_i^2}, \tag{65}$$

where an estimate of w_i $(\hat{w}_i)$ can be written as:

$$\hat{w}_i = \frac{1}{\sigma_\rho^2 + \dfrac{g_i^2 r_{x_i x_i} r_{y_i y_i} (r_{x_i x_i} - r_{x_i y_i}^2)(r_{y_i y_i} - r_{x_i y_i}^2)}{(n_i - 1)\hat{V}_i^3}}. \tag{66}$$

Equations 64 and 65 will need to be solved iteratively for obtaining the maximum likelihood estimates of the mean and variance of ρ. As in the previous models, the sampling variance of $\hat{\mu}_\rho$ within the ML framework may be expressed as:

$$\hat{\sigma}_{\hat{\mu}_\rho}^2 = \frac{1}{(\sum\limits_{i=1}^{k} \hat{w}_i)}. \tag{67}$$

Appropriate confidence intervals for μ_ρ can be developed using an equation similar to the one given in Equation 21.

As previously noted, VG with direct corrections assumes that predictor and criterion reliabilities and range restriction values are available at the individual study level. It is quite possible in practice for some studies to have complete artifact information, while other studies to have only partial artifact information. Raju et al. (1991) explained how to estimate the (unattenuated and unrestricted) population validity (Equation 58) and its sampling variance (Equation 62) when complete artifact information is unavailable for a given study. According to Raju et al., even when artifact information is unavailable for all studies included in a VG study, it is still possible to obtain adequate estimates of population validity (Equation 58) and its sampling variance (Equation 62), provided a reasonable set of estimates of predictor reliability, criterion reliability, and range restriction can be generated or proposed for use across all studies.

According to Raju et al. (1991), the sampling variance formula in Equation 62 assumes that the range restriction value (u_i) is fixed within a study; that is, the sampling error associated with the range restriction value is not reflected in Equation 62. Also, Equation 62 assumes that u_i is derived from the unattenuated sample. If a range restriction value is only available for the attenuated sample (and let this be denoted by u'_i), then the unattenuated u_i can be obtained by multiplying u'_i and the ratio of (sample-based) restricted reliability to (sample-based) unrestricted reliability of the predictor. Formulas for obtaining an unrestricted reliability from a restricted reliability are available in Lord and Novick (1968). Interested readers may want to refer to Raju et al. for additional information.

CONCLUDING REMARKS

In this chapter, we have briefly outlined the advantages of ML estimation methods over other estimation methods (e.g., the method of moments) and then presented procedures for estimating the mean and variance of population validities within this framework. ML-based VG estimates are presented for three different scenarios: bare-bones (uncorrected correlations), artifact distributions (correlations corrected with hypothetical artifact distributions), and direct corrections (correlations corrected with sample-based artifact data at the study level). All three models are expressed in terms of observed correlations without any transformations.

The ML estimation results are new for VG with artifact distributions and VG with direct corrections, while some of the results for bare-bones VG have been known for sometime (Erez et al. 1996; Hedges & Olkin, 1985).

Although it is aesthetically pleasing to derive new estimators for important VG parameters, it is also important to consider the "So what?" question. Specifically, do the ML estimators described herein for VG with artifact distributions and VG with direct corrections provide improved estimation of the mean and variance of population correlations? One clear benefit is that we know the sampling distribution of ML estimates (i.e., they are asymptotically normal); consequently we can legitimately construct confidence intervals for VG parameters based on our sample estimates. In contrast, the sampling distributions of estimates based on the method of moments may not be (asymptotically) efficient or BAN and so the resulting confidence intervals need to be interpreted with caution (Mood & Graybill, 1963).

There is a pressing need for assessing empirically the accuracy of the ML estimates for the three models studied here. In addition to accuracy, there is a need for assessing the relative accuracy of the ML estimates and the estimates from other methods, such as the method of moments. Large scale, Monte Carlo studies are needed for a comprehensive assessment of the accuracy and utility of these estimations. Such studies would reveal whether our ML estimates are more precise for the types of data typically analyzed by applied psychologists.

Simulation studies will determine whether the statistical optimality of the ML methodology—consistency, asymptotic efficiency, and asymptotic normality—justifies its computational complexity. Although we do not view these computations overly complex (e.g., the computations required for maximum likelihood factor analysis are much more complicated), they are certainly more challenging than earlier methods based on the method of moments. Noniterative methods for estimating the VG parameters, especially in the bare-bones, random-effects VG model, are available (DerSimonian & Laird, 1986; Hedges & Vevea, 1998; Overton, 1998) and may be employed when deemed appropriate. With the readily available sampling variance of an ML estimate of the mean of population validities, it should be possible to combine data from a new validation study with data from a previously conducted meta-analysis to come up with a revised meta-analytic estimate or result, using the Bayesian procedures described by Brannick (2001). Such continuous updating, without a full blown meta-analysis, should be very beneficial to practitioners.

REFERENCES

Brannick, M. T. (2001). Implications of empirical Bayes meta-analysis for test validation. *Journal of Applied Psychology, 86,* 468–480.

Callender, J. C., & Osborn, H. (1980). Development and test of a new model for validity generalization. *Journal of Applied Psychology, 65,* 543–558.

DerSimonian, R., & Laird, N. M. (1986). Meta-analysis in clinical trials. *Controlled Clinical Trials, 7,* 177–188.

Erez, A., Bloom, M. C., & Wells, M. T. (1996). Using random than fixed effects models in meta-analysis: Implications for situational specificity and validity generalization. *Personnel Psychology, 49,* 275–306.

Hedges, L. V. (1989). An unbiased correlation for sampling error in validity generalization studies. *Journal of Applied Psychology, 74,* 469–477.

Hedges, L. V., & Olkin, I. (1985). *Statistical methods for meta-analysis*. New York: Academic Press.

Hedges, L. V., & Vevea, J. L. (1998). Fixed and random effects models in meta-analysis. *Psychological Methods, 3*, 486–504.

Hunter, J. E., & Schmidt, F. L. (1990). *Methods of meta-analysis*. Beverly Hills, CA: Sage.

Hunter, J. E., & Schmidt, F. L. (2000). Fixed effects vs. random effects meta-analysis models: Implications for cumulative research knowledge. *International Journal of Selection and Assessment, 8*, 275–292.

James, L. R. J., Demaree, R. G., Mulaik, S. A., & Ladd, R. T. (1992). Validity generalization in the context of situational models. *Journal of Applied Psychology, 77*, 3–14.

Kendal, M., & Stuart, A. (1977). The advanced theory of statistics (Vol. 1, 4th Ed.). New York: Macmillan.

Kendall, M., & Stuart, A. (1979). The advanced theory of statistics (Vol. 2, 4th Ed.). New York: Macmillan.

Law, K., Schmidt, F. L., & Hunter, J. E. (1994). Nonlinearity of range restriction in meta-analysis: Test of an improved procedure. *Journal of Applied Psychology, 79*, 425–438.

Lehmann, E. L. (1983). *Theory of point estimation*. New York: Wiley.

Lord, F. M., & Novick, M. R. (1968). *Statistical theories of mental test scores*. Reading, MA: Addison-Wesley.

Mendoza, J. L. (1993). Fisher transformations for correlations corrected for selection and missing data. *Psychometrika, 58*, 601–615.

Mood, A. M., & Graybill, F. A. (1963). *Introduction to the theory of statistics* (2nd Ed.). New York: McGraw-Hill.

Overton, R. C. (1998). A comparison of fixed-effects and mixed (random-effects) models for meta-analysis tests of moderator variable effects. *Psychological Methods, 3*, 354–379.

Pearlman, K., Schmidt, F. L., & Hunter, J. E. (1980). Validity generalization results for tests used to predict job proficiency and training success in clerical occupations. *Journal of Applied Psychology, 65*, 373–406.

Raju, N. S., Anselmi, T. V., Goodman, J. S., & Thomas, A. (1998). The effect of correlated artifacts and true validity on the accuracy of parameter estimation in validity generalization. *Personnel Psychology, 51*, 453–465.

Raju, N. S., & Burke, M. J. (1983). Two new procedures for studying validity generalization. *Journal of Applied Psychology, 68*, 382–395.

Raju, N. S., Burke, M. J., Normand, J., & Langlois, G. M. (1991). A new meta-analytic approach. *Journal of Applied Psychology, 76*, 432–446.

Raju, N. S., Pappas, S., & Williams, C. P. (1989). An empirical Monte Carlo test of the accuracy of the correlation, covariance, and regression slope models for assessing validity generalization. *Journal of Applied Psychology, 74*, 901–911.

Rao, C. R. (1973). *Linear statistical inference and its application* (2nd Ed.). New York: Wiley.

Schmidt, F. L., Gast-Rosenberg, I., & Hunter, J. E. (1980). Test of a model of validity generalization: Results for computer programmers. *Journal of Applied Psychology, 65*, 643–661.

Schmidt, F. L., & Hunter, J. E. (1977). Development of a general solution to the problem of validity generalization. *Journal of Applied Psychology, 62*, 529–540.

Schmidt, F. L., Hunter, J. E., & Raju, N. S. (1988). Validity generalization and situational specificity: A second look at the 75% rule and the Fisher's z transformation. *Journal of Applied Psychology, 73*, 665–672.

Shohoji, T., Yamashita, Y., & Tarumi, T. (1981). Generalization of Fisher's z-transformation. *Journal of Statistical Planning and Inference, 5*, 347–354.

Thomas, A. L., & Raju, N. S. (1998, April). *An examination and evaluation of James et al. (1992) VG estimation procedure when artifacts are corrected.* Paper presented at the annual meeting of the Society for Industrial and Organizational Psychology, Dallas, TX.

Wilks, S. S. (1962). *Mathematical statistics*. New York: Wiley.

10

Methodological and Conceptual Challenges in Conducting and Interpreting Meta-Analyses

Michael J. Burke
Ronald S. Landis
Tulane University

Meta-analysis has proven to be a powerful tool for researchers from a variety of social science disciplines interested in testing whether bivariate relationships or effects generalize across conditions or settings. In addition to examining such relatively simple relations, researchers are beginning to use meta-analysis to address broader research questions and hypotheses including the use of meta-analytic results as input to structural equation models. Because the ultimate goal of most research is to develop an understanding of the associations among constructs, meta-analysis represents a powerful technique for explicating nomological networks. The use of meta-analytic procedures to test broader research hypotheses than posited in primary studies as well as the diverse applications of meta-analytic procedures present new methodological challenges and construct validity issues.

The purpose of this chapter is to discuss five important issues that can affect the use of meta-analytic procedures in making inferences about relations between constructs or the effectiveness of behavioral interventions, and to offer suggestions for dealing with these issues. More specifically, this chapter presents discussions of three topics that are likely to affect the conduct of meta-analyses: the estimation of effect size in studies that use repeated measures designs, the use of hypothetical artifact distributions versus sample-based artifacts when making corrections for statistical artifacts, and assessments of interrater agreement when identifying and classifying studies that are included in meta-analyses. The discussion then moves to two topics that are likely to be relevant to drawing inferences about construct-level relations on the basis of meta-analytic studies, specifically questions about the definition of constructs and the relation between the operational procedures employed in the studies that are meta-analytically combined and the constructs those procedures are designed to tap and the emerging use of multivariate techniques for analyzing meta-analytic findings. Other methodological issues identified in earlier critiques of meta-analytic procedures (see Burke, 1984; Hedges, 1992) such as missing data, possible publication biases, and combining estimates of effects that are not independent continue to be the subject of considerable research, yet are not the focus of this commentary. That is, this chapter is not intended to be an exhaustive discussion of methodological and construct validity issues related to present applications of meta-analytic procedures but rather is intended to discuss issues or problems that are more central to realizing the potential of meta-analytic studies for advancing knowledge in various disciplines.

OPERATIONAL ISSUES
IN CONDUCTING META-ANALYSES

Despite the widespread use of meta-analysis, the available computer software, and the numerous books and articles describing meta-analytic techniques, there are still a number of questions about how to best structure a meta-analysis, and even how to extract appropriate information from primary studies. This section deals with three issues that are often encountered when carrying out meta-analyses, the problems in estimating effects when repeated measures designs are used, difficulties in estimating the size and effects of statistical artifacts, and the problems in establishing and documenting interrater agreement in the judgment calls that are often a part of meta-analysis, especially those that involve making judgments about study characteristics.

Computing Effect Sizes for Experiments with
Matched Groups or Repeated Measures Designs

Many primary studies report inferential test statistics (e.g., a *t-statistic* or an *F*-ratio) and fail to include descriptive statistics such as means and standard deviations. A result is that meta-analysts often need to use the inferential test statistic to estimate the correlation or effect and, thus, use the effect size estimate from that primary study in the meta-analysis. Such estimation is particularly problematic for meta-analyses applied to studies involving experimental effects with *correlated designs* (i.e., matched groups or repeated measures designs, for which there exists a correlation between measures). Specifically, the critical concern related to these meta-analyses is that the *d* value, the standardized mean difference, is often incorrectly computed from the *t* statistic. For estimating the standard effect size (*d*) from the test statistic (t_c) for a *correlated design*, many researchers have relied on suggestions and incorrect equations presented in Glass, McGaw, and Smith (1981), Rosenthal (1991, 1994), Mullen and Rosenthal's (1985) meta-analytic software, or texts adopting Rosenthal's suggestions (e.g., Cooper, 1998). As demonstrated in Dunlap, Cortina, Vaslow, and Burke (1996), reliance on these incorrect formulae results in considerable overestimation of effect sizes. For instance, using data reported in Driskell, Copper, and Moran's (1994) meta-analysis as an example, effect sizes incorrectly computed from t-statistics for *correlated designs* overestimated, on average, the correct effect sizes by .57. The overestimation of the strength of experimental manipulations based on incorrect computations of *d* values is a serious problem in meta-analysis with *correlated designs*. Given the magnitude of overestimation of effect sizes and the dozens of meta-analyses that have employed incorrect equations for estimating effect sizes from t_c statistics from *correlated designs*, the conclusions of many of these meta-analyses are questionable.

Authors of methodological papers in this area have not always discussed the general matter of *designs with correlated measures*, but many have provided discussions of the analysis of gain scores (see Hunter & Schmidt, 1990; Lipsey & Wilson, 2001). Unfortunately, these discussions of gain scores have not consistently dealt with the problem of using test statistics from *correlated study designs* to estimate effect sizes. A notable exception is the ES program documentation and algorithm for computing various types of effect sizes (see Shadish, Robinson, & Lu, 1999).

The correct formula for estimating an effect size (*d*) from t_c is

$$d = t_c \sqrt{\frac{2(1 - r)}{n}} \tag{1}$$

where *r* is the correlation across pairs of measures and *n* is the sample size per group (Dunlap et al., 1996, p. 171). In dealing with studies that only report t_c and do not report descriptive statistics or the correlation between the measures, the researcher should consider estimating the correlation between the measures from previous findings and employ Equation 1 for estimating d (e.g., see Finkelstein, Burke, & Raju, 1995). However, if the correlation between the measures cannot be approximately estimated, then we would suggest excluding the study from the meta-analysis rather than risk considerable overestimation of effect sizes.

Conducting Meta-Analyses With Hypothetical Artifact Distributions Versus Sample-Based Artifacts

Using Hypothetical Artifact Distributions. By correcting individual study effects for various methodological and statistical artifacts (e.g., unreliability of measures, range restriction), a more accurate estimate of the population relationship between variables of interest may be obtained. Most meta-analytic procedures involving corrections for statistical artifacts are based on the observed correlation model, which can be expressed as

$$r_{xy} = \rho\sqrt{\rho_{xx}}\,\sqrt{\rho_{yy}}\,\frac{u}{\sqrt{1 + (u^2 - 1)\rho^2\rho_{xx}\rho_{yy}}} + e, \qquad (2)$$

where r_{xy} is the observed correlation between the predictor (x) and criterion (y), ρ is the unattenuated and unrestricted population correlation between x and y, ρ_{xx} and ρ_{yy} are the unrestricted reliabilities of x and y, respectively, u is the ratio of restricted population standard deviation to unrestricted population standard deviation on the predictor, and e is the sampling error. The sampling variance for the observed correlation is defined as

$$\hat{V}_e = \frac{(1 - r_{xy}^2)^2}{(N - 1)}. \qquad (3)$$

Notably, three of the statistical artifacts in Equation 2 (predictor reliability, criterion reliability, and range restriction) are expressed as population parameters. Thus, any solution to the mean and variance of ρ across a set of studies will be functionally dependent on these population parameters.

Given the unavailability of population artifact values, the meta-analytic procedures based on Equation 2 (i.e., independent multiplicative procedure, see Callender & Osburn, 1980; noninteractive, Pearlman, Schmidt, & Hunter, 1980; interactive procedure, Schmidt, Gast-Rosenberg, & Hunter, 1980; TSA1 and TSA2 procedures, see Raju & Burke, 1983) rely on hypothetical (population-level) distributions of statistical artifacts. Hence, these procedures are commonly referred to as *distributional meta-analysis*. Because distributional meta-analytic procedures incorporate corrections for measurement artifacts, the use of these procedures is sometimes referred to as *psychometric meta-analysis*. Empirical and Monte Carlo studies (Burke, Raju, & Pearlman, 1986; Mendoza & Reinhardt, 1991; Raju & Burke, 1983) indicate that five of the most widely cited distributional procedures yield comparable estimates of the mean and variance of ρ. With the exception of a special case involving nonlinear range restriction corrections (Law, Schmidt, & Hunter, 1994), TSA1 provides slightly more accurate estimates of the mean and variance of ρ (Linn & Dunbar, 1986; Mendoza & Reinhardt, 1991; Raju & Burke, 1983). However, the accuracy of these results may depend substantially on the accuracy of assumptions that are made about the unknown population artifact values.

Paese and Switzer (1986) and Raju, Pappas, and Williams (1989) demonstrated that the accuracy of distributional meta-analytic procedures in estimating the mean and variance of ρ is affected by how closely the hypothetical or assumed artifact distributions match the population distributions of artifacts. Given the virtual impossibility of knowing the population artifacts and the extent to which the assumed artifact distributions match the population artifact distributions, the degree to which the use of assumed artifact distributions has affected the conclusions of many meta-analyses is unknown. The most commonly employed hypothetical artifact distributions are those presented in Pearlman et al. (1980) and were developed for standardized cognitive ability tests and supervisory performance ratings. Even if these distributions were accurate for estimation of the effects in employment test settings, the conceptual appropriateness and accuracy of the Pearlman et al. hypothetical artifact distributions to many nonselection test meta-analyses is questionable. Unfortunately, their uncritical use continues unabated in the behavioral and social sciences, with resulting uncertainty as to what we are learning about corrected relationships in many domains outside of employment testing.

Assuming That Statistical Artifacts and Situational Variables Are Independent. An important assumption of distributional meta-analytic procedures is that statistical artifacts and situational variables such as criterion unreliability are independent. Several authors including James, Demaree, Mulaik, and Ladd (1992) and Russell and Gilliland (1995) have questioned this assumption. More specifically, James et al. (1992) proposed that the independence assumption might be violated when situational variables such as organizational climate act as "common causes" of both differences in correlation coefficients and the magnitudes of one or more statistical artifacts. If a causal relation exists between a key situational variable and the range, or reliability, of the criterion (or predictor) measure, this effect would be masked or covered-up by distributional meta-analytic procedures. Furthermore, if the situational variable operated through mechanisms that are treated as artifactual within applications of distributional meta-analytic procedures, then these meta-analytic procedures might serve to obscure the very situational specificity they are intended to identify.

Burke, Rupinski, Dunlap, and Davison (1996) reported the results of two large-scale studies designed to investigate the hypothesized effects of common-cause models of situational variables (i.e., organizational climate and business unit situational constraints). The results did not support the notion that situational variables act as common causes of both substantive differences in relationships among individual difference measures and statistical artifacts associated with these measures. However, failure to find empirical support for common-cause models should not minimize the role of situational variables in primary or meta-analytic studies. Researchers should attend to the description, measurement and test of theoretically relevant situational variables in primary studies. Likewise, meta-analytic researchers should conduct their studies with consideration given to theoretical hypotheses that explicitly consider the role of situational variables. Concurrent with this suggestion is the need for meta-analytic researchers to carefully define situational variables to assist in the coding of studies and situations. Recent advances in taxonomic research on work environment characteristics might provide a starting point for classifying situational characteristics or studying situational variables in primary studies (e.g., see Burke, Borucki, & Hurley, 1992; James & McIntyre, 1996; Peters & O'Connor, 1988).

In addition to examining assumptions about the role of situational variables in applications of distributional meta-analytic procedures, the assumption that ρ and e are uncorrelated has been debated and found to be reasonable (Hedges, 1989; Raju et al., 1989; Schmidt, Hunter, & Raju, 1988). Furthermore, researchers have investigated a host of other issues with distributional procedures including bias in parameter estimates, the resistance of these procedures to Type I error, the statistical power for detecting moderator variables, and the effects of nonlinear range restriction corrections (Kemery, Mossholder, & Dunlap, 1989; Kemery, Mossholder, & Roth, 1987; Law et al., 1994; Oswald & Johnson, 1998; Rasmussen & Loher, 1988; Sackett, Harris, & Orr, 1986). Although these latter studies have contributed to our knowledge of both the strengths and limitations of distributional meta-analytic procedures, issues with the use of hypothetical artifact distributions remain a central concern.

Using Sample-Based Artifact Data. The emergence over the last 10 years of alternative correlation or regression models and the use of meta-analytic procedures that do not rely on distributions of hypothetical population artifacts offer promise as meta-analytic procedures. Notably, the population correlation model and sampling variance formulae for different types of corrected correlations derived by Raju, Burke, Normand, and Langlois (1991) permitted statistical significance tests of individually corrected, study-based correlation coefficients. In Raju et al., the relation between the unattenuated and unrestricted population correlation (ρ_i) and the estimated population correlation ($\hat{\rho}_i$) can be expressed by the equation

$$\hat{\rho}_i = \rho_i + e_i, \tag{4}$$

where e_i is the sampling error associated with $\hat{\rho}_i$. Computationally, $\hat{\rho}_i$ may be obtained through the application of the following formula:

$$\hat{\rho}_i = \frac{k_i r_i}{\sqrt{r_{x_i x_i} r_{y_i y_i} - r_i^2 + k_i^2 r_i^2}}. \tag{5}$$

In the preceding formula, $k_i = \dfrac{1}{u_i}$ (u_i is the ratio of the restricted predictor standard deviation to the unrestricted predictor standard deviation), r_i is the correlation between the predictor measure and the criterion measure in a sample from population i, and $r_{x_i x_i}$ and $r_{y_i y_i}$ are the sample-based predictor and criterion reliability, respectively. We refer the reader to Bobko, Roth, and Bobko (2001) for issues and procedures for correcting d-statistics for statistical artifacts.

Once the values of $\hat{\rho}_i$ have been computed, an asymptotic estimate of the sampling variance of an individually corrected correlation $(\hat{V}_{e_i})^1$ can be computed using

$$\hat{V}_{e_i} = \frac{k_i^2 r_{x_i x_i} r_{y_i y_i} (r_{y_i y_i} - r_i^2)(r_{x_i x_i} - r_i^2)}{(N_i - 1)\hat{D}_i^3} \, , \tag{6}$$

where N_i is the number of participants in sample i, and $\hat{D}_i$ is computed as

$$\hat{D}_i = r_{x_i x_i} r_{y_i y_i} - r_i^2 + k_i^2 r_i^2 \, . \tag{7}$$

Notably, the square root of the quantity in Equation 6 is the standard error of a corrected correlation coefficient. Variations or special cases of Equation 6 (presented in Raju et al., 1991) can be employed to estimate the standard error of different types of corrected correlations (e.g., a correlation that is only corrected for criterion unreliability). Also, one should note that when predictor and criterion reliability are perfect (i.e., equal to one) and there is no range restriction on the predictor, Equation 6 reduces to the well-known sampling variance estimation equation for the observed correlation (i.e., Equation 3; Kendall & Stuart, 1977).

These procedures, which are collectively referred to as the Raju, Burke, Normand, and Langlois (RBNL) meta-analytic procedures, offer a means for using sample-based statistical artifacts (i.e., sample-based predictor and criterion reliability values) whenever they are available and in whatever proportions along with observed correlations for estimating the mean and variance of ρ. Even when the researcher needs to substitute for missing sample artifact values (i.e., assume a sample-based artifact value), the RBNL meta-analytic procedures have been shown to be more accurate in estimating the mean and variance of ρ in computer simulations than distributional meta-analytic procedures for typical corrections to correlations (Raju et al., 1991).

Furthermore, an asymptotic estimate of the sampling variance of the mean corrected correlation (and its square root, the standard

---

[1]This formula differs from the one initially reported by Raju et al. (1991) in that the denominator includes the quantity $(N_i - 1)$ as opposed to simply (N_i). Although there is likely to be little empirical difference between the two formulas, the version presented in this chapter is consistent with how standard errors are computed for observed correlation coefficients.

error of the mean corrected correlation) has been presented for the RBNL procedure (Finkelstein, Burke, & Raju, 1995), which permits hypothesis testing and the construction of confidence intervals around mean corrected correlations as well as statistical test of hypothesized moderators (e.g., see Davison & Burke, 2000; Dorman & Zapf, 2001; Organ & Ryan, 1995; Quinones, Ford, & Teachout, 1995). That is, the sampling variance of the mean of $\hat{\rho}$ ($V_{M_{\hat{\rho}}}$) can be written as

$$V_{M_{\hat{\rho}}} = W_1^2 V_{e_1} + W_2^2 V_{e_2} + \ldots + W_k^2 V_{e_k}, \tag{8}$$

where

$$W_i = \frac{N_i}{N_1 + N_2 + \ldots + N_k}. \tag{9}$$

In the preceding equations, N_i is the number of participants in Study i and V_{e_i} is computed for each study effect using the previously mentioned Equation 6.

The sampling variance for the mean corrected correlation was presented in fixed-effect form in Finkelstein et al. (1995). For a fixed effects conceptualization of validity, the researcher assumes that the population value of the study effects is fixed, but unknown. Furthermore, an observed effect or correlation is assumed to estimate the population effect or correlation with random error that stems only from subject-level sampling error in the study.

Alternatively, a random effects conceptualization would not assume a common ρ across studies. That is, a random effects model would assume that the observed effects will have subject-level sampling error for each study as well as study-level sampling error associated with them. Recently, the computer program, MAIN (Raju & Fleer, 1997), for the RBNL meta-analytic procedures and equations have been updated to include the random effects equation for estimating the sampling variance of the mean corrected correlation and its square root, the standard error of the mean corrected correlation (N. S. Raju, 2001, personal communication), where the sampling variance of mean ρ would be defined as

$$V_{M_{\hat{\rho}}} = \frac{\sigma_\rho^2 + \dfrac{\sum\limits_{i=1}^{k} V_{e_i}}{k}}{k}. \tag{10}$$

In situations in which the researcher does not believe that the fixed assumption is appropriate, the fixed effects formula for the standard error of the mean corrected correlation will result in an underestimation of this quantity and a smaller confidence interval. These latter procedural developments and others related to the use of fixed, random and mixed effects models offer further promise for meta-analyses of correlations and experimental effects (see Brannick, 2001; Erez, Bloom, & Wells, 1996; Field, 2001).

In concluding this discussion of correlations estimated via applications of meta-analytic procedures, researchers are cautioned to attend to issues concerning the meaningfulness of sample-based or meta-analytic based corrected correlation coefficients (Murphy & DeShon, 2000) and the inappropriateness of using disattenuated correlation coefficients, individually corrected or meta-analytically based, in decision-theoretic utility analyses (Raju, Burke, Normand, & Lezotte, 1993).

Assessing Intercoder Agreement

A common practice in meta-analyses is to test the hypothesis that characteristics of studies (e.g., their design, different operational definitions of important variables, etc.) affect the outcomes of studies, perhaps yielding different effect size estimates for studies that vary along any of a number of methodological or substantive dimensions. Tests of these hypotheses usually require the meta-analyst to categorize studies and to code and record information about study characteristics. Although this process is sometimes a simple clerical task, there is often a need to make judgments in coding study characteristics, and these judgments are often surprisingly subjective. Despite widespread recognition by writers on meta-analysis of the need to assess intercoder agreement on the ratings of characteristics of each study (see Orwin, 1994), a cursory scan of the meta-analytic literature reveals that systematic assessments of intercoder agreement are the exception rather than the rule.

Intercoder agreement refers to the degree to which independent coders tend to make exactly the same judgment or rating of a characteristic or set of characteristics of a single study. Typically, the researcher computes and reports an overall (across all coded items in the meta-analysis) agreement rate, ranging somewhere between 80% and 100% of the coded items. There are at least three problems with this practice. First, this practice does not make psychometric sense, given that the coded items represent discrete ratings of a single target (i.e., discrete characteristics of a single study), which are not part of some overall scale. Second, many study characteristics that are being coded and suggestions for coding study characteristics such as rating the "confidence in effect size computation" (see Lipsey & Wilson, 2001, p. 232) or providing "confidence ratings for the most important items in a coding protocol" (Orwin & Cordray, 1985, p. 137) are made on categorical Likert-type or continuous scales for which simple assessments of agreement are inappropriate. Third, an overall assessment of agreement does not inform the researcher as to specific construct categories or variables that are problematic and in need of refinement or deletion.

We concur with Orwin (1994) that assessments of intercoder agreement should be conducted on an item-by-item basis within each study. However, we recognize that a researcher may choose to assess intercoder agreement in a hierarchical manner by attending to key items such as coded effects that enter tests of meta-analytic hypotheses. Yet, we disagree with the common suggestion in most meta-analytic texts that randomly selecting a percentage of studies from the meta-analysis to examine the issue of intercoder agreement is adequate. Assessments of intercoder agreement, although extremely tedious, can and must follow a systematic assessment in order to ensure the quality of the meta-analytic data.

To date, four indices have been discussed as potentially useful methods for assessing intercoder agreement: agreement rate, kappa and weighted kappa, intercoder correlation, and intraclass correlation (see Orwin, 1994). Although assessments using agreement rate, kappa, intercoder correlation, and intraclass correlation may yield some useful information, these indices are not necessarily appropriate for assessing within-group interrater agreement of a single target (in this case a study; see Burke, Finkelstein, & Dusig, 1999; James et al., 1984). Recently, Burke et al. (1999) argued that, in comparison to other indices for estimating interrater agreement for judges' ratings of a single target on a single occasion, the average absolute deviation computed relative to the mean of an item (AD_M) provides a more direct conceptualization and assessment of interrater agreement in the metric or units of the original measurement scale. Although the AD index is used as a measure of agreement, the quantity AD actually reflects the level of disagreement. If AD were equal to zero (no disagreement), one would conclude that there is perfect agreement among coders regarding the rated characteristic of a study. Interpretive standards for the AD index with respect to response scales that involve percentages or proportions, discrete categories or Likert-type items, and dichotomous items (e.g., yes–no, true–false) are presented in Burke and Dunlap (2002).

Burke and Dunlap (2002) also presented critical values for tests of statistical significance with AD indices. However, assessments of intercoder agreement within meta-analyses do not call for such statistical significance tests. Nevertheless, assessments of coder ratings should be treated as a standard exercise in gathering data for a study of interrater agreement of judges' ratings of characteristics of a single target. The results of these assessments will likely inform follow-up discussions where disagreement was found and lead to improvements in the meta-analytic database.

MAKING INFERENCES ABOUT UNDERLYING CONSTRUCTS

As noted at the beginning of this chapter, the ultimate purpose of most scientific research is to draw inferences about the constructs that underlie primary research studies. Meta-analytic research, however, is sometimes cavalier in its treatment of construct-related issues. In particular, there sometimes is an apparent assumption that superficially similar studies, or those that claim to be dealing with the same set of constructs, can be easily combined to draw meaningful construct-level inferences. This is not true. Rather, careful thought needs to go into decisions about how to link study outcomes with constructs.

Second, there is an increasing trend to use multivariate methods in conjunction with meta-analysis (e.g., applying structural equations modeling to meta-analytic estimates of correlations). Such methods do have the potential to strengthen the links between the primary study data that are the basis of meta-analysis and the sort of construct-level inferences that meta-analysts hope to make, but these methods also present some unique challenges and issues.

Defining Constructs

Meta-analysis is typically characterized as the statistical integration of results from similar studies. Although this characterization is partially correct, meta-analytic studies should be more than mere statistical integrations of prior research. That is, meta-analyses as studies and meta-analysts as researchers are not exempt from the requisite tenet of scientific research of formulating testable hypotheses or exploratory research questions, and following through with a study methodology to appropriately address such hypotheses or questions. Formulating testable hypotheses or research questions necessitates that careful attention be given to defining predictor and criterion constructs or independent and dependent variables. In the absence of clearly defined constructs, the inferences that can be made from any meta-analysis will remain ambiguous.

Carefully developing conceptual definitions for constructs is particularly relevant to meta-analytic studies given that it is not un common for meta-analyses to include different measures of the same construct, none of which may adequately represent the construct as defined by the meta-analyst. For instance, a meta-analytic researcher might define a construct such as negative affectivity (i.e., the disposition to experience aversive emotional states) and find that very few operationalizations provide complete measurement of this construct domain; yet, hundreds of studies with various scales called trait anxiety, neuroticism, ego strength, general maladjustment, repression-sensitization, and so on could be considered potentially useful indicators of the construct. In these cases, there exists a need for the meta-analytic researcher to carefully define the construct or category so as to assist coders in including and properly classifying all eligible studies and for readers to eventually be able to understand what inferences are being made.

The issue of properly defining constructs is not only an issue for meta-analysts dealing with continuous measures in field studies. Manipulations in experiments can vary in important ways from study to study as can experimental dependent variables, which are often answers to single questions or discrete behaviors. That is, experimental dependent variables can differ in the length in delay before they are measured, their sensitivity, their reactivity, and so on. The extent to which the meta-analyst's definition of the dependent variable captures these aspects of the construct domain and permits the appropriate inclusion–exclusion of theoretically relevant studies will have an important impact on the inferences to be made.

The argument being advanced for carefully defining constructs within meta-analyses should not be construed as a revival of the composite vs. multiple criteria debate of the 1960s (see Schmidt & Kaplan, 1971). One would not be developing composite measures by placing markedly different types of measures or experimental manipulations into ill-defined construct categories as were done in many early meta-analyses. Furthermore, although one might attempt to justify inferences to ill-defined criterion categories based on some underlying economic criterion, the scope of the meta-analytic research effort, or for policy considerations, such attempts do little to advance our knowledge of predictor–criterion relations or the effectiveness of interventions in the social sciences. In fact, one could argue that inferences to ill-defined criterion or dependent variable categories erroneously imply that our predictors and independent variables "have validity," a notion that is clearly rejected by current professional testing and validation standards (American Educational Research Association, American Psychological Association, and National Council on Measurement in Education, 1999). In sum, the degree to which inferences from experimental manipulations or measured variables can be made from meta-analytic efforts is critically dependent on the nature of construct definitions within the meta-analysis and the extent to which these construct definitions assist in the consistent classifying of primary studies and study characteristics.

Use of Meta-Analytically Derived Correlations as Input to Regression Analysis and Structural Equation Models

The nature of the research questions addressed in most meta-analyses is generally narrow. To date, meta-analyses have emphasized understanding simple, bivariate relations. Hunter (1983) provided an early example of how meta-analysis could be extended and combined with path modeling techniques. Relatively few applications of the technique, however, had been reported in the literature during the 1980s and early 1990s (e.g., Hom, Caranikas-Walker, Prussia, & Griggeth, 1992; Premack & Hunter, 1988; Schmidt, Hunter, & Outerbridge, 1986). In the past several years, meta-analytically derived correlations have been used as input to regression analysis (e.g., Colquitt, LePine, & Noe, 2000), structural equation modeling (e.g., Lance & Bennett, 2000), and confirmatory factor analysis (Klein, Wesson, Hollenbeck, Wright, & DeShon, 2001).

Viswesvaran and Ones (1995) evaluated this practice and offered suggestions for conducting such analyses along with a discussion of the important decisions that must be made. They emphasized that a chief benefit of using meta-analytically derive correlations in tests of structural equation models is the ability to test relatively complex models when information from individual studies may not be available for such tests. In the following paragraphs, we review and comment on some of these key decisions that confront researchers attempting to conduct multivariate analyses with meta-analytically derived correlation or covariance matrices.

Pairwise Versus Listwise Deletion of Studies. One important issue with respect to the practice of analyzing the pattern of relations among meta-analytically derived correlations is whether one should engage in pairwise versus listwise deletion of cases or studies. If one is simply interested in the correlation between two variables, the question is rendered moot. Although the decision may influence the observed *r*, interpretation still is done only at the bivariate level. When multiple relations are considered simultaneously, however, serious problems can occur if pairwise deletion of cases is practiced. Consider that if the relationship between A and B is positive, as is the relation between variables B and C, then the relation between A and C cannot be negative. In short, particular relations among variables constrain other relationships. When pairwise deletion of cases or studies is used, the possibility exists that because different studies are being used to assess different relations, impossible values may be observed in the meta-analytically derived correlation matrix. As a result, parameter estimates may not accurately reflect the tested relationships. Related, Kuncel, Hezlett, and Ones (2001) cautioned researchers to consider the homogeneity of the meta-analytic correlations in the resulting matrix. Because the correlations are derived from potentially different populations, use of the resulting matrix of relationships as input to SEM could produce results that are inaccurate.

Covariance Versus Correlation Matrix as Input. Another question that naturally arises in applications of structural equation modeling (SEM) is whether the variance–covariance matrix or the correlation matrix is used as input. Although this issue has been discussed elsewhere with respect to the application of SEM to observed correlations (see Cudek, 1989), several points deserve special comment. First, the use of correlations fixes the variances of all the latent variables to unity and, in turn, disregards important information about the scaling of these variables. Second, the chi-square (χ^2) test of overall model fit is affected to the extent that the model tested is not scale invariant. Thus, use of a correlation, as opposed to a covariance, matrix will lead to different values, and, potentially different conclusions (Cudek, 1989). Finally, standard errors of parameter estimates will be inaccurate when a model that is not scale invariant is applied to a correlation matrix. Researchers interested in applying SEM techniques to meta-analytically derived covariance matrices should refer to Raju, Fralicx, and Steinhaus (1986) for procedures to meta-analyze covariances.

OLS Versus ML. Still another important decision that must be addressed in these types of analyses is whether the meta-analytic correlations will be analyzed using ordinary least squares (OLS) regression or maximum likelihood (ML) techniques as commonly associated with SEM. Because ML procedures are more appropriately used with covariances (Colquitt, Conlon, Wesson, Porter, & Ng, 2001; Cudek, 1989), the choice of OLS generally makes sense given that meta-analysis produces correlations. Whereas some applications, in fact, have relied on OLS analyses (e.g., Colquitt et al., 2000, 2001), others (e.g., Chen, Casper, & Cortina, 2001) have used ML techniques. Logically, the OLS techniques would seem the more appropriate choice when correlations based on one or more meta-analyses are analyzed within an SEM framework.

Two examples of the appropriate application of ML techniques are Klein et al. (2001) and Lance and Bennett (2000). Klein et al. applied meta-analytic results to evaluate a measurement model associated with a commonly used measure of goal commitment. These authors located 17 data sets that used at least some of the items from the scale of interest and then meta-analyzed the relationships among all original nine items. They then converted the correlations derived through meta-analysis back to covariances using the observed correlations and item standard deviations (both weighted for sample size). Similarly, Lance and Bennett (2000) evaluated several alternative models related to supervisor performance ratings. They too used the average correlations and standard deviations as input to the path analysis and fixed the paths from each measure to its underlying construct by setting the factor loading to the square root of the estimated reliability.

Sample Size. Several authors (e.g., Colquitt et al. 2001; Viswesvaran & Ones, 1995) have raised the question of what the appropriate sample size is for use in such analyses. Although some possibilities include the smallest cell sample size or the mean sample size, the harmonic mean appears to be the alternative of choice. Another way of thinking about this issue is related to how the model is tested. Specifically, should the entire model be tested at once (as in SEM) or should segments of the model be tested one at a time? The former strategy forces the selection of a single sample size whereas the latter allows for sample sizes to vary based on the segment of the model being tested. As an example of the latter strategy, Colquitt et al. (2000) chose to test segments of their model and, thus, use sample sizes as appropriate for the segments.

A related issue is how to deal with cells in a meta-analytically derived matrix that lack correlations. Because each cell represents a meta-analytically derived correlation, it is possible that some of the bivariate relations have not been studied within any individual study. For instance, in the Colquitt et al. (2000) study, 21% of the cells in the matrix had no values. Possible solutions identified by these authors were using the average correlation in the matrix as a replacement value or having subject matter experts estimate the correlation. Colquitt et al., (2000) dealt with this issue by first trimming the matrix by getting rid of variables that had a large number of missing relationships or those based on only a single study. For those still empty cells, the authors went to other, related literatures to generate estimates. This strategy is consistent with the aforementioned suggestions for handling missing data problems in meta-analysis.

Additional Issues. Oswald and Johnson (1998) reported a Monte Carlo analysis related to the robustness of meta-analytically derived correlations that points to other important issues to consider. First, when small numbers of studies (k) are used as input, meta-analytically derived estimates were much more variable. This situation has been common in studies that have attempted to integrate meta-analysis and SEM techniques. Conducting factor analysis or path analysis on such estimates would thus be an unwise move. Second, if there are moderator effects present, the direct paths will necessarily be misspecified unless the moderators are actually included in the path model. This inclusion is not likely to be practical. They suggested that given these potential challenges, correlations based on large samples are the optimal strategy.

Given the interest in testing broader and more complex (i.e., mediated) relations, the integration of SEM techniques and meta-analytic procedures is likely to become even more widespread. The aforementioned decisions represent factors that future research must consider in subsequent uses of meta-analytic findings. Because the ultimate goal of psychological research is to develop an understanding of the associations among constructs, the wedding of SEM and meta-analysis represents a potentially useful technique for explicating nomological networks.

CONCLUSION

Making accurate inferences about construct relations is at the heart of scientific research. Presently, meta-analysis provides a powerful methodological tool that can assist researchers in making such inferences, with an emphasis on bivariate relations and tests of simple moderation. This chapter highlights select methodological and conceptual issues that currently confront meta-analysts and offered suggestions for dealing with these issues. By way of summary, we offer the *checklist* contained in Table 10.1 of select

TABLE 10.1
Suggestions for Handling Select Issues in Applications of Meta-Analysis

---

Computing Effect Sizes for Matched Groups or Repeated Measures Designs

- Effect sizes computed from test statistics with equations presented by Glass, McGaw, and Smith (1981), Rosenthal (1991, 1994), Mullen and Rosenthal's (1985) software, or texts adopting Rosenthal's suggestions (e.g., Cooper, 1998) are incorrect and should not be employed.
- The correct formula to use for computing the standard effect (d) from the test statistic for a *correlated study design* (t_c) is: $d = t_c \sqrt{\dfrac{2(1-r)}{n}}$.

  where r is the correlation across pairs of measures and n is the sample size per group.

Using Sample-Based Artifact Data

- When sample-based artifact data are available in any proportion, the use of distributional meta-analytic procedures should be avoided.
- When conducting meta-analyses that incorporate sample-based artifact data in any proportion, use procedures that correctly compute standard errors for the individually corrected correlations and the mean corrected correlation.
- When testing hypotheses concerning the mean corrected correlation, consider the relevance of a fixed versus a random effects model for the computation of the standard error of the mean corrected correlation.

Assessing Intercoder Agreement

- Overall assessments of intercoder agreement are deficient and should be avoided.
- The reported index of intercoder agreement should provide for an assessment of agreement of judges' ratings of characteristics of a single study, with consideration given to the use of the AD index for computing interrater agreement.

Defining Constructs

- Conceptual definitions of constructs are necessary for making inferences about relations between variables and for assisting in the coding of measures and manipulations from primary studies.

Integrating Meta-Analysis and Structural Equation Modeling

- Possible empirical problems resulting from pairwise deletion of cases or studies should be considered.
- Use meta-analytically derived correlation matrix as input if OLS procedures are to be used and covariance matrix as input for ML procedures.
- Sample size issues and missing cells in correlation or covariance matrices must be defended.

---

issues that are likely to bear on the execution and interpretation of meta-analyses and suggestions for assisting researchers in making more informed inferences about construct relations.

REFERENCES

American Educational Research Association, American Psychological Association, and National Council on Measurement in Education (1999). *Standards for educational and psychological testing*. Washington, DC: APA.

Bobko, P., Roth, P., & Bobko, C. (2001). Correcting the effect size of d for range restriction and unreliability. *Organizational Research Methods, 4*, 46–61.

Brannick, M. T. (2001). Implications of empirical Bayes meta-analyses for test validation. *Journal of Applied Psychology, 86*, 468–480.

Burke, M. J. (1984). Validity generalization: A review and critique of the correlation model. *Personnel Psychology, 37*, 93–115.

Burke, M. J., Borucki, C. C., & Hurley, A. E. (1992). Reconceptualizing psychological climate in a retail service environment: A multiple stakeholder perspective. *Journal of Applied Psychology, 77*, 717–729.

Burke, M. J., & Dunlap, W. P. (2002). Estimating interrater agreement with the Average Deviation (AD) Index: A user's guide. *Organizational Research Methods, 5*, 159–172.

Burke, M. J., Finkelstein, L. M., & Dusig, M. S. (1999). On average deviation indices for estimating interrater agreement. *Organizational Research Methods, 2*, 49–68.

Burke, M. J., Raju, N. S., & Pearlman, K. (1986). An empirical comparison of the results of validity generalization procedures. *Journal of Applied Psychology, 71*, 349–353.

Burke, M. J., Rupinski, M. T., Dunlap, W. P., & Davison, H. K. (1996). Do situational variables act as substantive causes of relationships between individual difference variables? Two large-scale tests of "common cause" models. *Personnel Psychology, 49*, 573–598.

Callender, J. C., & Osburn, H. G. (1980). Development and test of a new model for validity generalization. *Journal of Applied Psychology, 65*, 543–558.

Chen, G., Casper, W. J., & Cortina, J. M. (2001). The roles of self-efficacy and task complexity in the relationships among cognitive ability, conscientiousness, and work-related performance: A meta-analytic examination. *Human Performance, 14*, 209–230.

Colquitt, J. A., Conlon, D. E., Wesson, M. J., Porter, C. O. L. H., & Ng, K. Y. (2001). Justice at the millennium: A meta-analytic review of 25 years of organizational justice research. *Journal of Applied Psychology, 86*, 425–445.

Colquitt, J. A., LePine, J. A., & Noe, R. A. (2000). Toward an integrative theory of training motivation: A meta-analytic path analysis of 20 years of research. *Journal of Applied Psychology, 85*, 678–707.

Cooper, H. (1998). *Synthesizing research*. Thousand Oaks, CA: Sage.

Cudek, R. (1989). Analysis of correlation matrices using covariance structure models. *Psychological Bulletin, 105*, 317–327.

Davison, H. K., & Burke, M. J. (2000). Sex discrimination in simulated employment contexts: A meta-analytic investigation. *Journal of Vocational Behavior, 56,* 225–248.

Dorman, C., & Zapf, D. (2001). Job satisfaction: A meta-analysis of stabilities. *Journal of Organizational Behavior, 22,* 483–504.

Driskell, J. E., Copper, C., & Moran, A. (1994). Does mental practice enhance performance? *Journal of Applied Psychology, 79,* 481–492.

Dunlap, W. P., Cortina, J. M., Vaslow, J. B., & Burke, M. J. (1996). Meta-analysis of experiments with matched groups or repeated measures designs. *Psychological Methods, 1,* 170–177.

Erez, A., Bloom, M. C., & Wells, M. T. (1996). Using random rather than fixed effects models in meta-analysis: Implications for situational specificity and validity generalization. *Personnel Psychology, 49,* 275–306.

Field, A. P. (2001). Meta-analysis of correlation coefficients: A Monte Carlo comparison of fixed- and random-effects models. *Psychological Methods, 6,* 161–180.

Finkelstein, L. M., Burke, M. J., & Raju, N. S. (1995). Age discrimination in simulated employment contexts: An Integrative Analysis. *Journal of Applied Psychology, 80,* 652–663.

Glass, G. V., McGaw, B., & Smith, M. L. (1981). *Meta-Analysis in Social Research.* Beverly Hills, CA: Sage.

Hedges, L. V. (1989). An unbiased correlation for sampling error in validity generalization studies. *Journal of Applied Psychology, 74,* 469–477.

Hedges, L. V. (1992). Meta-analysis. *Journal of Educational Statistics, 17,* 279–296.

Hom, P. W., Caranikas-Walker, F., Prussia, G. E., & Griffeth, R. W. (1992). A meta-analytical structural equations analysis of a model of employee turnover. *Journal of Applied Psychology, 77,* 890–909.

Hunter, J. E. (1983). A causal analysis of cognitive ability, job knowledge, job performance, and supervisor ratings. In F. J. Landy, S. Zedeck, & J. Cleveland (Eds.), *Performance measurement and theory* (pp. 257–266). Hillsdale, NJ: Lawrence Erlbaum Associates.

Hunter, J. E., & Schmidt, F. L. (1990). *Methods of meta-analysis.* Beverly Hills, CA: Sage.

James, L. R., Demaree, R. G., Mulaik, S. A., & Ladd, R. T. (1992). Validity generalization in the context of situational models. *Journal of Applied Psychology, 77,* 3–14.

James, L. R., Demaree, R. G., & Wolf, G. (1984). Estimating within-group interrater reliability with and without response bias. *Journal of Applied Psychology, 69,* 85–98.

James, L. R., & McIntyre, M. D. (1996). Perceptions of organizational climate. In K. R. Murphy (Ed.), *Individual differences and behavior in organizations* (pp. 416–450). San Francisco: Jossey-Bass.

Kemery, E. R., Mossholder, K. W., & Dunlap, W. P. (1989). Meta-analysis and moderator variables: A cautionary note on transportability. *Journal of Applied Psychology, 74,* 168–170.

Kemery, E. R., Mossholder, K. W., & Roth, L. (1987). The power of the Schmidt and Hunter additive model of validity generalization. *Journal of Applied Psychology, 72,* 30–37.

Kendall, M., & Stuart, A. (1977). *The advanced theory of statistics* (Vol. 1, 4th Ed.). New York: Macmillan.

Klein, H. J., Wesson, M. J., Hollenback, J. R., Wright, P. M., & DeShon, R. P. (2001). The assessment of goal commitment: A measurement model meta-analysis. *Organizational Behavior and Human Decision Processes, 85,* 32–55.

Kuncel, N. R., Hezlett, S. A., & Ones, D. S. (2001). A comprehensive meta-analysis of the predictive validity of the graduate record examinations: Implications for graduate student selection and performance. *Psychological Bulletin, 127,* 162–181.

Lance, C. E., & Bennett, W., Jr. (2000). Replication and extension of models of supervisory job performance ratings. *Human Performance, 13,* 139–158.

Law, K. S., Schmidt, F. L., & Hunter, J. E. (1994). Nonlinearity of range corrections in meta-analysis: Test of an improved procedure. *Journal of Applied Psychology, 79,* 425–438.

Linn, R. L., & Dunbar, S. B. (1986). Validity generalization and prediction bias. In R. A. Berk (Ed.), *Performance assessment: Methods and applications* (pp. 203–236). Baltimore, MD: Johns Hopkins.

Lipsey, M. W., & Wilson, D. B. (2001). *Practical meta-analysis.* Thousand Oaks, CA: Sage.

Mendoza, J. L., & Reinhardt, R. N. (1991). Validity generalization procedures using sample-based estimates: A comparison of six procedures. *Psychological Bulletin, 110,* 596–610.

Mullen, B., & Rosenthal, R. (1985). *BASIC meta-analysis: Procedures and programs.* Hillsdale, NJ: Lawrence Erlbaum Associates.

Murphy, K. R., & DeShon, R. (2000). Interrater correlations do not estimate the reliability of job performance ratings. *Personnel Psychology, 53,* 873–900.

Organ, D. W., & Ryan, K. (1995). A meta-analytic review of attitudinal dispositional predictors of organizational citizenship behavior. *Personnel Psychology, 48,* 775–802.

Orwin, R. G. (1994). Evaluating coding decisions. In H. Cooper & L. V. Hedges (Eds.), *The handbook of research synthesis* (pp. 139–162). New York: Russell Sage.

Orwin, R. G., & Cordray, D. S. (1985). Effects of deficient reporting on meta-analysis: A conceptual framework and reanalysis. *Psychological Bulletin, 97,* 134–147.

Oswald, F. L., & Johnson, J. W. (1998). On the robustness, bias, and stability of statistics from meta-analysis of correlation coefficients: Some initial Monte Carlo findings. *Journal of Applied Psychology, 83,* 164–178.

Paese, P. W., & Switzer, F. S. (1988). Validity generalization and hypothetical reliability distributions. *Journal of Applied Psychology, 73,* 267–274.

Pearlman, K., Schmidt, F. L., & Hunter, J. E. (1980). Validity generalization results for tests used to predict job proficiency and training success in clerical occupations. *Journal of Applied Psychology, 65,* 373–406.

Peters, L. H., & O'Connor, E. J. (1988). Measuring work obstacles: Procedures, issues, and implications. In F. D. Schoorman & B. Schneider (Eds.), *Facilitating work effectiveness* (pp. 105–123). Lexington, MA: Lexington Books.

Premack, S. L., & Hunter, J. E. (1988). Individual unionization decisions. *Psychological Bulletin, 103,* 223–234.

Quinones, M. A., Ford, J. K., & Teachout, M. S. (1995). The relationship between work experience and job performance: A conceptual and meta-analytic review. *Personnel Psychology, 48,* 887–910.

Raju, N. S., & Burke, M. J. (1983). Two new procedures for studying validity generalization. *Journal of Applied Psychology, 68,* 382–395.

Raju, N. S., Burke, M. J., Normand, J., & Langlois, G. M. (1991). A new meta-analytic approach. *Journal of Applied Psychology, 76,* 432–446.

Raju, N. S., Burke, M. J., Normand, & Lezotte, D. V. (1993). What would be if what is wasn't? Rejoinder to Judiesch, Schmidt, and Hunter (1993). *Journal of Applied Psychology, 78,* 912–916.

Raju, N. S., & Fleer, P. F. (1997). *MAIN: A computer program for meta-analysis.* Chicago, IL: Illinois Institute of Technology.

Raju, N. S., Fralicx, R., & Steinhaus, S. (1986). Covariance and regression slope models for studying validity generalization. *Applied Psychological Measurement, 10,* 195–211.

Raju, N. S., Pappas, S., & Williams, C. P. (1989). An empirical Monte Carlo test of the accuracy of the correlation, covariance, and regression slope models for assessing validity generalization. *Journal of Applied Psychology, 74,* 901–911.

Rassmussen, J. L., & Loher, B. T. (1988). Appropriate critical percentages for the Schmidt-Hunter procedure: Comparative evaluation of Type I error rate and power. *Journal of Applied Psychology, 73,* 683–687.

Rosenthal, R. (1991). *Meta-analytic procedures for social research.* Newbury, CA: Sage.

Rosenthal, R. (1994). Parametric measures of effect size. In H. Cooper and L. V. Hedges (Eds.), *The handbook of research synthesis* (pp. 231–244). New York: Russell Sage.

Russell, C. J., & Gilliland, S. W. (1995). Why meta-analysis doesn't tell us what the data really mean: Distinguishing between moderator effects and moderator processes. *Journal of Management, 21,* 813–831.

Sackett, P. A., Harris, N. M., & Orr, J. M. (1986). On seeking moderator variables in the meta-analysis of correlational data: A Monte Carlo investigation of statistical power resistance to Type I error. *Journal of Applied Psychology, 71,* 302–310.

Schmidt, F. L., Gast-Rosenberg, I., & Hunter, J. E. (1980). Validity generalization results for computer programmers. *Journal of Applied Psychology, 65,* 643–661.

Schmidt, F. L., Hunter, J. E., & Outerbridge, A. N. (1986). The impact of job experience and ability on job knowledge, work sample performance, and supervisory ratings of job performance. *Journal of Applied Psychology, 71,* 432–439.

Schmidt, F. L., Hunter, J. E., & Raju, N. S. (1988). Validity generalization and situational specificity: A second look at the 75% rule and Fisher's z transformation. *Journal of Applied Psychology, 73,* 665–678.

Schmidt, F. L., & Kaplan, L. B. (1971). Composite vs. multiple criteria: A review and resolution of the controversy. *Personnel Psychology, 24,* 419–434.

Shadish, W. R., Robinson, L., & Lu, C. (1999). *ES: A computer program for effect size calculation.* St. Paul, MN: Assessment Systems Corporation.

Viswesvaran, C., & Ones, D. S. (1995). Theory testing: Combining psychometric meta-analysis and structural equations modeling. *Personnel Psychology, 48,* 865–885.

11

Meta-Analysis and the Art of the Average

Frederick L. Oswald
Michigan State University

Rodney A. McCloy
Human Resources Research Organization (HumRRO)

Since its introduction into the organizational research literature 25 years ago (Schmidt & Hunter, 1977), meta-analysis has been the focus of numerous conceptual and methodological controversies and developments. Before we delve into some of those issues, let us first remember that meta-analysis can be seen as essentially two things: (a) statistically, it provides an estimate of the mean and variance of the effect size estimates across studies (e.g., correlations, *d*-values, odds ratios); and (b) more broadly, it provides a statistically *and* rationally driven process of identifying, gathering, coding, combining, and interpreting results across studies. Clearly these two characterizations of meta-analysis are interrelated: Conceptual and practical considerations inform the decision points regarding what research data to summarize and how to summarize them (Matt, 1989; Wanous, Sullivan, & Malinak, 1989), and in turn, the statistical results and substantive interpretation from meta-analysis inform further research and practice.

In the sections that follow, the popularity of meta-analysis in psychological research is briefly documented first; meta-analysis is clearly here to stay for a long time, at least in some form, even if not in the exact statistical forms we use today. Second, how the meta-analytic mean is computed is discussed and, consequently, how researchers and practitioners should interpret it. Third, several considerations when making statistical artifact corrections in a meta-analysis are reviewed—an important topic because so many meta-analyses summarizing organizational research follow the conventions of the Schmidt and Hunter model in attempting to remove these artifacts before interpreting meta-analytic findings (Mohr, Zickar, & Russell, 2000). Fourth, the statistical power of meta-analysis is examined, particularly for detecting true variance across a set of study statistics after statistical corrections have been made. Finally, related to detecting true variance statistically, a set of critical conceptual issues is presented that address the detection of moderator effects across studies in a meta-analysis.

Note that many points that tend to be associated with meta-analysis could just as well be profitably applied to individual research studies, and vice versa. Both meta-analysis and individual studies must summarize and interpret data at an aggregate level, and therefore both confront similar issues, such as applying statistical corrections, preventing threats to internal and external validity, and generalizing beyond the data at hand (see Cooper & Hedges, 1994).

POPULARITY OF META-ANALYSIS
IN PSYCHOLOGY

Figure 11.1 illustrates the rise in the number of published meta-analyses in psychology-related journals from 1978 until 2000. The figure is based on a search of the PsychFIRST database with the keywords *meta-analysis* or *validity generalization* in the title or abstract, including 1,531 articles that performed meta-analyses and excluding 1,045 commentaries on meta-analysis (unless they performed a reanalysis), book chapters, theses, computer programs, and methodological papers. The figure illustrates the unabating positive trend in meta-analysis publications, supporting what you might have predicted from a similar figure presented more than a decade ago by Guzzo, Jackson, and Katzell (1985). Several reasons are offered that, either singularly or in combination, could explain this phenomenon: (a) individual studies constituting the "fossil fuel" of meta-analysis are in large supply and remain to be exhausted; (b) meta-analysis explores distinct but related constructs, thus permitting individual studies to serve in multiple meta-analyses; (c) the popularity and use of meta-analysis have spread to different areas within psychology; (d) more researchers have been recognizing and acting on a reinforcement contingency that a meta-analysis generally will not be denied a publication, given the time, effort, and sheer weight of the research literature behind it; and (e) organizations, policy makers, and granting agencies require greater accountability or value added for the research and systems

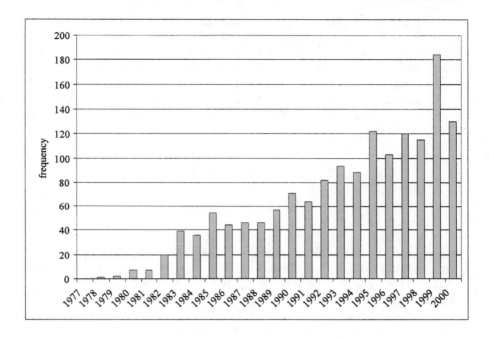

FIG. 11.1. Histogram of published meta-analysis articles in psychology, 1977–2000.

in which they invest, and the mean and variance from meta-analysis provide that accountability by summarizing a research literature that, at the individual-study level, may seem to show highly variable or conflicting results due to sampling error variance and other statistical artifacts (Hunter & Schmidt, 1996).

Whatever the reasons, the trend in the publication rate of meta-analyses shows no evidence of a downturn, which seems to merit the focus of this chapter (and this book, in fact) on the past, present, and future of meta-analysis. The following discussion is framed in the context of the meta-analysis of criterion-related validity coefficients across personnel selection studies; however, many of the points made are generally relevant to the meta-analysis of other types of statistics and research settings.

THE MEAN FROM META-ANALYSIS

All meta-analytic methods start by computing the mean of the effect size estimates present in the literature that the analysis seeks to summarize. As discussed in detail later, the mean may be interpreted either *descriptively* as the overall relationship found across studies, or it may be interpreted *inferentially* as the overall relation that one would find across all settings, perhaps even those that were not explicitly represented by the studies included in the meta-analysis. Typically, the meta-analytic mean is computed as some sort of weighted composite of the statistics gathered across k studies ($i = 1, 2, \ldots, k$). For example, in meta-analyzing correlation coefficients:

$$\bar{r} = \frac{\displaystyle\sum_{i=1}^{k} w_i r_i}{\displaystyle\sum_{i=1}^{k} w_i} \tag{1}$$

where $\bar{r}$ is the meta-analytic mean, r_i is the correlation coefficient for study i, and w_i is the corresponding weight for that study correlation. The weight w_i is almost always a function of the study sample size n_i, but it can also represent a multiplicative combination of factors that includes n_i (e.g., $n_i \times r_{xx-i} \times r_{yy-i}$, where r_{xx-i} and r_{yy-i} are study-specific estimates of the reliability of measures x and y, respectively; see Hunter & Schmidt, 1990).

For the moment, the focus is solely on the sample-size-weighted mean from meta-analysis, which can be computed in two cases. The first case is the *homogeneous case* (Hunter & Schmidt, 1994), where there is a set of studies that are either strict replications or, more realistically, close replicates of one another (i.e., the same or similar organizations, jobs, measures, and samples). Here, it makes complete sense that study correlations with higher N contribute more to the meta-analytic mean because all study samples come from essentially the same population; therefore, the N-weighted mean is a maximum-likelihood estimate of the population correlation (Hedges & Olkin, 1985).

By contrast the second case is the *heterogeneous case*, in which studies gathered for meta-analysis are thought *a priori* to differ in important ways (e.g., types of tasks that workers perform, worker and supervisor characteristics, organizational cultures). In this case, although the meta-analytic mean is computed in the same way as in the first case, its interpretation is much more difficult—or even impossible. To understand why, here is a simple but illustrative example. Say you are meta-analyzing the relation between conscientiousness and job performance, and you include two studies that are rather different in both a substantive and statistical sense:

a military study with $N = 10,000$ and $r = .24$, and a study in a small organization with $N = 100$ and $r = .08$. If these two studies are included in the same meta-analysis, then when you compute the sample-size weighted mean correlation (other statistical artifacts aside), the military study receives 100 times more weight than the small-organization study does. This means that the weighted mean correlation reflects characteristics of the military sample much more than characteristics of the small-organization sample, to the extent that their respective characteristics affect the differences in study correlations. Despite the fact that the contexts of the two studies may be equally important to researchers and practitioners, the statistical weights are unequal, creating a weighted mean that comes with a very serious interpretation problem.

Again, support for sample-size weighting in the aforementioned homogeneous case is straightforward. Similar support for the heterogeneous case may lie in an assumption that the unique characteristics of studies somehow balance out when computing the mean. The statistical formula for the sample-size-weighted mean directly challenges this assumption, however, because for the unique characteristics of studies to balance out, the effects of all variations across studies would have to be completely crossed with variations in sample size (and other statistical artifacts used for weighting the correlations). There is no guarantee that this would happen in your sample of studies for meta-analysis—and if in fact it did, the weighted mean would be the same as the unweighted mean. In the heterogeneous case, the meta-analytic mean statistically weights some studies more than other studies when, substantively, studies may be equally important.

The bottom line here is that the meta-analytic mean is interpretable when studies are strict replications or bear close similarity to one another. In this case very few studies—even two studies—can be meta-analyzed, and the result is a population correlation that is readily interpretable and more informative than the estimates from each study alone. Conversely, the meta-analytic mean is extremely difficult to interpret when constituent study correlations are influenced by different study characteristics (and/or different levels of those characteristics). In this case, a large number of studies—possibly more than the research literature offers at the time—may be required to obtain a meta-analytic mean that appropriately represents the overall correlation across study populations. Note that the estimated true variance of study correlations is similarly distorted in the heterogeneous case, because it uses the weighted meta-analytic mean in its computation (Hunter & Schmidt, 1990).

STATISTICAL CORRECTIONS

Meta-Analytic Approaches that Incorporate Statistical Corrections

In contrast with other meta-analysis methods, the two major meta-analysis methods developed by Hunter and Schmidt (1990) emphasize applying statistical corrections to observed validity coefficients to obtain reasonable estimates of the meta-analytic mean and variance. The first method, by far the most popular in organizational research, is called the *artifact distribution* (AD) method in which, essentially, the average of observed validity coefficients is corrected by using average values of the available artifact information (sampling error variance, measurement unreliability, range restriction, etc.). This method differs from the second method, the *individual correction* (IC) method, in which each study correlation is corrected individually by its own artifact information. In principle, the IC method is probably more accurate, but it is rare that every study provides information on statistical artifacts, so most meta-analyses using Schmidt and Hunter procedures have adopted the AD method (Hunter & Schmidt, 1990). As a compromise between the AD and IC methods, Hunter and Schmidt briefly presented a *mixed method* of meta-analysis. In the mixed method, IC is used for studies having all statistical artifact information available, and then AD is used for studies having only partial statistical artifact information available. This approach requires further statistical development, but it is a promising method that could lead to more accurate results than the AD method alone, because in most meta-analyses, artifact information may be missing from some studies, but not all.

The Purpose of Statistical Correction

Regardless of whether a study is used for a meta-analysis, statistically correcting an observed correlation for measurement unreliability can be of important theoretical and practical use: (a) to estimate the strength of a relation between two constructs (i.e., correcting a validity coefficient for measurement unreliability on both the x and the y measures), and (b) to determine how well test scores, with their attendant measurement error variance, will predict individuals on a latent job performance construct (i.e., correcting a validity coefficient for measurement unreliability in the y measure only; see Binning & Barrett, 1989). Correction for measurement unreliability can make perfect psychometric sense, so long as you select and calculate the appropriate reliability coefficient, which in turn requires understanding of what causes observed measures to be unreliable (e.g., item content, test format, test-taker fatigue). Test–retest reliability, alternate-forms reliability, internal consistency reliability, and interrater reliability are four well known ways to estimate different types of measurement error variance, and other systematic (as opposed to random) sources of variance can be identified and measured, too, further reducing the measurement error variance that remains (DeShon, 2002; Murphy & DeShon, 2000). Not thinking about reliability seriously can misguide one's opinion about the psychometric quality of a measure (Muchinsky, 1996), and using the wrong reliability coefficient for statistical correction in meta-analysis can lead to serious over- or under-correction of the observed correlation coefficients (Schmidt & Hunter, 1996).

In addition to corrections for measurement unreliability, corrections for direct and/or incidental range restriction can be important, especially in personnel selection studies, serving to estimate the overall relation between predictor and criterion within the full range of job applicants from the restricted range of those hired for a job. Researchers and practitioners can select and apply the appropriate correction by understanding the processes that lead to range restriction (James, Demaree, Mulaik, & Ladd, 1992; Linn, Harnisch, & Dunbar, 1981; Russell & Gilliland, 1995). Range restriction is not discussed in this chapter. Instead, the reader is referred to Sackett and Yang (2000), who used a comprehensive framework to organize the types of situations in which direct and incidental range-restriction effects occur, and outlined a variety of procedures for statistically correcting correlations for range-restriction effects.

Whether statistical corrections are for measurement unreliability, range restriction, dichotomization of the predictor, or any number of other factors (see Hunter & Schmidt, 1990), the purpose of making statistical corrections to correlations is the same: to replace the sample-based variance or covariance of x and y with better estimates of its value in the population. In the end, statistical corrections are no magical replacement for conducting studies with larger samples, better measures, and so on, but practically speaking, while research pushes ahead to improve itself, applying statistical corrections in meta-analysis can be a much more sensible practice than not doing so. The corrections incur a cost, however, namely an increased standard error associated with the corrected meta-analysis statistics (Bobko, 1983). The tradeoffs when making statistical corrections in meta-analysis remain an important topic of discussion (e.g., Murphy, 1993).

What Can and Cannot Be Statistically Corrected?

To introduce the sorts of concepts that neither meta-analysis nor any individual study can address or correct for statistically, it is useful to hearken back to Brogden and Taylor (1950), who discussed irrelevant systematic variance in criterion measures in terms of biasing factors, or "any variable, except errors of measurement and sampling error, producing a deviation of obtained criterion scores from a hypothetical 'true' criterion score" (p. 161). Note that the correction for measurement unreliability only corrects for irrelevant *unsystematic* variance that attenuates correlations between measures. Unsystematic variance is not due to the constructs of interest and is random error (i.e., the error term in true-and-error score theory). These corrections do not (and, in fact, cannot) address irrelevant *systematic* variance in either measure.

Irrelevant systematic variance can either artificially increase or decrease the amount of observed covariance between the two variables being meta-analyzed, thereby producing a validity coefficient with an unknown amount of positive or negative bias. For instance, when irrelevant systematic variance in the criterion measure is unrelated to systematic variance (relevant or irrelevant) in the predictor measure, the correlation between the measures is reduced (e.g., Brogden and Taylor's "predictor-free" criterion bias). In this case, criterion contamination contributes to variance in the criterion without contributing to the covariance between the predictor and criterion, thereby attenuating the correlation. As a related example, if the criterion contains irrelevant systematic variance that *is* related to the systematic variance in the predictor measure, then the resulting correlation between the criterion and predictor is either higher or lower than it would be otherwise, depending on whether the contaminating variance was positively or negatively related to the predictor (e.g., Brogden and Taylor's "predictor-related criterion bias").

Those ideas, most notably the ideas of criterion deficiency and criterion contamination, can be extended to the context of predictor and criterion variables being correlated in meta-analysis. Please refer to Fig. 11.2, which diagrams the relations between the measures and constructs for predictor and criterion variables x and y (the figure does not depict random measurement error). Variance in each observed measure appears in the areas A + B. Variance in each con-

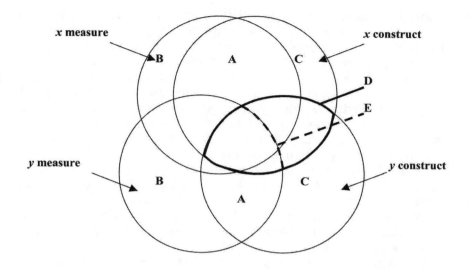

A = relevant construct variance measured

B = construct contamination in the measures

C = construct deficiencies in the measures

D = desired covariance estimate in meta-analysis

E = best-case covariance estimate in meta-analysis

FIG. 11.2. How deficiency and contamination of x and y measures affect observed correlations.

struct appears in the areas A + C. The B areas represent contamination in the observed measures—the extent to which the measures capture systematic construct-irrelevant variance (e.g., when high verbal ability is required of a mechanical knowledge test). The C areas represent the extent to which the observed measures are deficient—the extent to which the measures fail to tap construct-relevant variance (e.g., when a mechanical knowledge test measures knowledge of straight-line forces on objects but not rotational forces). The A areas are the two almond-shaped areas, and they represent valid (i.e., construct-relevant) measurement, in which measure and construct overlap. These are the areas that reliability coefficients are meant to estimate (i.e., that they estimate ideally)—the valid portion of the true score variance (i.e., the relevant variance). In true-and-error score theory, however, reliability coefficients esti-

mate the area given by A and B (i.e., all systematic observed variance, relevant or otherwise), although other approaches to reliability work toward addressing the contributions of these systematic
sources of error (e.g., Murphy & DeShon, 2000).

Reliability coefficients are *not* able to estimate (or correct for) the
degree to which observed measures are deficient in measuring their
respective constructs. Ideally, a statistically corrected validity coefficient in meta-analysis would be based on the *x construct* and *y construct* circles, where the covariance would be represented by the entire area where those circles overlap (area D). At best, however, a
statistically corrected validity coefficient can be based only on the
covariance in the central triangular area labeled *E*, the construct-
relevant covariance that the measures tap, and usually, the observed covariation is based on the overlap between the *x measure*
and *y measure* circles, which reflect all systematic covariance, regardless of its relevance.

Assessing the relationships among constructs more accurately requires developing better measures of those constructs—measures
that are less contaminated and less deficient—rather than relying
on statistical corrections. This measurement development task requires researchers to spend more time and attention on construct
validation that links measures back to constructs and to the
nomological networks in which they are embedded. Theoretical and
empirical efforts from individual studies *and* from meta-analysis inform this process, not just results from meta-analysis (cf. Schmidt,
1992). This process appears essential for generating correct estimates of a mean correlation because corrections for measurement
error assume that all remaining variance in each measure is relevant variance, which then implies that all remaining corrected
covariation is desired covariation. In truth, covariances—including
their standardized versions known as correlations—are black boxes:
They tell us how much observed measures covary, but they do not
tell us the sources of that covariation.

The implication of using such correlations as grist for the meta-
analytic mill is that one may be tricked into thinking that one has
the best estimate of the correlation between the constructs of interest, when that estimate is actually biased to an unknown degree by
an undetermined amount of irrelevant variance in (and deficiency
of) the measures appearing in each study: Do these corrected correlations reflect only desired covariation (i.e., the covariation of the
relevant variance in the *x* construct with the relevant variance in the
y construct)? To what extent are they biased upward because of un-
desired covariation (any covariation involving irrelevant variance)?

To what extent are they biased downward due to irrelevant variance in one or both measures, which serves as unexplained variance (and thus, from the standpoint of a prediction model, error variance)? The only way to begin answering such questions is to define what the relevant variance in each measure should be and then to treat all other sources of variance as irrelevant—something that requires construct validation of clearly and carefully defined constructs that are embedded within strong theories. This *a priori* conceptual approach complements the *post hoc* mathematical approach of meta-analysis, which takes the opposite tack of identifying relevant variance as the residual of a subtractive process (i.e., taking the estimate of true variance across studies as what remains after subtracting the sampling error variance from the observed variance).

Meta-Analysis Confronts a Large Missing-Data Problem

Possible biases in the results from meta-analysis even go beyond this two-construct/two-measure situation because each study may use different measures of the x and y constructs, and on a theoretical level, the x and y constructs themselves may differ across studies somewhat (see Hunter & Schmidt, 1990). For the sake of discussion, say there are five studies, each based on an independent sample, and each using a different measure of x and a different measure of y. Table 11.1 presents the correlations between the x and the y measures across studies. First, notice that this matrix is missing 80% of the potential correlational information—a percentage that would be higher if the meta-analysis comprised more than five studies (which is often the case in meta-analysis). Next realize that, for two reasons, the matrix of correlational information is even sparser than what you see. First, no study contains any information on correlations be-

TABLE 11.1
Correlations in a Hypothetical Five-Study Meta-Analysis

	y_1	y_2	y_3	y_4	y_5
x_1	r_1	—	—	—	—
x_2	—	r_2	—	—	—
x_3	—	—	r_3	—	—
x_4	—	—	—	r_4	—
x_5	—	—	—	—	r_5

Note. Studies are based on independent samples. The symbol — indicates missing correlations between the x and the y measures.

tween all the x measures and correlations between all the y measures. Second, each correlation is from an independent sample, which implies two things: (a) Study 1 yields an estimate of r_1 but not of r_2 through r_5, Study 2 estimates r_2 but not of r_1 and r_3 through r_5, and so on; and (b) no study yields estimates of the off-diagonal correlations in the matrix. In fact, if one did have all this information between and within the set of x and y measures—even within one study—then any of several multivariate measures of association (e.g., canonical correlation or set correlation; see Cohen, 1982; Skinner, 1978) would incorporate the available information and would likely be more sensible than the meta-analysis approach of averaging the x–y correlations.

Having full information on multiple measures of the x and y constructs is rare in practice but would be an ideal construct validation approach that would inform a better understanding and estimation of a mean correlation. The matrix in Table 11.1 is a marked departure from this ideal, showing us that meta-analyzing the information provided across studies leaves a lot of water in the well.

STATISTICAL POWER

Even if it is assumed that corrected correlations across studies correctly estimate their respective population correlations, and there is heterogeneity (i.e., true variance) across study correlations, then two problems remain regarding the capacity of meta-analysis to detect that heterogeneity. The first problem is statistical: The statistical power of a meta-analysis of small-sample studies may be high for estimating the mean correlation, but it can be extremely low for detecting true variance across studies (i.e., heterogeneity in effect sizes; Hedges & Pigott, 2001). A meta-analyst with a set of small-sample studies (e.g., each study with the median N of 68 from Lent, Aurbach, & Levin, 1971) might tend to be led to the conclusion of across-study homogeneity, whereas the same meta-analysis with a similar collection of large-N studies (e.g., each study with $N = 6{,}800$) might lead the meta-analyst to the opposite conclusion that heterogeneity exists. It is somewhat ironic that meta-analysis has been viewed as an alternative approach to statistical significance testing, yet the meta-analysis of small-N studies relies on its high sampling error variance to support the null hypothesis—namely, the strong conclusion that no moderator effects exist across studies.

For the sake of discussion, consider the simple case of two studies with observed validity coefficients of .25 and .35. Extending the previous example for the N-weighted mean, if the two studies were conducted in two small organizations, and each study had $N = 20$, then meta-analysis would conclude that both studies could have come from the same underlying population validity coefficient. On the other hand, if the two studies were conducted in two branches of the U.S. military and both studies had $N = 20,000$, then the opposite conclusion—that study populations were different—would be upheld. These are two very different conclusions from meta-analysis, although the conclusions differ only because of the predictable effects of statistical artifacts (namely, that of sampling error variance) in small- versus large-sample studies.

Many meta-analyses of organizational research have reported that a high percentage of the variation in observed correlation coefficients can be accounted for by sampling error variance (e.g., meta-analyses supporting the "75% rule," in which at least 75% of the variance observed is sampling error variance; see Hunter & Schmidt, 1990). Such a large percentage of artifact-based variance is not good for a conservative test of validity generalization because it leads to the bias that all studies in the meta-analysis have essentially the same underlying population correlation. The level of statistical power for finding variation among true correlations when it exists tends to be embarrassingly low regardless of the statistical test or estimate of heterogeneity (Harwell, 1997; Kemery, Mossholder, & Roth, 1987; Koslowsky & Sagie, 1993; Murphy, 1997; Oswald & Johnson, 1998). There is hope, however, because sample sizes in published criterion-related validity studies in applied psychology have tended to increase over time. Salgado (1998) reported a median sample size of 113, compared with Lent et al.'s (1971) reported median of 68. Much larger sample sizes are needed, however, to find support for differences in validity coefficients between studies, as opposed to simply finding support that validities are nonzero (Trattner & O'Leary, 1980).

More ideal, although rarely possible, would be to determine whether the variance in validity coefficients from a set of large-sample studies is large or small—a substantive decision, not an automatic statistical decision. In the absence of large-sample studies, however, it is nearly impossible to distinguish sampling error variance from true variance. Ghiselli (1966) examined trends in validity coefficients across studies in a way similar to meta-analysis, and although often quoted for strongly advocating the position of situational specificity across validity coefficients, he realized that sampling error variance was "unquestionably" one source of variation (p. 28). What his analyses lacked (that Schmidt and Hunter, 1990, supplied) was a way of estimating the amount of variance in study outcomes that one might expect on the basis of factors other than simple sampling error. Small-sample studies contain so much sampling error that real differences in study outcomes can be obscured.

The second problem is more conceptual than statistical: Moderating effects, when found, have been said to be due to situations within studies, almost as if "the situation" were one thing. Moderator effects on correlation coefficients often comprise multiple variables that should be identified and perhaps modeled in a meta-analysis (Steel & Kammeyer-Mueller, 2002; Viswesvaran & Ones, 1995). There may also be important mean differences in predictor and criterion measures across studies—and even within studies (e.g., in data collected across multiple organizations)—that would go unnoticed in a meta-analysis of correlation coefficients. Those level effects may be important to understand and model, as well (Light & Pillemer, 1984; Ostroff & Harrison, 1999).

MODERATOR EFFECTS AND "TRUE VARIANCE"

Assuming you can measure true variance accurately as an index for the presence of moderators, how can one decide what a practical amount of true variance is? The amount of true variance one calls "small" may be called "large" by someone else, and so this decision is somewhat arbitrary, just as the conventions suggested by Cohen (1988) were for defining a small, moderate, and large effect size. The decision should be made, nevertheless, because it focuses your attention on the size of the true variance, not just whether it is zero or non-zero as determined by a statistical significance test. To assist in determining some benchmarks for the true variance of correlations, consider the following example.

Assume a normal distribution for the true values of correlation coefficients across studies in a meta-analysis. To determine a large amount of variance, let us say (somewhat arbitrarily) that a difference of 50 correlation units between study correlations (i.e., .50) is a large difference. About 95% of the normal curve is represented by 4 (i.e., ± 2) standard deviations around the mean. Therefore, the standard deviation associated with this large difference is $\frac{.50}{4} = .125$, and the variance associated with this difference is thus $(.125)^2$, or .0156. Using similar computations, let us say that a difference of 30 correlation units (i.e., .30) translates into a "moderate" true variance of .0056 (SD = .075), and a difference of 10 correlation units translates into a small true variance of .000625 (SD = .025). Of course, different values could be set as standards. Oswald (1999) used .0200, .0050, and .00125 as large, moderate, and small true variance levels for an approximately normal distribution of correlation coefficients. Notice that what researchers might take to be a small number at first glance, .0200, is by our definition a large amount of true variance and should not be overlooked. To capture accurately the range of potentially meaningful true variance, estimates of true variance from meta-analysis should probably be reported to four decimal places.

In estimating true variance, the general conceptual formula in meta-analysis is:

$$\text{true variance} = \text{weighted observed variance} - \\ \text{weighted average sampling error variance}$$

(see Hedges & Olkin, 1985; Hunter & Schmidt, 1990). Using ANOVA-like terms, this can be rewritten as:

$$\text{true variance} = \text{across-studies variance} - \\ \text{average within-studies variance}$$

Meta-analysis estimates of true variance obtained by subtraction have different distributions than do ANOVA F ratios (Thomas, 1988), but clearly their ingredients are similar. The subtraction of variances (instead of the ratio of variances) is useful because it places the focus on the amount of true variance remaining instead of simply whether a statistical-significance test indicates nonzero variance. However, because the homogeneity of within-studies variances is assumed in ANOVA, one might want to assume the same in meta-analysis. It is known, however, that the sampling error variance within studies in meta-analysis can vary widely because variations in sample size, which correspond roughly to variations in sampling error variance, commonly reach a factor of 10 (e.g., sample sizes across studies can easily vary by a factor of 10). Such heterogeneity of sampling error variance may have implications for meta-analysis estimates of true variance.

In some circumstances this estimate of true variance can be accurate *on average* (Hunter & Schmidt, 1994), but what you might get in the average meta-analysis may not be what you would get in any particular meta-analysis. In fact, there is often a high standard error associated with the true variance estimate, which means that although the average true variance estimate may be accurate, any estimate of true variance in any particular meta-analysis would tend to be inaccurate. Even statistical significance tests that simply test for the presence or absence of true variance, regardless of the size of the true variance, are not very powerful in most meta-analyses, leading to potentially inaccurate inferences about validity generalization (Cornwell & Ladd, 1993; Law, 1992; Oswald & Johnson, 1998; Sackett, Harris, & Orr, 1986). Perhaps organizational researchers should adopt the practice followed in the medical research literature (Biggerstaff & Tweedie, 1997; DerSimonian & Laird, 1986), in which confidence intervals are reported around the point estimate of true variance, thus allowing readers to determine the stability of the estimate and therefore whether and how it should be interpreted. The present authors could not find a single meta-analysis in the organizational research literature in which a confidence interval was reported around the estimate of true variance.

As for moderator effects lurking behind the true variance estimates, these may exist in any of several different ways: (a) across all studies, (b) in some subset of studies, (c) in one particular study, (d) in a study outside the meta-analysis, or (e) in life, but not in any study that can generalize to it. The search for moderators based on the true variance estimate in meta-analysis is typically limited to points (a) and (b), which can lead one to cross-study moderators that are only weakly related to the phenomenon of interest (e.g., year of publication, sex of the researcher). As for point (c), this refers to studies that have specific moderator effects modeled explicitly within the study, or to studies that implicitly have "the study" as the moderator because its correlation value is an outlier compared with other values. In either case, a meta-analysis typically will not take a serious look at individual studies like this, focusing instead on the mean correlation, possibly even conducting a statistical test for homogeneity and deleting outlier studies like this, never examining studies that may have the most interesting effects due to the influence of moderators. Points (d) and (e) are to say that no meta-analysis is comprehensive, because usually not all good research can be obtained, and often more good research is yet to be done.

RECOMMENDATIONS AND DISCUSSION:
IMPROVING THE PRACTICE OF META-ANALYSIS

Schmidt and Hunter have done our field an enormous service by emphasizing the detrimental impact of statistical artifacts on investigations of the relation between constructs (e.g., cognitive ability and job performance). They have soundly condemned the perceived need for local validity studies—studies typically characterized by low statistical power and large amounts of sampling error—arguing instead for the merits of meta-analysis of numerous studies as the correct method for investigating the degree to which validity generalizes across settings. Figure 11.1 shows that the idea has caught on, but there is considerable room for improvement in the way meta-analyses are conducted.

Focus on the Descriptive Nature of Meta-Analysis

It is certainly true that applying statistical corrections to studies has led us to understand that relations between cognitive ability and job performance, the effects of programmed-instruction training interventions, and so on, are likely larger than traditionally assumed because of our previous failure to recognize the presence of statistical artifacts. Further, surveying those effects across studies via meta-analysis has led us to realize that effects may be consistent across a variety of researchers' attempts to capture similar phenomena across different measures, samples, and situations— perhaps more consistent than anticipated when examining the results from many individual studies (see Murphy, 2000). In the initial search for studies for meta-analysis, you should be thorough in your search, and you should apply (and codify) your expert knowledge and judgment in the selection and subgrouping of different types of studies. The quantitative meta-analysis that follows should be seen as descriptive and exploratory in nature, at least in the initial stages.

That is, at the descriptive level a meta-analysis provides a historical snapshot of effects observed in a particular research domain. Interpreting a meta-analysis is perhaps somewhat simpler and safer when the resulting snapshot serves a retrospective function in surveying exactly where the research has been, or when it serves a sort of prospective function, finding substantive gaps in the literature where future research and stakeholders in research might want to allocate their time and resources (Hedges, 1990). Stronger interpretations and inferences may be more challenging to support, and as with any individual study, you should be cautious about making any inference about broader populations (real or hypothetical) to the extent the inferences about generalizability stretch beyond the set of studies used in the meta-analysis.

Examine the Track Record of Research and Define Practical Generalizability

A meta-analysis cannot always be informative about exactly how study characteristics such as predictors, criteria, and sampling design can be improved, but it can be informative about the track record across studies in a particular area and how concerned you should be about it as a researcher or practitioner. Whether you find enough homogeneity depends on your intents and purposes; the true variance does not have to be exactly zero. When observed heterogeneity falls below some practical minimum you set beforehand (per our discussion about determining what a small true variance might be), then you can conclude that validity generalizes enough.

Inspect Data Visually

Examining and exploring one's data visually has been recommended as a good way to summarize and understand a wealth of quantitative information (Task Force on Statistical Inference, 1999; Tukey, 1977). Rothstein, McDaniel, and Borenstein (2002) provided a clear example of what we might call a *pancake plot*, where each study's point estimate and confidence interval are plotted and stacked on top of one another. It is richer in information than any summary statistic addressing true variance (e.g., the true variance estimate, the Q test of homogeneity, the "75% rule") because it can be seen exactly where subsets of studies overlap, partially overlap, or are independent from one another. One could also run a regression line through this stack to account for any fixed effects across studies that predict variability across effect sizes (see Thompson, 1993). Ghiselli (1966) and Ackerman and Heggestad (1997) also provided good examples of studies in which the distribution of validity coefficients is presented and explored using histograms. Researchers have long noted the importance of using various tools to explore and understanding the nature of variability across studies (e.g., Light, 1979), though Glass (2000), in his recent retrospective on meta-analysis, noted that unfortunately "Little effort is invested in trying to plot the complex, variegated landscape that most likely underlies our crude averages."

Supplement Meta-Analysis With the Use of Complementary Sources of Evidence

A meta-analysis may support an overall theoretical relation across a set of studies, but any important disparities that can be noticed between the studies that went into the meta-analysis and the situation at hand should be reported (see the American Educational Research Association, American Psychological Association, & National Council on Measurement in Education *Standards*, 1999). Strong empirical *and* rational support are needed for good validity generalization. Evidence for validity generalization can come from all angles (Schmitt & Landy, 1993). For example, in supporting the use of cognitive ability tests in personnel selection, Hoffman, Holden, and Gale (2000) brought together evidence from meta-analyses, in-house validation studies conducted on other jobs, job component validity estimates, and job clustering using job analysis information to make inferences about testing in jobs that had very small N and no direct evidence. Brannick (2001) presented an empirical Bayesian meta-analysis framework that incorporates information from meta-analysis and a local validity study (e.g., from your own organization), and then informs you how best to weigh the meta-analysis and the validity study information. Howard, Maxwell, and Fleming (2000) noted that different methodologies (point estimates and confidence intervals, meta-analysis, and Bayesian models) are complementary approaches in understanding research data.

Conduct "Local Meta-Analyses"

Meta-analyses designed to include all relevant work, published or unpublished, on a given research phenomenon have been common since the initial introduction of meta-analytic methods in the social sciences (e.g., Smith & Glass, 1977). Such meta-analyses have been described with such terms as *comprehensive*, *robust*, or even *unbiased*. Although the comprehensiveness of these studies may sometimes be questioned (e.g., they rarely include studies published in languages other than English), the most critical question is whether it is better to attempt to provide a comprehensive coverage of all available studies, or to focus only on studies that meet some minimal standards of quality. Comprehensive meta-analyses do not require researchers to make (admittedly subjective) judgments about which studies to include or exclude and thus might appear to be more objective. It can be argued, however, that avoiding making sensible judgments about the methodological rigor in the sample of studies for meta-analysis is as inappropriate as avoiding making judgments about which individuals are sampled in a study. In both cases, your decision to include studies or subjects in an analysis that arguably do not belong there creates threats to your ability to make high-quality generalized inferences (see Cooper, 1998; Shadish, Cook, & Campbell, 2001; Wortman, 1994). Some aspects of research quality can be analyzed in the meta-analysis, such as comparisons between quasi-experimental and experimental studies, or examinations of the effects of the methods used to gather information on the variables of interest. Studies are often categorized on these types of variables, and thus they may be rated on quality and weighted accordingly (Rosenthal & DiMatteo, 2001).

The quality of studies is an important issue for meta-analysis, but study quality is multidimensional (Becker, 1991; Gottfredson, 1978), so it is not an easy issue to address conceptually or quantitatively. Regardless of whether studies are weighted or included or excluded based on quality, having good rules for determining study quality, and applying those rules systematically to the set of candidate studies for meta-analysis, is important so that (a) different study coders can be trained in a standardized way, (b) coding rules can be applied consistently across studies, and (c) those rules can be reported to the interested reader. Accumulating a large collection of poorly conducted studies—whether or not the effect sizes reported are large or small, heterogeneous or homogeneous, and so on—leads to uninterpretable results.

Restricting a meta-analysis to methodologically rigorous studies, however, does not guarantee interpretable results. Anyone conducting a meta-analysis should examine *a priori* those facets across jobs that may have an impact (e.g., type of job, job complexity; see Hunter & Hunter, 1984) and then keep those facets relatively constant so that the meta-analytic results are more interpretable. Historically, however, researchers have frequently cast a very broad net across the ocean of research literature when identifying studies to include in their meta-analysis. This quest for statistical power in determining the mean effect size has led to instances in which one or more of the constructs of interest in the meta-analysis has been operationalized in so many ways across studies that the results and implications of the meta-analysis are nearly uninterpretable. For instance, job performance is known to be multidimensional (Campbell, Gasser, & Oswald, 1996; Campbell, McCloy, Oppler, & Sager, 1992; Viswevaran, Ones, & Schmidt, 1996), yet some meta-analyses have accumulated studies that reflect and operationalize job performance in a variety of ways (e.g., ratings, work samples, productivity, absenteeism), and then have treated the studies as if they were similar. This practice is virtually useless for helping advance theories of job performance and the improved practice that can result. The estimate of the mean correlation, for instance, is thus obtained with great statistical power but at the expense of interpretability. More specifically, the accuracy of the mean value (say, between cognitive ability and job performance) is dubious: The value might be too high or too low, depending on the previously discussed effects of contamination, deficiency, and variation in construct definitions across the studies included in the meta-analysis. Ironically, the strategy of including as many studies as possible to maximize the accuracy of our estimates of effect sizes can actually decrease their accuracy because it results in pooling studies that may be quite heterogeneous with regard to their operational definitions of the constructs of interest. Returning to job performance, cognitive ability has been shown to be a stronger predictor of "can-do" performance (e.g., work sample measures) than temperament has, but temperament is the better predictor of "will-do" performance (e.g., supervisor ratings of typical job performance; see Campbell, 1986; McHenry, Hough, Toquam, Hanson, & Ashworth, 1990). Including both types of measures in a meta-analysis will result in a muddy interpretation of how strongly cognitive ability predicts job performance because it depends on the type of performance measure used. The situation becomes ineffably murky when studies are included that operationalize performance in ways that are inconsistent with our theories of performance (e.g., absenteeism, productivity; see Campbell et al., 1992).

We instead advocate that researchers narrow the universe of studies for any given meta-analysis—*not* down to the individual study ("Yes, Virginia, validity does generalize"), but rather down to a subset of studies that bear rational and theoretical similarity to each other. Thus, we likewise eschew the local validity study with small sample sizes, but we heartily endorse the *local meta-analysis*. Clearly, this notion of conducting local meta-analyses runs counter to the traditional diffuse approach to conducting meta-analysis in which the studies to be analyzed are aggregated across a wide array of settings, measurement conditions, measures, and samples.

Employ Mixed-Effects Models

We know that meta-analysis provides improved statistical estimates when small-sample studies are strict replications of one another (e.g., same predictor and criterion within the same organization and type of sample), but when they are not, the local meta-analysis may be the best we can do. When studies are known to vary on dimensions that are theoretically or empirically relevant to the correlation between x and y, a meta-analysis of these studies must start with the assumption that effects vary across studies (i.e., a random-effects model) and proceed to careful tests of the advisability of aggregating effects across those studies. Although random-effects models have been used extensively in validity generalization research, there are statistical drawbacks to this model. Estimates of random effects can be unstable, and even when they can be quantified accurately, it is difficult substantively to specify the universe to which random effects generalize (Hedges, 1992). If you have a heterogeneous set of studies, and you are examining heterogeneity in a *post hoc* way (instead of an a priori way via a local meta-analysis) then a single study with a sample size much larger than other studies can greatly affect the meta-analytically estimated mean and the variance of study correlations, because they both use sample size weighting.

Fixed- and random-effects models of meta-analysis have appeared in the psychology literature (Erez, Bloom, & Wells, 1996; Hedges, 1992; Hunter & Schmidt, 2000), but this literature is now moving toward the more integrated mixed-effects model (Hedges & Vevea, 1998; Kalaian & Raudenbush, 1996; Overton, 1998). Mixed-effects models, which have been widely used in educational research (Raudenbush & Bryk, 1985) and medical research (Stram, 1996), integrate random and fixed-effects models into a single overarching framework. Mixed-effects models are now well established in the analysis of longitudinal data (e.g., Cudeck, 1996) and are beginning to gain a foothold in the meta-analysis literature. Mixed-effects models lead to intermediate-sized confidence intervals, somewhere between fixed-effects (all variation is captured within the studies at hand by known study characteristics) and random effects (all variation comes from the studies being sampled from some larger universe of studies).

SUMMARY

The purpose of this chapter was to make several simple points regarding meta-analysis, the inferences it can (and, importantly, cannot) support, and how it might be more profitably conducted. Meta-analysis has served as a double-edged sword. The method has clearly aided the research enterprise in several ways, in particular by (a) explicitly recognizing the biasing effects of statistical artifacts, and (b) improving the quality of research studies (Murphy, 1997). Even so, meta-analysis arguably has had several unintended negative effects, chief among which are the following:

- A meta-analysis of small-N studies will tend to lead to statistical results and conclusions that discourage the search for moderator effects. By tending to support the null hypothesis of homogeneity across study statistics, meta-analysis has swung the pendulum strongly away from situational specificity, perhaps too far in the direction of generalizability. A slight adjustment might be in order where both researchers and practitioners can decide on levels of generalizability (i.e., levels of true variance) sufficient for their purposes.

- Meta-analysis has not noticeably sparked theory development and indeed may have stunted it. Because meta-analysis frequently rests on a heterogeneous collection of studies (e.g., different operational definitions of the constructs of interest, different definitions of the constructs themselves), the descriptive statistics it yields have limited application to testing particular theoretical relations. To the extent that meta-analysis findings have muted investigations of moderator effects, theory testing and refinement has been likewise muted. For example, how should one interpret a mean correlation and estimate of variability computed from a meta-analysis comprising studies from competing theories (e.g., those who espouse the merits of the general factor of intelligence, those who instead espouse the triarchic theory)? Substantively testing for moderators beforehand yields more interesting and more statistically powerful possibilities than the information provided by any index or statistical test for true variance.

The points raised in this chapter are meant to improve both the conduct of meta-analysis and the interpretation of the descriptive statistics such an analysis provides. As the number of meta-analyses increases, the contribution they will make to the literature will likewise increase if researchers bear in mind the following:

- True variance is not the same thing as relevant variance.
- Total sample size is not the same thing as representativeness.
- Meta-analysis yields two descriptive statistics with which we are all familiar—a mean and a variance—and both can be flawed due to the effects of weighting some heterogeneous studies more than others, the effects of contamination and deficiency on the mean correlation, and the potential variability around the estimate of the true variance across study populations. Adjust your interpretations accordingly.

- Local meta-analyses will yield descriptive statistics that lead to stronger interpretations and inferences, based on fewer relevant studies that are more substantively focused.

REFERENCES

Ackerman, P. L., & Heggestad, E. D. (1997). Intelligence, personality, and interests: Evidence for overlapping traits. *Psychological Bulletin, 121*, 219–245.

American Educational Research Association, American Psychological Association, National Council on Measurement in Education, & Joint Committee on Standards for Educational and Psychological Testing. (1999). *Standards for educational and psychological testing.* Washington, DC: AERA.

Becker, B. J. (1991). The quality and credibility of research reviews: What the editors say. *Personality & Social Psychology Bulletin, 17*, 267–272.

Biggerstaff, B. J., & Tweedie, R. L. (1997). Incorporating variability in estimates of heterogeneity in the random effects model in meta-analysis. *Statistics in Medicine, 16*, 753–768.

Binning, J. F., & Barrett, G. V. (1989). Validity of personnel decisions: A conceptual analysis of the inferential and evidential bases. *Journal of Applied Psychology, 74*, 478–494.

Bobko, P. (1983). An analysis of correlations corrected for attenuation and range restriction. *Journal of Applied Psychology, 68*, 584–589.

Brannick, M. T. (2001). Implications of empirical Bayes meta-analysis for test validation. *Journal of Applied Psychology, 86*, 468–480.

Brogden, H. E., & Taylor, E. K. (1950). The theory and classification of criterion bias. *Educational and Psychological Measurement, 10*, 159–186.

Campbell, J. P. (1986). *Improving the selection, classification, and utilization of Army enlisted personnel: Annual report, 1986 fiscal year* (ARI technical report 813101). Alexandria, VA: U.S. Army Research Institute for the Behavioral and Social Sciences.

Campbell, D. T., & Fiske, D. W. (1959). Convergent and discriminant validation by the multitrait-multimethod matrix. *Psychological Bulletin, 56*, 81–105.

Campbell, J. P., Gasser, M. B., & Oswald, F. L. (1996). The substantive nature of job performance variability. In K. R. Murphy (Ed.), *Individual differences and behavior in organizations* (pp. 258–299). San Francisco: Jossey-Bass.

Campbell, J. P., McCloy, R. A., Oppler, S. H., & Sager, C. E. (1992). A theory of performance. In N. Schmitt & W. Borman (Eds.), *Personnel selection in organizations* (pp. 35–70). San Francisco, CA: Jossey-Bass.

Cohen, J. (1982). Set correlation as a general multivariate data analytic method. *Multivariate Behavioral Research, 17*, 301–341.

Cohen, J. (1988). *Statistical power analysis for the behavioral sciences* (2nd ed.). Hillsdale, NJ: Lawrence Erlbaum Associates.

Cooper, H., & Hedges, L. V. (1994). Research synthesis as a scientific enterprise. In H. Cooper & L. V. Hedges (Eds.), *The handbook of research synthesis* (pp. 3–14). New York: Sage.

Cooper, H. M. (1998). *Synthesizing research: A guide for literature reviews* (3rd ed.). Thousand Oaks, CA: Sage.

Cornwell, J. M., & Ladd, R. T. (1993). Power and accuracy of the Schmidt and Hunter meta-analytic procedures. *Educational & Psychological Measurement, 53,* 877–895.

Cudeck, R. (1996). Mixed-effects models in the study of individual differences with repeated measures data. *Multivariate Behavioral Research, 31,* 371–403.

DerSimonian, R., & Laird, N. M. (1986). Meta-analysis in clinical trials. *Controlled Clinical Trials, 7,* 177–188.

DeShon, R. P. (2002). Generalizability theory. In F. Drasgow & N. Schmitt (Eds.), *Measuring and analyzing behavior in organizations: Advances in measurement and data analysis* (pp. 189–220). San Francisco: Jossey-Bass.

Erez, A., Bloom, M. C., & Wells, M. T. (1996). Using random rather than fixed effects models in meta-analysis: Implications for situational specificity and validity generalization. *Personnel Psychology, 49,* 275–306.

Ghiselli, E. E. (1966). *The validity of occupational aptitude tests.* New York: Wiley.

Glass, G. V. (2000, January 12). Meta-analysis at 25. Retrieved from http:// glass.ed.asu.edu/gene/papers/meta25.html

Gottfredson, S. D. (1978). Evaluating psychological research reports: Dimensions, reliability, and correlates of quality judgments. *American Psychologist, 33,* 920–934.

Guzzo, R. A., Jackson, S. E., & Katzell, R. A. (1987). Meta-analysis analysis. In L. L. Cummings & B. M. Staw (Eds.), *Research in Organizational Behavior* (Vol. 9). Greenwich, CT: JAI Press.

Harwell, M. (1997). An empirical study of Hedges's homogeneity test. *Psychological Methods, 2,* 219–231.

Hedges, L. V. (1990). The future of meta-analysis. In K. W. Wachter & M. L. Straf (Eds.), *The future of meta-analysis* (pp. 11–26). New York: Sage.

Hedges, L. V. (1992). Meta-analysis. *Journal of Educational Statistics, 17,* 279–296.

Hedges, L. V., & Olkin, I. (1985). *Statistical methods for meta-analysis.* Orlando, FL: Academic Press.

Hedges, L. V., & Pigott, T. D. (2001). The power of statistical tests in meta-analysis. *Psychological Methods, 6,* 203–217.

Hedges, L. V., & Vevea, J. L. (1998). Fixed- and random-effects models in meta-analysis. *Psychological Methods, 3,* 486–504.

Hoffman, C. C., Holden, L. M., & Gale, K. (2000). So many jobs, so little "N": Applying expanded validation models to support generalization of cognitive test validity. *Personnel Psychology, 53,* 955–991.

Howard, G. S., Maxwell, S. E., & Fleming, K. J. (2000). The proof of the pudding: An illustration of the relative strengths of null hypothesis, meta-analysis, and Bayesian analysis. *Psychological Methods, 5,* 315–332.

Hunter, J. E., & Hunter, R. F. (1984). Validity and utility of alternative predictors of job performance. *Psychological Bulletin, 96,* 72–98.

Hunter, J. E., & Schmidt, F. L. (1990). *Methods of meta-analysis: correcting error and bias in research findings.* Newbury Park: Sage.

Hunter, J. E., & Schmidt, F. L. (1994). Estimation of sampling error variance in the meta-analysis of correlations: Use of average correlation in the homogeneous case. *Journal of Applied Psychology, 79,* 171–177.

Hunter, J. E., & Schmidt, F. L. (1996). Cumulative research knowledge and social policy formulation: The critical role of meta-analysis. *Psychology, Public Policy, & Law, 2,* 324–347.

Hunter, J. E., & Schmidt, F. L. (2000). Fixed effects vs. random effects meta-analysis models: Implications for cumulative research knowledge. *International Journal of Selection & Assessment, 8,* 275–292.

James, L. R., Demaree, R. G., Mulaik, S. A., & Ladd, R. T. (1992). Validity generalization in the context of situational models. *Journal of Applied Psychology, 77,* 3–14.

Kalaian, H. A., & Raudenbush, S. W. (1996). A multivariate mixed linear model for meta-analysis. *Psychological Methods, 1,* 227–235.

Kemery, E. R., Mossholder, K. W., & Roth, L. (1987). The power of the Schmidt and Hunter additive model of validity generalization. *Journal of Applied Psychology, 72,* 30–37.

Koslowsky, M., & Sagie, A. (1993). On the efficacy of credibility intervals as indicators of moderator effects in meta-analytic research. *Journal of Organizational Behavior, 14,* 695–699.

Law, K. S. (1992). Estimation accuracy of Thomas's likelihood-based procedure of meta-analysis: A Monte Carlo simulation. *Journal of Applied Psychology, 77,* 986–995.

Lent, R. H., Aurbach, H. A., & Levin, L. S. (1971). Research design and validity assessment. *Personnel Psychology, 24,* 247–274.

Light, R. J. (1979). Capitalizing on variation: How conflicting research findings can be helpful for policy. *Educational Researchers, 8,* 3–11.

Light, R. J., & Pillemer, D. B. (1984). *Summing up: The science of reviewing research.* Cambridge, MA: Harvard University Press.

Linn, R. L., Harnisch, D. L., & Dunbar, S. B. (1981). Corrections for range restriction: An empirical investigation of conditions resulting in conservative corrections. *Journal of Applied Psychology, 66,* 655–663.

Matt, G. E. (1989). Decision rules for selecting effect sizes in meta-analysis: A review and reanalysis of psychotherapy outcome studies. *Psychological Bulletin, 105,* 106–115.

McHenry, J. J., Hough, L. M., Toquam, J. L., Hanson, M. A., & Ashworth, S. (1990). Project A validity results: The relationship between predictor and criterion domains. *Personnel Psychology, 43,* 335–354.

Mohr, D. C., Zickar, M. J., & Russell, S. S. (2000, April). An analysis of historical trends in meta-analytic research. Poster presented at the 15th Annual Conference of the Society of Industrial and Organizational Psychology, New Orleans, LA.

Muchinsky, P. M. (1996). The correction for attenuation. *Educational & Psychological Measurement, 56,* 63–75.

Murphy, K. R. (1997). Meta-analysis and validity generalization. In N. Anderson & P. Herriot (Eds.), *International Handbook of Selection and Assessment* (Vol. 2, pp. 323–342). New York: Wiley.

Murphy, K. R. (1993). The situational specificity of validities: Correcting for statistical artifacts does not always reduce the trans-situational variability of correlation coefficients. *International Journal of Selection and Assessment, 1,* 158–162.

Murphy, K. R. (2000). Impact of assessments of validity generalization and situational specificity on the science and practice of personnel selection. *International Journal of Selection and Assessment, 8,* 194–206.

Murphy, K. R., & DeShon, R. (2000). Progress in psychometrics: Can industrial and organizational psychology catch up? *Personnel Psychology, 53,* 913–924.

Ostroff, C., & Harrison, D. A. (1999). Meta-analysis, level of analysis, and best estimates of population correlations: Cautions for interpreting meta-analytic results in organizational behavior. *Journal of Applied Psychology, 84,* 260–270.

Oswald, F. L. (1999). On deriving validity generalization and situational specificity conclusions from meta-analysis: A conceptual review and some empirical findings. *Dissertation Abstracts International: Section B: The Sciences & Engineering, 60*(1-B), 0399.

Oswald, F. L., & Johnson, J. W. (1998). On the robustness, bias, and stability of results from meta-analysis of correlation coefficients: Some initial Monte Carlo findings. *Journal of Applied Psychology, 83,* 164–178.

Overton, R. C. (1998). A comparison of fixed-effects and mixed (random-effects) models for meta-analysis tests of moderator variable effects. *Psychological Methods, 3,* 354–379.

Raudenbush, S. W., & Bryk, A. S. (1985). Empirical Bayes meta-analysis. *Journal of Educational Statistics, 10,* 75–98.

Rosenthal, R., & DiMatteo, M. R. (2000). Meta analysis: Recent developments in quantitative methods for literature reviews. *Annual Review of Psychology, 52,* 59–82.

Rothstein, H. R., McDaniel, M. A., & Borenstein, M. (2002). Meta-analysis: A review of quantitative cumulation methods. In F. Drasgow & N. Schmitt (Eds.), *Measuring and analyzing behavior in organizations: Advances in measurement and data analysis* (pp. 534–570). San Francisco: Jossey-Bass.

Russell, C. J., & Gilliland, S. W. (1995). Why meta-analysis doesn't tell us what the data really mean: Distinguishing between moderator effects and moderator processes. *Journal of Management, 21,* 813–831.

Sackett, P. R., Harris, M. M., & Orr, J. M. (1986). On seeking moderator variables in the meta-analysis of correlational data: A Monte Carlo investigation of statistical power and resistance to Type I error. *Journal of Applied Psychology, 71,* 302–310.

Sackett, P. R., & Yang, H. (2000). Correction for range restriction: An expanded typology. *Journal of Applied Psychology, 85,* 112–118.

Salgado, J. F. (1998). Sample size in validity studies of personnel selection. *Journal of Occupational & Organizational Psychology, 71,* 161–164.

Schmidt, F. L. (1992). What do data really mean? Research findings, meta-analysis, and cumulative knowledge in psychology. *American Psychologist, 47,* 1173–1181.

Schmidt, F. L. (1996). Statistical significance testing and cumulative knowledge in psychology: Implications for training of researchers. *Psychological Methods, 1,* 115–129.

Schmidt, F. L., & Hunter, J. E. (1977). Development of a general solution to the problem of validity generalization. *Journal of Applied Psychology, 62,* 529–540.

Schmidt, F. L., & Hunter, J. E. (1996). Measurement error in psychological research: Lessons from 26 research scenarios. *Psychological Methods, 1,* 199–223.

Schmitt, N., & Landy, F. (1993). The concept of validity. In. N. Schmitt, W. Borman, & Associates (Eds.), *Personnel selection in organizations* (pp. 275–309). San Francisco: Jossey-Bass.

Shadish, W. R., Cook, T. D., & Campbell, D. T. (2001). *Experimental and quasi-experimental designs for generalized causal inference.* Boston: Houghton-Mifflin.

Skinner, H. A. (1978). The art of exploring predictor-criterion relationships. *Psychological Bulletin, 85,* 327–337.

Smith, M. L., & Glass, G. V. (1977). Meta-analysis of psychotherapy outcome studies. *American Psychologist, 32,* 752–760.

Stram, D. O. (1996). Meta-analysis of published data using a linear mixed-effects model. *Biometrics, 52,* 536–544.

Steel, P. D., & Kammeyer-Mueller, J. D. (2002). Comparing meta-analytic moderator estimation techniques under realistic conditions. *Journal of Applied Psychology, 87,* 96–111.

Task Force on Statistical Inference, American Psychological Association Science Directorate. (1999). Statistical methods in psychology journals: Guidelines and explanations. *American Psychologist, 54,* 594–604.

Thomas, H. (1988). What is the interpretation of the validity generalization estimate $S_o^2 = S_r^2 - S_e^2$? *Journal of Applied Psychology, 73,* 679–682.

Thompson, S. G. (1993). Controversies in meta-analysis: The case of the trials of serum cholesterol reduction. *Statistical Methods in Medical Research, 2,* 173–192.

Trattner, M. H., & O'Leary, B. S. (1980). Sample sizes for specified statistical power in testing for differential validity. *Journal of Applied Psychology, 65,* 127–134.

Tukey, J. W. (1977). *Exploratory data analysis.* Reading, MA: Addison-Wesley.

Viswesvaran, C., & Ones, D. S. (1995). Theory testing: Combining psychometric meta-analysis and structural equations modeling. *Personnel Psychology, 48,* 865–885.

Viswesvaran, C., Ones, D. S., & Schmidt, F. L. (1996). Comparative analysis of the reliability of job performance ratings. *Journal of Applied Psychology, 81,* 557–574.

Wanous, J. P., Sullivan, S. E., & Malinak, J. (1989). The role of judgment calls in meta-analysis. *Journal of Applied Psychology, 74,* 259–264.

Wortman, P. M. (1994). Judging research quality. In H. Cooper & L. V. Hedges (Eds.), *The handbook of research synthesis* (pp. 97–109). New York: Sage.

12

Validity Generalization From a Bayesian Perspective

Michael T. Brannick
University of South Florida

Steven M. Hall
Embry-Riddle Aeronautical University

Early papers on validity generalization referred to the Schmidt-Hunter calculations as Bayesian (e.g., Algera, Jansen, Roe, & Vijn, 1984; Schmidt & Hunter, 1977; Schmidt, Hunter, Pearlman, & Shane, 1979). Subsequent papers dropped the Bayesian label (e.g., Hunter & Schmidt, 1990), instead describing the calculations as a method of meta-analysis. Although methods labeled as Bayesian were not applied subsequently to validity generalization problems, researchers continued to develop such methods. Currently available techniques include empirical Bayes meta-analysis (Brannick, 2001; Raudenbush & Bryk, 1985) and some applications of hierarchical linear models (e.g., Bryk & Raudenbush, 1992; Selzer, Wong, & Bryk, 1996).

This chapter attempts to re-establish connections between Bayesian aspects of meta-analysis and validity generalization. The first half of the chapter emphasizes statistics and calculations. The chapter begins by describing empirical Bayes meta-analysis and linking it to validity generalization. We then extend previous work by showing how empirical Bayes meta-analysis might be based on r rather than the Fisher transformed z. This is important for two reasons. First, it allows the incorporation of previous meta-analyses using the Schmidt-Hunter methods into current Bayesian calculations without having to locate the original data and recompute the analysis in z. Second, it allows us to provide a means for a Bayesian combination of the results of a meta-analysis with a local validation study when the local study is disattenuated for reliability and direct range restriction, which has not been accomplished in previous Bayesian applications.

The second half of the chapter is more methodological and deals less with the analysis of the data but more with the design of the study and the influence of design on inference. In general, we tackle the problem of the legitimacy of inference in meta-analysis. In particular, we consider the commensurability problem, the homogeneity of study characteristics, and legal issues.

STATISTICS AND CALCULATIONS

Bayesian Jargon

Bayesian statistics provide a method for the revision of belief. Before we begin a study, we have some initial idea about the outcome of the study. Then we collect some new data that are relevant to our research question. Bayesian statistics show how to combine the new information with the initial idea in an optimal way. Suppose we are going to conduct a validation study to see whether a clerical aptitude test predicts bank tellers' job performance. Before we do our local validation study, suppose that we discover a meta-analysis of correlations between a test of clerical speed and accuracy and a measure of the job performance of bank tellers. The meta-analysis will contain a distribution of coefficients that can be analyzed to provide our initial idea of what we expect in our local validation. The initial idea is called the *prior distribution* (or just *prior*) in Bayesian statistics. After we collect the data for our local validation study, we will compute a local *r*. This item is called the *likelihood* in Bayesian statistics. Then we can combine the data from the prior and the likelihood to provide an optimal (from the statistician's view) estimate of our local validity taking into account both the previous studies in the meta-analysis and our local validation result. This last item is called the *posterior distribution* (or just *posterior*) in Bayesian statistics.

One of the criticisms of Bayesian statistics is that the initial idea (prior) can come from anywhere, including hard data, hunches, visions, and hallucinations. Thus, two people can begin an analysis with very different priors, collect exactly the same data for the likelihood and after calculating the posterior distribution, reach different or even opposite conclusions. Bayesians have responded to this criticism in two ways: (a) by the use of "flat" priors that have very little influence on the outcome, and (b) by the use of hard data, that is, the use of empirical data collected in scientific experiments (see Box & Tiao, 1973; Lee, 1989). When the latter approach is used, it is customary to label the analysis *empirical Bayes meta-analysis* (Raudenbush & Bryk, 1985).

What Is Empirical Bayes Meta-Analysis?

Empirical Bayes meta-analysis is composed essentially of two steps. The first step is common to all types of random-effects meta-analysis (e.g., Hedges & Vevea, 1998; Hunter & Schmidt, 1990; Raju, Burke, Normand, & Langlois, 1991). The purpose of the first step is to estimate the mean and standard deviation of the population of effect sizes. In validity generalization studies, we will estimate the mean test-criterion correlation, denoted $\bar{\rho}$, which is the population mean effect size. The standard deviation of population effect sizes in validity generalization is denoted σ_ρ, which indicates the variability around the mean that we would expect to see if we could collect the population of local studies and if each local study were composed of an infinite sample size. The local, infinite sample size correlations are denoted ρ_i; these are estimated by correlations obtained in local validation studies, r_i. The estimates of the mean and standard deviation of the population effect sizes are routinely reported in validity generalization studies. The mean and standard deviation are often used to compute credibility intervals such that the lower bound of the interval is used to infer whether validity generalizes (Hunter & Schmidt, 1990).

The second step in empirical Bayes meta-analysis is to combine the information from the first step with individual effect sizes to yield revised, Bayesian estimates of the individual effect sizes. The basic idea is that if an individual study's results are imprecise because of say, a small sample size, then the study's results should be adjusted to be nearer the mean of all effect sizes, that is, closer to $\bar{\rho}$. Results of studies with greater precision (larger sample size) will be adjusted less than the results of studies with lesser precision.

In terms of validity generalization, when we do a local validation study, we gather data to compute a local r. The value of r is used to estimate the value of ρ_i, the local population parameter (recall that there are both local population parameters ρ_i and a mean across all contexts, $\bar{\rho}$). If we collect many local r values, we can use empirical Bayes meta-analysis to estimate $\bar{\rho}$ and σ_ρ across localities and then to estimate the value of ρ_i for each location. To the best of our knowledge, the second step in empirical Bayes meta-analysis has not been taken in published applications of validity generalization research. However, the second step has important implications for applied work, that is, for interpreting the results of local validation studies and for deciding whether to conduct a local validation study (Brannick, 2001).

There appears to be a difference in philosophy between empirical Bayes applications and VG. In VG, one finds $\bar{\rho}$ and σ_ρ in order to compute a lower bound of a distribution of correlations. If the lower bound is suitably large, the analysis is complete, the test is thought to be useful across all contexts, and no further work need be done. The Bayesians will not be content to finish the analysis when finding a positive lower bound, however. They will note that if σ_ρ is positive, and we do not know the underlying distribution of the ρ_i (which is virtually always the case in applied work), then we must admit the possibility of a negative correlation. Therefore, it makes sense to inspect or test each local correlation to see whether the test appears useful in the given context. The best estimate of the local correlation is, of course, that which is obtained using the meta-analysis as the prior distribution, the local estimate as the likelihood, and the posterior as the local outcome.

Analyzing *r* Versus *z*

There has been a controversy about whether to base a meta-analysis on *r*, the observed correlation in validation studies, or *z*, the result of Fisher's *r* to *z* transformation (see James, Demaree, & Mulaik, 1986; Schmidt, Hunter, & Raju, 1988; Silver & Dunlop, 1987). The transformation is calculated by:

$$z = .5\ln\left\{\frac{(1 + r)}{(1 - r)}\right\} = \operatorname{atanh}(r). \tag{1}$$

where *r* is the observed correlation and *ln* stands for the natural logarithm. Proponents of *z* note that it has desirable statistical properties. The sampling variance of *z* depends only on the sample size, but the sampling variance of *r* depends on both the sample size and the value of ρ (Hunter & Schmidt, 1990). Furthermore, the sampling distribution of *z* is approximately normal even when $\rho \neq 0$, but the distribution of *r* becomes increasingly skewed as ρ departs from zero (Hays, 1981). On the other hand, the mean of the sampling distribution of *r* is typically less biased than the mean of the sampling distribution of z (Hunter & Schmidt, 1990). Furthermore, the estimate of σ_ρ will be in the units that form the basis of the meta-analysis (either r or z). If σ_ρ is computed in z, then the interpretation of the result in terms of the original (r) units is a problem. This is because unlike the mean, the standard deviation cannot easily be translated back into r. The recommended method for interpreting the results calculated in z in terms of r is to compute a credibility interval in z using the mean and standard deviation in z, and then translating the endpoints of the interval from z to r, which results in a credibility interval in r (Hedges & Vevea, 1998).

Bayesians have chosen to use z rather than r because the sampling distribution of z is approximately normal. It can be shown that if both the prior and likelihood distributions are normal, then the posterior will also be normal (Box & Tiao, 1973; Lee, 1989). However, the sampling distribution of r will not be normal, and so the posterior distribution in r is known not to be normal (Lee, 1989, pp. 169–172, provides an approximate posterior distribution of the correlation coefficient). However, it may be the case that for large samples, the results will be close enough that using the normal distribution will provide a practical approximation.

A Numerical Example in z

Suppose we have completed a meta-analysis according to method of meta-analysis provided in Hedges and Vevea (1998), and found that $\bar{\rho} = .40$ and $\sigma_\rho = .20$ (both expressed in z, not r). These numbers represent our prior. Further suppose that we have completed a local validation study with $N = 100$ and $r = .30$ (so that $z =$ atanh$(.30) = .30952$), which is the value of our likelihood. According to Bayesian analysis, the sampling variance of z is approximately $1/N$ (Lee, 1989, p. 173). Thus, we can express the variance of the likelihood as $1/100 = .01$ or we can express the variance of the prior as an equivalent sample size (see Brannick, 2001). In the present example for our prior, we have $\sigma_\rho = .20$, $\sigma_\rho^2 = .04$. This variance is equivalent to the sampling variance one would expect to see if $N = 1/.04 = 25$. This is the variance one would expect through sampling error, but not the size of the actual studies in the meta-analysis. In other words, the sampling variance in our local validation study is expected to be about .01, and the variance of the prior is about .04. Expressed as equivalent sample sizes, we have 100 for the local study and 25 for the prior. Note that the variance of the prior is determined by the variability of effect sizes and not the total sample size of the meta-analysis (unless σ_ρ^2 is estimated to be 0; see Brannick, 2001). To find the Bayesian estimate of the local validity we first find the variance of the posterior (Lee, 1989):

$$\sigma^2_{Posterior} = (N_{Prior} + N_{Likelihood})^{-1}. \tag{2}$$

In our example, we have $(25 + 100)^{-1} = 1/125 = .008$. Notice that this could be written as:

$$\sigma^2_{Posterior} = ([\sigma^2_{Prior}]^{-1} + [\sigma^2_{Likelihood}]^{-1})^{-1}. \tag{3}$$

Basically, Equation 3 says that information from independent studies is additive, so that the variance of the posterior (uncertainty) shrinks as studies accumulate. Our prior is already expressed in z and recall that our likelihood is atanh(.30) = .30952. The posterior estimate that yields the optimal estimate of ρ_l is (Lee, 1989):

$$\hat{\rho}_l = \sigma^2_{Posterior}\left[(N_{Prior})(z_{Prior}) + (N_{Likelihood})(z_{Likelihood})\right]. \tag{4}$$

Equation 4 is just a weighted average, which is equivalent to:

$$\hat{\rho}_l = \frac{\sum N_l z_l}{\sum N_l}. \tag{5}$$

In our example, we have

$$\hat{\rho}_l = .008[(25)(.40) + (100)(.30952)] = .3276 = .33.$$

Thus, the best estimate of our local ρ_l (in z) is .33. To compute a confidence interval about this estimate, use (Lee, 1989, pp. 174–175):

$$95\%CI = \hat{\rho}_l \pm 1.96\sigma_{Posterior}. \tag{6}$$

In our case, this amounts to a lower bound of .33 − 1.96sqrt(.008) = .154692 and an upper bound of .33 + 1.96sqrt(.008) = .505308. Now we can retranslate from z to r using the hyperbolic tangent function (tanh). The lower bound (rounded to two decimals) is thus calculated to be .15, the point estimate ($\hat{\rho}_l$) is .32, and the upper bound is .47.

Bayesian Analysis in r

The Bayesian analysis just provided is reasonable when the meta-analysis is computed in z rather than r. However, most VG studies are computed in r rather than z. Further, Schmidt and Hunter (1977) suggested that the local correlation be corrected for unreliability of the criterion and range restriction before combining it with the prior. To date, there are no meta-analyses that have employed z and also corrected correlations for range restriction and criterion unreliability (Hall & Brannick, 2002, provided an approximate solution for the results of an overall meta-analysis). Even if the meta-analysis for the prior is conducted in z, however, there remains the problem of the distribution of the disattenuated local correlation. The sampling distribution of the disattenuated correlation has a greater variance than does the sampling distribution of the attenuated (observed) correlation, so that although the local estimate will be larger when disattenuated (assuming that the observed correlation is positive), it will also be less precise, and thus deserving of less influence on the magnitude of the posterior.

We can use the meta-analytic estimates of $\bar{\rho}$ and σ_ρ in r just as we did when they were in z to represent our prior distribution. To compute the analysis in r rather than z, we must solve two problems. The first is an expression of the precision of the local r; the second is an expression for the distribution of the posterior. Fortunately, there are estimates available for the sampling variance of r, both attenuated and disattenuated (see Allen & Dunbar, 1990; Bobko, 1983; Duan & Dunlap, 1997; Millsap, 1988; Raju et al., 1991).

A Model for Disattenuation

In this section, an expression is developed for the precision of the estimate of the disattenuated correlation. Then we cope as best we can with the form of the posterior. It is often the case that a test being used for validation is also used for selection, thus resulting in direct range restriction in test scores. If we collect test data from our applicants, we can compare the standard deviation of those selected to the standard deviation those who apply to examine range restriction. The range restriction index u_i is the restricted SD divided by the unrestricted SD. Despite the range restriction, we can collect a sample of data for a local validation study in situation or context i, and compute r_i, the local correlation coefficient between a predictor or test (x) and a criterion or job performance measure (y). In the local sample, we will typically also estimate the sample restricted reliabilities of our predictor and criterion, which we will label r_{xx} and r_{yy}, respectively. An estimate of the disattenuated correlation (what would be obtained if $r_{xx} = 1$ and $u = 1$) is given by (Raju et al., 1991, p. 433):

$$\hat{\rho}_i = \frac{k_i r_i}{\sqrt{r_{xx} r_{yy} - r_i^2 + k_i^2 r_i^2}},$$ (7)

where $k_i = 1/u_i$. The estimate in Equation 7 is based on sample estimates, and r_i is first adjusted for reliability and then adjusted for range restriction (Raju et al., 1991). We can now write an expression for the relations between the statistic and its associated parameter:

$$\hat{\rho}_i = \rho_i + e_i,$$ (8)

where e_i is the sampling error associated with $\hat{\rho}_i$. What we want to know for our analysis is the size of the variance of e_i. Raju et al. (1991, p. 434) provided the following estimate of such a variance:

$$\hat{V}_{e_i} = \frac{k_i^2 r_{xx} r_{yy} (r_{yy} - r_i^2)(r_{xx} - r_i^2)}{N_i \hat{W}_i^3},$$ (9)

where N_i is the sample size and

$$\hat{W}_i = r_{xx} r_{yy} - r_i^2 + k_i^2 r_i^2.$$ (10)

If we will not be making an adjustment for unreliability of the predictor (we usually do not make such an adjustment in validation studies), then Equation 8 simplifies to (Raju et al., 1991):

$$\hat{V}_{e_i} = \frac{k_i^2 r_{yy} (r_{yy} - r_i^2)(1 - r_i^2)}{N_i \hat{W}_i^3},$$ (11)

and

$$\hat{W}_i = r_{yy} - r_i^2 + k_i^2 r_i^2$$ (12)

Thus, we now have two estimates (the prior and likelihood point estimates of ρ, and their respective precisions as given by $1/\sigma_\rho^2$ for the meta-analysis, and $1/\hat{V}_{e_i}$ for the local study).

For the second problem, that of expressing the distribution of the posterior, we note that ρ_t is assumed to be normal in the meta-analysis, and that the distribution of $\hat{\rho}_t$ (the local disattenuated r) will become increasingly normal as N increases. If N is large, the resulting posterior distribution should be approximately normally distributed. Bobko (1983) recommended a minimum sample size of $N = 100$ for the disattenuation formulas to be accurate. The effect the non-normality of the posterior will be quite small in terms of its influence of the point estimate of $\hat{\rho}_t$. The main effect will be to decrease the accuracy the confidence interval about the point estimate. Therefore, we suggest that our procedures not be applied to local samples smaller than 100.

A Numerical Example in r

Suppose we have found or computed a meta-analysis in r (see Hunter & Schmidt, 1990) such that our estimate of $\bar{\rho}$ is .50 and our estimate of σ_ρ is .10. Because σ_ρ is .10, our value of N for the prior is $1/.10^2 = 100$. Further suppose that we have conducted a local validation study where observed $r = .30$, $N = 100$, our criterion reliability estimate is $r_{yy} = .75$, and our range restriction index is $u = .80$. To estimate the disattenuated correlation, we would use:

$$\hat{\rho}_t = \frac{(1/.8)(.3)}{\sqrt{.75 - .3^2 + (1/.8)^2 \, .3^2}} = .42$$

To estimate the variance of the sampling distribution of the disattenuated r, we have

$$\hat{W}_t = .75 - .3^2 + (1/.8)^2 \, .3^2 = .800625,$$

and

$$\hat{V}_{e_t} = \frac{(1/.8)^2 \, (.75)(.75 - .3^2)(1 - .3^2)}{(100) \, .800625^3} = .013714.$$

The variance of the disattenuated r yields an N equivalent of $1/.013714 = 72.92$. To complete the illustration, we need to combine the prior and likelihood to produce posterior estimates. For the disattenuated correlation, our posterior variance is $(100 + 72.92)^{-1}$

= .005783. The posterior estimate of ρ_i is .005783[100(.50) + 79.92(.42)] = .48. The 95% confidence interval would range from .33 to .63.

It is instructive to consider the analysis in r without corrections for attenuation. The sampling variance of observed (attenuated) r is approximately (Hunter & Schmidt, 1990):

$$\hat{V}_{e_{Obs}} = \frac{(1 - r_i^2)^2}{N_i - 1},$$ (13)

which in the example would yield $\hat{V}_{e_{Obs}} = \dfrac{(1 - .3^2)^2}{100 - 1} = .008365$. Thus,

by disattenuating, we increased the local r from .30 to .42, but also increased the sampling variance from .008 to .014. The N equivalents that represent the precision of the estimates are 119.55 (observed) and 72.92 (corrected). To complete the computations with the observed correlation, we find that our posterior variance is 1/(100 + 119.55) = .004555. The posterior estimate of ρ_i is .004555[100(.50) + 119.55(.30)] = .39, and the confidence interval ranges from .26 to .52. The estimate and the confidence interval for the posterior using the disattenuated correlation are appreciably larger than those based on the observed (attenuated) correlation. The method we have provided can be applied widely. The relative impact of the prior and likelihood will depend upon the magnitude and precision of the particular estimates in practice.

Implications for Test Validation

Bayesian statistics allow us to improve local validity estimates by incorporating information for other similar studies. Doing so can be expected to yield local validation efforts that are more accurate in the sense that $\hat{\rho}_i$ will be closer on average to ρ_i than would be the case if the information in the prior was ignored and $\hat{\rho}_i$ was based solely on the likelihood. In addition, because information is additive, the confidence intervals for $\hat{\rho}_i$ based on Bayesian estimates will be smaller, and thus tests of the significance of the local r will be more powerful (Brannick, 2001).

The intended contribution of this portion of this chapter is to extend empirical Bayes meta-analysis to applications based on r rather than z, and to apply the analysis to disattenuated correlations. Doing so increases the practical utility of empirical Bayes meta-analysis. In the first case, r has been the basis of most previous meta-analyses, so applied researchers could use estimates of $\bar{\rho}$ and σ_ρ directly, rather than having to recomputed them in z. Because some authors do not provide their raw data, it may be difficult or impossible to recompute the analysis in z. The second case allows the use of disattenuated correlations in r. The distribution of disattenuated correlations in z is unknown, so at present there is no appropriate formula for combining the prior and the disattenuated likelihood in z.

METHODOLOGICAL CONSIDERATIONS

In the first half of the chapter, we described how to analyze data for a meta-analysis. In the second half of the chapter, we consider whether we should do the analysis at all, or at least what the requirements of the data might be. The numbers do not care what you do to them, but practitioners and theorists alike care a great deal about the meaning of the results of a meta-analysis.

Meta-analysis began essentially as a quantitative approach to the literature review (see, e.g., Bangert-Drowns, 1986; Glass, 1976; Rosenthal, 1991). Many studies attempted either to summarize broad literatures on the relations between two constructs using a single number (e.g., $\bar{\rho}$ = .37 over all correlations in the assessment center literature; Gaugler, Rosenthal, Thornton, & Bentson, 1987) or to show the correlation between effect size and study characteristics (e.g., assessment center validity is greater when psychologists are assessors than when managers are assessors; Gaugler et al., 1987). As methods for meta-analysis have advanced, the techniques have become seen simply as tools for research to answer questions posed by researchers. Such questions might be rather broad or rather narrow, depending on the researcher's interests.

Although a VG study is likely to begin with a search for as wide a set of measures and contexts as possible, a practical Bayesian approach to local validation is likely to begin with the local context and a narrow search to identify studies that most closely resemble the local context. Given either vantage point, however, it is reasonable to ask just how broad the inclusion of measures and contexts should be in order to reach the proper research conclusion (Lipsey & Wilson, 2001).

The discussion of study commensurability begins by examining the issue from the perspective of current meta-analysis models pertinent to industrial/organizational psychology. The discussion then examines the issue from the perspective of empirical Bayes meta-analysis.

Commensurability: Statement of the Problem

The commensurability problem is sometimes referred to as the apples-and-oranges problem (see Algera et al., 1984; Eysenck, 1995; Sharpe, 1997). If different studies use different measures, there could be a problem because the measures might mean different things. If they do, then averaging the effect sizes (validity coefficients) across studies will result in a number that summarizes the distribution of effect sizes but that has no substantive interpretation. One could, for example, compute the mean of all the correlations found in the *Journal of Applied Psychology* over a 10-year period. Such a mean would describe the average correlation found in the journal for the given period of time, but one would not be able to interpret the result as the average correlation between construct X and construct Y (there would, of course, be many constructs X and many constructs Y, and this is exactly the problem). Commensurability is not a problem so long as the aim is merely to describe a distribution. However, as soon as one begins to estimate a parameter such as $\bar{\rho}$ or to explain σ_ρ^2, then the problem is immediate and significant.

Our position is that current versions of meta-analysis (and VG) require measures of a single construct X and a single construct Y for the results to be meaningful (see Algera et al., 1984, for a more formal treatment). We do not require that all the measures of X be identical nor that all measures of Y be identical. Rather, each measure of X should be saturated with the same construct, and each measure of Y should be saturated with the same construct (X and Y stand for a predictor and a criterion, which typically are two different constructs, such as verbal reasoning and college grade point average). Because the correlation coefficient is free of units, one study could use height in inches as a predictor and another study could use height in centimeters as a predictor and it would make sense to combine the results of the two studies provided that the studies' criteria were measures of the same construct. However, there would be a commensurability problem if one study measured height in inches for the predictor and another study measured weight in pounds for the predictor. The problem would occur not because of the units of measurement but rather because the two predictors measure different constructs.

How to Determine Whether Commensurability is a Problem

Some have argued (Gaugler, et al., 1987; Hunter & Schmidt, 1990) that the commensurability problem can be examined as an empirical matter, and more specifically that the problem can be examined in terms of the homogeneity of effect sizes. The argument is that if we have different measures of say, personality as our predictors, and different measures of job performance as our criteria, there is no commensurability problem as long as all the observed correlations are approximately the same size (after adjusting for artifacts). In other words, if effect sizes are homogeneous, there is no commensurability problem. However, it is easy to show that the homogeneity of effects sizes is not the key issue here (e.g., Algera et al., 1984, Sharpe, 1997). Suppose that validity studies linking *Graduate Record Examination* (GRE, a cognitive ability test) scores with job performance and age with job performance are combined with one another in one meta-analysis. Suppose that both measures (GRE and age) have the same true validity coefficient of .30 but that they possess different functional relations with job performance. When the studies are combined and the observed variance analyzed, only a small amount of variance between studies will exist. Does this provide evidence that GRE and age are commensurable? Such a conclusion would be illogical because age and GRE have a very small correlation in the U.S. adult working population. Note that the mean of the distribution of correlations (some with age, some with GRE) would have no substantive interpretation (it would describe the correlation between job performance and an ill-defined mixture).

The meta-analyst must make a determination as to the equivalency of different tests serving as measures of the same construct. The key to the commensurability problem is the correlation of the X variables with one another and the correlation of the Y variables with one another, not the correlation of the X variables with the Y variables. Suppose we have completed two studies. In the first study, we have observed measures X_1 and Y_1; in the second study, we have X_2 and Y_2. If all we have is the two observed correlations, one for each study, then we cannot examine the commensurability problem empirically. In such a case, Algera et al. (1984) argued for a strict a priori rules for study inclusion, and we agree for cases in which empirical data are unavailable. However, suppose we can do additional studies or find previous studies in which scores were compared for measures X_1 and X_2 and for measures Y_1 and Y_2. Then we might see relations such as those depicted in Table 12.1.

All of the correlations shown in Table 12.1 are corrected for unreliability of measurement and for direct range restriction. Three different scenarios are depicted. In the first scenario (A), the disattenuated correlations between X_1 and X_2 and also for Y_1 and Y_2 approach 1.0. This is the crucial result necessary to avoid the

TABLE 12.1
Hypothetical Correlations for a Meta-Analysis

	X1	X2	Y1	Y2
A				
X1	—			
X2	.95	—		
Y1	.40	NA	—	
Y2	NA	.40	.98	—
B				
X1	—			
X2	.95	—		
Y1	.50	NA	—	
Y2	NA	.20	.90	—
C				
X1	—			
X2	.25	—		
Y1	.30	NA	—	
Y2	NA	.30	.00	—

commensurability problem. The correlations for both studies between X and Y are .40, so the effect sizes are homogeneous and there is no indication of a moderator present.

In the second scenario (B), the corrected correlations between X_1 and X_2 and also between Y_1 and Y_2 are quite high, indicating that commensurability is not an issue. However, in this scenario, the correlations between X and Y vary considerably between studies. Thus, it appears that the correlations are heterogeneous and that a moderator appears to be operating (to be sure, one would ordinarily use a larger number of studies and evaluate the influence of sampling error in a more rigorous way; the current results are for illustrative purposes only).

In the third scenario (C), the corrected correlation between X_1 and X_2 is quite low, and the corrected correlation between Y_1 and Y_2 is zero. In this case, commensurability is a serious issue, even though the correlations between X and Y are the same for both studies. Consider as a thought experiment a single Y variable paired with X_1 and X_2 in the same study. If X_1 and X_2 are uncorrelated with one another, they might still both be correlated with Y at say .30. But if X_1 and X_2 are uncorrelated (assume linear relations and reliable measures), then they do not share common causes and they will relate to Y for different reasons. Uncorrelated measures have different antecedents and tend to have different consequents. Combining such variables is likely to impede scientific progress because variables that operate differently will be understood mistakenly to be equivalent.

Perfect independence and perfect correlation among predictors (and analogously among criteria) are two ends of a continuum. When the measures are independent, they have different causes and effects (or similar effects for different reasons). When they are perfectly correlated, they have identical causes and effects (at least empirically). The commensurability problem diminishes as the corrected correlations of predictors with predictors and the corrected correlation of criteria with criteria approach unity. When the corrected correlation is not near 1.0, the results of a meta-analysis will be ambiguous at best. Therefore, researchers should search for and present data that indicates the magnitude of the correlations of the X variables with the other the X variables and of the Y variables with the other Y variables.

Our argument, therefore, is that the commensurability problem can and should be addressed through empirical data. The homogeneity of effect sizes, however, is not the key issue. The necessary data involves the correlations of the X variables with one another and the correlations of the Y variables with one another. Other data that speak to the same issue might also be used. For example, one might examine the correlations of several predictors with a well-known standard. Cognitive ability tests might be correlated with the WAIS, for example. Or the results of factor analysis in which several of the measures to be used in the meta-analysis have been shown to load heavily on the same factor might be informative.

It is sometimes the case that the information needed to detect the commensurability problem is scarce. Such cases will require a judgment call. It is hazardous to ignore the commensurability problem and to combine studies simply because the variables share the same name or label. For example, Ones, Vishwesvaran and Schmidt (1993) reported an overall correlation between integrity tests and various criteria, but the different integrity tests do not correlate with one another highly so the overall correlation has no substantive interpretation. Similarly, Guagler et al. (1987) reported an overall correlation for assessment center research, but that average has no substantive interpretation. The commensurability problem occurs in most VG applications because tests measuring different constructs are used, various criteria are used, or both.

Dealing With Multidimensional Data

In a few lucky cases, the meta-analyst can find data in which each study uses the same independent and dependent variables. The study of the effects of aspirin on mortality of heart attack patients is an example (e.g., National Research Council, 1992). In psychology generally and in VG specifically, it is usually the case that several different independent and dependent variables are discovered when collecting data for a meta-analysis. Such data present commensurability problems. Several means of dealing with such data have been proposed, including ignoring the problem, coding for variable type, factor analyzing the constituent variables and analyzing each variable separately (e.g., Gaugler et al., 1987; Glass, 1976). Only the last approach results in meaningful estimates and is therefore the only viable candidate to date.

Despite the commensurability problem, it is tempting to throw all available data into a meta-analysis because either the data on the correlations among the predictors (criteria) are unavailable, or because it is obvious that there are only a small number of studies that would be likely to pass a reasonable test of commensurability. This is the most common response to the problem. However, it is not the fault of the data that there are few studies. The remedy to such a situation is not to combine studies measuring other constructs but rather to collect more data.

Consider meta-analysis in relation to other statistical tools. At one level, we can divide statistics into two broad categories: univariate and multivariate. *Multivariate statistics* are defined as those having more than one dependent variable or criterion variable. *Univariate statistics* are limited to having only one dependent variable or criterion variable. Many univariate and multivariate methods have provisions for multiple independent variables. The data for meta-analysis are typically composed of multiple independent variables and multiple dependent variables. What would be important is some multivariate version of meta-analysis analogous to canonical correlation so that the multivariate nature of the analysis could be properly modeled from a statistical standpoint. To date, however, the most sophisticated models consider in one model only a single X, a single Y, and an unlimited host of third variables $Z_1 - Z_n$ that moderate the relations between X and Y (e.g., Overton, 1998).

The Homogeneity of Studies

The commensurability problem deals with the comparability of studies only in the respect that the predictors measure a common construct and the criteria measure a common construct. Studies vary in many other ways. In VG applications, such differences include the demographics of the samples (e.g., age, race, tenure on the job, sex of the participants, sample size), characteristics of the host organization (including its size, geographical location, age, quality and style of management), human resource practices (selection, training, benefits, job design), type of industry (retail, manufacturing, service, etc.), and the task content of the job. Some authors have argued that most such differences are inconsequential (e.g., Schmidt et al., 1980, 1993). On the other hand, some differences between studies have been associated with differences in the magnitude of the observed validity. For example Brown (1981) found that the quality of management in life insurance offices was associated with the magnitude of observed validity, and Gaugler et al. (1987) found that psychologists produced ratings that were more highly correlated with criteria than were ratings produced by managers.

The homogeneity of studies, that is, their similarity across the entire range of possible differences, is interesting from several vantage points (e.g., Algera et al., 1984; Hunter & Schmidt, 1990). First, we suspect that Bayesian statistics are not commonly used in psychology because it is difficult to tell when one study qualifies as a replication of another. In the strictest sense, validation studies are probably never actual replications because they vary so much in terms of the study characteristics previously mentioned. However, with the advent of meta-analysis has come the widespread belief that studies contain at least some relevant information about the parameters of interest, that is, that studies are in some sense exchangeable (National Research Council, 1992). If it makes sense to meta-analyze data, then it makes sense to apply Bayesian statistics to the same data (and vice versa).

The second reason the homogeneity of studies is of interest is that, with one exception, homogeneous studies (not effect sizes) are of interest for applied work, but heterogeneous studies are of interest for theoretical work. We also expect that effect sizes taken from homogeneous studies would themselves be more homogeneous than those taken from more heterogeneous studies. That is, we expect σ_ρ^2 to increase as the differences among studies increase (but this is an empirical question).

Applied Work

In developing a testing program, the researcher is usually trying to demonstrate the validity of a specific instrument for predicting some future outcome in a specific context. That is, the researcher's first interest is not "personality tests" or "jobs that also involve typing." Instead, the researcher wants to understand the relation between scores on a specific test and specific job-related outcomes. Additionally, the researcher needs to establish the utility of the measure in question and determine whether or not the measure is legally defensible. The researcher might turn to VG as an alternative to a time-consuming and expensive local validation study.

As the studies in the meta-analysis more and more closely resemble the local context of interest to the applied researcher, the greater will be the apparent exchangeability and the easier it will be to argue that the studies in the meta-analysis are representative of the local context. That is, it will become easier to argue for the transportability of the test as the validation results appear more exchangeable with the local context.

The Bayesian perspective on validity generalization offers some additional insight into how similar studies should be before they are aggregated, but the Bayesian analysis begins with the assumption that the included studies are exchangeable. In the random-effects case, the Bayesian analysis uses information about effect size homogeneity, not about study characteristic homogeneity. Bayesian meta-analysis as applied to VG uses prior information and local information to estimate the local population validity coefficient. The weight or impact of the prior depends upon the estimate of the variability of the population effect sizes (that is, $\hat{\sigma}_\rho^2$). In the simplest case, a fixed-effects model can be used, which assumes that the true population validity coefficient is constant. In such a case, the weight of the prior is equal to the sum of all samples in the prior, that is, the total N of the meta-analysis. In practice, this assumption is very difficult to meet, as there are many different things that can differ from situation to situation, and differences in study characteristics may lead to larger values of $\hat{\sigma}_\rho^2$ (Hunter & Schmidt, 2000). However, by selecting a smaller number of similar studies it may be possible to reduce the size of the estimate of σ_ρ^2 such that the posterior is actually more precise based on a smaller number of similar studies than it would be based on a larger number of studies in which the effect sizes were variable.

As σ_ρ^2 increases (the prior flattens), the Bayesian model places more weight on local information and less weight on prior information. At the limit, as variance in the true validity coefficient increases, the local point estimate of the validity coefficient will approach the value of the validity coefficient found in the local situation, regardless of the information stored in the prior distribution. In other words, the more variability across studies, the more important the information from the local validation study becomes. In applied work, the research question tends to be very specific:

"Will this test predict job performance on this job?" In such cases, we encourage practitioners to find studies that are as close in study characteristics to the local situation as possible.

It will often be possible to select studies that use the same predictor or else predictors that are known to be highly correlated (e.g., most professionally developed tests of g are highly correlated). More problematic is congruency across criterion measures. Outcomes such as job performance are often tailored to a specific work situation or are constructed around the organization's specific definition of productivity. Unlike predictor measures, it is impossible in most cases to determine empirically the extent to which specific criterion measures are similar. In the absence of empirical data showing the equivalence of criterion measures, criterion measures across studies should define performance in some common way (i.e., number of widgets produced, sales volume, supervisor ratings, etc.) and should be based on the same basic measurement methodology (i.e. supervisory reports, self-reports, archival data).

Theoretical Work

As we mentioned previously, for applied work it is helpful to have homogeneous studies and to have small values of σ_ρ^2 (homogeneous effect sizes). For theoretical work, however, we would like heterogeneous studies. If we complete a VG study and find that σ_ρ^2 is small, we would like to conclude that validity generalizes and that no further local validation work is necessary because the effect sizes vary so little that the context cannot have a large effect. However, this last statement can only follow from a meta-analysis if the context varies in the meta-analysis and there are enough studies to show that context matters (it is doubtful that σ_ρ^2 can be estimated with any accuracy if the number of studies is less than 25; good power for tests of the homogeneity of effect sizes does not emerge until the number of studies approaches 100 unless σ_ρ^2 is very large). That is, we cannot see an impact of context if it is restricted in range, nor can we detect an effect of context (reliably, with any power) with a small number of studies. If we conduct a meta-analysis in which the context is restricted or the number of studies is small, we will not be able to conclude anything about the effect of context. It is only reasonable to conclude that validity generalizes across context on the basis of a study that gives context a chance to show an effect.

Therefore, if we wish to make a statement such as "vocabulary tests predict reading comprehension scores" across contexts, then our meta-analysis needs lots of studies that examine the relationship between reading comprehension and vocabulary in different contexts.

Mixed Models

Truly random-effects models (such models are also known as *random coefficients* models; Bryk & Raudenbush, 1992) for meta-analysis can be unsatisfying from a theoretical standpoint. The results of such an analysis are estimates of $\bar{\rho}$ and σ_ρ. The estimate of $\bar{\rho}$ is of direct theoretical interest (how well does vocabulary predict reading comprehension?), but the estimate of σ_ρ indicates unexplained variance. In essence, σ_ρ says that there are influences on ρ_i, but we do not know what they are. To continue our example, we might discover that vocabulary predicts reading comprehension ($\bar{\rho}$ is positive), but for unknown reasons, vocabulary is a better predictor of reading comprehension in some situations than it is in other situations (σ_ρ is positive). Although the random-effects model does provide a good description of the idea of situational specificity (i.e., validity varies by context for some unknown reason), situational specificity is also unsatisfying from a scientific standpoint. If it is true that σ_ρ is positive, then we want to explain why.

From a theoretical standpoint, we would like to explain the variance in the ρ_i. Mixed models (e.g., Overton, 1998) that allow one to estimate the effects of study context variables within the random-effects framework can be used to explain variance in ρ_i. Doing so has important advantages. First, it allows us to make better, more precise estimates of ρ_i in any given location (context). Second, it allows us to eliminate context variables that do not have any impact on ρ_i. Mixed models can help us to be more precise about the degree to which validity generalizes across various contexts. There are also drawbacks to such models, including power and Type I errors (Hunter & Schmidt, 1990). In our view, however, the ultimate goal in test validation is to understand the role of individual differences in explaining variance in job performance. Such an understanding will be incomplete if local context plays an unexplained role in test validation.

Legal Issues

Test validation studies have serious organizational and legal implications. Test users must be able to demonstrate the validity and usefulness of a test in the event of adverse impact. Ideally, a local validation study should be conducted to establish test validity, but this is not always possible. Consequently, the *Standards for Educational and Psychological Testing* allow test developers to argue test validity by way of validity generalization. When validity generalization is used to support test validity, the exchangeability of the studies in the meta-analysis with the local study becomes important. Additionally, the methodology used to estimate true effect size must also be sound and defensible. Specifically, red flags will be raised by the use of artifact correction procedures, especially if the corrected validity coefficient is much larger than the uncorrected coefficient (Seymour, 1988).

We encourage practitioners to provide multiple lines of test validity evidence, as suggested by the *Standards for Educational and Psychological Testing*, and urge caution when relying on validity generalization alone as the basis of a legal defense for test validity. When feasible, local validation studies should be completed and the practitioner may also want to consider finding an appropriate meta-analysis or conducting one to add additional support to the local validation. We now offer ways in which empirical Bayes meta-analysis can be used to provide additional evidence of test validity.

Local validation studies are feasible in many situations and are commonly conducted as part of implementing an assessment process. A well-done local validation study may provide sufficient evidence for a legal defense; the defense can be strengthened with a validity generalization argument based on the results of a meta-analysis. These two lines of evidence can be combined to form a third line of validity evidence by mathematically combining the local results with the results of a previous meta-analysis, effectively increasing the statistical power of the local validation study. The beauty of the Bayesian approach in this situation is that the practitioner need not acquire the original meta-analysis data to successfully combine the results. We do suggest that the practitioner be very careful with the selection or construction of the meta-analysis as study commensurability and proper usage of artifact correction is likely to be of interest to the court.

Empirical Bayes meta-analysis can sometimes be used to bolster a weak local empirical validation effort. Consider the case of a local validation study that results in an unacceptably low validity coefficient when the results of an applicable meta-analysis were much stronger. The practitioner could combine the local and prior results to find the posterior, which may indicate an acceptable validity coefficient. Such an outcome could mean that the local validation study was flawed either methodologically or computationally, or that the meta-analysis is not commensurable with the local situation. Or it could simply be a matter of sampling error, that is, the researcher in the local context was unlucky. As was demonstrated earlier, a local study with a small or even zero validity coefficient could be combined with a prior and result in an acceptable posterior validity coefficient estimate. Although statisticians would probably accept this posterior estimate as accurate, in remains to be seen how the courts would respond to such a line of evidence. We suspect that the legal battle would not involve the statistics but rather the data in the prior. How were the studies in the prior selected? How can it be shown that the studies in the prior are relevant to or exchangeable with the local context?

A similar application of empirical Bayes meta-analysis also applies to the situation in which a meta-analysis is available but a local study is either not feasible or has yet to be conducted. The Bayesian approach can be used to estimate the local parameters required to produce a posterior distribution that is unfavorable (the logic is similar to that used by Rosenthal (1979) in developing his response to the file drawer problem). That is, one could compute the sample size required in a local validation study, assuming a local validity coefficient of zero or some other small or negative number, to result in an unacceptably low estimate of the validity coefficient in the posterior distribution. The validity generalization defense would be strengthened if the results indicated that a very large sample size and a zero or negative validity coefficient would be required in the local validation study to result in an unacceptably low posterior validity coefficient estimate.

For example, suppose we found a validity generalization study in which $\hat{\rho} = .50$ and $\hat{\sigma}_\rho = .05$. Suppose we conducted a local validation study and found that r = 0. What sample size would be needed such that the lower bound of the confidence interval includes zero? Note that such an outcome would be equivalent to finding that the posterior local r is not significantly different from zero. Suppose for sake of argument that our study that showed r = 0 was based on a sample of N = 100. Then our prior variance would be $.05^2 = .0025$ and our N equivalent for the prior would be $1/.05^2 = 400$. For our local sample the N equivalent would be 99 (see Equation 13) and the expected sampling variance for the likelihood would be $1/99 = .0101$. Our posterior variance would be $1/499 = .002004$. Our posterior estimate of r would be (99 * 0 + 400 * .5)/499 = .400802. The lower bound would be 400802 − 1.96 * sqrt(.00204) = .31306. It would require an N greater than 10,000 to find a lower bound less than zero in such a scenario. Such a result might be used to bolster the claim that a local validation study could not reasonably reverse the conclusion based on the prior.

Empirical Bayes meta-analysis could be used in the opposite direction. That is, a plaintiff could argue that the results of a local validation study in which test validity was found to be adequate are not consistent with the current literature. Although this scenario is probably rare when the local validation study has been conducted properly, it is possible that a practitioner provides local results that are just too good to be true. For example, the local study may have used liberal artifact correction or capitalized on chance by including only high and low performers in the validation study. Empirical Bayes meta-analysis could be used to demonstrate that the local validity coefficient, r_i, is substantially larger than it should be. That is, estimated ρ_i, as computed by combining prior studies with the local study, may be much smaller than r_i, indicating a possible problem with the local study and opening a window of doubt.

Although we feel that the Bayesian approach to meta-analysis has practical and theoretical benefits, we urge caution in using Bayesian methods to legally defend or attack test usage. Although Bayesian statistics are not new, to the best of our knowledge they have not been used to support test usage in legal cases. Gutman (1993) warned that newer strategies for demonstrating test validity are particularly risky and should be avoided until the courts have ruled on them.

SUMMARY

Empirical Bayes meta-analysis is relevant to the study of validity generalization. We illustrated how to combine a meta-analysis with a local validation study to yield a statistically optimal local estimate of the test's validity. The work in this chapter extended previous work by showing how to use a Bayesian procedure on correlations expressed in r rather than z, and by showing how to combine local correlations corrected for unreliability and range restriction.

We then turned from the analysis of data to questions of study design. We described the commensurability problem, which exists when measures of different constructs are combined into a single meta-analysis. We noted that commensurability problem precludes a meaningful substantive interpretation of the results. We showed that the key to detecting and avoiding the commensurability problem is to examine the empirical relations among the predictors and the empirical relations among the criteria rather than the relations of the predictors with the criteria.

We next considered the homogeneity of study characteristics as distinct from the effect sizes. We argued that studies become increasingly exchangeable as the homogeneity of study characteristics increases. Homogeneous studies are desirable for applied work, but heterogeneous studies are desirable for theoretical work. If we want to know the magnitude of test validation results in a specific context, then we want to find lots of studies in that specific context. If we want to understand the impact of context on the magnitude of test validation results, then context has to vary so we want studies from many different contexts.

Finally, we considered legal issues in the application of empirical Bayes meta-analysis to validity generalization. In our view, the statistical calculations may prove fairly innocuous because Bayesian statistics are well accepted (although the use of r instead of z and also the use of corrected correlations could raise some eyebrows). We suspect, however, that issues around study design such as the choice of studies to include in the prior will prove contentious.

REFERENCES

Allen, N. L., & Dunbar, S. B. (1990). Standard errors of correlations adjusted for incidental selection. *Applied Psychological Measurement, 14*, 83–94.

Algera, J. A., Jansen, P. G., Roe, R. A., & Vijn, P. (1984). Validity generalization: Some critical remarks on the Schmidt-Hunter procedure. *Journal of Occupational Psychology, 57*, 197–210.

Bangert-Drowns, R. L. (1986). Review of developments in meta-analytic method. *Psychological Bulletin, 9*, 388–399.

Bobko, P. (1983). An analysis of correlations corrected for attenuation and range restriction. *Journal of Applied Psychology, 68*, 584–589.

Box, G. E. P., & Tiao, G. C. (1973). *Bayesian inference in statistical analysis.* New York: Wiley.

Brannick, M. T. (2001). Implications of empirical Bayes meta-analysis for test validation. *Journal of Applied Psychology, 86*, 468–480.

Brown, S. H. (1981). Validity generalization and situational moderation in the life insurance industry. *Journal of Applied Psychology, 66*, 664–670.

Bryk, A. S., & Raudenbush, S. W. (1992). *Hierarchical linear models: Applications and data analysis methods.* Newbury Park, CA: Sage.

Duan, B., & Dunlap, W. P. (1997). The accuracy of different methods for estimating the standard error of correlations corrected for range restriction. *Educational and Psychological Measurement, 57*, 254–265.

Eysenck, H. J. (1995). Meta-analysis squared—Does it make sense? *American Psychologist, 50*, 110–111.

Gaugler, B. B., Rosenthal, D. B., Thornton, G. C., & Bentson, C. (1987). Meta-analysis of assessment center validity. *Journal of Applied Psychology, 72*, 493–511.

Glass, G. V. (1976). Primary, secondary, and meta-analysis of research. *Educational Researcher, 5*, 3–8.

Gutman, A. (1993). *EEO law and personnel practices*. Newbury Park, CA: Sage.

Hall, S. M., & Brannick, M. T. (2002). Comparison of two random-effects methods of meta-analysis. *Journal of Applied Psychology, 87*, 377–389.

Hays, W. L. (1981). *Statistics* (3rd ed.). New York: Holt, Rinehart & Winston.

Hedges, L. V., & Vevea, J. L. (1998). Fixed- and random-effects models in meta-analysis. *Psychological Methods, 3*, 486–504.

Hunter, J. E., & Schmidt, F. L. (1990). *Methods of meta-analysis: Correcting error and bias in research findings*. Newbury Park, CA: Sage.

Hunter, J. E., & Schmidt, F. L. (2000). Fixed effects vs. random effects mata-analysis models: Implications for cumulative research knowledge. *International Journal of Selection and Assessment, 8*, 275–292.

James, L. R., Demaree, R. G., & Mulaik, S. A. (1986). A note on validity generalization procedures. *Journal of Applied Psychology, 71*, 440–450.

Lee, P. M. (1989). *Bayesian statistics: An introduction*. New York: Halsted.

Lipsey, M. W., & Wilson, D. B. (2001). *Practical meta-analysis*. Thousand Oaks, CA: Sage.

Millsap, R. E. (1988). Sampling variance in attenuated correlation coefficients: A Monte Carlo study. *Journal of Applied Psychology, 73*, 316–319.

National Research Council (1992). *Combining information: Statistical issues and opportunities for research*. Washington, DC: National Academy Press.

Ones, D. S., Viswesvaran, C., & Schmidt, F. L. (1993). Comprehensive meta-analysis of integrity test validities: Findings and implications for personnel selection and theories of job performance. *Journal of Applied Psychology, 78*, 679–703.

Overton, R. C. (1998). A comparison of fixed-effects and mixed (random-effects) models for meta-analysis tests of moderator variable effects. *Psychological Methods, 3*, 354–379.

Raju, N. S., Burke, M. J., Normand, J., & Langlois, G. M. (1991). A new meta-analytic approach. *Journal of Applied Psychology, 76*, 432–446.

Raudenbush, S. W., & Bryk, A. S. (1985). Empirical Bayes meta-analysis. *Journal of Educational Statistics, 10*, 75–98.

Rosenthal, R. (1979). The "file darwer problem" and tolerance for null results. *Psychological Bulletin, 86*, 638–641.

Rosenthal, R. (1991). *Meta-analytic procedures for social research* (Rev. ed.). Thousand Oaks, CA: Sage.

Schmidt, F. L., & Hunter, J. E. (1977). Development of a general solution to the problem of validity generalization. *Journal of Applied Psychology, 62*, 529–540.

Schmidt, F. L., Hunter, J. E., & Pearlman, K. (1980). Task differences and the validity of aptitude tests in selection: A red herring. *Journal of Applied Psychology, 66*, 166–185.

Schmidt, F. L., Hunter, J. E., Pearlman, K., & Shane, G. S. (1979). Further tests of the Schmidt-Hunter Bayesian validity generalization procedure. *Personnel Psychology, 32*, 257–281.

Schmidt, F. L., Hunter, J. E., & Raju, N. S. (1988). Validity generalization and situational specificity: A second look at the 75% rule and Fisher's *z* transformation. *Journal of Applied Psychology, 73*, 665–672.

Schmidt, F. L., Law, K., Hunter, J. E., Rothstein, H. R., Pearlman, K., & McDaniel, M. (1993). Refinements in validity generalization methods: Implications for the situational specificity hypothesis. *Journal of Applied Psychology, 78,* 3–12.

Seltzer, M. H., Wong, W. H., & Bryk, A. S. (1996). Bayesian analysis in applications of hierarchical models: Issues and methods. *Journal of Educational & Behavioral Statistics, 21,* 131–167.

Seymour, R. T. (1988). Why plaintiffs' counsel challenge tests, and how they can successfully challenge the theory of "validity generalization." *Journal of Vocational Behavior, 33,* 331–364.

Sharpe, D. (1977). Of apples and oranges, file drawers and garbage: Why validity issues in meta-analysis will not go away. *Clinical Psychology Review, 17,* 881–901.

Silver, N., & Dunlop, W. (1987). Averaging coefficients: Should Fisher's z-transformation be used? *Journal of Applied Psychology, 72,* 146–184.

Standards for educational and psychological testing. (1999). Washington, DC: American Educational Research Association.

13

A Generalizability Theory Perspective on Measurement Error Corrections in Validity Generalization

Richard P. DeShon
Michigan State University

In the 1960s and 1970s individuals in the field of Industrial and Organizational Psychology grappled with a major dilemma. It was unclear whether the results of a local validation study, used to support selection decisions, were specific to the particular situation (e.g., job and organization) or whether they could be generalized to other types of jobs and organizations. Ghiselli (1966, 1970) concluded that the validity coefficients varied considerably across settings and therefore demonstrated substantial "situational specificity."[1] If his conclusion was correct and validity results were not generalizable, then it would be necessary to engage in the highly undesirable process of conducting a new validation study every time a selection test was used in a new context. To determine whether validities were situationally specific, a new methodology was needed that could integrate validity results from numerous studies and estimate the average validity and the variance of the validities while accounting for study artifacts known to affect these quantities such as sampling error, measurement error, and range

---

[1]Ghiselli (1966) also highlighted that much of the situational specificity was likely due to sample size and reliability differences across studies. However, this important insight appears to have been overlooked and he is now commonly portrayed as an advocate of situational specificity. The accuracy of this portrayal is questionable.

restriction. To fill this need, Schmidt and Hunter (1977) developed the first set of techniques specifically designed to address this important issue, which they termed validity generalization (VG).

At roughly the same time that Schmidt and Hunter were developing their methods for studying the generalizability of validities across situations in the field of Industrial and Organizational Psychology, many others were developing similar techniques to integrate quantitative results across studies in other areas of inquiry. In 1976, Glass coined the term *meta-analysis*, developed the concept of effect size (e.g., d), and highlighted the importance of differentially weighting results from studies having low sample sizes. Around the same time, Rosenthal and Rubin (1979) were developing methods for comparing the significance levels (e.g., p-values) of results across studies. A few years later, Rosenthal and Rubin (1982) moved away from comparing significance levels and developed a method that extended Glass's technique and generalized this technique to other measures of effect size (e.g., proportions). Hedges (1981; 1982; 1983) extended Glass's procedures to random effect models and developed more rigorous methods for determining the average effect size and the variance of effect sizes across studies. Finally, Raudenbush and Bryk (1985) developed an empirical-bayes approach to performing meta-analysis based on the mixed-effect linear model. These methods were all developed as general techniques that could be used to integrate research results across studies, irrespective of the particular research question.

There are two important philosophical differences between the methods of meta-analysis developed in other areas and Schmidt and Hunter's VG techniques. First, VG was originally developed to address a specific research issue—the generalizability of validities across situations. Virtually every other meta-analytic method was focused on the general question of how to integrate research findings across studies. This subtle difference in focus resulted in a substantial difference in the emphasis placed on parameters in the two approaches. Most methods of meta-analysis focused on the estimation of the average effect size across studies and estimated the variance or homogeneity of the effect sizes as a secondary issue. However, VG was developed to address the issue of situational specificity and therefore, the variance of the effect sizes was of much greater importance. Of course, it was important to demonstrate that the average validity was positive but the variance of the effect sizes across studies addressed the primary research question in this area, i.e. the situational specificity of test validities.

The second philosophical difference between VG and the other methods of meta-analysis resulted from the long history of psychometric methods used when developing and evaluating selection tests. Again, VG was developed to determine whether the validity of selection inferences, based on test scores, differed across situations. In this context, it was well known that factors such as measurement error and range restriction systematically affected the validity estimates. Therefore, VG incorporated corrections for these artifacts when estimating the average validity coefficient and the variance of the validity coefficients across studies. To date, the Schmidt and Hunter approach represents the only systematic attempt to integrate the procedures of meta-analysis with the psychometric techniques dealing with measurement error and range restriction.

The impact of this critical difference between VG and the other methods of meta-analysis—the integration of psychometrics—on the use of the VG procedures and the quality of inferences based on the procedures is somewhat ambiguous. On the one hand, VG has been extraordinarily successful in answering the question it was designed to address. The question of whether selection test validities are situationally specific has been answered so thoroughly that it is rarely, if ever, raised and the generalizability of validity is now the default assumption. The fact that this massive swing in opinion occurred over the short time span of 20 years is a clear testament of the impact resulting from the VG approach.

On the other hand, the utility of the VG procedure for answering questions beyond the domain of the validity of inferences based on selection tests is less clear. In the 1980s and early 1990s, there was a flurry of research designed to develop and evaluate VG procedures (e.g., Callender & Osburn, 1980; James, Demaree, & Mulaik, 1986; Raju, & Burke, 1983; Schmidt, Hunter, & Pearlman, 1981; Schmidt, Hunter, Pearlman, & Shane, 1979). Research on the techniques of validity generalization continues today (e.g., Oswald & Johnson, 1998) but at a much slower pace. In contrast, the number of research papers addressing other meta-analytic techniques is much greater and the rate of research on non-VG methods of research synthesis continues to increase (e.g., Aguinis & Pierce, 1988; Morris & DeShon, 1997). Perhaps more telling, the VG procedure is used predominantly by individuals in the fields of Industrial and Organizational Psychology and Organizational Behavior (Murphy, 1997). In virtually all other research fields, the techniques developed by Glass (Glass, McGaw, & Smith, 1981) and Hedges (1983; Hedges & Olkin, 1985) clearly dominate. The relative lack of attention given to VG in other fields of inquiry might be explained in one of two ways. First, it is possible that researchers in other areas are not aware of the advantages of the VG method. Second, it is possible that researchers in other areas are not convinced about the appropriateness or the perceived usefulness of the corrections for artifacts used in VG.

If the integration of psychometric theory into the methods of meta-analysis is such a good idea, why then are the Schmidt and Hunter VG techniques the exception rather than the norm for meta-analytic investigations? Why is the majority of quantitative research focused on the other techniques that do not incorporate psychometric theory? Why do most users of meta-analysis choose to use methods that do not incorporate corrections for artifacts known to impact the effect sizes in studies? Are the advantages of the VG procedures simply unknown by both methodologist and users of meta-analysis or is there a deeper reason for the relative lack of use?

The purpose of this presentation is to evaluate the advantages and disadvantages of integrating psychometric corrections into the VG model from a conceptual perspective. Generalizability theory (G-theory) is used as a framework for evaluating the strengths and limitations of measurement error corrections in VG. As Murphy and DeShon (2000b) pointed out, the treatment of measurement error used in VG is based on classical test theory and much can be gained by switching to a more modern and comprehensive perspective for evaluating measurement error. The psychometric theory underlying the VG model is sound, if one accepts a number of assumptions that are the subject of some controversy in the literature, but even if this measurement model is accepted the appropriate implementation of the corrections for measurement error in the VG model is extraordinarily difficult and fraught with numerous inferential hazards. A key point in this presentation is that the very aspects of VG that made it so effective when evaluating the issue of situational specificity (i.e., psychometric corrections) may be the source of real difficulties when the method is used to address other types of research questions. Finally, suggestions are provided for implementing corrections for measurement error in the VG model based on G-theory to reduce inferential errors.

The focus of the present discussion is limited to the meta-analysis of correlations across studies (other models based on the Fisher-Z transformation, e.g., Hedges, 1982; will not be considered here). This presentation will focus exclusively on the corrections for measurement error that occur in the VG model and will not address other artifacts such as range restriction. Where possible, the focus is on corrections for measurement error using individual effect sizes rather than corrections based on an artifact distribution. The issues discussed here apply to both types of corrections, but the use of artifact distributions to make psychometric corrections raises complex problems that are beyond the scope of this presentation. The focus on measurement error corrections is not such a large limitation because, in actual use, relatively few validity generalization studies correct for artifacts beyond sampling and measurement error, and in cases where additional corrections are made, their effects are typically small. Before discussing the difficulties of correcting correlation coefficients for measurement error, it is necessary to have a working knowledge of the basics of VG and G-theory.

VG OVERVIEW

The purpose of VG is to estimate the average correlation and the variance of the correlations across studies (situations). If the variance of the correlations is sufficiently large, it is concluded that there is evidence of situational specificity and that moderators of the correlations exist. When estimating the mean and variance of the distribution of correlations, all methods of meta-analysis make provisions for the effects of sampling error by weighting the observed correlations by some function of the sample size, such that correlations based on smaller samples are given less weight than correlations based on larger samples. The VG procedure not only employs differential weighting but also proposes specific methods for estimating the variance in correlation coefficients that cannot be explained in terms of measurement error. More important for the purpose of this chapter, the VG method goes beyond the correction for sampling error to also incorporate corrections for measurement error, range restriction, and numerous other factors (i.e., artifacts) that affect the mean and variance of the correlation.

In the VG model, corrections for measurement error can be accomplished in one of two ways. The most straightforward technique is to correct each coefficient included in the meta-analysis individually using reliability information provided for the particular correlation. Unfortunately, the reporting of reliability information remains sporadic and it is often impossible to correct each coefficient individually. In this case, Hunter and Schmidt (1990) recommended constructing an artifact distribution based on the reliability information that is available from a subset of the studies. The meta-analysis is conducted on the uncorrected correlation coefficients and then the average reliability from the artifact distribution is used to correct the meta-analytically derived average correlation coefficient. The standard deviation of the reliability coefficients in the artifact distribution is also used to correct the observed variance in the correlation coefficients in the meta-analysis to achieve a more accurate estimate of the variance in the population correlations (i.e., situational specificity). This chapter will focus on corrections for individual studies, but as previously noted, the concerns raised here apply to all methods of VG analysis.

Correcting Correlations Individually

When sampling error and measurement error are considered as the only reasons for observed correlations to differ from the corresponding population coefficients, the VG model may be represented as,

$$r_i = \rho_i \sqrt{\rho_{xx_i} \rho_{yy_i}} + \varepsilon_i \tag{1}$$

where r_i is the observed correlation for the ith study, ρ_i is the population correlation for the ith study, ρ_{xx_i} is the reliability of the predictor for the ith study, ρ_{yy_i} is the reliability of the criterion for the ith study, and ε_i is sampling error for the ith study. It is further assumed that the sampling error and the population correlation are independent. Given this model, any variance in observed correlations across studies can be explained in terms real variance in the population correlations (i.e., situation specificity) and artifactual variance due to sampling error and differences in measurement error across studies. After correcting each observed correlation for measurement error in the predictor and criterion (using sample estimates of reliability in the standard disattenuation formula) the variance in the corrected correlations may be represented as,

$$\sigma_{r_c}^2 = \sigma_\rho^2 + \sigma_{\varepsilon_c}^2, \tag{2}$$

where $\sigma_{r_c}^2$ is the variance of the observed correlations corrected for measurement error, σ_ρ^2 is the population variance of the true correlations, and $\sigma_{\varepsilon_c}^2$ is the sampling error variance of the corrected correlations. The estimate of the observed variance of the corrected correlations is,

$$\hat{\sigma}_{r_c}^2 = \sum \omega_i (r_{c_i} - \bar{r}_c)^2 / \sum \omega_i, \tag{3}$$

where all summation occurs across the k correlation coefficients included in the meta-analysis, $\omega_i = N_i r_{xx} r_{yy}$ (r_{xx} and r_{yy} are sample estimates of the population reliability, and N_i is the sample size for the ith study), and $\bar{r}_c = \sum \omega_i r_i / \sum \omega_i$ (r_i is the uncorrected sample estimate of the population correlation). Inspection of the ω_i indicates that correlation coefficients are weighted by both the sample size and the reliability such that correlation coefficients based on smaller samples and measures with poorer reliability contribute less to the computation of the average correlation coefficient. The estimate of the sampling error variance is,

$$\hat{\sigma}^2_{\varepsilon_c} = \sum \left(\frac{N_i (1 - \bar{r}^2)^2}{N_i - 1} \right) / \sum \omega_i, \tag{4}$$

where $\bar{r} = \sum N_i r_i / \sum N_i$. Then, using subtraction, the variance of the population correlations (i.e., the effect of situation specificity) can be estimated as,

$$\hat{\sigma}^2_\rho = \hat{\sigma}^2_{r_c} - \hat{\sigma}^2_{\varepsilon_c}. \tag{5}$$

To evaluate the validity generalization hypothesis, the magnitude of the population correlation variance may be tested using the Chi-Square test,

$$Q = k\hat{\sigma}^2_{r_c} / \hat{\sigma}^2_{\varepsilon_c}, \tag{6}$$

which is referenced to a Chi-Square distribution with $k - 1$ degrees of freedom. Alternatively, Schmidt and Hunter (1977) recommend using the 75% rule to determine whether validities generalize across situations by forming the ratio,

$$\hat{\sigma}^2_\rho / \hat{\sigma}^2_\rho < .25 \tag{7}$$

If this ratio is less than 25% it implies that more than 75% of the variance in observed correlations is due to artifacts and that the true population correlation is reasonably homogenous across settings or studies.

GENERALIZABILITY THEORY

To understand the complexities of correcting for measurement error in the VG model, it is critical to understand measurement error itself. Unfortunately, it is not possible to provide a complete overview of the theory and procedures of G-theory in the space available. A general introduction to G-theory, in the context of measurement error corrections, may be found in DeShon (2001). More complete presentations may be found in Cronbach, Glaser, Nanda, and Rajaratnam (1972) and Shavelson and Webb (1991). The current presentation will focus on the three central concepts of G-theory that are relevant to evaluating the corrections for measurement error used in VG procedures: multifaceted error structures, generalizability of inferences, and importance of the research design for estimating measurement error.

Multifaceted Error Structures

G-theory (Cronbach et al., 1972) is an insightful extension of classical test theory that explicitly models the multiple sources of error that impact measurement. In classical test theory, an individual's observed score (O) resulting from a measurement process is comprised of the individual's true score (T) for the construct being measured and random error (E) that is responsible for the observed score differing from the true score. This implies the well-known relation, O = T + E. The reliability of a measure is then defined as the ratio of true score variance over the sum of the true score variance and the error variance,

$$\rho_{xx} = \sigma_t^2 / (\sigma_t^2 + \sigma_e^2). \tag{8}$$

In classical test theory, this quantity is typically estimated by examining the correlation between parallel measures of the same construct.

The key difference between classical test theory and G-theory is the treatment of error. In classical test theory, error is undifferentiated, considered to be random, and simply reflects any factor that results in the observed score differing from the true score. In contrast, G-theory explicitly recognizes that the error term (E) in classical test theory is comprised of a multitude of systematic, unmeasured, and perhaps interacting error sources. So, for instance, a researcher might be interested in the extent to which a measurement system is able to differentiate individuals with respect to their job performance. If the researcher collects data on individual differences in job performance using multiple raters who each complete multiple items designed to evaluate job performance, then a complex error structure can be estimated using the G-theory procedures.

Based on this design, it is possible to decompose the error that occurs when attempting to differentiate job performance across individuals into the respective sources due to differences in: (a) the average rating provided by raters across individuals and items (*Rater error*), (b) the average level of item endorsement across raters and individuals (*Item Error*), (c) each rater's relative ranking of individuals' job performance averaged across items (*Person* × *Rater*), (d) each rater's relative rankings of items averaged across individuals (*Items* × *Raters*), (e) the relative ranking of each aspect of the individuals' job performance averaged across raters (*Person* × *Item*), and (f) a *residual error* term that represents all of the factors resulting in rater disagreements that cannot be further decomposed given the research design. It is important to recognize that this partially decomposed error term might be further decomposed into other sources of error if additional factors (e.g., time periods, administrators, or time of day) are incorporated into the research design.

G-theory provides a set of rigorous procedures, based on the decomposition of variance through the Analysis of Variance (ANOVA), to estimate the magnitude of error due to each of these sources; these estimates are typically framed in terms of variance components associates with each possible source of error. In contrast, classical theory simply assumes that all factors other than the residual error have a value of zero. Applications of ANOVA that are most common in G-theory are no more difficult to perform or interpret than any other simple and familiar ANOVA (see e.g., DeShon, 2001). Once the magnitude of the components of error variance have been estimated, it is possible to flexibly form intra-class correlations (G-theory coefficients) that reflect the ability of the measurement system to dependably differentiate job performance levels across individuals for a variety of situations in which inferences about those individuals might be made. The formation and interpretation of these coefficients, which represent the effects of measurement error on inferences, is discussed in the following section.

Generalizability of Inferences

When developing G-theory, Cronbach et al. (1972) noted that the assumption of parallel measures used in classical test theory was too restrictive and that it was difficult to defend in many contexts, impossible to justify in others (i.e., rater judgments), and rarely satisfied in practice. Given this difficulty, the coefficients used in most VG analyses to estimate reliability can often be substantially inaccurate (Murphy & DeShon, 2000a). G-theory was developed under the less restrictive assumptions of domain sampling, and no attempt was made to derive reliability coefficients that parallel those most familiar to the users of VG. In G-theory, the levels of the facets of measurement (e.g., survey items, raters, observational periods) used to obtain measurements are viewed as being randomly sampled from a population of potential facet levels. The population of potential facet levels is typically assumed to follow a normal distribution. So, in the example presented earlier, it is assumed that there is a population of potential raters from which to sample and that the scores that would be obtained if all raters in the population provided responses would be normally distributed. Similarly, it is assumed that the particular items used in the measurement system represent a random sample of items from a population of potential items that might be used to reflect job performance and that the scores obtained if all items were assessed would follow a normal distribution.

Instead of focusing on the proportion of observed variance that is true variance (reliability), G-theory focuses on the more relevant issue of the exchangeability of measurement facets. In other words, the focus of G-theory is on estimating the population variance associated with the various facets of measurement (e.g., raters, time periods, or items) that are used to obtain scores upon which decisions will be based. If the variance associated with a particular component of measurement (e.g., raters) is large, then it means that the ratings obtained from different raters are not very exchangeable and the decisions based on scores obtained from the particular set might not generalize to decisions that would be made on the basis of scores obtained using a different set of raters. Obviously, this is not a desirable result for a measurement system and it would not be wise to depend on the particular scores obtained. The smaller the variance component associated with an aspect of measurement, the better. Small variance components suggest that the levels of the particular facet of measurement (e.g., items) are exchangeable and that virtually identical scores would be obtained if a different set of items were used in the measurement process. Therefore, the inferences that can be justified based on this perspective are ones of dependability or generalizability of measurements, not reliability as defined in the classical theory.

By estimating the magnitude of error associated with each component in the measurement system, it is possible to identify the problematic areas of measurement and take action to remedy these problematic aspects of the measurement system. The components of variance associated with the different facets of a measurement system provide information concerning the exchangeability of measures for each facet of measurement (e.g., raters, time periods, or items). This information is very useful in determining how much confidence should be placed in each of the different facets of the measurement system. However, it is also important to integrate the information across the different facets of the measurement system to determine the dependability or generalizability of scores for the entire measurement system. In other words, how generalizable are the scores obtained using a particular set of raters, items, etcetera.

Generalizability coefficients are used to determine the dependability or generalizability of scores obtained using the entire measurement system by integrating the components of variance associated with each facet of the measurement system into a single number (e.g., raters using multiple items across time). The computation of generalizability coefficients is straightforward and involves calculating an intra-class correlation. The general form of the intra-class correlation is,

$$\rho^2 = \frac{\sigma_t^2}{\sigma_t^2 + \sigma_e^2}, \tag{8}$$

where σ_t^2 is the variance of the target (i.e., person) and σ_e^2 is the error variance. In G-theory, the goal is to decompose the error variance into its constituents and so it is very common to obtain more complex intra-class correlations when computing G-theory coefficients. When the data meet the additional assumptions required for parallel tests, the G-theory coefficients are equivalent to reliability coefficients and may be interpreted as such.

How should the error term be represented and decomposed when forming the G-theory coefficients? In G-theory there is a distinction between *relative* and *absolute* definitions of error depending on the type of decision a researcher or practitioner wishes to generalize. If the researcher is only interested in whether or not the relative ranking of persons stays the same across measurement conditions (e.g., time, raters, tasks, contexts, etc.), then a *relative definition* of error is used when constructing the G-theory coefficient. For instance, this would be the relevant error term if top-down selection were used to fill positions in an organization. The ranking of applicants determines selection, not the actual magnitude of the score obtained by the person. In this case, only the sources of variance that contain interactions with the individual (i.e., target) are included in the error term. So, for the job performance example presented previously, the generalizability coefficient for relative decisions would be,

$$\rho^2 = \frac{\sigma_t^2}{\sigma_t^2 + [\sigma_{tr}^2 + \sigma_{ti}^2 + \sigma_{tri,e}^2]},$$
(9)

where σ_t^2 is the variance component associated with individuals, σ_{tr}^2 is the variance component associated with the interaction between raters and individuals, σ_{ti}^2 is the variance component associated with the interaction between individuals and job performance items, and $\sigma_{tri,e}^2$ is the residual part of the error that cannot be further decomposed using this research design. The quantity inside the brackets represents the relative error present when attempting to differentiate individuals with respect to their job performance using a single rater and a single job performance item.

If, on the other hand, it is important to the researcher that the differences between individuals remain constant across conditions, then an *absolute definition* of error is used. Absolute error terms are used when the magnitude of the score is important, such as in a pass–fail cutoff situation. In this case both the relative standing of the individual and the magnitude of the score must generalize across the measurement conditions. Otherwise, the person's score might fall above the cutoff on one administration of the measurement system and then fall below the cutoff on a different administration of the measurement system despite maintaining the same rank order. The error term corresponding to the absolute decisions consist of all sources of variance other than the target variance. In the scenario presented above, the generalizability coefficient for absolute decisions would be,

$$\rho^2 = \frac{\sigma_t^2}{\sigma_t^2 + [\sigma_r^2 + \sigma_i^2 + \sigma_{tr}^2 + \sigma_{ti}^2 + \sigma_{ri}^2 + \sigma_{tri,e}^2]}.$$
(10)

In words, all sources of error contribute to the error involved in generalizing inferences across the conditions in the measurement system. Generalizability coefficients will clearly be larger when based on the relative definition of error than when based on the absolute error definition reflecting the fact that absolute decisions are less dependable than relative decisions.

A comparison of the generalizability coefficients for relative and absolute decisions points to an important assumption of G-theory, that reliability is not simply a function of the test or measure, but rather, it also depends on what inferences the test user is attempting to draw. From the perspective of classical theory, it makes sense (and it is common practice in VG research) to use a single number as an estimate of the reliability of a measure. From the perspective of G-theory, it is clear that a particular test or measure might have as many levels of reliability as it has uses.

In addition to the need to distinguish between relative and absolute decisions, two more complications in the computation of generalizability coefficients need to be considered. First, the generalizability coefficients presented above represent the generalizability of ratings to a single, randomly sampled level of either raters or items. In other words, they describe how confident an investigator could be that the decisions or inferences based on a single rater using a single item would generalize to the larger population of raters or items. Suppose, however, that decisions will be based on more than one rater or more than one item and the resulting average of the ratings across raters or items is what the researcher intends to generalize. In this case, we need to consider generalizing the ratings from one set of conditions (e.g., raters, items, etc.) to a different, but equally large, set of conditions in the population.

Assume that we intend to make a top-down selection decision in a work context (an inference about the best person for a promotion) based on the average rating provided by a single rater who uses three items to represent job performance. How confident should we be that this decision would generalize to other ratings of job performance by a different rater across a different set of three items? In this case, the generalizability coefficient, based on absolute error, would be computed as,

$$\rho^2 = \frac{\sigma_t^2}{\sigma_t^2 + \left[\sigma_r^2 + \dfrac{\sigma_i^2}{3} + \sigma_{tr}^2 + \dfrac{\sigma_{ti}^2}{3} + \dfrac{\sigma_{ri}^2}{3} + \dfrac{\sigma_{tri,e}^2}{3}\right]}. \tag{11}$$

In words, the variance components that include items (i) are divided by the number of items on which the decision will be based. What if we were also interested in the average performance across a set of raters? Assume that we intend to make a top-down selection decision concerning promotion based on job performance information reflecting the average rating of two raters across the average performance on four job performance items. The corresponding generalizability coefficient, based on the absolute error, would be computed as,

$$\rho^2 = \frac{\sigma_t^2}{\sigma_t^2 + \left[\dfrac{\sigma_r^2}{2} + \dfrac{\sigma_i^2}{4} + \dfrac{\sigma_{tr}^2}{2} + \dfrac{\sigma_{ti}^2}{4} + \dfrac{\sigma_{ri}^2}{2 \cdot 4} + \dfrac{\sigma_{tri,e}^2}{2 \cdot 4}\right]}. \tag{12}$$

In estimating the generalizability of ratings where there are multiple raters, each variance component containing a term for raters is divided by the number of raters. Similarly, any variance component containing a term for items is divided by the number of items. When both raters and items are represented in the same variance component, the number of raters and items is multiplied. Clearly, the error terms based on generalizing to sets of raters or sets of items will be smaller than those based on generalizing to a single rater or item. As a result, the generalizability coefficient will be greater and the user should have more confidence in the results of the measurement system for this type of inference.

Second, placing conceptual constraints on the population of interest may increase the confidence that a researcher has in generalizing the results of a particular study to a larger population. For instance, restricting inference to only the particular raters included in the study may narrow the scope of generalization in a supervisory rating study, because raters will serve as a fixed rather than a random effect. The same raters will be used in future decisions and the variance in the population of raters is not relevant to the conclusions drawn from the study. When inferences will not be generalized to a broader sample of measurement conditions, then the variance associated with the particular aspect of measurement (e.g., raters) does not contribute to the error variance and the corresponding generalizability coefficient will be larger. Details on this procedure may be found in DeShon (2001) or Shavelson and Webb (1991). It should also be highlighted that this is not an all or none decision. A researcher may consider an aspect of measurement to be fixed in repeated applications of the measurement system and a different researcher (or the same researcher at a different time) may consider the same aspect of measurement to be a random sample from a population. The two researchers will likely end up with substantially different coefficients of generalizability as a result of the different perspectives on the measurement process.

In addition, the use of these techniques can be prospective or retrospective. In other words, once you have estimated the variance components you can answer questions about how much confidence you should have in generalizing the results of a particular study that has already been conducted based on a different number of measurement facets or treating some of the measurement components as fixed. By experimenting with the numbers used to divide the variance components, you can also answer questions about how many raters or tasks need to be averaged to achieve desired levels of generalizability for future decisions. This is referred to as a decision study in G-theory. One implication of this issue is that the same data structure may result in very different estimates of generalizability depending on the current and future inferential desires of the investigator.

Importance of Research Design

Another important issue highlighted by G-theory is the fundamental impact of the research design used to collect measurements when estimating the reliability, dependability, or generalizability of scores. As an example, consider the modal approach to measurement error in Industrial and Organizational Psychology. In the vast majority of studies conducted, self-report assessments using multiple, Likert-scaled items are obtained at a single time period to reflect constructs of interest. Scales are formed from the self-reports on the multiple items and these scale scores are compared to other self-report scales or objective indicators of relevant variables. Coefficient alpha (α) is computed and reported as the estimate of reliability for each of the self-report scales. Finally, the relation between the scales and other measures of interest is corrected for unreliability using the traditional disattenuation formula or by forming a measurement model using structural equation modeling. What can be said about the measurement error for the self-report assessments based on this research methodology?

One of the central principles of G-theory is that the error term can only contain sources of error that are freely manifested in scores using a particular research design. So, for instance, in this design observations were not assessed at multiple time periods and, therefore, any error due to instability of response across time cannot enter into the scores or the error term associated with these scores. In this case, examining the internal consistency of a measure only provides information on the extent to which research inferences may be generalized across items in the domain of items that might possibly be used to assess the construct. The internal consistency of the measure provides no information on whether inferences may be safely generalized across time, research settings, contexts, time of day, raters, or methods of administration—to mention just a few inferential hazards.

Figure 13.1 presents a graphic representation of this concept. On the left side of the figure is the desired inference space or scope of generalization. In this case, the researcher wishes to generalize inferences based on test scores across time periods, raters, items, methods of administration, and five other miscellaneous conditions that are not as central (e.g., time of day, test administrators, or the media used to present test material). This defines a scope of generalization with a large but unspecified amount of error. Now, if the researcher restricts the research design so that observations are only collected at a single time point using a single rater then the magnitude of the error observed in the test scores will be substantially and artificially reduced. This outcome is represented by the scope of generalization on the right side of the graph. Error due to both time and raters will not contribute to the variance of the test scores. It should be pointed out that this process functions the same irrespective of whether the total error is undifferentiated (reliability theory) or is decomposed into its constituents (G-theory). The key point being made

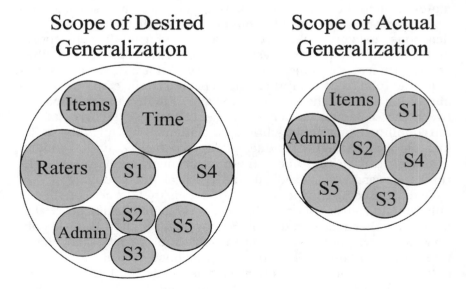

FIG. 13.1. Example of desired and actual inference spaces depending on the research design.

is that if you wish to generalize across a facet of measurement (e.g., time) but you don't include the potential source of error in your research design, then neither reliability theory nor G-theory can be used to estimate the impact of this error source on inferences (DeShon, 1998).

To summarize, one of the key implications of the G-theory approach to measurement error is that no single reliability coefficient is capable of representing the effect of measurement error on inferences. In other words, there is no such thing as the reliability of a measure. Instead, there exist a multitude of indices that reflect the exchangeability of measurement conditions (i.e., facet levels) relevant to the specific inferential goals of the researcher. Further, unless the purpose of measurement (i.e., the desired inference) is clearly specified, it is virtually impossible to identify the relevant measure of reliability or dependability of the measurement process. Ignoring this critical issue results in many misconceptions concerning reliability, and as Thompson (1992) stated, "this is not just an issue of sloppy speaking—the problem is that sometimes we unconsciously come to think what we say or what we hear, so that sloppy speaking does sometimes lead to a more pernicious outcome, sloppy thinking and sloppy practice" (p. 436).

EVALUATING MEASUREMENT ERROR CORRECTIONS IN VG

Now that the basics of VG and G-theory have been presented, it is possible to finally get to the business at hand and evaluate the effect of measurement error corrections in the VG model. In theory, correcting the magnitude of the correlation coefficients for measurement error and correcting the variance in correlation coefficients for the variance in reliability coefficients across studies are good ideas. However, implementing these ideas in a reasonable way is extraordinarily difficult. This section highlights problematic aspects of integrating measurement error corrections into VG analyses from a G-theory perspective. After presenting these issues, an example of an actual validity generalization study is used to demonstrate how problematic the VG process can become if careful attention is not paid to the incorporation of measurement error. This presentation is organized in terms of the two major benefits of correcting for measurement error: the disattenuation of validity coefficients and the reduction in the variance associated with observed validities.

Disattenuating the Magnitude of the Observed Validities for Measurement Error

It is well known that correlation coefficients are biased toward zero when the variables are measured with error. It is also well known that using the disattenuation formula to correct correlation coefficients for measurement error removes this bias (if appropriate reliability estimates are used) and results in a larger correlation coefficient, representing the relationship that would have been observed if the source of error did not have an effect on the measurement process (Lord & Novick, 1968).

However, the practical effects of using the disattenuation formula on the standard error of the resulting, corrected coefficient are not as well understood. Forsythe and Feldt (1969) demonstrated that the disattenuation formula increases the magnitude of the correlation coefficient but that the standard error of the corrected coefficient is also substantially increased. In other words, the disattenuation formula shifts the effects of uncertainty due to measurement error from the size of the correlation coefficient to the standard error of the correlation coefficient. This means that confidence intervals placed around the corrected coefficient will be substantially larger than the corresponding confidence intervals around the uncorrected correlation coefficient. Assuming the reliability coefficient is known a priori, Bobko and Rieck (1980) demonstrated that the standard error of the corrected coefficient equals the standard error of the uncorrected coefficient divided by the square root of the reliability (see also Murphy, 1993).

From a practical perspective, if the observed (biased) correlation coefficient is relatively small then the correction for measurement error will result in a larger coefficient, but one that also has a larger confidence interval and that may not be clearly differentiated from zero. Therefore, from an inferential perspective, there may not be as much to be gained by correcting the magnitude of the correlation coefficient as is commonly assumed: The parameter estimate may be unbiased and larger but the confidence interval around the unbiased estimate will also be proportionally larger.

In addition to this practical limitation, there are numerous theoretical reasons for urging caution when correcting the magnitude of the correlation coefficients for measurement error. First, as I have argued elsewhere (DeShon, 1998; 2001), correcting a correlation for measurement error, whether it is a zero-order correlation or a meta-analytically derived correlation, is of dubious merit in many situations. Typically, it is assumed that the corrected correlation coefficient reflects the level of correlation that would be obtained if the measures functioned perfectly (i.e., if there was no measurement error). But what does it mean for a measurement system to function perfectly? One need only consider the causes of measurement error in a given research context to understand the magnitude of the problem and the folly inherent in asking this question.

Murphy and DeShon (2000a) provided a substantive example of this issue in the context of supervisory ratings. We highlighted that the causes of disagreements between raters were likely due to systematic differences in the behaviors observed by the different raters, systematic differences in access to information beyond the observations, systematic differences in expertise related to interpreting the observed behaviors, and systematic differences in the evaluation of the same behaviors. In other words, the reasons for disagreements (i.e., errors) between raters almost certainly include systematic and important differences between the raters and do not reflect a random response pattern in any way. If this is accurate, then correcting a correlation coefficient for the disagreements between raters does not correct for measurement error. Rather this should be thought of as a correction for lack of knowledge (i.e., ignorance) concerning the factors that systematically influence ratings (Cronbach, 1947). This interpretation is a stark contrast to the typical interpretation of the disattenuation correction. Understanding all of the factors that combine to result in rater disagreements is certainly a laudable goal but correcting for this ignorance when studying variables related to supervisory ratings is not a recipe for scientific progress.

A second reason for caution that arises when correcting the magnitude of the correlation coefficient for measurement error is the scope of generalization desired by the investigator. If validities are going to be corrected for measurement error then it is important that the estimates of reliability consistently reflect the inferential goals of the meta-analyst. Consider the case of correcting a single correlation coefficient for unreliability from a G-theory perspective. G-theory highlights the fact that there is no single number that can represent the reliability of a test or set of scores. Instead, the index of measurement error must capture the specific measurement conditions over which the meta-analyst wishes to generalize inferences, including both sources of error and the number of observations obtained for each source (e.g., number of items or number of raters). So, in other words, the reliability coefficient reported in the study may or may not reflect the scope of generalization desired by the investigator. For instance, it seems reasonable to assume that in most cases investigators hope that the processes studied generalize (or are stable) over time. If a researcher finds a relation between a set of test scores and a set of supervisory ratings of performance, he or she hopes and believes this relation will be maintained over time. However, if the researcher only has access to an internal consistency measure of reliability for a set of items measured at a single point in time, or interrater correlations obtained at one point in time, he or she can not assess, or correct for, the generalizability of the findings over time.

Now, what happens when this perspective is generalized to the case where you have multiple correlation coefficients across studies and wish to compute the average, corrected correlation coefficient? In this case, the researcher may correct each of the coefficients for unreliability using the reliabilities reported in the studies or by constructing an artifact distribution of reliabilities and using the average reliability value to correct the average correlation coefficient for unreliability. The corrections utilized should represent the error present when attempting to generalize inferences over a set of measurement conditions that are relevant to the meta-analyst. Corrections should be based on the inferential goals of the investigator and should reflect the same sources of error and be based on using the same number of desired items, raters, or other numbers related to the aspects of measurement. The problem is that reliability coefficients found in the research literature usually reflect a hodgepodge of measurement conditions, and the inferential purposes of the original research are almost never specified. As a result, it is nearly impossible to connect evaluations of reliability and the impact of measurement error on scores for a particular study to the inferential goals of the meta-analyst.

As an example of these inferential problems, consider the frequent finding that corrected correlation coefficients that are greater than 1.0. The math supporting the disattenuation formula is straightforward: The observed correlation coefficient is biased toward zero as a direct function of the amount of measurement error present in the sample data. The correlation between true scores can not be greater than 1.0, which means that any disattenuated correlation that is greater than 1.0 is simply wrong—it is an inaccurate, overestimate of the correlation between true scores. If it occurs, the only reasonable interpretation is that the estimate of error used to disattenuate the correlation coefficient is an overestimate of the magnitude of measurement error (i.e., the reliability coefficient is too small).

How can the magnitude of measurement error in a set of measures be overestimated? Unfortunately, it is all too easy to overestimate the magnitude of measurement error. Alpha is the most commonly used estimate of measurement error and it is well known that, under the best of conditions, it is the lower bound of the reliability among a set of items (Cronbach, 1951; Novick & Lewis, 1967). Even worse, under very reasonable conditions alpha will be less than 1.0 for a set of perfectly reliable and homogeneous items (Miller, 1995; Novick & Lewis, 1967).

The overestimation of measurement error (or the underestimation of reliability) is even worse when estimates of reliability are considered based on factors other than the internal consistency of items. Consider the common situation in which a researcher wishes to generalize inferences concerning job performance across items, raters, and time. However, the measure of job performance is obtained from a single rater who completes the multiple items at a single point in time. In this case, the effects of variables that cause differences in ratings over raters, and time will not be present in the observed data. In other words, the error due to differences in ratings across raters and time can not be present in the observed set of scores due to limitations in the research design. Even so, the investigator wishes to generalize inferences over measurement conditions that were not represented in the research design. Given the inferential goals of the investigator, the appropriate index of generalizability would contain error due to raters, time, and items, along with their interactions, for a specified number of raters, items, and time periods. The problem is that the sources of error the investigator wishes to generalize over could not be responsible for attenuating the relation between variables in the research design utilized. Therefore, a correction based on a more complex error structure than was present when the original data were collected would substantially overestimate the correlation among true scores. In other words, the disattenuated estimate of validity would be a substantial overestimate and could easily be larger than 1.0.

And so the meta-analyst who wishes to correct for measurement error is presented a double-edged sword. If measurement error is going to be corrected, then each correlation coefficient should be corrected for the sources of error and the number of measurement conditions (e.g., items, raters, time periods) in the desired scope of generalization. However, many of the correlation coefficients will come from studies in which the sources of error (e.g., instability across time) could not have impacted scores because the measurement condition was not allowed to vary (e.g., scores collected at a single point in time). If corrects are made for sources of error that could not have impacted the obtained correlation coefficient, then the resulting corrected correlation coefficient will overestimate the true correlation coefficient.

Rosenthal (1984) lucidly summarized many of these issues when he stated:

> correcting for the artifacts is not the proper goal of meta-analysis. The purpose of meta-analysis is to teach us what is, not what might be some day in the best of all possible worlds when all of our variables might be perfectly measured. Even when the corrections can be used to set an upper limit on what might occur in some future research, the corrections need to be used very cautiously because it is well known that the corrections can yield coefficients that are greater than 1.0. (p. 25)

Correcting the Variance in Observed Validities for Measurement Error

Although the magnitude of the average correlation is important, the assessment of the variability of the correlation coefficients across studies is the most important aspect of a VG analysis. As stated earlier, the variance of the correlation coefficients addresses the central question of the VG model concerning the homogeneity of the correlations (i.e., situationally specific) across studies. What are the effects of measurement error corrections on inferences of concerning the heterogeneity or homogeneity of the correlation coefficients? Unfortunately, the complexities previously highlighted, when correcting the mean of the correlation coefficients, are simple in comparison to the problems encountered when the effects of measurement error corrections on the variance of the observed correlation coefficients is considered.

There is little doubt that differences in measurement error across studies contribute to some of the observed variance in correlation coefficients. This fact was known as early as the 1960s when Ghiselli (1966) reviewed hundreds of validity studies and concluded that artifacts such as measurement error and range restriction were responsible for some of the observed variance in validity across situations. Even Hedges (1988) explicitly recognized the importance of accounting for differences in reliability when evaluating the variance of correlation coefficients across studies. However, incorporating the variance due to differences in measurement error across studies into the estimation of the correlation coefficients across situations is remarkably difficult.

Unfortunately, the VG procedure (e.g., Hunter & Schmidt, 1990; Schmidt & Hunter, 1994) does not provide an explicit measurement error model for disattenuation corrections. This makes it difficult to identify the correct model to use as a base when evaluating measurement error corrections to the variance of the correlation coefficients. To fill this void, I provide the assumptions that I believe represent the functioning of classical test theory in the VG procedure. As a starting point, it seems reasonable to assume that situational factors that might affect the magnitude of the correlation coefficients should not also be responsible for differences in the reliability of the measures. If the same situational factors affected both correlation coefficients and reliability coefficients, it would be entirely inappropriate to correct the variance among the observed correlation coefficients for the variance in the reliability coefficients when assessing situational specificity. As a result, it is appropriate to assume that there is a single, true reliability underlying the observed reliabilities and that sampling error leads to differences in the observed reliabilities. Any other model allowing for heterogeneity among the true reliabilities across studies would introduce the need to demonstrate that the same situational factors are not responsible for variance in both the correlation and reliability coefficients. The following sections describe problems associated with the use of reliability coefficients representing different inference spaces and the need to demonstrate that the reliability coefficients are homogenous themselves before using them to correct observed correlations for measurement error.

Inference Space Consistency. As shown earlier, there is no such thing as the reliability of a set of test scores. Instead, the desired inference space determines the generalizability or dependability of inferences based on the scores. Inference spaces that allow more facets of measurement to impact scores and are based on fewer numbers of observations from each facet of measurement (e.g., a single rater instead of the average score based on 3 raters) result in scores that are less dependable for the particular inference. The implication of this perspective is that the reliability coefficients used to correct correlation coefficients for unreliability should represent the same sources of error and should be consistent with the desired inference space of the meta-analyst.

There are at least two undesirable effects on the variance of correlation coefficients when reliability coefficients, representing a hodgepodge of inference spaces, are used to correct correlations for measurement error. First, the corrected correlations will not be directly comparable because they will represent correlations corrected for different sources of error that either implicitly or explicitly represent fundamentally different research questions. As a result, the variance among the corrected correlations will not be easily interpretable. Is there any reason to believe that a set of correlations that generalize across one type of measurement error (e.g., time) should be equal to another set of correlations that generalize across a different source of measurement error (e.g., internal consistency) even if the underlying population correlation is the same?

Second, the variance of the reliability coefficients that reflect different inference spaces will be too large. If subsets of the reliability coefficients reflect different inference spaces (e.g., raters, items, time periods) then the reliability coefficients will probably differ systematically both between and within the subsets. The result of ignoring difference in the inference spaces represented by the different reliability coefficients will be an overestimation of the variance associated with this measurement error artifact and a corresponding overcorrection of the variance in the observed correlations due to the measurement error. In other words, the variance attributable to artifacts will be overestimated and the meta-analyst will be more likely to conclude that there is no situational specificity.

So, for instance, if the researcher wishes to generalize across item content, then reliability estimates such as Cronbach's alpha and parallel forms coefficients should be used. If the researcher wishes to generalize across time, then test–retest forms of reliability should be used. It makes no sense whatsoever to correct some correlation coefficients for error due to time and others for error due to item content. If the researcher wishes to examine correlation coefficients that correct for both sources of error, then every reliability coefficient should reflect both sources of error. If the reliability coefficients reflect different sources of error, they will almost certainly be more heterogeneous than if they reflected a single source of error. However, it is inappropriate to partial the variance of the reliability coefficients due to the use of different scopes of generalization in the primary studies from the variance in the obtained correlation coefficients and refer to this as a situational artifact.

To illustrate these problems, assume that the true population correlation between two variables is .50. Samples of 1,000 observations are used to study the relation between the two variables in 100 independent studies. The large and equal sample sizes are used to minimize the impact of sampling error so attention may be focused on the effects of measurement error corrections. Further assume that the data contains error due to disagreements between raters and items such that the population G-coefficient for generalizing over scores obtained from a single rater using a single item is 0.40 for the criterion variable (with only one rater and only one item, values this low are entirely plausible). Of course the sample estimates of the G-coefficient will vary randomly around this population value. A simulation study using this generalizability coefficient and Hunter and Schmidt's (1990) estimate of the variance in the observed correlations after accounting for sampling and measurement error produces reasonable results. The estimated population correlation is a very accurate (.499) and 132% of the observed variance is estimated to be caused by sampling and measurement error. In other words, there is a slight bias toward accounting for more variance than actually exists among the observed coefficients but the results are actually quite close to the known characteristics of the population.

Now, what happens if the same example is used but reliability coefficients representing restricted inference spaces are used in the analysis? For ease of demonstration, assume that 50 of the samples only reported an internal consistency estimate of reliability with an average value of .85. Similarly, the remaining 50 studies reported interrater reliability estimates with an average value of .55. These two coefficients reflect a more restricted estimate of error than the first example and so both estimates of reliability are higher than the G-theory coefficient of .40 and both are consistent with actual values reported in the literature. The coefficients differ substantially because they reflect very different sources of error. If the Hunter and Schmidt (1990) VG methods are applied to this data, the results are not so encouraging. The average, corrected correlation coefficient is .38, which is a substantial underestimate of the population correlation (.50). This is not surprising because the reliability coefficients used to correct the observed correlations were larger than the G-coefficient reflecting the actual error in the data. A much more substantial problem occurs with the variance attributed to artifacts. In this case, the variance attributable to sampling and measurement error is 332% of the actual variance among the observed coefficients and the majority of this is due to the variance in reliability coefficients. In other words, the variance due to artifacts is substantially overestimated when reliability coefficients reflecting different inference spaces are used in the analysis.

Do researchers actually use reliability coefficients representing different inference spaces when conducting VG analyses? As an example of this issue, Schmidt, Viswesvaran, and Ones (1997) examined validity generalization for the prediction of drug and alcohol abuse using integrity tests. Of the 124 integrity test reliabilities used to construct the reliability artifact distribution, 68 were coefficient alphas, 47 were test–retest coefficients, and 9 coefficients were used despite having no idea what type of error they represented. The authors clearly stated that the most desirable type of reliability for their purpose was coefficient alpha (item content) but argued that it was fine to incorporate the test–retest reliability information since "the means of the two types of reliability were similar" (pp. 82). In this study, the variance in reliability coefficients that reflected entirely different sources of error was subtracted from the observed variance of the correlation coefficients to estimate the variance in the true coefficients. As shown earlier, this process results in an overcorrection of the observed variance in validities and in an underestimation of the true variance in correlation coefficients.

Reliability Coefficient Homogeneity. Perhaps an even more problematic issue that exists when correcting observed correlation coefficients for measurement error in the validity generalization model is whether the correction accounts for some of the variance due to real differences across situations, rather than simple statistical artifacts. In other words, the situational factors that are responsible for situational specificity in correlation coefficients (i.e., moderators) may also result in differences in the amount of measurement error encountered in different studies. If this is the case, correcting correlation coefficients for measurement error will confound variance due to random fluctuations in reliability across similar situation with variance due to situations, and the variance in true correlation coefficients will be underestimated. James, Demaree, Mulaik, and Ladd (1992) provided the most cogent discussion of this critical issue. As they stated, it is surprising that the situational specificity hypothesis has been refuted without ever providing a theory of situations or measuring a single situational variable. Unless theory and measures of situations are incorporated into the VG model, it is impossible to determine whether the situational variables affect the artifacts (e.g., measurement error) and therefore, whether it is appropriate to correct for the artifacts when assessing the generalizability of correlation coefficients. James et al. (1992) used a restrictiveness of climate example to demonstrate how an important situational variable may affect both the reliability of measurement and the correlation coefficient. They further demonstrated that correcting for measurement error would result in an underestimate of the effect of situations on validities. Similarly, Murphy (1989) argued that the relation between cognitive ability tests and job performance depends in part on the amount of change present in the situation. In both these cases, situational variability is a substantive variable of real interest, not just a statistical artifact to be subtracted out.

The potential impact of situational variables on the error variance associated with particular measurement system highlights the importance of demonstrating that the coefficients representing measurement error are homogeneous before using the coefficients to disattenuate the correlation coefficients. In other words, one must first perform a meta-analysis on the reliability coefficients before using this information to correct correlation coefficients in a validity generalization study. To the best of my knowledge, not a single VG study has evaluated the homogeneity of the reliability coefficient across situations before using the reliability coefficients to correct the correlation coefficients included in the study.

The burgeoning field of reliability generalization provides an excellent example of the analyses that are needed before incorporating reliability information into a VG study. For instance, Vacha-Haase, Kogan, Tani, and Woodall (2001) examined the situational moderators of the reliability of the various MMPI scales. Similarly, Caruso, Witkiewitz, Belcourt-Dittloff, and Gottlieb (2001) examined the situational determinants of variation in the internal-consistency reliability indices of the Eysenck personality questionnaire. In contrast, Viswesvaran, Ones, and Schmidt (1996) did not evaluate the homogeneity of reliability coefficients before using the average level of reliability in an artifact distribution to correct for measurement error in ratings provided by multiple raters. Similarly, the example used previously by Schmidt et al. (1997) did not attempt to determine whether the reliability coefficients were homogeneous before applying the correction to the variance of the observed coefficients.

In summary, when correcting both the mean of the correlation coefficients and the variance among the correlation coefficients, it is critical that the reliability coefficients used to make those corrections represent the same inference space. It makes little sense to correct one correlation coefficient for error due to instability over time and another correlation coefficient (from a different study) for error due to disagreements between raters. The resulting correction would result in correlation coefficients that reflect substantially different research questions and assumptions. At the same time, correlation coefficients should not be corrected for sources of error that could not possibly have affected observed scores in the design used. Finally, it is important to demonstrate that the situation does not affect reliability coefficients by testing for homogeneity before using the variance in reliability coefficients to correct the variance in correlation coefficients. All of the issues described previously are demonstrated in the following example.

EXAMPLE

To demonstrate the difficulties encountered when attempting to correct correlation coefficients in VG studies, the recent meta-analysis on the relation between job satisfaction and job performance by Judge, Thoresen, Bono, and Patton (2001) is evaluated in light of the issues previously raised. The use of this meta-analysis as an example is based primarily on the authors' superb reporting of data and procedures used to incorporate measurement error into the validity generalization process. Most authors fail to provide this information, making it impossible to evaluate the decisions made in the VG study. The Judge et al. (2001) analysis is an exemplar of the thorough application of a confusing and difficult set of measurement error correction procedures in VG studies.

Judge et al. (2001) used the Hunter and Schmidt (1990) VG procedure to examine the relation between job satisfaction and job performance using 312 independent correlation coefficients found in 254 research studies. Measurement and sampling error were the only artifacts considered in the meta-analysis, and the correlation coefficients were corrected individually for these artifacts. In the following sections, the estimates used to correct correlations for measurement error in the job performance and job satisfaction measures are reviewed. Then issues concerning inference space heterogeneity and heterogeneity of the reliability coefficients are discussed. The implications of using inappropriate estimates of measurement error when correcting correlation coefficients using reliability estimates that represent different inference spaces are highlighted.

Job Performance Reliability Estimates. More than 80% of the job performance data was obtained through supervisory ratings ($k =$ 242), but only four of these studies provided reliability information for the raters. When job performance was assessed using supervisory ratings but no estimate of interrater reliability was provided for the study, the Vis, wesvaran et al. (1996) estimate of the reliability of supervisory ratings was used (.52). The remaining measures of job performance were obtained through peer ratings, objective measures, subordinates, students, clients, or customers. For the vast majority of the studies, artifact information from other sources was used to correct the correlation studies for measurement error. When job performance was assessed using peer ratings, the Viswesvaran et al. (1996) estimate of the reliability of peer ratings was used (.42). The reliability of objective measures of job performance was estimated by forming a composite of the multiple measures of objective job performance. Some studies used a composite of supervisory and peer ratings as the measure of job performance. In this case, a composite estimate of reliability for studies using both supervisory and peer ratings was taken from the Harris and Schaubroeck (1988) meta-analysis of this relation. Other studies provided both supervisor ratings and objective measures of job performance. In these studies, the meta-analytic correlation between supervisory ratings and objective measures of job performance from Bommer, Johnson, Rich, and Podsokoff (1995) was used in estimating the reliability for these correlation coefficients. Finally, for the remaining 34 correlation coefficients that did not report a reliability coefficient, the estimated reliability was based on the studies that did report reliability information in the meta-analysis. In sum, 270 correlation coefficients were corrected using an estimate of .52 for the reliability, 13 were corrected using an estimate of .62 for the reliability, 12 were corrected using an estimate of .39 for the reliability, 7 were corrected using an estimate of .42 for the reliability, and the 10 remaining correlation coefficients were corrected using unique estimates of reliability ranging from .17 to .92.

Job Satisfaction Reliability Estimates. For the measures of job satisfaction, an internal consistency measure of reliability was used to correct for error in the job satisfaction measure if it was reported ($k = 105$). If correlations between multiple measures of job satisfaction were available, then they were used to compute the reliability of an equally weighted composite of overall job satisfaction ($k = 97$). When job satisfaction was assessed using a single item, the reliability of a single item measure was used based on the findings of Wanous, Reichers, and Hudy (1997). Longitudinal information was used to estimate reliability for five of the correlation coefficients. The reliability of the remaining 105 correlation coefficients was based on the information contained in the available reliability estimates yielding a value of .74. Overall, the reliability coefficients used for job satisfaction ranged from .18 to .97 with a mean of .75 and an SD of .10.

Magnitude Corrections

The impact of using inappropriate estimates of reliability when correcting correlation coefficients can be highlighted by examining the outcomes of this process in the Judge et al. (2001) meta-analysis.

Seven of the corrected correlation coefficients reported by Judge et al. (2001) are greater than 1.0 with the highest correlation coefficient being 1.43. This is an unambiguous indication that the wrong estimate of reliability was used in the correction process. Furthermore, more than 5% of the corrected coefficients are greater than .80. Could it be possible that a complex variable such as job performance can be so highly related to another single variable, even if that variable is job satisfaction? All too frequently it is necessary to suspend disbelief when correcting correlation coefficients for measurement error.

Many of the very large or impossible corrected coefficients likely result from the use of the Viswesvaran et al. (1996) estimates of measurement error for the supervisory ratings of job performance measures. As previously discussed, Murphy and DeShon (2000a) raised numerous concerns about the use of this estimate in correcting correlations for measurement error. Judge et al. (2001) were clearly aware of this issue but chose to use the interrater reliability estimate from Viswesvaran et al. (1996) and supported the choice by stating that their practice was "consistent with all contemporary (post-1990) meta-analyses involving job performance" (p. 384). Apparently, the use of a poor procedure in the past is justification for perpetuating the use of an inaccurate procedure in the future. Again, this does not seem like a good recipe for scientific progress.

Similar issues can be raised with respect to the correction for measurement error in the job satisfaction measures. Some of the correlation coefficients are corrected to reflect the situation where items are perfectly exchangeable whereas other correlation coefficients reflect the relation that would occur if job satisfaction were perfectly stable over time. The former correction for measurement error might make some sense. The latter correction for stability over time makes little sense based on what we know about the stability of job satisfaction over time (e.g., Weiss & Cropanzano, 1996; Weiss, Nicholas, & Daus, 1999). Why ask what the relation would be if job satisfaction were stable when we know it is not stable?

Inference Space Heterogeneity

The reliabilities used in this meta-analysis support substantially different inference spaces and, because Judge et al. (2001) did not specify a desired inference space, it is not clear which is most appropriate. For instance, the reliability estimates used to correct job performance reflect such diverse inference spaces as supervisory ratings, peer ratings, objective measures, clients, and customers. For a small subset of the studies, a reliability coefficient was computed that reflected the agreement between the different sources such as supervisor–peer or supervisor–objective measures. This source of error reflects a generalization over various sources of information rather than agreement within a particular source of information. In terms of the job satisfaction measures, the vast majority of the reliability coefficients reflect internal consistency estimates of error across items. However, there are a number of reliability coefficients that reflect longitudinal estimates of error (e.g., test-retest reliability).

As previously highlighted, it makes little conceptual sense to correct one set of correlation coefficients for the lack of generalizability across raters, another set of correlation coefficients for the lack of generalizability across peers, and yet another set of correlation coefficients for the lack of agreement between supervisory and objective measures of performance. Again, the meta-analyst should clearly specify the desired scope of generalizability and make sure that the corrections to the correlation coefficients represent a consistent scope of generalization. If they represent different inference spaces, then the coefficients should be analyzed separately or no correction should be utilized. Otherwise, the resulting corrected coefficients will be difficult to interpret and the variance attributable to artifacts will be overestimated.

Another issue related to inference spaces is the number of facet levels used to collect the desired measurements. Judge et al. (2001) made great efforts to assure that the reliability coefficients were based on the same number of observations (e.g., single rater) where possible. Despite this laudable effort, some of their correlation coefficients were based on the average of multiple raters, and they reflected this in the computation of the associated coefficient. This correction certainly makes sense for the case of a single correlation coefficient where the number of raters in the inference space can be consistent with the particular study. However, corrections based on the average of a set of raters reflect a very different inference space than those based on a single coefficient. It would probably be best to leave out the problematic reliability coefficients or not correct for measurement error in the meta-analysis. The complete scope of generalization (i.e., the inference space) including facets and the number of facet levels should be consistent for all measurement error corrections.

Homogeneity of Reliability Estimates

Another issue related to the reliability coefficients used to correct the correlation coefficients is whether they represent a homogeneous set of reliability coefficients. Recall the earlier discussion of the importance of demonstrating homogeneity of the reliability coefficients before correcting the correlation coefficients to avoid the inappropriate removal of variance due to situations. If the reliability coefficients are not homogeneous, after accounting for sampling error, then they should not be used to correct correlation coefficients unless it can clearly be established that the source of heterogeneity in the reliability coefficients is not a source of heterogeneity in the correlation coefficients. In the case of job performance, 270 of the 312 correlation coefficients were corrected using the reliability value of .52. Hence, there is virtually no variance among the coefficients to be analyzed. However, enough data are available for the reliability of the job satisfaction measure to evaluate this issue by performing a meta-analysis on the reliability coefficients similar to the process used by Viswesvaran et al. (1996) and then testing for homogeneity.

The 105 studies that did not provide reliability information used a substituted reliability value based on the reliability data reported in the other studies. If these substituted values are removed from the analysis, 207 reliability coefficients are available for the evaluation of homogeneity. The average, sample-size weighted reliability coefficient from this analysis is .78 with a standard deviation of .13. The Q test for homogeneity yields a value of 4371.03 based on 206 degrees of freedom, which is highly significant at any conventional level ($Q_{206} = 4371.03$, p < .01). Thus it may safely be concluded that the reliability coefficients are not homogeneous across situations, after correcting for sampling error, and therefore the situational causes of heterogeneity in the reliability coefficients could potentially overlap with the situational influences on the correlation coefficients. As a result, it is unwise to correct the correlation coefficients for heterogeneity in the reliability coefficients until it can be unambiguously demonstrated that the causes for heterogeneity in the reliability coefficients are not the causes for heterogeneity in the correlation coefficients. A follow-up analysis of the reliability coefficients was performed to see if any of the coded variables in the Judge et al. (2001) meta-analysis served as a moderator of the reliability coefficients. None of the potential moderators coded in the meta-analysis was a significant moderator of the reliability coefficients and so the reasons for heterogeneity in the reliabilities remain unclear. A similar analysis could have been performed on the job performance reliabilities had sufficient data been reported and similar conclusions would likely have been reached.

One final issue that has not been raised to this point is how to correct correlation coefficients when reliability data is not available for all of the correlation coefficients. In this case, Hunter and Schmidt (1994) recommended the construction of an artifact distribution and that the mean reliability and the variance of the reliabilities be used to correct the results of a standard meta-analysis of the uncorrected coefficients. Given this, it is interesting to note that the process used by Judge et al. (2001) to correct for measurement error reflects a hybrid approach that performs corrections to individual coefficients using a mixture of artifact estimates of reliability and reliability information from particular studies when available. The basis for this procedure is not clear. Hunter and Schmidt (1990) did not provide mathematics to support this approach to performing measurement error corrections in a VG study and it has received virtually no statistical evaluation. Raju, Burke, Normand, and Langlois (1991) provided a rigorous method for attacking this problem, but that does not appear to be the method used by Judge et al (2001). Much work is needed to evaluate a hybrid approach that mixes corrections to individual correlation coefficients using reliability estimates where reported and artifact information when the study does not report reliability information before this procedure could be recommended as general practice.

CONCLUSION

The purpose of this presentation is to examine the measurement error corrections used in VG studies from a G-theory perspective. G-theory highlights the multidimensional nature of error, the importance of the research design used to collect observations, and focuses attention on the generalizability of inferences based on scores. G-theory also provides a rigorous and highly flexible set of procedures for estimating the generalizability of inferences or decisions across the various sources of error. It has been said numerous times in the past, but the lack of attention paid to basic issues concerning measurement error necessitates saying it again. Internal consistency, parallel forms, test–retest, and interrater estimates are not alternative methods for estimating the amount of measurement error present in a measurement process. Instead, they are all very simplistic estimates of highly distinct sources of error that may or may not affect the generalizability of inferences in a particular situation. There is no such thing as the reliability of a test, and combining estimates of reliability that address fundamentally different forms of generalization when combining correlation coefficients cannot support good inference.

Given the importance of using estimates of error that reflect desired inference spaces, it is instructive to evaluate the patterns of reporting measurement error information in the literature. Hogan, Benjamin, and Brezinski (2000) evaluated the reporting of reliability coefficients for tests appearing in 37 psychology journals from 1991 to 1995. They found that 75% of the studies reported only a single reliability coefficient representing a single source of measurement error and that the vast majority of these reported coefficients (66.5%) were coefficient alpha. Only 19% of the studies reported two or more reliability coefficients and only about 20% of the coefficients reported reflected test–retest or interrater reliability. Based on this information, it is reasonable to conclude that researchers are making an effort to evaluate error due to item content (the easiest form of error to estimate) and paying virtually no attention to other sources of error that affect inference.

So, what are the implications of this presentation for correcting correlation coefficients for measurement error in VG analyses? There is little doubt that actual validities are larger and less variable across studies than an examination of observed correlations would suggest. However, unless great care is used when correcting for measurement error, it is quite easy to make the interpretation of correlation coefficients more difficult after the correction than before the correction was applied. It should also be highlighted that there is no statistical solution to this problem. Every single method of meta-analysis that corrects for measurement error when aggregating effects sizes across studies suffers from these problems.

Some general guidelines should be clear at this point. First, when conducting a VG study, it is important to clearly specify the research question and the sources of error to be generalized over. The source of error should be something that is reasonably generalized over in a scientific investigation. For instance, it does not make sense to correct for instability in scores over time, manifested through a measurement process, if it is known that the fundamental process being assessed is unstable over time. Once the sources of error have been identified, it is important to make sure that all of the measurement error estimates used to correct correlation coefficients reflect the relevant sources of error related to this research question. This is much easier said than done. Second, before correcting correlation coefficients for measurement error, the homogeneity of the reliability coefficients should be clearly established. Otherwise, there is virtually no way to demonstrate that the situational (i.e., study) differences in reliability coefficients are unrelated to situational differences in uncorrected correlation coefficients. Third, if a correction for measurement error results in a very high correlation (e.g., greater than .80) the correction should be regarded with skepticism, particularly if the estimate of reliability used is very low. If the corrected coefficient is greater than 1.0, it is certain that the estimate of reliability does not reflect the actual sources of error impacting scores.

In conclusion, the huge impact of VG analyses on thinking and research within the field of Industrial and Organizational Psychology is indisputable. However, it is quite possible that the very factor that set VG apart from other methods of meta-analysis, namely the correction for artifacts other than sampling error, is responsible for the lack of impact this technique has had outside of Industrial and Organizational Psychology. For VG to gain more widespread acceptance, it will be necessary to clearly demonstrate that better inferences result from the careful incorporation of artifact information and that the reported reliability data is precise enough to make this possible. Even if the clear theoretical benefits of measurement error corrections in VG analyses can not be realized in practice, due to limitations of the data, the impact of this technique within the field has been substantial and perhaps that is more than enough.

REFERENCES

Aguinis, H., & Pierce, C. A. (1998). Testing moderator variable hypotheses meta-analytically. *Journal of Management, 24*, 577–592.

Bobko, P., & Rieck, A. (1980). Large sample estimators for standard errors of functions of correlation coefficients. *Applied Psychological Measurement, 4*, 385–398.

Bommer, W. H., Johnson, J., Rich, G. A., Podsokoff, P. M., & MacKenzie, S. B. (1995). On the interchangability of objective and subjective measures of employee performance: A meta-analysis. *Personnel Psychology, 48*, 587–605.

Callender, J. C., & Osburn, H. E. (1980). Development and test of a new model for validity generalization. *Journal of Applied Psychology, 65*, 543–558.

Caruso, J. C., Witkiewitz, K., Belcourt-Dittloff, A., & Gottlieb, J. D. (2001). Reliability of scores from the Eysenck personality questionnaire: A reliability study. *Educational and Psychological Measurement, 61*, 675–689.

Cronbach, L. J. (1947). Test "Reliability" Its meaning and determination. *Psychometrika, 12*, 1–16.

Cronbach, L. J. (1951). Coefficient alpha and the internal structure of tests. *Psychometrika, 12,* 1–16.

Cronbach, L. J., Gleser, G. C., Nanda, H., & Rajaratnam, N. (1972). *The dependability of behavioral measurements: Theory of generalizability for scores and profiles.* New York: Wiley.

DeShon, R. P. (1998). A cautionary note on measurement error corrections in structural equation models. *Psychological Methods, 3,* 412–423.

DeShon, R. P. (2001). Why do we keep spinning our wheels? Using Generalizability Theory to Understand Error. In F. Drasgow & N. Schmitt (Eds.), *Advances in Measurement and Data Analysis* (pp. 189–220). San Francisco: Jossey-Bass.

Forsyth, R. A., & Feldt, L. S. (1969). An investigation of empirical sampling distributions of correlations coefficients corrected for attenuation. *Educational and Psychological Measurement, 29,* 61–71.

Glass, G. V. (1976). Primary, secondary, and meta-analysis of research. *Educational Researcher, 5,* 3–8.

Glass, G. V., McGaw, B., & Smith, M. L. (1981). *Meta-analysis in social research.* Beverly Hills, CA: Sage.

Ghiselli, E. E. (1966). *The validity of occupational aptitude tests.* New York: Wiley.

Ghiselli, E. E. (1970). The validity of aptitude tests in personnel selection. *Personnel Psychology, 26,* 461–477.

Harris, M. M., & Schaubroeck, J. (1988). A meta-analysis of self-supervisor, self-peer, and peer-supervisor ratings. *Personnel Psychology, 41,* 43–62.

Hedges, L. V. (1981). Distribution theory for Glass's estimator of effect size and related estimators. *Journal of Educational Statistics, 6,* 107–128.

Hedges, L. V. (1982). Estimation of effect size from a series of experiments. *Psychological Bulletin, 92,* 490–499.

Hedges, L. V. (1983). A random effects model for effect size. *Psychological Bulletin, 93,* 388–395.

Hedges, L. V. (1988). Meta-analysis of test validities. In H. Wainer & H. Braun (Eds.), *Test validity* (pp. 191–212). Hillsdale, NJ: Lawrence Erlbaum Associates.

Hedges, L. V., & Olkin, I. (1985). *Statistical methods for meta-analysis.* New York: Academic Press.

Hogan, T. P., Benjamin, A., & Brezinski, K. L. (2000). Reliability methods: A note on the frequency of use of various types. *Educational and Psychological Measurement, 60,* 523–531.

Hunter, J. E., & Schmidt, F. L. (1990). *Methods of meta-analysis: Correcting error and bias in research findings.* Newbury Park, CA: Sage.

Hunter, J. E., & Schmidt, F. L. (1994). Correcting for sources of artifactual variation across studies. In H. Cooper & L. V. Hedges (Eds.), *The handbook of research synthesis* (pp. 323–336). New York: Russell Sage.

James, L. R., Demaree, R. G., & Mulaik, S. A. (1986). A note on validity generalization procedures. *Journal of Applied Psychology, 71,* 440–450.

James, L. R., Demaree, R. G., Mulaik, S. A., & Ladd, R. T. (1992). Validity generalization in the context of situational models. *Journal of Applied Psychology, 77,* 3–14.

Judge, T. A., Thoresen, C. J., Bono, J. E., & Patton, G. K. (2001). The job satisfaction-job performance relationship: A qualitative and quantitative review. *Psychological Bulletin, 127*, 376–407.

Lord, F. M., & Novick, M. R. (1968). *Statistical theories of mental test scores*. Reading, MA: Addison-Wesley.

Miller, M. B. (1995). Coefficient alpha: A basic introduction from the perspective of classical test theory and structural equation modeling. *Structural Equation Modeling, 2*, 255–273.

Morris, S. B., & DeShon, R. P. (1997). Correcting effect sizes computed from factorial ANOVA for use in meta-analysis. *Psychological Methods, 2*, 192–199.

Murphy, K. R. (1989). Is the relationship between cognitive ability and job performance stable over time? *Human Performance, 2*, 183–200.

Murphy, K. R. (1993). The situational specificity of validities: Correcting for statistical artifacts does not always reduce the trans-situational variability of correlation coefficients. *International Journal of Selection and Assessment, 1*, 158–162.

Murphy, K. R. (1997). Meta-analysis and validity generalization. In N. Anderson & P. Herriot (Eds.), *International handbook of selection and assessment* (Vol. 2, pp. –). New York: Wiley.

Murphy, K., & DeShon, R. (2000a). Inter-rater correlations do not estimate the reliability of job performance ratings. *Personnel Psychology, 53*, 873–900.

Murphy, K., & DeShon, R. (2000b). Progress in psychometrics: Can industrial and organizational psychology catch up? *Personnel Psychology, 53*, 913–924.

Novick, M. R., & Lewis, C. (1967). Coefficient alpha and the reliability of composite measurements. *Psychometrika, 32*, 1–13.

Oswald, F. L., & Johnson, J. W. (1998). On the robustness, bias, and stability of statistics from meta-analysis of correlation coefficients: Some initial Monte Carlo findings. *Journal of Applied Psychology, 83*, 164–178.

Raju, N. S., & Burke, M. J. (1983). Two new approaches for studying validity generalization. *Journal of Applied Psychology, 68*, 382–395.

Raju, N. S., Burke, M. J., Normand, J., & Langlois, G. M. (1991). A new meta-analytic approach. *Journal of Applied Psychology, 76*, 432–446.

Raudenbush, S. W., & Bryk, A. S. (1985). Empirical Bayes meta-analysis. *Journal of Educational Statistics, 10*, 75–98.

Rosenthal, R. (1984). *Meta-analysis procedures for social research*. Beverly Hills, CA: Sage.

Rosenthal, R., & Rubin, D. B. (1979). Comparing significance levels if independent studies. *Psychological Bulletin, 86*, 1165–1168.

Rosenthal, R., & Rubin, D. B. (1982). Comparing effect sizes of independent studies. *Psychological Bulletin, 92*, 500–504.

Schmidt, F. L., & Hunter, J. E. (1977). Development of a general solution to the problem of validity generalization. *Journal of Applied Psychology, 62*, 643–661.

Schmidt, F. L., Hunter, J. E., & Pearlman, K. (1981). Task differences as moderators of aptitude test validity in selection: A red herring. *Journal of Applied Psychology, 66*, 166–185.

Schmidt, F. L., Hunter, J. E., Pearlman, K., & Shane, G. S. (1979). Further tests of the Schmidt–Hunter Bayesian validity generalization procedure. *Personnel Psychology, 32*, 257–281.

Schmidt, F. L., Viswesvaran C., & Ones, D. S. (1997). Validity of integrity tests for predicting drug and alcohol abuse: A meta-analysis. In W. J. Bukovski (Ed.), *Meta-analysis of drug abuse prevention programs* (pp. 69–95). Rockville, MD: U.S. Dept of Health and Human Services, National Institute of Drug Abuse.

Shavelson, R. J., & Webb, N. M. (1991). *Generalizability theory: A primer*. Newbury Park, CA: Sage.

Thompson, B. (1992). Two and one-half decades of leadership in measurement and evaluation. *Journal of Counseling and Development, 70*, 434–438.

Vacha-Haase, T., Kogan, L. R., Tani, C. R., & Woodall, R. R. A. (2001). Reliability generalization: Exploring variation of reliability coefficients of the MMPI clinical scale scores. *Educational and Psychological Measurement, 61*, 45–59.

Viswesvaran, C., Ones, D. S., & Schmidt, F. L. (1996). Comparative analysis of the reliability of job performance ratings. *Journal of Applied Psychology, 81*, 557–574.

Wanous, J. P., Reichers, A. E., & Hudy, M. J. (1997). Overall job satisfaction: How good are single-item measures? *Journal of Applied Psychology, 82*, 247–252.

Weiss, H. M., & Cropanzano, R. (1996). Affective events theory: A theoretical discussion of the structure, causes, and consequences of affective experiences at work. In B. M. Staw & L. L. Cummings (Eds.), *Research in Organizational Behavior* (Vol. 18, pp. 1–74). Greenwich, CT: JAI.

Weiss, H. M., Nicholas, J. P., & Daus, C. S. (1999). An examination of the joint effects of affective experiences and job beliefs on job satisfaction and variations in affective experiences over time. *Organizational Behavior & Human Decision Processes, 78*, 1–24.

14

The Past, Present, and Future of Validity Generalization

Kevin R. Murphy
Daniel A. Newman
Pennsylvania State University

Chapters 1 through 13 of this volume document an eventful past, a vibrant present, and an intriguing future for validity generalization. The aim of this chapter is to highlight some important themes running through this book and the literature on which these chapters are based. The aim is not to provide a comprehensive history of validity generalization (VG), a complete picture of its present status, or a detailed road map of where this field is heading; chapters 1 through 13 do a better job than could possibly be done here. Rather, the aim is to extract and discuss some of the key issues in the development and application of VG analyses, and to make some suggestions about important issues that remain to be resolved.

THE PAST

The history of VG research has followed a similar path to that carved out by other methodological advances, most notably the application of factor analysis in the earlier history of psychology. When factor analysis first burst onto the scene, there was a mad rush to factor analyze as many things as possible (mainly in the 1930s to 1950s), followed by a long period of discussion of alternate analytic methods and decision rules for interpreting factor analyses (1960s and 1970s), followed by a long period (extending into the present) of widespread acceptance of this method, occasional misuse or misinterpretation of factor analytic results, and occasional reminders to potential users of what factor analysis can and cannot do. Research and application in the area of VG seems to be tracing a similar trajectory.

Following the introduction of VG, there was a flurry of excitement and a rush to apply this method to a wide range of datasets (e.g., Brown, 1981; Callender & Osburn, 1981; Pearlman, Schmidt, & Hunter, 1980; Schmidt, Gast-Rosenberg, & Hunter, 1980; Schmidt, Hunter, & Caplan, 1981; Schmidt, Hunter, Pearlman, & Shane, 1979). Then came controversy, discussion, and some sense of resolution in the professional community about what this method could and could not do (e.g., the "Forty Questions," *Personnel Psychology*, Schmidt et al., 1985; Hunter & Schmidt, 1990). Finally, a set of refinements, new approaches, and tests of robustness appeared (e.g., Brannick, 2001; Millsap, 1988, 1989; Oswald & Johnson, 1998; Schmidt et al., 1993). At present, the method is widely used and widely appreciated, but it is also clearly understood that VG is not a panacea (Algera, Jansen, Roe, & Vijn, 1984; Bobko & Stone-Romero, 1998).

Over the last 25 years, hundreds of papers dealing directly or indirectly with VG have been published, and it would be difficult to produce a comprehensive summary of all of the issues covered. We will not even try. Rather, we will comment on the two issues that have dominated the methodological literature in validity generalization: (1) attempts to extend and develop new methods of estimating VG parameters, and (2) attempts to identify or rule out moderator variables in validation research.

A Proliferation of Estimation Procedures

Schmidt and Hunter (1977) laid out procedures for estimating the statistical and psychometric corrections that distinguish VG from the broader family of meta-analytic procedures used in other areas of social and behavioral science. Many of the VG papers published since then have featured or included corrections, refinements, or extensions of this original model. Some refinements have involved differential weighting of study information (e.g., weighting by sample size; Pearlman et al., 1980), whereas others involved better estimation of specific components of the basic VG model (Millsap, 1988). Others provided possible solutions for problems like the presence of non-Pearson r values in validity distributions (e.g., some studies report biserial or tetrachoric correlations; Schmidt et al., 1993). The theme of many of the papers in this tradition has been that by cleaning up specific components of the original Schmidt and Hunter (1977) equations, it should be possible to develop increasingly accurate estimates of the mean and the variance of the distribution of validities being studied.

Callender and Osburn (1980) proposed a multiplicative model that was, in some sense, a harbinger of things to come. This model introduced a set of terms into equations for the variance in validities that might, given specific sets of assumptions and patterns of data, lead to more accurate estimation. Variations on this and other models followed in short order, ranging from Schmidt, Gast-Rosenberg, and Hunter's (1980) interactive model to Callender, Osburn, Greener, and Ashworth's (1982) multiplicative independent model. By the time Callender and Osburn (1982) appeared, there were already at least four competing models, each providing its own estimate of the variance in validities due to different statistical artifacts.

Raju and Burke (1983) added two new estimation procedures to the mix, each based on Taylor Series approximations. Raju and his colleagues (Raju, Fralicx, & Steinhaus, 1986; Raju, Pappas, & Williams, 1989) extended VG-like models to covariance and regression slope models, whereas Thomas (1990) demonstrated the application of mixture models to the problem of validity generalization. Erez, Bloom, and Wells (1996) illustrated the advantages and application of random effect models. Oswald and Johnson (1998) examined the effect of violations of common statistical assumptions on the robustness and accuracy of various estimation procedures.

The proliferation of VG models led to a large number of Monte Carlo studies comparing models, or evaluating conditions under which specific models performed well or poorly, which in turn often led to commentaries, rebuttals, and exchanges of opinion (exemplars of this somewhat tedious literature include Burke, Raju, & Pearlman, 1986; Callender & Osburn, 1982; Hunter, Schmidt, & Pearlman, 1982). A number of well-conceived and well-executed studies have been carried out, and proponents of different models often argue that their own favorite has fared better than others. On the whole, however, it does not seem like variations in models seem to make all that much difference; in many contexts, especially when average sample sizes are small to moderate, "bare bones" approaches that make minimal corrections work about as well as their most complex rivals. The only important finding that emerges consistently from the literature is that there seem to be many domains where fixed effects models (e.g., Hedges, 1988) are not adequate, because of substantial variation in the levels of validity across settings.

Beyond this, it is hard to see how the proliferation of VG and VG-like models in the 20 years that followed the publication of Schmidt and Hunter (1977) has really accomplished much.

This entire literature has the look and feel of a Rube Goldberg contraption. That is, one refinement has been piled on another, leading to an increasingly complex and unwieldy set of equations for estimating VG parameters. This then led to dueling Monte Carlo studies and to increasingly arcane commentaries and rebuttals (Algera, Jansen, Roe, & Vijn, 1984; Callender & Osburn, 1981; Law, 1992; Osburn & Callender, 1990; Schmitt & Noe, 1986). Although many of these studies attacked important topics, often with considerable ingenuity and analytic skill, the overall thrust of this set of papers was nevertheless somewhat depressing. Although they reported and debated progress in validity generalization, it was hard to sustain the impression that the methodological work in this area was really going anywhere.

In this context, Raju and Drasgow (chap. 9, this volume) is like a breath of fresh air. Unlike earlier papers that attempted to patch holes in the original set of VG equations, Raju and Drasgow have taken on the formidable task of putting the whole affair on a solid mathematical footing. It has long been argued (e.g., Thomas, 1988, 1990) that the failure to develop a coherent mathematical model for VG has hindered progress in this area. Raju and Drasgow's chapter provides the first set of mathematically consistent equations for attacking the entire range of questions that are common in VG research.

Detecting Moderators

It is now obvious that validity is more generalizable than a simple examination of observed correlation coefficients would suggest. If Schmidt and Hunter (1977) had done nothing more than remind us that the results of small-sample validity studies *should* vary considerably and that this variance might not indicate meaningful differences in the way tests work from setting to setting, their paper would have made a major contribution. Their analyses have turned the question around. Instead of asking whether there is any consistency in validity, personnel psychologists now wrestle with the question of whether there are any meaningful differences in validity across jobs, organizations, settings, and so forth. Even small changes in validity from one setting to the next can make a practical difference (Brown, 1981), so the question of what variables, if any, moderate the validity of tests and other selection instruments has been an important one throughout the history of VG research.

Schmidt and Hunter (1977) suggested that if the residual variance in a distribution of validities (after having adjusted for statistical artifacts) is zero or near zero, it is reasonable to infer that validity is essentially constant across situations. Schmidt, Hunter, Pearlman, and Shane (1979) proposed a simpler and more lenient decision rule, that the hypothesis of situational specificity could be rejected if statistical artifacts accounted for 75% or more of the variance in validity coefficients. In part this was based on the assumption, which the authors have always admitted was untestable, that other artifacts would probably explain what little variance remained once the main VG corrections had wiped away the bulk of the observed variance in validity. In part, this assumption probably reflects the standards applied psychologists have been conditioned to pay attention to. In just about any context where applied psychologist work, accounting for 75% of the variance would be an noteworthy event. If VG models can meet this very high standard simply by taking sampling error and a few other minor artifactual sources of variance into account, this would be big news indeed, and it might support the inference that there was little real variability in validities.

The 75% rule has been the focus of a substantial body of research, and on the whole has probably been a source for confusion about the generalizability of validity rather than a workable and accurate rule of thumb. There is clear evidence that the 75% rule lacks statistical power, and that it leads to incorrect and indefensible inferences about the variability in validity across studies (Callender & Osburn, 1981; James, Demaree, & Mulaik, 1986; James, Demaree, Mulaik, & Mumford, 1988; Kemery, Mossholder, & Roth, 1987; Osburn, Callender, Greener, & Ashworth, 1983; Paese, & Switzer, 1988; Sackett, Harris, & Orr, 1986; Switzer, Paese, & Drasgow, 1992; see, however, Schmidt, Hunter, & Raju, 1988). In the first few years of VG, proponents of this method were likely to conclude that validity was essentially constant across jobs, settings, studies, etcetera. It is now clear that this conclusion says more about the 75% decision rule (which biases investigators to conclude that no differences in validity exist) than about the data. The more important question that has emerged in this literature is the definition of moderators versus artifacts. James, Demaree, Mulaik, and Ladd (1992) noted that one person's moderator might be another person's artifact and demonstrated how meaningful differences across situations might lead to variability in validities we would normally sweep away as statistical artifacts. This title suggested possible routes for developing meaningful moderator hypotheses, but to date, there have been few successful efforts in this area.

Like so many other aspects of the VG model, the early connection between VG and studies of the validity of cognitive ability tests set the stage for many misleading assumptions about moderator research. The studies that were most intensely analyzed in the early years of VG had two features in common (i.e. small sample size and variable results). This led to the assumption that most of the variance in validities was likely to be due to simple sampling error. Against this background, Schmitt, Gooding, Noe, and Kirsch's (1984) analysis, which suggested that sampling error might not explain such a large percentage of variance seemed to signal an important change in VG research. What became clear after the publication of this title, and the commentaries that followed, was that the assumptions that the validity of cognitive ability tests varies considerably across settings, and that simple sampling error explains virtually all of this variability were both themselves artifacts of a large but fairly lousy database. Schmidt and Hunter (1977) showed that if you attempted to draw conclusions about the validity of cognitive ability tests on the basis of a set of studies with an average N in the 1960s and 1970s, bad things would happen. Schmitt et al. (1984) showed that validity studies published in leading journals (which typically had much larger Ns) did not produce such inconsistent results. They also showed that variation in outcomes of published validity studies (small though it may be) was not simply a matter of sampling error.

There is an important lesson to be learned by comparing Schmitt et al. (1984) with the majority of the VG studies published prior to 1984. The sorts of conclusions you reach about the level of validity, the consistency of validity across studies, and the importance of sampling error in interpreting the results of those studies depends substantially on the quality of the original database. The 75% rule might have been acceptable for the studies that were the focus of the earliest VG research, but the conclusion that validities vary greatly and that sampling error explains almost of this variation turned out to be an artifact of the data, not a unifying principle for understanding primary research studies.

THE PRESENT

As in the previous section, there are a number of themes that could be chosen to summarize the present status of validity generalization, and rather than attempting a comprehensive coverage, the focus is on three broad issues that seem especially relevant for understanding the current status of validity generalization: (1) the success story of VG, (2) the revival of Bayesian thinking in meta-analysis, and (3) the need to define more precisely exactly what inferences you are attempting to make in a VG analysis.

The Success of VG

Methodological advances are sometimes like shooting stars. They usually appear suddenly, shine brightly a for a while, and they go away. Schmidt and Hunter (chap. 2, this volume) noted that validity generalization methods, which are now more than 25 years old, have certainly survived the test of time. Rothstein (chap. 5, this volume) catalogs the extraordinary breadth and popularity of this method. In applied psychology, it is rare to encounter a quantitative summary of the research literature that does not rely heavily (if not exclusively) on the methods developed by Schmidt, Hunter, and their colleagues.

The accomplishments of VG research have been documented in Chapters 1 through 13, and they are remarkable. First, this research has changed the face of personnel selection (Murphy, 2000). Prior to 1977, personnel selection systems were something like a vintage automobile. They were custom built from the ground up, relying on procedures that consumed lots of time and money, and nobody was sure whether they would really work. Psychologists armed with the results of VG research have a pretty good idea how various types of tests and assessment methods are likely to work in specific populations, and the broad principles for building a valid selection system seem simpler and more robust than they were prior to VG.

Second, VG has revitalized whole areas of inquiry. Twenty-five years ago, it would have been hard to find more than a handful of personnel psychologists interested in and optimistic about the use of personality inventories in predicting job performance. Now, the relation between personality and behavior in organizations is one of the most widely studied topics in applied psychology. The revival of interest in personality is the direct result of a number of meta-analyses that applied VG methods to the body of research linking personality and job performance (see chaps. 7 and 8, this volume).

The Reemergence of Bayesian Approaches

Bayesian statistics distinguish between prior and posterior outcomes or results. Priors, defined most broadly, describe your knowledge or beliefs before the results of a study are obtained, whereas posterior outcomes are based on a combination of what you knew before doing the study and what you learned on the basis of a study. The focus of Bayes theorem is on the best way of combining what you knew before conducting a study with what you learned on the basis of that study. One of the critical factors in Schmidt and Hunter's (1977) critique of then-current techniques for interpreting validity research was that researchers tended to ignore the body of available theory and research when interpreting the results of their own validation studies. One obvious way to correct this weakness would be to adopt a Bayesian approach to interpreting validities.

Several early validity generalization titles described this model as Bayesian. For example, Schmidt and Hunter (1977) noted that the best estimate of the validity of a test is obtained from a posterior distribution rather than from the observed validity coefficients, and that the prior distribution of validities contained essential information for evaluating the hypothesis that validities vary across situations. Schmidt et al. (1979) included suggestions for obtaining a better estimate of the Bayesian prior distribution, and Pearlman et al. (1980) included suggestions for further refinements. After about 1980, the term *Bayesian* rarely appeared in the validity generalization literature, at least until the publication of Brannick (2001), who showed how to estimate validity in any particular context, given a particular set of priors and the results of a local validation study. One question that is worth considering is why the Bayesian emphasis dropped from the vocabulary of VG researchers for so long and what implications its return might have.

One possible explanation for the long disappearance of explicitly Bayesian thinking in VG research is that VG models have generally been Bayesian in spirit rather than in fact. That is, Schmidt and Hunter (1977), Schmidt et al. (1979), and Pearlman et al. (1980) all use Bayesian concepts and terms, but none provide actual estimates of posterior validities. In our judgment this failure to carry out true Bayesian analyses says more about the researchers' beliefs about the prior distribution of validity coefficients rather than any specific distaste for Bayesian estimation procedures. In particular, proponents of VG have long argued that there is little or no real variation in the distribution of validity coefficients when cognitive ability tests are used to predict job performance, especially if jobs are equated for complexity (Gutenberg, Arvey, Osburn, & Jenneret, 1983). If this is true, one implication is that the prior distribution of validity coefficients probably has a very small variance. If the results of several hundred previous validity study produce near-constant estimates of validity (i.e., near-uniform priors), Bayes theorem suggests that your best estimate of posterior validity will match the prior, almost regardless of the results of your own validity study. In other words, if the priors are essentially uniform, there is no real need to perform Bayesian calculations, or for that matter, additional validity studies.

As Hunter and Schmidt (2000) noted, it is unrealistic to assume that true effects are constant in any research domain; on this basis, they recommend that researchers use random effects models rather than fixed effects models in their meta-analyses. However, if one assumes that the validities, the effects of interventions, etc. are in fact likely to differ in meaningful ways across settings, this implies that there will be some variability in the prior distribution, which makes it necessary to consider true Bayesian analytic methods for integrating prior information (e.g., information or theory about the true distribution of validities) with information provided by a local validation study. Brannick (2001) showed that if there is even a small amount of uncertainty about the prior (i.e., if the variance of the prior distribution of validities is not zero), the results of local validity studies might make a real difference in evaluating a test, intervention, and so forth. Perhaps the most significant contribution of that study is the demonstration that Bayesian calculations are informative in a much wider range of situations than the early papers on validity generalization might have suggested. It seems likely that future research on VG will profit from a careful reintroduction of Bayesian methods. Brannick's (2001, chap. 7, this volume) chapters in this area should make that work considerably easier.

As Rothstein and Jelley (chap. 8, this volume) and others (e.g., Landy, chap. 6, this volume) note, many aspects of the VG model and the style of research that grew up around this model are artifacts of its early focus on the validity of cognitive ability tests. In particular, the United States Employment Service (USES) database that was the focus of much of the early VG research included a large number of studies, many of which produced relatively large and consistent validity estimates. When statistical artifacts were taken into account, it seemed reasonable to believe that the prior distribution had a large mean and a small variance. It is unlikely that many other research domains would have yielded a similar prior distribution (especially one based on such a large number of studies). It is likely, therefore, that if VG research had started with virtually any other content domain, the decision to abandon Bayesian procedures would not have been so lightly taken, and it might not have taken two decades to reintroduce Bayesian notions to validity generalization researchers.

What Inferences Can Be Made on the Basis of VG Studies?

One of the most critical issues in understanding the strengths and weaknesses of meta analysis and validity generalization analysis is the difficulty in specifying exactly what inferences can and cannot be supported on the basis of this sort analysis. There have been two variations on this theme in the VG literature. First, questions have been raised about what population the sample of available validity studies included in a meta-analysis represents. Second, questions have been raised about the links between the variables actually measured in individual studies and the constructs a research literature hopes to address. Both of these are critically important issues, and neither has been adequately addressed in the 25-year history of VG.

It is useful to provide a specific example to illustrate the issues that are involved in answering these two questions. Murphy and Lee (1994) used meta-analytic methods to address the question of whether conscientiousness explained the relation between integrity test scores and measures of job performance (they concluded it did not). In particular, they attempted to use partial correlation to determine whether the correlation between integrity and performance (itself estimated from a meta-analysis) would diminish if the correlations of both integrity and performance with conscientiousness were taken into account. One part of their study involved estimating the correlation between measures of integrity and measures of conscientiousness. They relied on nine studies that correlated well-validated measures of these two constructs; these studies yielded 46 separate correlations, which were averaged. Their study also included a sensitivity analysis to determine whether heterogeneity in any of the three correlations that go into the partial correlation formula might materially affect their conclusions (it did not). There are two questions that are worth considering in evaluating this study: (1) were these nine studies all sampled from the same population, and if so, what population is that?; and (2) were these studies all looking at the same latent parameter (i.e., the correlation between the constructs of integrity and conscientiousness?).

One of the recurring frustrations in statistics is that the term *the population* is routinely used as if its meaning were obvious. In reality, all studies can be thought of as being sampled from some population, but it is often unclear exactly which one. In our example, it might be possible to think of these nine studies as being a sample of all studies that examine the link between measurers of conscientiousness and integrity. It might even be possible to think of them as a sample from the hypothetical population of studies that have been done or might be done on this topic. Alternately, they might represent a sample of studies from easily accessible sources (mostly American journals) that examined the correlations between a handful of conscientiousness measures and a handful of integrity measures. No matter which definition of the population you choose, these might be considered a random sample, or they might be a convenience sample whose representativeness is difficult to determine. These nine studies do allow one to make an inference to some population, but it might be difficult to determine which one or to determine whether the inference is any good (if the studies are indeed random samples, statistical theory helps in making such a determination, but the likelihood that they are indeed random samples probably very low). Several chapters in this volume (e.g., chaps. 1, 3, 4, 8, and 11, this volume) comment on the difficulty of specifying the populations to which inferences can and cannot be made.

We have only one piece of advice to offer in dealing with this issue. Any meta-analysis that fails to specify the population (meta-analyses that simply state that they will make inferences to the population without further elaboration fail this screen) and the method of sampling from that population (e.g., are studies to be interpreted as a stratified random sample, and if so, how are strata defined) is likely to lead to unwarranted inferences about what the data mean. That is, meta-analyses that fail to specify the population or the method of sampling are likely to lead to generic inferences to studies in general, to the constructs themselves, or to truth. The only meta-analyses that can be interpreted correctly are those that specify the population sampled and the relation between that sample and the population. Unfortunately, meta-analyses like this are few and far between. In practice, it is best to treat the discussion section of most meta-analyses like you would treat a report from a financial analyst who is trying to sell you some stock. It will probably be overly optimistic about what the analysis really has to say.

The second concern has to do with the pitfalls of aggregating studies that may or may not be sufficiently similar to allow you to draw meaningful conclusions from a averaged outcome (see chaps. 4, 10, & 11, this volume for discussions of issues in aggregation). The studies examined by Murphy and Lee (1994) correlated one of four conscientiousness measures (the conscientiousness scale from the NEO Personality Inventory, the superego strength scale from the Sixteen Personality Factors Questionnaire, the socialization scale from the California Personality Inventory or the prudence scale from the Hogan Personality Inventory) with one of four integrity measures (Employee Reliability Index, Reid Report, Personnel Attitude Screening System–II, or Personnel Decisions Inc. Employment Inventory). These are not, by any stretch of the imagination, parallel measures, and so the decision to aggregate results of studies using these measures must be based on evidence that they tap their respective constructs well enough to justify averaging correlations that involve differing pairs of tests. Murphy and Lee (1994) restricted their search to a small number of studies that used reasonably good measures of both constructs, but other meta-analyses in this area (e.g., Ones, Viswesvaran, & Schmidt, 1993) have employed different search rules and have considered a much larger (but arguably more heterogeneous) set of studies.

It is reasonable to hypothesize that the larger the number of studies included in a meta-analysis, the higher the likelihood that you will end up aggregating studies that do not really belong together because they do not really involve the same core constructs (in conference presentations, Murphy has referred to this at the "Cecil B. DeMille Effect"). We do not know of any empirical confirmation of this hypothesis, but if it is correct, it suggests fundamental tension between the desire to produce meta-analyses that are comprehensive and meta-analyses that are interpretable (see also Oswald & McCloy, chap. 11, this volume). It is very hard to make sense of a meta-analysis if the only thread holding the studies together is that all of the variables on the X and Y sides of the equation have the same word in their title. For example, if several hundred studies each claim to measure ability and performance, but they use wildly different measures of one or both constructs, the average ability-performance correlation across those studies might be hard to interpret.

THE FUTURE

Our selection of issues that are likely to be important in the future is even more limited and idiosyncratic than our characterization of the past and present of validity generalization. Most generally, the future looks bright. The methods are thoroughly researched and widely studied, and the current and future generation of researchers should have little difficulty applying these methods to new research domains. Two issues strike us as particularly important problems that have still not been resolved in the literature on validity generalization: (1) the shifting meaning of key terms in validity generalization, and (2) the limitations placed on inferences by the quality of the available validity studies.

The Problem of Fuzzy Definitions

It is depressing to realize that after 25 years, some of the most important terms in validity generalization are still poorly or incompletely defined. First and foremost, what does *validity* mean in validity generalization research? As Landy (chap. 6, this volume) notes, validity is sometimes discussed as a binary variable, in the sense that a test is either valid or not valid (see also Murphy, 1994). This way of thinking is a regrettable hold-over from decades of loose thinking about validity, but it has caused no end of trouble. One can argue that even the term *validity generalization* itself is an anachronism that reflects the argument that might have been made decades ago, when tests seemed to be valid sometimes and not valid other times. We return to this idea later.

It is time for psychologists to get over thinking about tests in terms of a valid–nonvalid dichotomy; methodologists have been trying to talk us out of this way of thinking for decades. First, validity is not a property of the test, it is a property of the inferences one makes on the basis of a test (Standards for Educational and Psychological Tests, 1999). For example, if I score in the 85th percentile on a test of three-dimensional spatial visualization, you might infer that I have good spatial skills, that I would perform well as an outfielder on a softball team, or that I have potential as a fighter pilot. Any or all of those inferences might turn out to be correct, or valid. Thus, every test has as many validities as it has uses. Second, some inferences will turn out to be more correct than others. Validity is not an all-or-none state, but a continuum. It is therefore more sensible to ask how well validity generalizes than to ask whether or not it generalizes. It is also more sensible to ask *which* validity generalizes (i.e., validity of which inferences?) rather than asking *whether* validity generalizes.

As we noted earlier, the term *validity generalization*, which made perfect sense 25 years ago, seems almost irrelevant today. VG methods are designed and used for a much wider set of purposes than for integrating traditional validity studies (Rothstein, chap. 5, this volume), and the title is no longer fully adequate. Many more recent applications of this set of methods describe their work in terms of psychometric meta-analysis (e.g., Viswesvaran & Ones, 1995), and this title not only provides a clear indication of the unique features of the methods that have grown out of Schmidt and Hunter's (1977) article, it also frees users from the linguistic shackles that are imposed by asking whether validity generalizes. We now know that validity often generalizes well, that it sometimes generalizes poorly, and that variables can be identified that influence or limit the generalizability of validity (e.g., job complexity appears to moderate the relationship between cognitive ability tests and measures of job performance). The VG label should be retired; "psychometric meta-analysis" is a much better description of this whole line of work.

There is a second term widely used in VG research that has been the focus of a great deal of angst and debate (i.e., the term *true score*). The problem is that even well-trained psychologists sometimes take this term at face value. If some parameter is labeled the true score correlation or the true variance, readers seem to think that the label means just what it seems to mean (i.e., that the parameter in question is correct or true). As Murphy and DeShon (2000a, 2000b) noted, it requires many leaps of faith to believe that even the best meta-analytic estimate is true in any meaningful sense. An example helps to illustrate this point.

Suppose you read a meta-analysis of 25 studies that examine the relation between verbal ability (measured in various ways across studies) and performance in managerial jobs (the jobs and the performance measures vary across studies). The average observed correlation is .24, and after the usual psychometric corrections, the estimate of the correlation in this population (which, as is normal in meta-analyses, is only fuzzily defined) is .44. The studies included in the meta-analysis are generally weak ones that use unreliable measures and small samples, and the observed correlations vary extensively. However, the observed variance in correlations is not much greater than the variation you would expect on the basis of sampling error. The results section of this meta-analysis refers to .44 as the true score correlation, and in the discussion, this is shortened further to the true correlation. How should we interpret this statement?

Terms like *true correlation* or *true score correlation* are in fact shorthand for something like:

> The best estimate of the correlation between tests of this sort and performance measures like these, corrected for measurement error in the criterion, is .44. Our estimate of measurement error is based on a model of reliability that we know is not strictly correct (e.g., one that treats raters like parallel tests), but we think it is a pretty good approximation, and we prefer this approach to others that might have been applied. We think of .44 as an estimate of a population correlation, but we don't have a clearly-articulated population in mind, other than the statement that this estimates the results we

would expect in a population of studies pretty much like the 25 we were able to locate.

Unfortunately, the discussion section of this chapter is likely to be interpreted as: "The correlations between these two things *is* .44, and we don't need any more research on the topic. The first 25 studies found the same thing, so we can be pretty sure that our conclusion about the real relationship between verbal ability and managerial performance would not change with more studies."

We suggest that the term *true* should be dropped from the lexicon of meta-analytic researchers. It can only serve to mislead readers, even those who understand all of the assumptions that go into the leap from the observed distribution of study validities to conclusions about the fundamental relationships between constructs. When a salesman is nicknamed *Honest John*, it is wise to assume that he is not trustworthy. When a statistical parameter is called *true* it is wise to assume that it might not be.

Can We Make Strong Statements Based on Weak Data?

There are at least two reasons for the long and bitter controversy over validity generalization. First, the outcomes of VG research contradicted widely held opinions about the validation process. At the time Schmidt and Hunter (1977) was published, it was assumed that the validity of personnel tests was simply unpredictable, and that a local validity study was needed in virtually any new setting where a test was applied. Furthermore, there was no apparent way of telling what features of situations might or might not materially affect validity, suggesting that the transportation of validity evidence across settings would always be hazardous at best. As depressing as these principles might have been, they did have a silver lining, at least for personnel psychologists. That is, they represented something close to the "Personnel Psychologists Full Employment Act," because they suggested that organizations would continuously need our services.

The second reason for the controversy over VG has little to do with the substantive meaning of validity generalization, and lots to do with the way this research was presented. Proponents of validity generalization have not been shy about making sweeping claims about the implications of their findings (see, e.g., Schmidt, 1992; Schmidt & Hunter, 1981; Schmidt, Hunter, & Pearlman, 1981). Nor have they been shy about making strong claims about the superiority of meta-analytic methods over other methods of doing research. For example, Schmidt (1992) suggested that in the future, it would be the meta-analysts who made the important discoveries, and that the main function of primary researchers would be to provide grist for the mills of their meta-analytic colleagues. This suggestion was not always welcomed with open arms (Bobko & Stone-Romero, 1998).

This tendency to make strong claims represented a strategic choice on the part of Schmidt, Hunter, and their colleagues (Schmidt et al., 1985), and it is probable that this choice was a major factor in much of the angst that accompanied each new VG paper (cf. Landy, chap. 6, this volume). In some ways, this was a brilliant choice, because it guaranteed that virtually every paper in this series would be examined closely and talked about in great detail. Authors in other areas of psychology would love to get the sort of attention the most pedestrian VG paper was likely to receive. On the other hand, it contributed substantially to the unhealthy ratio of heat to light that surrounded early discussions of VG. Every minor error, as well as every judgment call about how to conduct and interpret VG studies became fodder for the body of studies examining the bias, accuracy, robustness, etcetera, of every inch of the VG model. It is hard to escape the feeling that we all might have been spared about three quarters of the available body of Monte Carlo studies of minor variations in the VG model if only all authors had been less confrontational in the early years of VG research.

In recent years, there seems to be less concern with style and more concern with substance. Proponents of VG are less confrontational in their papers and critics of specific applications of the model are less apocalyptic in their assessments of the weaknesses of this approach. In our view, this cooling-down period offers a real opportunity for serious discussion of the problems in trying to draw strong conclusions from weak data. In particular, is it possible to rise above the limitations and weaknesses of the primary research in one's area and to draw conclusions about fundamental principles of behavior by averaging and correcting the results of multiple studies, each of which might be deeply flawed?

For example, suppose that you start off with a set of 50 studies, 35 of which employ small convenience samples that might or might not differ from the population you want to make inferences about. They employ a wide range of instruments and techniques that all purport to measure the construct spatial visualization, and each of them relates spatial visualization to task performance, a construct that is also operationalized in widely differing ways across the studies. The correlations between spatial visualization and task performance are often quite small and they vary extensively from study to study. After doing the standard VG corrections, you conclude that the mean rho value is about .20, and that the variation in correlations is not much greater than you should expect on the basis of sampling error and study differences in things like criterion reliability. What should you conclude? An old-fashioned narrative review would probably conclude "garbage in–garbage out." An enthusiastic VG researcher might conclude that we now had a pretty good handle on the relationships between these two constructs, and perhaps might also conclude that we do not need to do any more research on the topic. Neither of these approaches strikes us as reasonable.

The middle ground is that we often do not need more research but rather need better research. The fundamental insight of Schmidt and Hunter's (1977) volume was that the low quality of the available body of research muddied the water so much that it was hard to draw useful conclusions from research on topics like test validity. They proposed, and over the years have refined techniques for extracting as much information as possible from these studies, but the nagging doubt about the conclusions reached from meta-analyses will always remain if we rest our laurels on weak research. Murphy and Myors (1998) suggested that the ultimate contribution of techniques such as statistical power analysis might be to encourage researchers to do better work in the first place, and the same is possibly true of VG research. Once you understand just how badly the use of small samples, unreliable criteria, etcetera can mislead you, it is unlikely that you will be so willing to design future studies that look anything like the bulk of the studies that defined the early years of VG research (e.g., the USES validity studies).

It is possible, however, that meta-analytic methods could lead to complacency rather than spurring us on to do better research. That is, these methods seem to promise to help us turn lead into gold (i.e., to extract high-quality information from low quality studies). Furthermore, they can lead to the conclusion (which is sometimes entirely justified) that there is no need for more research. No matter how arcane the question, it is often possible to locate a body of relevant studies, and if you obtain better information by cumulating the results from existing studies than you could obtain by doing a study yourself, why bother to do primary research at all? In the late 1800s, there was a call to close the U.S. Patent Office, on the grounds that everything that could be invented already had been invented. Should we call a moratorium on primary research in some areas, on the grounds that enough studies already exist? The answer might sometimes be yes; it is hard to imagine what could be learned by running another study correlating measures of cognitive ability with measures performance in training or on the job (although it might be informative to determine whether this well-established finding holds up across cultures or across emerging methods of organizing training and work). In other cases, the answer might be that the available body of research is so full of holes that no firm conclusions can be reached, even if the results of a psychometric meta-analysis suggest consistent, nontrivial validities.

SUMMARY

The accomplishments of meta-analytic research in general, and VG research in particular have been little short of amazing. These methods allow researchers to pull together the findings of diverse studies, and to make sense of what often appear to be inconsistent results. Like many other important methodological advances, VG seems to be following a predictable cycle of excitement, controversy, application, and stabilization. At one time, VG seemed to many to be a panacea, and many of the early papers in this area were marked by more optimism and less caution than the method probably justified. As the field has matured, researchers have started to develop a firmer understanding of the strengths and weaknesses of this method of cumulating research. As it currently stands, psychometric meta-analysis represents an extremely valuable part of the researcher's toolkit. It allows us to address questions that are sometimes impossible to address with primary research, and it provides fresh insight in evaluating familiar data.

There are still many important challenges to interpreting the results of a VG analysis, especially in determining exactly what inferences can and cannot be supported using this method. Many of the chapters in this volume outline promising avenues for improving this method and for structuring future research on validity generalization. This method has an eventful and distinguished past, a vibrant and optimistic present, and, most important, an exciting future. We close by offering a few pieces of advice to meta-analysts and VG researchers; these are displayed in Table 14.1. Regardless of whether these suggestions are followed, it is probably safe to assume that VG will be with us for some time to come. It is possible that the suggestions in this chapter can further enhance the contributions of the VG method.

TABLE 14.1
Five Suggestions for Improving Validity
Generalization Research and Applications

1. Become Bayesian: In most areas of research, there is some variability in study outcomes that cannot be explained by statistical artifacts. Schmidt and Hunter were right in 1977 to think of the problem of interpreting study outcomes in Bayesian terms, and it is time to get back to our Bayesian roots.
2. Define the Population: There is no such thing as *the population*, and it is the researcher's job to define the population he or she wishes to generalize to and to justify that definition. It always pays to be skeptical in evaluating these definitions.
3. Care About Quality: Meta-analyses that attempt to be comprehensive usually end up giving more weight to bad studies than to good ones, simply because there are so many bad ones out there. The excuse is that evaluations of study quality are subjective. They are. Get over it. Ten good studies are usually more useful than sixty bad ones.
4. Change the Name: It is time to retire the jersey "Validity Generalization." "Psychometric Meta-Analysis" conveys the idea quite nicely.
5. Reform the Language: Stop calling parameter estimates *true*. They aren't.

REFERENCES

Algera, J. A., Jansen, P. G. W., Roe, R. A., & Vijn, P. (1984). Validity generalization: Some critical remarks on the Schmidt-Hunter procedure. *Journal of Occupational Psychology, 57*, 197–210.

Bobko, P., & Stone-Romero, E. (1998). Meta-analysis is another useful research tool but it is not a panacea. In J. Ferris (Ed.), *Research in personnel and human resources management* (Vol. 16, pp. 359–397). Greenwich, CT: JAI Press.

Brannick, M. T. (2001). Implications of empirical Bayes meta-analysis for test validation. *Journal of Applied Psychology, 86*, 468–480.

Burke, M. J., Raju, N. S., & Pearlman, K. (1986). An empirical comparison of the results of five VG procedures. *Journal of Applied Psychology, 71*, 349–353.

Brown, S. H. (1981). Validity generalization and situational moderation in the life insurance industry. *Journal of Applied Psychology, 66*, 664–670.

Callender, J. C., & Osburn, H. G. (1980). Development and test of a new model for validity generalization. *Journal of Applied Psychology, 65*, 543–558.

Callender, J. C., & Osburn, H. G. (1981). Testing the constancy of validity with computer-generated sampling distributions of the multiplicative model variance estimate: Results for petroleum industry validation research. *Journal of Applied Psychology, 66*, 274–281.

Callender, J. C., & Osburn, H. G. (1982). Another view of progress in validity generalization. *Journal of Applied Psychology, 67*, 846–852.

Callender, J. C., & Osburn, H. G. (1988). Unbiased estimation of sampling variance of correlations. *Journal of Applied Psychology, 73*, 312–315.

Erez, A., Bloom, M. C., & Wells, M. T. (1996). Using random rather than fixed effects models in meta-analysis: Implications for situational specificity and validity generalization. *Personnel Psychology, 49*, 275–306.

Gutenberg, R. L., Arvey, R. D., Osburn, H. G., & Jeanneret, P. R. (1983). Moderating effects of decision-making/information processing job dimensions on test validities. *Journal of Applied Psychology, 68,* 602–608

Hedges, L. V. (1988). Meta-analysis of test validities. In H. Wainer & H. Braun (Eds.), *Test validity* (pp. 191–212). Hillsdale, NJ: Lawrence Erlbaum Associates.

Hedges, L. V. (1989). An unbiased correction for sampling error in validity generalization studies. *Journal of Applied Psychology, 74,* 469–477.

Hunter, J. E., & Schmidt, F. L. (1990). *Methods of meta-analysis: Correcting error and bias in research findings.* Beverly Hills, CA: Sage.

Hunter, J. E., & Schmidt, F. L. (2000). Fixed effects vs. random effects meta-analysis models: Implications got cumulative research knowledge. *International Journal of Selection and Assessment, 8,* 275–292.

Hunter, J. E., Schmidt, F. L., & Pearlman, K. (1982). History and accuracy of validity generalization equations: A response to the Callender and Osburn reply. *Journal of Applied Psychology, 67,* 853–856

James, L. R., Demaree, R. G., & Mulaik, S. A. (1986). A note on validity generalization procedures. *Journal of Applied Psychology, 71,* 440–450.

James, L. R., Demaree, R. G., Mulaik, S. A., & Ladd, R. T. (1992). Validity generalization in the context of situational models. *Journal of Applied Psychology, 77,* 3–14.

Kemery, E. R., Mossholder, K. W., & Roth, L. (1987). The power of the Schmidt–Hunter additive model of validity generalization. *Journal of Applied Psychology, 72,* 30–37.

Law, K. S. (1992). Estimation accuracy of Thomas's likelihood-based procedure of meta-analysis: A Monte Carlo simulation. *Journal of Applied Psychology, 77,* 986–995.

Millsap, R. E. (1988). Sampling variance in attenuated correlation coefficients: A Monte Carlo study. *Journal of Applied Psychology, 73,* 316–319.

Millsap, R. E. (1989). Sampling variance in the correlation coefficient under range restriction: A Monte Carlo study. *Journal of Applied Psychology, 74,* 456–461.

Murphy, K. R. (1994). Advances in meta-analysis and validity generalization. In N. Anderson & P. Herriot (Eds.), *Assessment and selection in organizations: First update and supplement, 1994* (pp. 57–76). Chichester, UK: Wiley.

Murphy, K. R. (2000). The impact of assessments of validity generalization and situational specificity on the science and practice of personnel selection. *International Journal of Selection and Assessment, 8,* 194–206.

Murphy, K. R., & DeShon, R. (2000a). Inter-rater correlations do not estimate the reliability of job performance ratings. *Personnel Psychology, 53,* 873–900.

Murphy, K. R., & DeShon, R. (2000b). Progress in psychometrics: Can industrial and organizational psychology catch up? *Personnel Psychology, 53,* 913–924.

Murphy, K. R., & Lee, S. (1994). Does conscientiousness explain the relationship between integrity and performance? *International Journal of Selection and Assessment, 2,* 226–233.

Murphy, K. R., & Myors, B. (1998). *Statistical power analysis: A simple and general model for traditional and modern hypothesis tests.* Mahwah, NJ: Lawrence Erlbaum Associates.

Ones, D. S., Viswesvaran, C., & Schmidt, F. L. (1993). Meta-analysis of integrity test validities.*Journal of Applied Psychology, 78,* 679–703.

Osburn, H. G., & Callender, J. C. (1990). Bias in validity generalization estimates: A reply to Hoben Thomas. *Journal of Applied Psychology, 75,* 328–333.

Osburn, H. G., Callender, J. C., Greener, J. M., & Ashworth, S. (1983). Statistical power of tests of the situational specificity hypothesis in validity generalization studies: A cautionary note. *Journal of Applied Psychology, 68,* 115–122.

Oswald, F. L., & Johnson, J. W. (1998). On the robustness, bias, and stability of statistics from meta-analysis of correlation coefficients: Some initial Monte Carlo findings. *Journal of Applied Psychology, 83,* 164–178.

Paese, P. W., & Switzer, F. S. (1988). Validity generalization and hypothetical reliability distributions: A test of the Schmidt-Hunter procedure. *Journal of Applied Psychology, 73,* 267–274.

Pearlman, K., Schmidt, F. L., & Hunter, J. E. (1980). Validity generalization results for tests used to predict job proficiency and training success in clerical occupations. *Journal of Applied Psychology, 65,* 373–406.

Raju, N. S., & Burke, M. J. (1983). Two new procedures for studying validity generalization. *Journal of Applied Psychology, 68,* 382–395.

Raju, N. S., Fralicx, R., & Steinhaus, S. D. (1986). Covariance and regression slope models for studying validity generalization. *Applied Psychological Measurement, 10,* 195–211.

Raju, N. S., Pappas, S., & Williams, C. P. (1989). An empirical Monte Carlo test of the accuracy of the correlation, covariance, and regression slope models for assessing validity generalization. *Journal of Applied Psychology, 74,* 901–911.

Sackett, P. R., Harris, M. M., & Orr, J. M. (1986). On seeking moderator variables in the meta-analysis of correlational data: A Monte Carlo investigation of statistical power and resistance to Type I error. *Journal of Applied Psychology, 71,* 302–310.

Schmidt, F. L. (1992). What do data really mean? Research findings, meta-analysis, and cumulative knowledge in psychology. *American Psychologist, 47,* 1173–1181.

Schmidt, F. L., & Hunter, J. E. (1977). Development and a general solution to the problem of validity generalization. *Journal of Applied Psychology, 62,* 529–540.

Schmidt, F. L., & Hunter, J. E. (1981). Employment testing: Old theories and new research findings. *American Psychologist, 36,* 1128–1137.

Schmidt, F. L., Gast-Rosenberg, I., & Hunter, J. E. (1980). Validity generalization results for computer programmers. *Journal of Applied Psychology, 65,* 643–661.

Schmidt, F. L., Hunter, J. E., & Caplan, J. R. (1981). Validity generalization results for two jobs in the petroleum industry. *Journal of Applied Psychology, 66,* 261–273.

Schmidt, F. L., Hunter, J. E., & Pearlman, K. (1981). Task differences as moderators of aptitude test validity in selection: A red herring. *Journal of Applied Psychology, 66,* 166–185.

Schmidt, F. L., Hunter, J. E., Pearlman, K., & Shane, G. S. (1979). Further tests of the Schmidt–Hunter Bayesian validity generalization procedure. *Personnel Psychology, 32,* 257–281.

Schmidt, F. L., Hunter, J. E., Pearlman, K., Hirsch, H. R., Sackett, P. R., Schmitt, N., Tenopyr, M. L., Kehoe, J., & Zedeck, S. (1985). Forty questions about validity generalizations and meta-analysis with commentaries. *Personnel Psychology, 38*, 697–798.

Schmidt, F. L., Hunter, J. E., & Raju, N. S. (1988). Validity generalization and situational specificity: A second look at the 75% rule and Fisher's z transformation. *Journal of Applied Psychology, 73*, 665–672.

Schmidt, F. L., Law, K., Hunter, J. E., Rothstein, H. R., Pearlman, K., & McDaniel, M. (1993). Refinements in validity generalization methods: Implications for the situational specificity hypothesis. *Journal of Applied Psychology, 78*, 3–12.

Schmitt, N., Gooding, R. Z., Noe, R. A., & Kirsch, M. (1984). Metaanalysis of validity studies published between 1964 and 1982 and the investigation of study characteristics. *Personnel Psychology, 37*, 407–422.

Schmitt, N., & Noe, R. A. (1986). On shifting standards for conclusions regarding validity generalization. *Personnel Psychology, 39*, 849–851.

Standards for educational and psychological testing. (1999). Washington, DC: American Psychological Association.

Switzer, F. S. III, Paese, P. W., & Drasgow, F. (1992). Bootstrap estimates of standard errors in validity generalization. *Journal of Applied Psychology, 77*, 123–129.

Thomas, H. (1988). What is the interpretation of the validity generalization estimate $S_p^2 = S_r^2 - S_e^2$? *Journal of Applied Psychology, 73*, 679–682.

Thomas, H. (1990). A likelihood-based model for validity generalization. *Journal of Applied Psychology, 75*, 13–20.

Viswesvaran, C., & Ones, D. (1995). Theory testing: Combining psychometric meta-analysis and structural equations modeling. *Personnel-Psychology, 48*, 865–885.

Author Index

Subject Index